Foundations *of* Theology

Foundations *of* Theology

Biblical and Systematic Adventism

JOHN PETER LEWIS

RESOURCE *Publications* • Eugene, Oregon

FOUNDATIONS OF THEOLOGY
Biblical and Systematic Adventism

Copyright © 2022 John Peter Lewis. All rights reserved. Except for brief quotations in critical publications or reviews, no part of this book may be reproduced in any manner without prior written permission from the publisher. Write: Permissions, Wipf and Stock Publishers, 199 W. 8th Ave., Suite 3, Eugene, OR 97401.

Resource Publications
An Imprint of Wipf and Stock Publishers
199 W. 8th Ave., Suite 3
Eugene, OR 97401

www.wipfandstock.com

PAPERBACK ISBN: 978-1-7252-7872-1
HARDCOVER ISBN: 978-1-7252-7873-8
EBOOK ISBN: 978-1-7252-7874-5

JULY 8, 2022 11:31 AM

Scriptures taken from the Holy Bible, New International Version®, NIV®. Copyright © 1973, 1978, 1984, 2011 by Biblica, Inc.™ Used by permission of Zondervan. All rights reserved worldwide. www.zondervan.com The "NIV" and "New International Version" are trademarks registered in the United States Patent and Trademark Office by Biblica, Inc.™

Scripture quotations are taken from the (NASB®) New American Standard Bible®, Copyright © 1960, 1971, 1977, 1995, 2020 by The Lockman Foundation. Used by permission. All rights reserved. www.lockman.org

Contents

Preface | vii

Introduction | 1

CHAPTER 1   The Theologian's Task | 3
CHAPTER 2   Examples of Theological Method in Christianity | 6
CHAPTER 3   The Ground of Theology: Revelation | 10
CHAPTER 4   The Doctrine of God | 18
CHAPTER 5   The Person of Jesus Christ | 34
CHAPTER 6   The Deity of Jesus Christ | 44
CHAPTER 7   The Self-Awarness of Jesus | 47
CHAPTER 8   The Two Natues of Jesus Christ | 52
CHAPTER 9   The Holy Spirit | 57
CHAPTER 10   The Doctrine of the Trinity (The Divine Trio) | 62
CHAPTER 11   Humanity and the Problem of Sin | 67
CHAPTER 12   Jesus Christ: Saviour and Lord | 77
CHAPTER 13   Jesus Christ: Prophet, Priest and King | 80
CHAPTER 14   Atonement | 85
CHAPTER 15   Atonement and the Heavenly Sanctuary | 92
CHAPTER 16   Election and Predestination | 96
CHAPTER 17   Reconciliation | 104

CHAPTER 18	Justification	106
CHAPTER 19	Sanctification	118
CHAPTER 20	Glorification	135
CHAPTER 21	Pacifism	137
CHAPTER 22	The Church	141
CHAPTER 23	The History of the Church and Its Theological Development	153
CHAPTER 24	The Reformation	182
CHAPTER 25	The Radical Reformation- The Anabasptists	201
CHAPTER 26	Revival Movements	205
CHAPTER 27	The Practical Marks of the Church	218
CHAPTER 28	The Church in the Plan of Salvation	230
CHAPTER 29	The Three Angels Message	234
CHAPTER 30	Church Ordinances	237
CHAPTER 31	Worship	253
CHAPTER 32	The Sabbath	256
CHAPTER 33	Spiritual Agents	260
CHAPTER 34	Eschatology	265

Bibliography | 281

Preface

THIS VOLUME IS THE RESULT of over ten years of study, research, reflection and writing. While I have sought to be thorough and approach each topic in an academic manner, I have also sought to render this publication accessible to a broad readership. My hope is that this publication will encourage others to take on the challenge to write theologically and express their beliefs in a way that will spur others to deeper thinking, or to be challenged by new ideas and expressions of faith.

The Authorized Version is used without reference. Copyright for the New International Version (NIV) and the New American Standard Bible (NASB) is found on the last age.

In writing this book I acknowledge the contribution of my family to my faith development. To my children, Sophia, Gabriella, Christian and Charlotte. Importantly, to my wife, Marife, who opened the door to deeper thinking.

J.P.L

INTRODUCTION

IN THE EMERGING META-MODERNISTIC CONTEXT, with its complex vacillation between the determinism of modernism and the relativism and narrative style of post-modernism, there appears to be a need for a restating of Seventh-day Adventist theology that provides a resource for further discussion.

Therefore, the purpose of this book is to produce a systematic theology that is unashamedly Seventh-day Adventist and which stands within the context of the narrative of church history and determinism of biblical Christianity. The following pages provide an outline of the central beliefs of Christianity in a systematic manner that bears a resemblance to other systematic theologies. However, while sharing this common format, this book differs significantly.

This publication aims at a broad readership, as it seeks to engage with a variety of theological experiences. Also, it is a Seventh-day Adventist systemic theology, with a regard for the foundational and central importance of the Bible, as it has been insightfully exposited within the story of the Seventh-day Adventist movement from its formation. For this reason, Ellen White is extensively quoted and often utilized to provide concluding comments on a particular topic. Many quoted authors are not Seventh-day Adventist, nor share any affinity with the movement. The aim of quoting non-Seventh-day Adventist authors is not to commend everything that these authors stand for, but to highlight their helpful biblical insights. This is not new. For example, Seventh-day Adventists freely quote Martin Luther, without reference to numerous assertions he made that are at variance with Seventh-day Adventist beliefs. Indeed, this is how systematic theology works. Authors are quoted for their contribution to an argument and not for the totality of all they have written or asserted. The point of drawing on a wide authorship is also to place the message of the Seventh-day Adventist movement within the context of the wider church, notably biblical Christianity, and those aspects which support the core message of Seventh-day Adventism. These shared characteristics are primarily due to a shared heritage in one of the antecedents to the Advent Message, whether that be the theology of the early church, the Reformation, the radical Anabaptist Reformation, Pietism,

FOUNDATIONS OF THEOLOGY

Methodism or Revivalism. The view here is that Seventh-day Adventism is a movement at the apex of history, within the context of historical Protestantism. Finally, the chapters on the Sabbath and Eschatology are not as extensive as they could have been, since numerous fine monographs on these subjects have already been published.

CHAPTER 1
==========

THE THEOLOGIAN'S TASK

THEOLOGIANS ARE LIKE COOKS; THEY use different ingredients and put them together in a certain manner for a final outcome. They follow a set format, refer to a variety of sources and discuss them in order.[1] However, theology is often done spontaneously and without reference to a certain methodology. None-the-less, the study of theological method, particularly in the context of the theologian's biography, has the potential to open the door to self-understanding and the ways in which God's people are able to formulate belief structures that genuinely reflect their search for the truth. Post-modernism also leads one to the topic of method. The post-modernist worldview will not accept truth uncritically. In such a system of thought it is assumed that every proclamation of truth is based on a series of assumptions that must firstly be assembled and explained. Significantly, in the emerging Meta-modernism[2], with its oscillation between modernism and post-modernism, and its reliance on the internet, reality should not be viewed uncritically. Indeed, the growing allure of untruth, without a thoroughly sourced investigation, necessitates an in-depth investigation into the origins of theological conclusions.

N. T. Wright has grappled with finding the ultimate truth, in a maze of subjectivity, in his widely discussed *Critical Realism*. This is a way of describing the process of "knowing" that acknowledges the *reality of the thing known, as something other than the knower* (hence "realism"), while fully acknowledging that the only access we have to this reality lies along the spiralling path of *appropriate dialogue or conversation between the knower and the thing known* (hence "critical").[3]

---

1. Pinnock, *New Directions in Theological Method*, 197.
2. Vermeulen, van den Akker, *Notes on Metamodernism*.
3. Wright, *The New Testament and the People of God*, 35.

Indeed, asserting objective truth within a society that maintains a predominately subjective worldview, is a complex and sometimes difficult undertaking. An apologetic arguing for the existence of an ultimate truth is often an essential preliminary step. Concurrently, the existence of influences that determine theological outcomes is an equally necessary discussion. However, a subjective view of reality, which determines that truth is relative, need not result in the assertion that all truth is subjective and impossible to grasp with any sense of certainty. To be sure, the existence of objective truth is of equal philosophical validity than that there is no ultimate truth. Therefore, one might conclude that through the lens of a subjective world view, objective truth is not only philosophically valid, but also possible. Indeed, discovering the Ultimate, cannot, with any philosophical certainty, be discounted. Theologically, there is every reason to assert that God draws together in a person's life a number of influences that, if responded to in faith and an openness to the guidance of God, will lead to theological outcomes that not only fulfil a Divine agenda for that person, at that time, but embody the truth. Therefore, influence is an important factor in analysing a theologian's method.

One must ask what the various influences on a particular theologian have been, to uncover the particular rational behind their theological conclusions. There may have been a particular theology that was dominant in their upbringing, or at the time of their conversion. For a number of theologians, and indeed Christians, there have been significant people, whether in the church setting or through reading, that have become important influences. Some influences have been created over a number of years, while others come about at a single moment, perhaps in a crisis experience that plays a role in the theological development of the individual. Influences usually become sources, acknowledged or otherwise, that become predominant in the theologians' self-expression. Some writers are influenced by a single theologian and often quote that author. However, most have been exposed to a variety of influences that culminate in a number of key sources.

The language often used to explain a theological position usually gives an indication of the kind of influences that have led to the variety of sources the theologian relies upon. Often authors, as they express their beliefs, combine sources that can include Calvinism, Wesleyanism, Pietism, Revivalism, Pentecostalism, and others. Societal and cultural influences also have a part to play. However, in this array of influences, personal choice must also be considered, as ideas arise within the context of the complexity of the human psyche, with all its influences, experiences and characteristics. Indeed, the choice to pursue an objective belief, and have a conviction about that belief, is a perfectly legitimate, if not necessary, exercise. Indeed, embedded within the apparent subjectivity found in our global society, and the new unsourced or unverifiable determinism, is the longing for a truth that is genuine, well-researched and thoughtful. Philosophically, and certainly biblically, the total relativization of truth is unsustainable, as is the making of bold statements without due care. After all, the insistence that truth is relative is itself reflective of an objective worldview. Further, many contemporary assertions that cannot be verified by the usual conventions of investigation, and with a total disregard for a fair and open debate, will dissipate along with the emotions that created them.

In theological thinking, sources are often combined together for the purpose of constructing theological themes and for the pursuit of a certain theological agenda. Theologians usually have points they want to argue and issues they believe need to be addressed. Theological themes take a variety of forms, but may include: The sovereignty of God and God's grace, holiness and free will, justice for the poor, the expectation of the coming kingdom, or issues related to church and mission. Agendas are what theologians seek to pursue in their theologies. They may want to rejuvenate classic Calvinism or Arminianism, create biblical theology of justice, harmonize various strands of theology into one biblical theology, or create a theological system guided by post-modernist, or meta-modernist, philosophies.

Ultimately, influences become sources that lead to the construction of theological themes in the pursuit of a certain theological agenda.

Donald Bloesch, in his *Essentials of Evangelical Theology: Volume 1*, wisely framed our theological enterprises within the limits of human enterprise. Consequently, theology cannot be a static enterprise, but one that is always being revised and reformed. However, this does not mean that our theology should always be changing or that it lacks certainty. The revelation of the Bible reveals God's purposes as well as the human situation. Therefore, our human systems must always be open to revision in the light of new insights into the Word of God. Yet in the times in which we live, Bloesch believed that in order to safeguard the message of faith, some doctrines will need to be emphasized as essentials. By stating this, Bloesch did not suggest that the divinity of Christ, for example, may or may not be true, or that today we uphold it and tomorrow we may believe something else. What Bloesch stated was that, in the light of our human limitation we may find, on reflection of God's Word, better ways of expressing such a theology with greater clarity or depth within our current society or cross-culturally. This is essential, if new generations and people groups are to be engaged with the timeless truths of Scripture.

Chapter 2

EXAMPLES OF THEOLOGICAL METHOD IN CHRISTIANITY

DONALD BLOESCH

Donald Bloesch was raised in a denomination which traced its roots to the Reformational and Pietistic theology of central European evangelicalism. He was later influenced by an encounter with the theology of Karl Barth. These various influences led to a theology that utilized the kind of sources that enabled him to pursue a variety of themes and agendas. Bloesch sought to hold to the fundamentals of the faith. However, he was willing to diverge from contemporary fundamentalism and evangelicalism wherever he detected misunderstandings of the faith. He believed that the bane of much evangelicalism was a rationalism that denies the mystery in faith and a sectarianism that breaks continuity with the historic church. However, he also saw dangers in liberalism, which dissolves faith in the spirit of the times. He sought a theology that was radical as well as conservative, since he perceived the Bible to be the infallible rule of faith. He sought to be irenic wherever possible and build bridges between Calvinism and Arminianism, and Calvinism and Lutheranism. The influences of Reformed scholasticism and pietism in his upbringing led to a deep concern for a theology of the Word, but also the need to emphasize a theology of the heart. Consequently, Bloesch pursued a theology of "Word and Spirit".[1]

---

1. See Bloesch, *Essentials of Evangelical Theology: Vol. 1* and Bloesch, *A Theology of Word and Spirit*.

EXAMPLES OF THEOLOGICAL METHOD IN CHRISTIANITY

MILLARD ERICKSON

Millard Erickson was raised in a denomination formed by Swedish Baptist immigrants to the United States, who preached a moderate Calvinism. This influence is evident in Erickson's theology and methodology. Consequently, he followed a structured and rational approach to theology, but not a strictly rigid one. He believed that since theology is an art as well as a science, it cannot follow a rigid structure. However, he recognised that procedures need to be spelled out. The first of these procedures is the collection of biblical materials. Erickson's method, therefore, begins with the gathering of all relevant biblical passages on the doctrine being investigated. This step must also involve a thorough utilization of the very best tools and methods for getting the meaning of these passages. Erickson also suggested the unification of the biblical materials, which amounts to considering the whole of scripture and finding common themes. He advocated for an analysis of the meaning of biblical teachings. The expositor must ask what this collection of texts truly means before putting the meaning into clear and understandable language. Beyond this, is the recognition that we are not the first generation to examine a particular doctrine biblically. Consequently, he promoted an examination of historical treatments before an identification of the essence of the doctrine. This amounts to distinguishing a given text from the cultural environment in which it is written. Also, one should seek illumination from sources beyond the Bible.

In addition, Erickson encouraged the theologian to consider the context in which he or she must communicate his or her theology. Although, there is a note of warning here: theologies that seek to express concepts that are over familiar with contemporary expression soon appear out of date. Further, various doctrines within a single theological system must be seen to be in relationship with one another. However, he warned that passages should not be misinterpreted for the simple purpose of establishing, in spite of the meaning of the text, a consistent theological pattern. Finally, he advised that there be a delineation between major themes and sub-topics.[2]

THOMAS ODEN

Thomas Oden, raised a Methodist, pursued a theological method in the Wesleyan tradition. He asked by what authority, or on what ground, Christian teaching rests? Oden believed that the study of God relies upon an interdependent quadrilateral of sources from which the confessing community can articulate, make consistent, and integrate the witness of revelation. In this he alluded to four elements of the Wesleyan Quadrilateral: Scripture, tradition, experience, and reason. All of these depend on revelation. Oden further believed that all of these were operative in the writings

---

2. See Erickson, *Christian Theology*.

of the classical Christian teachers: Irenaeus, John Chrysostom, Ambrose, Augustine, and John of Damascus. All of these methods hinge on the fact that God has made himself known. The sequence of this revelation is important to this method. The original event of revelation is Christ, the Revealer of God and the Father, as proclaimed by the community, then recorded in Sacred Scripture.

Oden believed in a divinely inspired Scripture that is an utterly reliable source and the norm of Christian theology. From here follows the traditionalization of that word inter-generationally through time, which is tradition, or, the Word remembered. This elicits personal and social awareness and experience of the salvation event, or, the Word experienced and then the reflection required to think by reason upon the salvation event. That is, the Word made intelligible. Importantly, each layer depends on the previous one.[3]

ELLEN WHITE

Ellen White's theology is to be distinguished from the theologians mentioned already, since she possessed prophetic authority. Her theological method was highly influenced by her Methodist heritage. Indeed, her theology is profoundly Wesleyan and resonates with the overtones of a holiness worldview. She therefore sits within the Arminian branch of Protestantism. Her most enduring influence came from her parents, who were committed Methodists, before joining the Millerite movement. She was born at Gorham, Maine, November 26, 1827 to Robert and Eunice Harmon. Her parents

> *were for many years residents of this state. In early life, they became earnest and devoted members of the Methodist Episcopal Church. In that church they held prominent connection, and labored for the conversion of sinners, and to build up the cause of God, for a period of forty years. During this time, they had the joy of seeing their children, eight in number, all converted and gathered into the fold of Christ.*[4]

The influence of her parents further developed her theological perspective during the year of 1843, when they were removed from the Episcopal Methodist Church and joined the Millerite Movement. What emerged from this was a Wesleyan theology imbued with prophetic sentiments, marked by a concern for the soon return of Christ and guided by way of visions from God. I refer to this as a type of prophetic and apocalyptic Methodism. Importantly, her experience of conversion underpinned the infusion of these two theological orientations. She recalls a time, at a Methodist camp meeting her parents had taken her to, the experience of giving her life to Christ.

---

3. See Oden, *John Wesley's Scriptural Christianity: A Plain Exposition of His Teaching on Christian Doctrine*.

4. White, *Testimonies fo the Church: Vol. 1*, 9.

> *While bowed at the altar with others who were seeking the Lord, all the language of my heart was: 'Help, Jesus, save me or I perish! I will never cease to entreat till my prayer is heard and my sins forgiven!' I felt my needy, helpless condition as never before. As I knelt and prayed, suddenly my burden left me, and my heart was light. At first a feeling of alarm came over me, and I tried to resume my load of distress. It seemed to me that I had no right to feel joyous and happy. But Jesus seemed very near to me; I felt able to come to Him with all my griefs, misfortunes, and trials, even as the needy ones came to Him for relief when He was upon earth. There was a surety in my heart that He understood my peculiar trials and sympathized with me. I can never forget this precious assurance of the pitying tenderness of Jesus toward one so unworthy of His notice. I learned more of the divine character of Christ in that short period when bowed among the praying ones than ever before.*[5]

It would further appear that the influence of Wesleyan methodology, comprising of the quadrilateral (Scripture, tradition, reason and experience), led Ellen White to approach her "Great Controversy" from an historical perspective that is deeply grounded in Scripture and presented in a reasoned and logical format and reflecting her personal experiences of faith. Indeed, the bulk of her work is comprised of the elements of the quadrilateral. That is, scriptural exposition, as in the case of *The Desire of Ages*, *Patriarchs and Prophets* and *Prophets and Kings*; and reasoned responses to various personal issues, such as those found in *Testimonies for the Church*. Ellen White's experiences are conveyed in her *Early Writings* and *Life Sketches*, but also in her recollections of her visions. Therefore, her writings encompass biblical exposition of large sections of the Bible, both Old and New Testaments, as well as extensive literature on health, parenting, education, inter-personal relationships, and personal development.

In her ministry, she embodied the work of a prophet, in that she revived the truth of the Sabbath and the state of the dead found in Scripture, alerted people to its prophetic message regarding end time events, pointed to the signs that indicate the soon return of Christ, prophesied about events that came true, had divine insights into a number of people's individual circumstances, displayed a knowledge well beyond her education and the general knowledge of her time, and brought about a revival of faith in Christ. Therefore, the influences upon her life resulted in publications and correspondence rich with Arminian theology with a holiness emphasis, prophetic insights God had given her, and an emphasis on the biblical works of Daniel and Revelation which, synthesized, describe the events leading up to the soon return of Jesus Christ. She was, in no uncertain terms, an apocalyptic prophet who possessed a pastoral heart.

---

5. White, *Testimonies fo the Church: Vol. 1*, 17.

Chapter 3

THE GROUND OF THEOLOGY: REVELATION

IN BIBLICAL THEOLOGY, REVELATION DESCRIBES an encounter between God and humanity. God speaking to humanity forms the basis of the biblical narrative, which is further enhanced by humanity's response. The varying responses to God's commanding and objective voice weaved the history of the biblical narrative, which incorporates threads of God's wisdom, human sinfulness, faithfulness, and prophecy. While Scripture remains the founding and guiding principle of Christian theology, God is not limited to it. In addition to the written Word, God also reveals Himself to the human heart through a variety of means. Indeed, in addition to the spoken and written word, God also makes Himself known through creation (but does not inhabit creation), His actions of deliverance, healing, through the movement of the Holy Spirit and the life and works of Jesus Christ. Indeed, in Scripture, He communicates through the limitations of human language by way of the subjectivity of human feelings. Therefore, while the pure revelation of God in Scripture is to be taken as objective truth, with all revelation to be tested by it, a discussion of revelation is not limited to Scripture.

By its very nature, revelation from God cannot evade the human dimension. Since God's self-revelation seeks responsiveness, it is, therefore, only within a relational context that the sense of what is being imparted can truly be appreciated. This does not imply, however, that revelation is wholly, or even predominately, experiential. If a people are to move in a certain direction, obey various commands, or even re-orientate their very ground of being, then thought must take place that is grounded in a truth that can be spoken of with power. This is expressed clearly in Exodus 34:27: "Then the Lord said to Moses, "Write down these words, for in accordance with these words I have made a covenant with you and with Israel. (NASB)"

THE GROUND OF THEOLOGY: REVELATION

As a result, the act of revelation is designed to elicit a response. Indeed, God's revelation leads to a dialogue, which is potentially instructive, liberating, transforming, or condemnatory. Consequently, revelation implies communication in which information is imparted in the context of a relational dialogue that is transformative and tied in with God's redemptive will. Again, this concept is expressed in Exodus, as God spoke through Moses and sought a response from the people of Israel. "And all the people answered together, and said, all that the Lord hath spoken we will do. And Moses returned the words of the people unto the Lord (Exodus 19:8)."

There is also a strong sense of the spoken word in the New Testament. The words of the prophet directed the hearers to Jesus Christ and the need to make a response. "This is he who was spoken of through the prophet Isaiah: "A voice of one calling in the wilderness, 'Prepare the way for the Lord, make straight paths for him.'(NIV) (Matthew 3:3)". In John's Gospel, Mary Magdalene conveyed an urgency about the words that Jesus had spoken to her. "Mary Magdalene came and told the disciples that she had seen the Lord, and that he had spoken these things unto her (John 20:18)." A response to a declaration of the Gospel is found in the Book of Acts. After Peter's Pentecost sermon, the people felt compelled to respond to what they had heard. "Now when they heard this, they were pricked in their heart, and said unto Peter and to the rest of the apostles, Men and brethren, what shall we do (Acts 2:37)?"

Therefore, message, response, experience, relationship and dialogue are key terms that encompass the purpose and event of revelation. In the contemporary mind-set, the experience of relationship and the dynamics of feeling the truth can easily predominate. However, in biblical teaching, content always has precedence over feeling, since a feeling is responsive to a truth revealed. None-the-less, truth is always accompanied by feelings, since the context of God's self-disclosure to His people is a covenant, analogous to both a king and his subjects, and a marriage between a husband and wife. Isaiah presented this well: "For thy Maker is thine husband; the Lord of hosts is his name; and thy Redeemer the Holy One of Israel; The God of the whole earth shall he be called." (Isaiah 54:5) It is in the Book of Revelation that we find the fulfilment of human existence as being in the form of a marriage between Christ and His people;

> *Let us rejoice and be glad and give the glory to Him, for the marriage of the Lamb has come and His bride has made herself ready." It was given to her to clothe herself in fine linen, bright and clean; for the fine linen is the righteous acts of the saints. Then he said to me, "Write, 'Blessed are those who are invited to the marriage supper of the Lamb.'" And he said to me, "These are true words of God." (NASB) (Revelation 19:7–9).*

The core of objective truth, as it is revealed by God, can only be found in God Himself. What is ultimately revealed from God comes in the form of a person, Jesus

Christ, who is an embodiment of truth. He is the "way, the truth and the life (John 14:6)"; Divine wisdom in human form (John 1:1). Therefore, from God's perspective, revelation involves making known what is true and imparting the blessings of a loving God. However, revelation also includes admonition, rebuke and judgment, since it takes place within the context of a fallen world and a Creator's desire to see His creation perfected. Importantly, revelation includes prophecy, which points to Jesus Christ, in both His first and second appearing. Consequently, prophecy highlights the centrality of Jesus Christ to salvation and end-time events.

DEFINING REVELATION

The word, *revelation*, is derived from the Greek noun, *apokalypsis*, which is an *unveiling* or disclosure. The consequence of God's self-disclosure is a communication between two parties, the Divine and the human, which is often dynamic, informative and transformative. As James Garrett pointed out, revelation "involves both a Revealer and the recipient of the revelation."[1] The revealer is God and the recipients are usually His people, though not exclusively so, since He has commanded the universe into being, and sustains it by the power of His Word. To be sure, the heavens declare the glory of God (Psalm 19:1). Further, God communicated with heavenly beings before He spoke to His creation on earth (Ezekiel 28:14–15; Isa. 14:12–14; Rev. 12:7).

The wonder of revelation is that God makes Himself known. Therefore, Revelation is not doctrine, which proceeds from what has been made known, but an action from God that is efficacious in its intent. Indeed, doctrine arises as a consequence of revelation and, at its best, seeks to accurately convey the content of what has been revealed. Its weakness is found in the limitations of human language and the fact that what has been revealed must travel through the filter of the one who writes it down and conveys the message. Pure revelation therefore, can only be encountered at the event itself. None-the-less, what others come to hear and experience, albeit through the human medium, is sufficient for what is intended to be revealed. To be sure, God's revelation is always sufficiently expressed for the benefit of those who would read it so that it might go forward in power and achieve the purpose for which it was given. Indeed, doctrine, and explorative theology, must always be derived from the truth, which distinguishes it from philosophy, which "seeks after" the truth.[2] As humans, we hear and experience what is Divine, since revelation "is God entering human experience" to bring about a consciousness of His presence and power.[3] However, revelation is not raw energy, but a personal God seeking communication

---

1. Garrett, *Systematic Theology: Biblical, Historical and Evangelical: Vol. 1*, 44.
2. Weber, *Foundations of Dogmatics: Vol. 1*, 169.
3. Mullins, *The Christian Religion: In Its Doctrinal Expression*, 141.

with His created beings. Indeed, what is revealed comes from the storehouse of God's perfect wisdom and love that seeks to redeem a people that He might call His very own. Therefore, revelation must be referred to as an event. This is emphasized by the fact that as an event, there must be an actor and this leads to revelation belonging to God alone as holding the central part in the drama of redemption. As Otto Webber has averred, "revelation is in essence God's act."[4] This is clearly articulated by Isaiah. "But now, this is what the Lord says— he who created you, Jacob, he who formed you, Israel: 'Do not fear, for I have redeemed you; I have summoned you by name; you are mine' (NIV) (Isaiah 43:1)." Consequently, revelation is not a human announcement. In biblical revelation humanity does not speak, but is spoken about and to. Revelation is therefore received, and not created, by the Church.

Those who receive what is revealed must respond in some way. However, Revelation does not guarantee a specific outcome. There is a freedom to reject what has been declared. None-the-less, there is the possibility of acceptance, which amounts to a step of faith on the part of the recipient to trust the wisdom and truth of the One who has made it known. Consequently, revelation engages the mind in a relational encounter that seeks to draw the person, or people, on a pathway of faith that fulfils the agenda of God's redemptive purposes. Therefore, on the human side, revelation is foremost both a spiritual and intellectual event. To be sure, it is an event of the inner person, an act of one's whole being in response to God's self-disclosure.[5] Salvation, therefore, is not a mere intellectual ascent, the cognitive grasping of the concept of faith, or feelings that orientate one to the concept of God. Salvation is the surrender of the whole person, by which one, by the power of the Holy Spirit, is led to repentance of sin and immersion in the life of Jesus Christ. Therefore, we can conclude, along with Otto Weber, that revelation always leads to the knowledge of God, but also to the knowledge of self.[6]

Christian theology has traditionally divided revelation into two kinds: General and Special. General Revelation has to do with God revealing himself through nature, history and personal testimony. However, what is seen to be revealed through these means cannot contradict what has been revealed in Scripture, since "God cannot contradict His speech in Nature by His speech in Scripture. If the Author of Nature and Scripture are the same God, then the two books of God must eventually recite the same story."[7] That God reveals Himself in the created order is evident in Scripture. Psalm 19:1–6 embodies the Scriptural basis of this theology.

> *The heavens are telling of the glory of God;*
> *And their expanse is declaring the work of His hands.*

---

4. Weber, *Foundations of Dogmatics: Vol. 1*, 173.
5. Weber, *Foundations of Dogmatics: Vol. 1*, 141.
6. Weber, *Foundations of Dogmatics: Vol. 1*, 170.
7. Ramm, *The Christian View of Science and Scripture*, 25.

FOUNDATIONS OF THEOLOGY

Day to day pours forth speech,
And night to night reveals knowledge.
There is no speech, nor are there words;
Their voice is not heard.
Their line has gone out through all the earth,
And their utterances to the end of the world.
In them He has placed a tent for the sun,
Which is as a bridegroom coming out of his chamber;
It rejoices as a strong man to run his course.
Its rising is from one end of the heavens,
And its circuit to the other end of them;
And there is nothing hidden from its heat (NASB).

In Romans 1:18–20, Paul exhorts the reader to consider the moral nature of God as it has been revealed in creation. Therefore, regarding the necessity of salvation, there is no excuse.

General Revelation also refers to God making Himself known through the flow of history as His hand guides events, in conjunction with the free agency of humanity, to fulfil His purposes; particularly as He has outlined in prophecy. Again, we assert that in biblical faith the possible subjective insights of general revelation cannot contradict the teaching of Scripture, since the Canon of Scripture is objective. As well as historical events, God is seen, in the biblical account, to reveal Himself through prophecy. The Hebrew word for prophet is derived from a verb, *nabu*, which has the meaning of "to call" or "proclaim". The word is to be understood passively and not actively. That is, of one called and appointed by God and ministering totally on His behalf. Therefore, the prophet is not self-appointed, but has responded passively to the active call and equipping of God. As C.H. Peisker has concluded, behind "the passive form stands God as the agent, here the one who calls."[8] It is on this basis that the meaning of the prophet develops. The prophet is a called agent of God, who stands as the true author of the proclamation. From calling comes proclamation, since the prophet must show, present, or express him or herself as a prophet speaking what God has imparted. A number of prominent leaders in the early history of Israel are granted the title of prophet, including Abraham (Gen. 20:7), Moses (Deut. 34:10), Aaron (Ex. 7:1), and Miriam (Ex. 15:20). The major canonical prophets were Isaiah, Jeremiah and Isaiah, while the minor prophets include Amos, Micah, Hosea, Nahum, Joel, Obadiah, Zephaniah and Zechariah. The non-canonical prophets include Joseph, Samuel, Huldah and Nathan. Earlier forms of a prophetic ministry are found in the Old Testament before the so-called writing prophets took shape. One of these is the appearance of groups of ecstatics. Their presence was a cause of debate. In Numbers 11:10–30, seventy elders were seized by the Spirit of God and went into

---

8. Peisker, *Prophet*, 77.

THE GROUND OF THEOLOGY: REVELATION

ecstasy and Joshua responded critically. However, Moses said to him, "Are you jealous for my sake? Would that all the Lord's people were prophets, that the Lord would put His Spirit upon them! (NASB) (Num. 11:29)." As Gerhard von Rad has asserted, what we have here is the legitimation of the prophetic office.[9] The role of the prophet is to engage people with the veracity of the Bible and the commands of God. Biblically, this is exemplified through the prophet Nathan when he confronted King David over his sin with Bathsheba. He challenged David with the moral demands of the law, which had the result of renewal through repentance and faith.

Seventh-day Adventists view Ellen White to have met the prophetic requirements of the Bible, as she faithfully proclaimed the Gospel and renewed the biblical teaching of the Sabbath, the state of the dead, healthful living, the sanctuary service and the soon return of Jesus Christ. Yet while she is believed to have been a prophet inspired by God, she never considered her work to have been an extension of the Bible. By contrast, she believed her writings to primarily be a guide. "She saw her work as that of leading people back to the Bible. 'Little heed is given to the Bible,' she said, therefore 'the Lord has given a lesser light to lead men and women to the greater light.'"[10] Consequently, her writings are part of God's self-disclosure through General Revelation, since they are an inspired means to point humanity to the God of the Bible.

It is through Jesus Christ that God has ultimately revealed Himself in the course of human history. The Old Testament points to Jesus Christ and the New Testament testifies about Him. Consequently, we can assert that the Bible is the Christian's supreme and authoritative literary source of the revelation of God.[11] The Bible proclaims its own authority in both testaments. In Proverbs, Solomon announced every "word of God is pure: he is a shield unto them that put their trust in him. Add thou not unto his words, lest he reprove thee, and thou be found a liar (Proverbs 30:5–6)." Paul, in the New Testament affirmed that all "scripture is given by inspiration of God, and is profitable for doctrine, for reproof, for correction, for instruction in righteousness (2 Timothy 3:16)."

HISTORICAL DEVELOPMENT

The early church recognized the authority of the Scriptures. Justin Martyr (c. 160 AD) exhorted Christians to renounce the errors of their fathers and "read the prophecies of the sacred writers . . . (l)earn from them what will give you everlasting life."[12] Indeed, Clement of Rome (c. 96, AD) considered the emerging New Testament

---

9. Peisker, *Prophet*, 78.
10. White, *An Open Letter, Jan. 20, 1903*, 15.
11. Mullins, *The Christian Religion: In Its Doctrinal Expression*, 41.
12. Bercot, *A Dictionary of Early Christian Beliefs*, 598.

Canon to have been inspired; "(t)ake up the epistle of the blessed apostle Paul. What did he write to you at the time the Gospel first began to be preached? Truly, he wrote to you under the inspiration of the Spirit."[13]

The Reformers renewed the centrality of the Word of God after centuries of neglect. Martin Luther dealt with the question of how God may be known in his Galatians commentary of 1535. While affirming the validity of general revelation, Luther insisted that this is limited and inadequate, unless supplemented and corrected in the light of Scripture. However, it is the Scripture's capacity to unveil Jesus Christ as Lord and Saviour where its true authority lies. Luther asserted that: "God does not want to be known except through Christ; nor can he be known in any other way . . . Through Christ God declares his favour and mercy on us. In Christ, we see that God is not an angry master and judge but a gracious and kind father, who blesses us."[14] The Pietist, Philip Jakob Spener, upheld Scripture as the basis for Christian life. In his 1675 work, Pious Longings (Pia Desideria), Spener contended that,

> *thought should be given to the more extensive use of the Word of God among us . . . since faith must be enkindled through the gospel, and the law provides the rules for good works and many wonderful impulses to attain them. The more at home the Word of God is among us, the more we shall bring about faith and its fruits.*[15]

Further, Spener argued that sermons were not enough, since a diligent reading of Scripture, in addition to sermons, would give the people a deeper knowledge. Therefore, households should have their own Bible, which, in turn, would facilitate more private reading for personal edification and group reading for those who cannot read or have their own copy of the Bible.[16] In this matter Spener represented the Reformer's contention that the church must be the servant of the Word, not its master. Indeed, Donald Bloesch pointed to the Reformer's contention that "(s)cripture is to be and can be read by every person, who is able to find its clear message and directly search for the truth."[17]

In the twentieth century Karl Barth struck the same note of the Reformers when he formulated his doctrine of the Word of God. For Barth, the written word of Scripture is objective in that it leads the reader to God's revelation, because it bears witness to it. Indeed, Barth believed that the biblical writers, as such, are not the actual revelation itself, but "the witness to the revelation, and this expressed in human terms . . . "[18] Further, Bernard Ramm found, in a personal interview with

13. Bercot, *A Dictionary of Early Christian Beliefs*, 601.
14. McGrath, *The Christian Theology Reader*, 55.
15. McGrath, *The Christian Theology Reader*, 61.
16. McGrath, *The Christian Theology Reader*, 61
17. Bloesch, *Essentials of Evangelical Theology: Vol. 1*, 59.
18. Bloesch, *Essentials of Evangelical Theology: Vol. 1*, 52.

Barth (July 11, 1958), that the Basel theologian did in fact hold, more assuredly in his later thinking, that the revelation of God was still to be found in the written Word. As Ramm compared this comment with the *Church Dogmatics* he came to the conclusion that it is wrong to persist in affirming "that Barth's doctrine of inspiration is totally subjective and that he denies propositional revelation."[19] Indeed, Barth's theology of the Word testified that God is one who reveals Himself to humanity. Scripture bears witness to a Word that comes from above and so is an authority free from subjectivism. [20]

Ellen G. White, in contrast to Christian Fundamentalism, concurred with the Reformers that infallibility rests with God Himself, since "God and heaven alone are infallible."[21] Indeed, she rightly contended that God inspired the writers with the truth He sought to reveal, who, in turn, wrote in words of human origin.[22] Consequently, Ellen White's statements concerning the Bible, and her own work, indicate that the concept of verbal inspiration is without support in either the Bible writers' or her own word. This position was also clearly set forth at the General Conference session of 1883: "We believe the light given by God to His servants is by the enlightenment of the mind, thus imparting the thoughts, and not (except in rare cases) the very words in which the ideas should be expressed."[23] She also raised the issue in *The Great Controversy*. There she asserted that,

> *God has been pleased to communicate His truth to the world by human agencies, and He Himself, by His Holy Spirit, qualified men and enabled them to do this work. He guided the mind in the selection of what to speak and what to write. The treasure was entrusted to earthen vessels, yet it is, nonetheless, from Heaven. The testimony is conveyed through the imperfect expression of human language, yet it is the testimony of God; and the obedient, believing child of God beholds in it the glory of a divine power, full of grace and truth. In His Word, God has committed to men the knowledge necessary for salvation. The Holy Scriptures are to be accepted as an authoritative, infallible revelation of His will. They are the standard of character, the revealer of doctrines, and the test of experience.* [24]

---

19. Ramm, *After Fundamentalism: The Future of Evangelical Theology*, 119.
20. Ramm, *The Pattern of Religious Authority*, 21.
21. White, *Selected Messages: Book 1*, 37.
22. White, *Selected Messages: Book 1*, 24.
23. White, *Review and Herald*, Nov. 27, 1883.
24. White, *The Great Controversy*, vii.

Chapter 4

THE DOCTRINE OF GOD

When discussing the nature of God and His attributes, the possibility of actually knowing God must be the primary consideration. Surely there are two dangers to avoid; that of claiming to have a complete understanding of all aspects of God's being and attributes, or possessing a complete vagueness and uncertainty as to who God is, because He is too far removed from our limited comprehension. Alternatively, based on the biblical account, one can affirm that God can be known, and in some detail. However, He cannot be fully known, since His being is in many respects beyond the limitations of our comprehension and language. According to Ervene Bragg,

> *God is known and yet unknown. In His infinite perfection of being He dwells in the thick darkness. The mind cannot think of Him as He is in Himself. Through the impartations of some attributes of His in man, some revelations in nature, and through the Holy Scriptures, He has manifested enough of His incomprehensible reality upon which faith can rest. We can only know these things of which we have experience.*[1]

However, realizing the human predicament, "God, in His love and compassion, reached out to us in the Bible."[2] What we are able to assert is that the God of the Bible is a personal being. From Genesis 1:1 He is represented as one who speaks, acts and has dealings with humanity. As John Banks pointed out, all "the characteristics of personality are ascribed to him."[3] F.L Forlines further asserts that "(t)he fact that God is personal separates Him from the impersonal God of philosophy. He is not an

---

1. Bragg, *Systematic Theology—The Doctrine of God*, 11.
2. *Seventh-day Adventists Believe: An exposition of the fundamental beliefs of the Seventh-day Adventist Church*, 24.
3. Banks, *A Manuel of Christian Doctrine*, 77.

THE DOCTRINE OF GOD

impersonal object to be found by our searching. He is a personal God who cares and has declared Himself."[4]

Though not as prominent as the soteriological and ecclesiological arguments of the Reformation, the discussion of the knowledge of God featured in John Calvin's Institutes. He divided the topic between his two books and therefore gave two guiding headings to the discussion. In Book I, of the Institutes, he discussed "God the Creator", while in the second book, "God the Redeemer". By concentrating on the word "knowledge", Calvin did not mean to imply that simply knowing about God was sufficient. Nor did he seek to imply that a personal encounter was all that God looks for. According to David Steinmetz, Calvin's understanding of the knowledge of God involved "love, trust, fear, obedience, and worship of God. It embraced mind and heart, affections and will, worship and devout work. It rested on the gospel of God's free grace toward sinners and included the duties of both tables of the law, duties toward God and towards one's neighbours."[5] This knowledge of God is deepened over time, as is, consequently, the knowledge of self. According to Calvin, this knowledge of God is discovered through a variety of means. The historical figures of Adam and Eve "knew God through His self-revelation in nature and history."[6] Consequently, the possibility opens up for every natural process and historical event to give understanding as to the nature of the creative and providential care of God. Indeed, "The universe was a never-ending festival of divine self-revelation that stimulated the first human beings to the praise, thanksgiving, and love of God."[7] The devastating consequences of sin, however, resulted in the distortion of God's self-revelation. His voice that travelled through the wonder of creation was marred by the voice of rebellion and dissent. Consequently, a variety of responses now seek to echo the original revelation of God, with varying degrees of accuracy. None-the-less, God still reveals Himself. As Calvin put it, the fall muted rather than extinguished the revelation of God and His works. Though in his early reflections he referred to this predicament as blindness, he later softened this view to include limited possibilities: such as, "the scattered sparks of a fire that had all but gone out, a sudden flash of lightening on a dark night, and the reduced vision of an old man who could read a book only with the aid of spectacles."[8] According to Calvin, when humanity seeks to discover God in nature and history without correct vision they are unable to do so, and therefore construct idols in God's place. Importantly, the Bible is not the sole answer here, for what human reason requires is redemption, through which the human will is restored to harmony with the will of God. It is the Bible, together with the Holy Spirit,

---

4. Forlines, *Biblical Systematics*, 36.
5. Steinmetz, *The Theology of John Calvin*, 120.
6. Steinmetz, *The Theology of John Calvin*, 120.
7. Steinmetz, *The Theology of John Calvin*, 120.
8. Steinmetz, *The Theology of John Calvin*, 121.

that illuminates what is true and restores what is damaged. To use Calvin's imagery, they form the corrective lenses through which God's self-revelation begins to come into clarity. However, it is not mere knowledge that is attained, but an immersion in the love of God resulting in trust, fear, obedience and worship.[9]

Yet, while God is portrayed in human language, He is not confined to human life. To be sure, the "God of the Bible is depicted as the Creator of the universe and the Lord of history."[10] Therefore, He is to be characterised as powerful; the power that is above all other powers (1 Chron. 29:11; Isa. 40:22–23; Ps 22:28; 47:7–8). As Daniel proclaimed, "the most high God ruled in the kingdom of men, and that he appointeth over it whomsoever he will (Daniel 5:21)." God is the one who controls all wealth and honour, just as might and power are of His disposition (1 Chron. 29:12).

The majesty of God was explained by Theophilus, second-century bishop of Antioch, in terms of His omnipresence: "He is by no means to be confined in a place. For if he were, then the place containing Him would be greater than He."[11] Clement of Alexandria contended that God cannot be contained "either by limitation or by section . . . (t)hough heaven is called his throne, not even there is He contained."[12] John Owen, in exposition of Psalm 130, proclaimed that, "whatever God doth, and towards whomever, be they many or few, a whole nation, or city, or one single person, be they high or low, rich or poor, good or bad, all are the works of his hands, and he may deal with them as seems good unto him."[13]

In biblical theology, God is portrayed as the Lord of creation and the mover of history. He is not the "Idea of Good", as one might find in Plato, but the righteous sovereign who wills good. In contrast to Kant, who depicted God as the ideal of pure reason, He is a Supreme Intelligence who plans and shapes humanity's destiny.[14] God is the power above all powers. In 1 Chronicles 29:11 David decreed: " Yours, O Lord, is the greatness and the power and the glory and the victory and the majesty, indeed everything that is in the heavens and the earth; Yours is the dominion, O Lord, and You exalt Yourself as head over all (NASB)." Isaiah sought to comfort Israel with the scope of God's sovereign might when he declared: "It is he that sitteth upon the circle of the earth, and the inhabitants thereof are as grasshoppers; that stretcheth out the heavens as a curtain, and spreadeth them out as a tent to dwell in: That bringeth the princes to nothing; he maketh the judges of the earth as vanity (40:22–23)." Yet God

---

9. Steinmetz, *The Theology of John Calvin*, 122.
10. Bloesch, *Essentials of Evangelical Theology: Vol. 1*, 25.
11. Bercot, (ed), *A Dictionary of Early Christian Beliefs*, 312.
12. Bercot, (ed), *A Dictionary of Early Christian Beliefs*, 312.
13. McGrath, *The Christian Theology Reader*, 115.
14. Bloesch, *Essentials of Evangelical Theology: Vol. 1*, 25.

is known in His personhood. He is the living God who is the absolute personality in contrast to the finite.[15]

He is known in His church through the Word. To be sure, the "knowledge of God that is bound to the Word of God stands secure against every threat."[16] Apologetics must never lose sight of the actual ground of reality. The reality of God cannot be found in abstract possibilities, but only as God has ultimately chosen to reveal Himself. Indeed, when it comes to the knowledge of God, God Himself is the object who can only really be known as an object of faith. Therefore, a special kind of knowledge is sought after, namely, the knowledge of faith, "faith being the relation of the knower to the God who gives himself to be known."[17]

In our subjectivity and searching for the truth and self-devising solutions, it is only God who can intersect through the fog of uncertainty and demand a response as He shows Himself, opening our eyes to see Him as He is, "so that we may truly know Him as God."[18]

In biblical theology God is known by the names that are given to Him. In Psalm 50:1, three important words are used of God – *Yahweh* is God's designated name for Himself, which is most often translated LORD. Of particular importance is the revelation to Moses (Exodus 3:1316; 6:3). Exodus 3:14 appears to contain a play on words where *Yahweh* is interpreted by *ehyeh* (I am, or, I will be). The context suggests that God is who he is and does not need a name to identify him—there is no other like him—he stands alone. However, in his glorious condescension He takes on a name for the sake of humans to identify Him from among all others.

The proclamation of His name, because it presents God as a person and brings Him into relationship with other (human) personalities, is the offer of fellowship; the offer of a personal relationship, originally conveyed in the context of an ancient near eastern covenant. Therefore, it is a promise of God's presence and power. This name is also found in combination with other terms that reveal something of His character as the God who makes Himself present with whatever is needed for the occasion. *Yahweh Jireh*: *Yahweh* will see to it provide (Genesis 22:8,14) and *Yahweh Shalom*: *Yahweh* is Peace (Judges 6:24).

El is usually translated as God and has similar forms in other Semitic languages. It means "a god" in the widest sense, even if false or only an image. It is from a root indicating strength or might and speaks of a power which a person cannot master and which fills his/her religious consciousness. The translation of Psalm 50:1 ("The mighty God") is therefore a good one. In Israelite history, the term is usually found in conjunction with other titles or names. For example,

---

15. Hughes, *Christian Foundations*, 53.
16. Bromiley, *Introduction to the Theology of Karl Barth*, 57.
17. Bromiley, *Introduction to the Theology of Karl Barth*, 58.
18. Bromiley, *Introduction to the Theology of Karl Barth*, 58.

FOUNDATIONS OF THEOLOGY

El Elyon	God Most High	Genesis 14:1820
El Olam	God Everlasting	Genesis 21:33
El Shaddai	God Almighty	Genesis 17:1

Elohim, is a plural form of *el*, but may be used in the singular, in which case it is a reference to the one Supreme deity. It is usually translated as "God" (Genesis 1:1).

Another common title is *Adonai*, meaning "master" or "lord". The word is first found in Genesis 15:2, 8 on the lips of Abraham in address to God. Personal lordship is indicated by the use of this name. God is the ruler of all things and all are subject to Him. In the New Testament *Kyrios* is used in this sense. More often than not it refers to Jesus. Indeed, many texts in the Old Testament that speak of *Yahweh* are referred to Christ in the New Testament.

Typically, in systematic theology, God is described as having attributes. The older Reformed theology distinguished between the communicable and incommunicable attributes of God. According to the Lieden Synopsis, the former is life, wisdom, will and power and the latter simplicity, infinity, eternity and immensity. For J. H. Heiddegger the communicable attributes are life, intellect, will, goodness, justice, liberty, power and beatitude. The incommunicable include his independence, simplicity, infinity and immutability. His eternity and immensity are classed under infinity. Donald Bloesch believed that in our delineation of the attributes, or perfections, of God, we must guard against singling out any of them as giving an exhaustive definition of who God is. For example, if we say that God is exhaustive love, we are then neglecting his holiness and righteousness. It is also possible to magnify the holiness and majesty of God to such a degree that his love is relegated to secondary significance. Others emphasise God's sovereignty, as defined as absolute power, knowing and willing, to such an extent that there is no mention of love, mercy and grace.

John Miley identified the nature of God in terms of eternity. He asserted that God exists without beginning or end. In its deepest meaning this amounts to His endless existence in absolute unchangeableness of essence or attribute.[19] The Anabaptist, Daniel Kauffman, pointed to biblical references of the "eternal God" (Deut. 33:27), "The everlasting God" (Gen. 21:33), and the One who is from "everlasting to everlasting" (Psa. 103:17) and "For ever and ever" (Rev. 11:15).[20] Methodist theologian, Thomas Ralston, discussed the Hebrew theme of the unity of God, which he rightly believed to be essential to true worship.[21] Stanley Grenz elaborated by pointing to the center of Hebrew tradition, which bequeathed to the church "the belief in

---

19. Miley, *Systematic Theology: Vol. 1*, 214.
20. Kauffman, *Doctrines of the Bible: A Brief Discussion of the Teaching of God's Word*, 28.
21. Ralston, *Elements of Divinity*, 17.

one God and the rejection of the worship of many gods found among the surrounding nations. The Old Testament community asserted unequivocally that there is but one God and that he demanded loyalty (Deut.6:4–5)."[22] Fernando Canale, Professor of Theology and Philosophy at Andrews University, casted God's eternity in the context of His relationship with time. According to Canale, a biblical concept of God's eternity stands in relationship to our own understanding and experience of time. However, while humanity experiences the limitations of time, God transcends such limitations. "Our time is a very limited, finite sharing of time", therefore, to attempt to "define God's time would clearly be a speculative attempt in which we would be penetrating the mystery of His being. Here silence is eloquent."[23]

In keeping with his high view of the majesty and glory of God, John Calvin linked his understanding of God squarely to the witness of Scripture as apprehended in human experience. He is, the maker of heaven and earth and governs the universe founded by Him. Indeed, both his fatherly goodness and his beneficently inclined will are repeatedly extolled; and examples of his severity are given, which show him to be the righteous avenger of evil deeds, especially where his forbearance toward the obstinate is of no effect (Exodus 34:6–7; Psalm 145; Jer. 9:24; 1 Cor. 1:31).[24]

God is also commonly referred to as being omniscient. Indeed, Scripture clearly perceives God possessing the attributes of knowledge "in the highest possible perfection."[25] Further, there are no special or chronological limitations to His knowledge, for He knows all, in all places and throughout all time. That is, God knows all things that will occur in the future. This constitutes His foreknowledge. However, His foreknowledge is not an influencing agent in the course of events that will take place. God's foreknowledge points to His omniscience, not to His predetermination of all events that are yet to take place. In no way, therefore, does God's foreknowledge detract from freedom to human agency or the consequences of a corrupted and fallen creation. Indeed, events can be seen to transpire, as both God and humanity determine, within the creative context of a covenant. Ultimately, on a macro scale, God's will for His universe will be accomplished and His prophecy fulfilled. On a micro level, God is seen in Scripture, and in experience, to answer prayer. Miracles occur, people are healed, circumstances work in one's favour, care is provided and wisdom delivered. However, the consequences of human choice, the devices of Satan and the general outworking of a fallen world, are also seen to be active. It is through these complex lines that the garment of history is woven, and which, in various ways and times, we are called upon to wear. What the foreknowledge of God provides for us in this is the resolution of the complexity of a multitude of lines into a single

---

22. Grenz, *Theology for the Community of God*, 54.
23. Canale, *Doctrine of God*, 109.
24. Calvin, *Institutes* I.10.1–3, 76.
25. Ralston, *Elements of Divinity*, 19.

thread of God's perfect order, as the lines of sin and Satan are destroyed. God is able to accomplish this end because He is omnipotent.

Omnipotence is the infinity of God's power. The omnipotence of God was strongly affirmed in the early church. The Nicene Creed opens with the declaration: "I believe in God, the Father almighty." Yet does God's absolute power imply that He can do anything? If we affirm that God is not going to turn a circle into square or cancel His promise to establish a new heaven and earth, then we must come to the conclusion that His absolute power exists and operates within the framework of an existing order that He has already established. To be sure, God does not, and will not, act in contradictory ways outside the parameters of His logic or promise. Indeed, the omnipotence of God must be seen in the context of His whole being. Therefore, His power is not unrestricted and arbitrary, but rather in concord with His character. As Alister McGrath concluded, "God cannot do anything that is logically impossible." Nor can He do anything that is inconsistent with His nature. The point was made firmly by Anselm of Canterbury who, in his "Proslogion", prayed: "How can you be omnipotent, if you cannot do all things? But how can you do all things, if you cannot be corrupted, or tell lies, or make the true into the false?"[26] As Bloesch put it, "His power is not irresistibly efficacious, it is not naked freedom and sovereignty; rather it is in the service of His love."[27] It may well be true to say that God is capable of anything, but this should only be seen in the context of His desire to do everything to fulfil His redemptive purposes for creation. God's power must be distinguished from power itself, for God is in control of His power. Again, we must affirm that God, in all His power, does not stand as the direct or sole cause behind all events. However, He remains the Lord over every event. "It means that God is omnicompetent, capable of dealing with all circumstances", in such a way that nothing can defeat or change His plans for His creation.[28]

For the Reformers, God's omnipotence was "the explicit starting point of theological treatises on a variety of themes."[29] Indeed, they upheld the medieval notion that God is characterized by His intelligence and will, which itself was based on Augustine's axiom that "the will of God is the first and the highest cause of all bodily appearances and motions." The English medieval cleric, Thomas Bradwardine, affirmed that God's power was expressed in His will, which "is the efficient cause of anything whatever that is done." Such a will, Bradwardine concluded, was greater than anything humanity possesses.[30]

---

26. McGrath, *Christian theology: An Introduction*, 223–4.

27. Bloesch, *Essentials of Evangelical theology: Vol. 1*, 27.

28. McGrath, *Christian theology: An Introduction*, 28.

29. Pelikan, *The Christian Tradition (A History of the Development of Doctrine): Reformation of Church and Dogma (1300–1700)*, 25.

30. Pelikan, *Reformation of Church and Dogma (1300–1700)*, 25.

Because God is omnipotent, He is also omnipresent. Omnipresence declares that God is everywhere (2 Chron. 6:18; Amos 9:2-3). Indeed, as Ralston put it, His centre is everywhere but His circumference is nowhere." This would appear to be essential to God's character; "for without it we do not see the infinite power, wisdom, goodness, and other attributes, could be exercised."[31] Indeed, while Christ is at work in the Sanctuary, the Holy Spirit works in the hearts of His people everywhere.

Immutability points to the unchangeableness of God. The Book of Malachi has the most direct affirmation: "For I am the Lord, I change not (3:6)." This is responded to in the book of Hebrews with the assertion: "But thou art the same, and thy years shall not fail. (1:12)" The immutability of God "seems necessarily to result from the perfections of his character. As all his attributes are infinite, it is clear that they cannot be increased in perfection."[32] However, the unchangeableness of God should not imply the inability to express emotion. In contrast to classical theism, and the Westminster Confession of Faith, Scripture points to a God who clearly and freely involves himself in the travail of His creation. Therefore, God does not simply empathize with our pain, but enters into it and experiences it. As Bloesch put it, suffering "is not inherent in God, but God freely wills to enter into our suffering so that it can be overcome."[33] Therefore, in His relationship with humanity God, who does not change, alters His ways in conjunction with people's responses to His gracious invitation to enter into His life. Therefore, while God's purposes, particularly as outlined in prophecy, have certainty of fulfilment, His work in the world is in some way dependant on the faithfulness of His covenant partners, since He seeks to work through His people to accomplish His will. Consequently, while God's mission is determined by His will, each person's place in that mission is not in God's will, but contingent on human decision. It is for this reason that the love of God is expressed in both joy and grief.

The love of God is widely discussed in the scriptures. In Deuteronomy 4:37, His love is closely associated with His redemptive action. Here Moses announced to the people that "because he loved thy fathers, therefore he chose their seed after them, and brought thee out in his sight with his mighty power out of Egypt." In His proclamation to Moses of His Name, God characterizes Himself as "merciful, gracious, slow to anger, abounding in steadfast love and faithfulness, and as forgiving (Exodus 34:67)." Moreover, God's love is marked by His grace as it is bestowed freely upon those who do not merit it, (Mat.5:4348, Rom.3:2324, Hosea 14:47). God's love is also expressed in mercy and forgiveness. It is a love which is very ready to pardon sin and not to exact full punishment upon the sinner (Ezra 9:13, Isaiah 55:67). His love is also found in His longsuffering and forbearance. It is a love which is patient

---

31. Ralston, *Elements of Divinity*, 24.
32. Ralston, *Elements of Divinity*, 24.
33. Bloesch, *God the Almighty: Power, Wisdom, Holiness, Love*, 95.

with the sinner, primarily seen in that God is slow to anger and bears the pain of being sinned against for a long time (Rom.2:4, 2 Pet.3:89). It is for this reason that God defers His anger (Is. 48:911, Hos.11:811). The love of God is also to be witnessed in His faithfulness and steadfastness. It is a love that is always faithful and persists even in the face of unfaithfulness (Lamentations 3:22–23, Hosea 2:14:15). As these aspects of His love refer to His character, it can clearly be inferred that God's holiness and His love should not be separated. Indeed, His holiness and His love are complementary. This is evident in that God is a jealous God (Ex.20:5, 34:14, Deut.4:24, Ezek.16:3543) since He demands absolute commitment, which He seeks to be fulfilled and expressed by His people (1 John 4:12, Luke 10:27, 1 Peter 1:1416). In addition, God's Holy love is revealed relationally in different contexts.

On His part, God reveals Himself appropriately in pure and undefiled relationships; straight and without any hint of crookedness (Deut.32:3–4). Forlines pointed to the different aspects of God's love as it is expressed in different contexts. When God's love is expressed toward those in misery, it is referred to as mercy. However, when it is shared with those who are ill-deserving, it is seen as grace. When it is manifested to the good and bad alike it is called benevolence.[34] In drawing God's love and holiness together, in a dissolvable union, Forlines discussed the nature of God's grace. "The fact that grace is offered is owed to the love of God. That it is free is owed to the holiness of God."[35]

Donald Bloesch also pointed to the holy love of God. He expressed the essence of biblical revelation when he determined that "God in his essence is both love and holiness, and therefore it is of a holy love that we must speak when referring to divinity. God is love, but His love exists in tension with His holiness, indeed, it is informed by His holiness."[36] It was because "God so loved the world" that He saw it fit to send His Only Son, that in dying He might redeem those who are condemned in sin. Therefore, the love of God is generous, extensive and far-reaching, yet it is also sacrificial, self-giving and painful. It is a love that leads to forgiveness and reconciliation, and yet it is a costly expression of love that results in death, both for the Son of God and for those who remain estranged from God's covenant. As Bloesch reminded us, it is also costly for the Christian, since it calls for a life of discipleship under the cross.

The love that comes from God accepts sinners as they are, in their sin, but because it is holy love, it demands that sinners change their ways, since God's love not only calls, but also occupies those who open their hearts. Furthermore, holy love is not weak or submissive, but possesses a severity that is quite distinct from the popular understanding of love, since it stands in judgement, ready to destroy all that is not of God. To be sure, "holy love does not cancel the demands of the law

---

34. Forlines, *Biblical Systematics*, 47.
35. Forlines, *Biblical Systematics*, 47.
36. Bloesch, *Essentials of Evangelical Theology: Vol. 1*, 32.

but seeks the fulfilment of these demands."[37] The holy love of God is also inseparable from His wrath, since it is a reaction of His holiness to sin. "Wrath is not the basic disposition of God toward his people, since God is 'slow to anger', but nonetheless it connotes the searing reaction of God to continued violations of His law. It is His righteous indignation against wrongdoing"[38], since in God's restorative justice all sin is eliminated, together with its author. Therefore, God's love can be likened to a fiery flame, that either purifies, or utterly destroys. Richard Rice, in his The Reign of God, defined God's love in relation to the Greek word, agape. Unlike eros, agape does not depend on desirable qualities in its object, nor does it seek possession. It is self-giving, self-sacrificing and untainted by self-interest. It is unconditional. Indeed, Rice described such love as "aggressive, generous and uncalculating."[39] God's love is also related to His work of salvation. As Canale pointed out, divine love is more than just relational. "Divine love is spelled out when, according to the eternal predestination of God, the 'goodness and loving kindness of God our saviour appeared' (Titus 3:4) and the Father of Jesus Christ 'gave us eternal comfort and good hope through grace' (2 Thess. 2:16)."[40] Therefore, love sums up the being of God. This is why the Apostle John can say, "God is love", in 1 John 4:8.

THE PRE-EXISTENCE OF GOD

The pre-existence of God was asserted by the early Christian apologists. They wrote in response to accusations, by the pagans, that the Jewish and Christian notions of God were ridiculous. They claimed that Christians and Jews understood God to be omnipotent, and yet constantly delved into human affairs by going into "every home listening to what is said and even checking out what is being cooked."[41] In the second century the converted Greek philosopher of Athens, Aristides, declared that:

> *God is not born, nor made. He is of an ever-abiding nature without beginning and without end. He is immortal, perfect, and incomprehensible. Now, when I say He is 'perfect,' I mean that there is no defect in Him and that He is not in need of anything. Rather, all things are in need of Him . . . The heavens do not limit Him.*[42]

Irenaeus, second century bishop of Lyon, also emphasised the self-sufficiency of God when he stated that "He Himself does not receive any benefit from (humanity).

---

37. Bloesch, *Essentials of Evangelical Theology: Vol. 1*, 33.
38. Bloesch, *Essentials of Evangelical Theology: Vol. 1*, 34.
39. Rice, *The Reign of God*, 61.
40. Canale, *Doctrine of God*, 111.
41. González, *The Story of Christianity: Vol. 1*, 51.
42. Bercot, *A Dictionary of Early Christian Beliefs*, 309.

For He is rich, perfect, and in need of nothing."[43] These assertions lay in contrast to Gnosticism's threat to the early church. Gnosticism virtually removed God from the world of temporality and materiality. Its goal was to "break free from the bonds of the flesh and to ascend to the purely spiritual realm where we reunite with divine being. Redemption is from an evil material environment rather than from the perversion of sin, which for orthodox Christians originates in the realm of spirit."[44]

THE FATHERHOOD OF GOD

The fatherhood of God involves His creative work in the universe and His providence. The term finds its fullest meaning when used by Jesus Christ. The concept of the Father guiding the son was in stark distinction from the pagan nations, whose female deities give birth in the primordial chaos. Also, it is for purposes of establishing Israel's God as being in covenant with His people, as being distinct from the surrounding nations, that the masculine is used. That is, a male God is in relationship with a female people. In biblical imagery, the final chapter in this relationship culminates in a marriage (Ez. 16:8–14; Isa. 54:5; Eph. 5:25–33; Jn. 3:29; Rev. 19:7–9).

The fatherhood of God is a rare concept in the Old Testament. However, there are a number of passages that refer to God as the Father of angels and humanity. In Job (1:6; 2:1) the people are referred to as God's sons, however there are more allusions to the fatherhood of God in the Old Testament than there are direct references. God's fatherly regard for the people of Israel are found in God's watch care over them through the exodus, during which time they were chosen from among the nations to be Yahweh's adopted children. In Deuteronomy 14:1 God proclaims to them, "You are the sons of the Lord your God; you shall not cut yourselves nor shave your forehead for the sake of the dead (NASB)."

This filial relationship is more overtly declared in 2 Samuel 7:14 as God describes His future relationship with Solomon. "I will be his father, and he shall be my son. If he commits iniquity, I will chasten him with the rod of men, and with the stripes of the children of men". In Isaiah 1:2–31, God claims to be Father: "I have nourished and brought up sons—not, I have nourished and brought up slaves—or subjects—or creatures—or insects—or beasts of burden—I have nourished and brought up sons: I am the Father of creation, the fountain and origin of the paternal and filial religion."[45]

In the Old Testament God's fatherliness is also expressed in terms of His attributes as creator and provider. In the event of Moses passing on the leadership of God's people to Joshua in his one hundred and twentieth year, God's gracious

---

43. Bercot, *A Dictionary of Early Christian Beliefs*, 309.
44. Bloesch, *God the Almighty*, 81.
45. Parker, *The People's Bible*.

forbearance with the people of Israel is compared to the watch care of a father. "Is this the way you repay the Lord, you foolish and unwise people? Is he not your Father, your Creator, who made you and formed you? (NIV) (Deut. 32:6)?" Also, in Isaiah, God is portrayed as a father who moulds and shapes the character of His children. "But now, O Lord, thou art our father; we are the clay, and thou our potter; and we all are the work of thy hand (Isa 64:8)." The fatherhood of God is also found in the Old Testament expressed in relation to the Father's love and compassion. The Psalmist picked this up when he reflected that just "As a father has compassion on his children, so the Lord has compassion on those who fear him (NIV) (Ps 103:13)." In the Book of Jeremiah, the hope of Israel is expressed in terms of a perpetual and lasting covenant relationship between the father and His children. The fatherhood of God is here cast in the mould of grace, forbearance and the love that God has a people He has called. It expresses His longing to put an end to sin and establish an everlasting kingdom that embodies more than simple victory, but victory for the everlasting love the father longs to lavish on His people. "But I said, how shall I put thee among the children, and give thee a pleasant land, a goodly heritage of the hosts of nations? and I said, Thou shalt call me, My father; and shalt not turn away from me (Jer. 3:19)."

While rare in the Old Testament, there is a decided turn in the New Testament with the ministry of Jesus, for "Father" was his favorite term for addressing God. In the New Testament Jesus refers to God as father sixty-five times in the Synoptic Gospels and over one hundred times in John.[46] Further, Jesus' unique contribution was in referring to God as *Abba*. This is not a teaching found in the Old Testament, nor does it find a context within first century Palestine. It does in fact express Jesus' unique and unprecedented relationship with the Father. As the Son of God, Jesus created a persona in ministry that was within the context of the people of God in first century Palestine. Yet He embraced a new era He had come to proclaim that did not fit existing expectations. Central to this new era was His unique relationship with the Father and a new way of being the people of God that He had come to inaugurate. As a consequence, as the German Lutheran theologian Joacham Jeramias pointed out, "Jesus could not be content with the liturgically prescribed prayers of Palestinian Judaism." Therefore, He "introduced a new way of speaking about God and to God."[47] This new way of speaking, as a child to their father, characterized a new intimacy, security and love that had previously not been the experience of God's people up until this point. Jeramius affirmed that this new way of addressing God was a sign of a new age, "which celebrates the open door to God in Jesus whereby sinners may receive forgiveness and enjoy a new relationship with the Father through Christ."[48]

---

46. Stevick, *Jesus and His Own: A Commentary on John 13–17*, 178.
47. Jeramias, *The Prayers of Jesus*, 77.
48. Jeramias, *The Prayers of Jesus*, 77.

FOUNDATIONS OF THEOLOGY

Daniel Kauffman asserted that the fatherhood of God "is brought out in fuller light and prominence in the New Testament." The reason for this increase in prominence correlates with the centrality of the Son and His repeated references to the Father.[49] Indeed, it is in the teaching of Jesus Christ, the Son of God, that the clearest portrait of God the Father is found. Perhaps in no other place is this portrait better defined than in the Lord's Prayer (Matt 6:9–13). Its commencement with "Our Father", places the Christian's relationship with God the Father in the context with their relationship with Jesus Christ. Indeed, the sonship of Christ is the basis of the sonship of all believers, as all, in Christ, become sons and daughters of the Father. The born-again believer, in Jesus Christ, enters into a new existence by the baptism of the Holy Spirit. This new existence is characterized by union with Christ. In this union, the believer's status is altered to "child of God" and relationships are re-defined in terms of brothers and sisters, since God is now the Father of all His people. The Lord's Prayer adds to our relationship with the Father with the location of the Father. Our Father is in heaven, which is seen to be His eternal dwelling place. When the Father is addressed, it is not to one who became incarnate, like the Son, or present in our lives with power, as with the Spirit. Importantly, the presence of the Father in Heaven places Him beyond the limitations of this world and within the bounds of human creation and expression. This reminds us that our faith is not a "this earthly" business, but one that has its origins in a creator God who speaks to us from above us and seeks to draw us to an existence that is removed from personal striving and ability. To be sure, the kingdom of God belongs to the Father, and since the kingdom is His, then the will of the Father, who must rule over our lives, must have pre-eminence. Indeed, Saul of Tarsus, at his conversion, expressed the Christian attitude when he asked what God wanted him to do (Acts 9:6). "If we give the Father the proper recognition we will make His will supreme in our minds, in our lives, in our Christian service. The true child of God has no will save to do the will of the Father."[50] For this reason it must be the will of the Christian that the Father leads us, in the same way as Christ sought the leading of the Father during His earthly ministry.

Constant prayer, in petition and enquiry, was the hallmark of Christ's prayer as He often withdrew to lonely places to seek for strength, guidance and assurance. This relationship is particularly evident in the garden of Gethsemane, when Jesus sought that His cup of suffering be taken away from Him. However, it was not His own will that He sought, but the will of the Father. However, our desire to be led by the Father and to follow His will is meaningless and to no effect, unless we also desire to be delivered from evil, since it is Satan who seeks to undermine and shipwreck

---

49. Kauffman, *Doctrines of the Bible*, 55.
50. Kauffman, *Doctrines of the Bible*, 57.

THE DOCTRINE OF GOD

any relationship with the Father that is characterized by the faithfulness of the Son imprinted in the heart of the believer.[51]

In Ellen White's writings, we find an emphasis of the love of the Father for fallen humanity. Indeed, the formulation of the plan of salvation for humanity derives from the love of the Father. According to Fernando Canale, "She identified the central piece of the plan, Christ's covenant with the Father, to represent the love of God by taking human form (16MR 192)."[52] Further, Mrs White discussed the form of the Father. At a general conference at Sutton, Vermont, in September 1850, Ellen White received a vision. In it she recalls:

> I saw a throne, and on it sat the Father and the Son. I gazed on Jesus' countenance and admired His lovely person. The Father's person I could not behold, for a cloud of glorious light covered Him. I asked Jesus if His Father had a form like Himself. He said He had, but I could not behold it, for said He, if you should once behold the glory of His person, you would cease to exist.[53]

This significant vision highlights the prophetic nature of Ellen White's ministry. While not being a repetition of a biblical message, it certainly accords with Scripture and in no way, contradicts it. Indeed, it assists in our understanding of the Bible by providing a more in-depth understanding. In regard to not seeing His face, we can turn to two important texts that verify that not seeing the face of the Father is a biblical theme. Firstly, John 1:18: "No man hath seen God at any time; the only begotten Son, which is in the bosom of the Father, he hath declared him." Secondly, in John 6:46: "Not that any man hath seen the Father, save he which is of God, he hath seen the Father." Importantly, however, is the inference in these two verses that God the Father can ultimately be seen, but cannot be seen at this point in time. Therefore, God must have a form. This is accentuated in Revelation, which reveals that the time will come when believers in heaven will see his face. Rev. 22:3, 4: "There will no longer be any curse; and the throne of God and of the Lamb will be in it, and His bond-servants will serve Him; they will see His face, and His name will be on their foreheads (NASB)." Ellen White, through this vision, importantly pointed out that while the Father is now hidden, the time will come when all of His people will behold Him. The apparent distance of the Father, as one who was never incarnate on earth or who has ever been seen, will be resolved in a new heaven and earth. In this way, Heaven is not only a place where sin is removed, for sin has been destroyed along with its champion, but a full revelation of the Father is introduced as a subsequent blessing.

---

51. Kauffman, *Doctrines of the Bible*, 57.
52. *The Ellen G. White Encyclopedia*, 843.
53. White, *Early Writings*, 54.

FOUNDATIONS OF THEOLOGY
GOD AND SUFFERING

The love of God is also deeply intertwined with His suffering. This is seen in the writing of Martin Luther, who pursued a distinctive theology of the cross (1518–19). Luther's "theology of the cross" discerns God hidden in the suffering and humiliation of the cross of Christ. The Reformer apparently used the phrase *theology of the cross* for the first time in his *Lectures on Hebrews* (1517–1518). Commenting on Hebrews 12:11, Luther drew the contrast between discipline as an alien work of God (God sending pain) and a proper work of God (the pain is for our benefit). "Here we find the Theology of the Cross," says Luther, because the fruit of righteousness is "hidden" by pain, just as salvation is "hidden" by the cross. Thus, God's work among believers is hidden in the crosses they carry, and God's work of salvation is hidden in the cross of Christ. Luther further clarified his theology of the cross in his *Explanation of the Disputation Concerning the Value of Indulgences*, 1518:

> *From this you can see how, ever since the scholastic theology—the deceiving theology (for that is the meaning of the word in Greek)—began, the theology of the cross has been abrogated, and everything has been completely turned upside down. A theologian of the cross (that is, one who speaks of the crucified and hidden God) teaches that punishments, crosses, and death are the most precious treasury of all and the most sacred relics which the Lord of this theology himself has consecrated and blessed, not alone by the touch of his most holy flesh, but also by the embrace of his exceedingly holy and divine will, and he has left these relics here to be kissed, sought after, and embraced. Indeed, fortunate and blessed is he who is considered by God to be so worthy that these treasures of Christ should be given to him; rather, who understands that they are given to him. For to whom are they not offered? "Count it all joy, my brethren, when you meet various trials" [Jas. 1:2]. For not all have this grace and glory to receive these treasures, but only the most elect of the children of God.* [LW 31.225-6]
>
> *A theologian of glory does not recognize, along with the Apostle, the crucified and hidden God alone [I Cor. 2:2]. He sees and speaks of God's glorious manifestation among the heathen, how his invisible nature can be known from the things which are visible [Cf. Rom. 1:20] and how he is present and powerful in all things everywhere. This theologian of glory, however, learns from Aristotle that the object of the will is the good and the good is worthy to be loved, while the evil, on the other hand, is worthy of hate. He learns that God is the highest good and exceedingly lovable. Disagreeing with the theologian of the cross, he defines the treasury of Christ as the removing and remitting of punishments, things which are most evil and worthy of hate. In opposition to this the theologian of the cross defines the treasury of Christ as impositions and obligations of punishments, things which are best and worthy of love. Yet the theologian of glory still receives money for his treasury, while the theologian of*

> *the cross, on the other hand, offers the merits of Christ freely. Yet people do not consider the theologian of the cross worthy of consideration, but finally even persecute him.* [LW 31.227]

Luther saw the theology of the cross as the *only* correct way to view God and the only way to correctly view the life of the believer. Therefore, the cross stands as the bridge between both. God comes to humanity through the cross, and humanity, in turn, comes to God through the cross.

Alister McGrath further clarified the idea of God's "concealed revelation": Only those who have faith understand the true meaning of the cross. Where the unbeliever sees nothing but the helplessness and hopelessness of an abandoned man dying upon a cross, the theologian of the cross (*theologus cruces*) recognizes the presence and activity of the "crucified and hidden God (*Deus crucifixus et absconditus*)," who is not merely present in human suffering, but actively works through it. It is with this God, and none other, that Christian theology must come to terms. As Luther himself emphasized, faith is the only key by which the hidden mystery of the cross may be unlocked: "The cross is the safest of all things. Blessed is the man who understands this."[54]

In the late twentieth century Jürgen Moltmann's *The Crucified God* (1974) expounded this idea. In his conception, the cross must be seen as an event between the Father and the Son, in which the Father suffers the death of his Son in order to redeem sinful humanity. Moltmann argued that a God who cannot suffer is deficient and cannot be envisaged as a perfect God. Stressing that God cannot be forced to change or undergo suffering, Moltmann declared that God willed to undergo suffering. According to Bloesch, God remains above pain and suffering even while descending into the world of confusion and misery. He is not invulnerable to pain and suffering, but he rises above them. Contrary to Moltmann, Bloesch contended that a theology of the cross must be completed in a theology of glory. Furthermore, suffering is not inherent in God, but God freely wills to enter into our suffering so that it can be overcome.

---

54. McGrath, *Luther's Theology of the Cross: Martin Luther's Theological Breakthrough*, 149–50, 175.

Chapter 5

THE PERSON OF JESUS CHRIST

As James Leo Garrett has affirmed, the "doctrine of the person of Christ has been traditionally concerned with the deity and the humanity of Jesus and their interrelation."[1] While the work of Christ is concerned with what Jesus has done for us, His person relates to who He is. As with humanity, identity and action are unable to be separated, no matter how convenient this might be for a systematic theology. To be sure, who Jesus is, is not easily distinguished from what He does. Therefore, it is true to say that the work of Jesus Christ is an expression of His person, both human and divine.

The name Jesus Christ consists of a proper name, Jesus, and a title or descriptor, Christ. It stands as an expression of the early Christian's belief that their Master, Jesus of Nazareth, was their Lord, their Saviour and the promised Redeemer. The name, Jesus, is an anglicised form of a Greek name, which was derived from Hebrew, translated into English as Joshua. As a name among Jews it appears to have come into popular use around the time of the Babylonian exile as a replacement of the older Jehoshua. Indeed, among the Jews of the First Century, both in Palestine and throughout the Dispersion, the name was widely used. To be sure, the Jewish historian, Josephus, names no fewer than 19 bearers of the name Jesus in his writings.[2]

The humanity of Jesus is identified in the Gospels as being born, living and then dying, in Palestine. Indeed, the Gospels give no hint of Jesus being anything other than fully human. As Bernard Ramm contended, the clearest expression of the humanity of Christ is found in Philippians 2:5–11. "There are three expressions in the Philippian passage that speak to the humanity of Christ: firstly, He was in the form of a servant; secondly, He was in the likeness of men; and thirdly, He was in the

---

1. Garrett, *Systematic Theology*, 527.
2. Rengstorf, *Jesus Christ*, 335.

appearance of a man."³ However, His likeness is more than simply His appearance. His humanity also incorporated his thoughts and feelings, yet all without sin and in full and perfect subjugation to the Father.

The account of Jesus' birth is found in the Gospels of Matthew and Luke. Both accounts emphasise the virgin birth of Jesus Christ. This is particularly central to Matthew's account.

Matthew 1:18–25 states:

> *Now the birth of Jesus Christ was as follows: when His mother Mary had been betrothed to Joseph, before they came together she was found to be with child by the Holy Spirit. And Joseph her husband, being a righteous man and not wanting to disgrace her, planned to send her away secretly. But when he had considered this, behold, an angel of the Lord appeared to him in a dream, saying, "Joseph, son of David, do not be afraid to take Mary as your wife; for the Child who has been conceived in her is of the Holy Spirit. She will bear a Son; and you shall call His name Jesus, for He will save His people from their sins." Now all this took place to fulfill what was spoken by the Lord through the prophet: "BEHOLD, THE VIRGIN SHALL BE WITH CHILD AND SHALL BEAR A SON, AND THEY SHALL CALL HIS NAME IMMANUEL," which translated means, "GOD WITH US." And Joseph awoke from his sleep and did as the angel of the Lord commanded him, and took Mary as his wife, but kept her a virgin until she gave birth to a Son; and he called His name Jesus* (NASB).

The doctrine of the virgin birth infers that Jesus was conceived without a human father. This is not to suggest that the virgin birth refers to some kind of holy marriage between Mary and God, as one might find in ancient mythologies. What we have in this virgin conception and birth is a union between the divine and the human. John, in his gospel, conceptually points to this when he states that, "the Word was made flesh and dwelt among us (John 1:14)." As Donald Bloesch stipulated, "The virgin birth signifies the conception not of an independent human existence but of a human nature. The Son of God united human flesh with the divine person."⁴ Furthermore, the virgin birth takes God's work of redemption beyond the will of humanity. God's approach clearly signifies that He came into an incarnate form without male desire, pride, or a power that seeks to subdue and oppress. Therefore, the virgin birth "may be a sign of God's independence of ordinary human processes."⁵ Indeed, it is a powerful testimony to the majesty, wonder and magnificence of God's grace, whose immense love resulted in a divine mission to save. Therefore, salvation is not a human activity, but one that comes from above. Consequently, the source of our hope can only be found in God.

---

3. Ramm, *An Evangelical Christology: Ecumenic and Historic*, 75.
4. Bloesch, *Jesus Christ: Saviour and Lord*, 86.
5. Wakefield, in Bloesch, *Jesus Christ: Saviour and Lord*, 86.

That the virgin birth points to the sovereignty of God in matters of redemption, is found in it being a fulfilment of prophecy. Matthew's Gospel refers to Isaiah, who offers one of numerous prophecies that point to the person and work of Jesus Christ. "Therefore, the Lord himself shall give you a sign; Behold, a virgin shall conceive, and bear a son, and shall call his name Immanuel (Isaiah 7:14)." It may well have been the intention here to provide one representative example of a weight of prophetic evidence that pointed to Jesus Christ as the fulfilment of messianic prophecies. Micah 5:2 prophesies that the Messiah will be born in Bethlehem, which is found fulfilled in Luke's account of Jesus' birth (Luke 2:1–7). Hosea 11:1 points to the Messiah being called out of Egypt; a fact outlined in Matthew 2:13–15,

> *Now when they had gone, behold, an angel of the Lord appeared to Joseph in a dream and said, "Get up! Take the Child and His mother and flee to Egypt, and remain there until I tell you; for Herod is going to search for the Child to destroy Him."*
>
> *So Joseph got up and took the Child and His mother while it was still night, and left for Egypt. He remained there until the death of Herod. This was to fulfill what had been spoken by the Lord through the prophet: "Out of Egypt I called My Son (NASB).*

Even the crucifixion of Jesus finds detail in various Old Testament prophecies, including that He would be pierced in His hands and feet (Psalm 22:16), and in His side (Zechariah 12:10). However, the most striking prophecy is found in Daniel 9:25–27. This "70 Week Prophecy", starting with the decree to return and re-build Jerusalem in 457 B.C, leads to the baptism of the "Messiah the Prince" in A.D. 27, when He started His ministry and A.D. 31, when Christ's death on the cross caused an end to "sacrifice and the oblation".

In Luke's Gospel, there is an emphasis on the angelic announcement. The angel Gabriel is sent by God to announce to Mary events that are soon to take place, that will lead to the salvation of a people for God. Importantly, Gabriel had last appeared to Daniel with prophecies regarding these vary events about to unfold. In *The Sanctified Life*, Ellen White described Daniel's encounter with Gabriel;

> *As Daniel's prayer is going forth, the angel Gabriel comes sweeping down from the heavenly courts to tell him that his petitions are heard and answered. This mighty angel has been commissioned to give him skill and understanding—to open before him the mysteries of future ages. Thus, while earnestly seeking to know and understand the truth, Daniel was brought into communion with Heaven's delegated messenger. In answer to his petition, Daniel received not only the light and truth which he and his people most needed, but a view of the great events of the future, even to the advent of the world's Redeemer.*[6]

---

6. White, *The Sanctified Life*, 47.

THE PERSON OF JESUS CHRIST

It was this same messenger sent by God to inform Daniel of events that were to unfold in the future, who comes to inform Mary that these events are soon to be fulfilled. Therefore, Gabriel, the messenger on both occasions, draws these two events together into a single narrative, emphasising the key element of prophecy in biblical revelation and the centrality of Jesus Christ to these prophecies.

> *Now in the sixth month the angel Gabriel was sent from God to a city in Galilee called Nazareth, to a virgin engaged to a man whose name was Joseph, of the descendants of David; and the virgin's name was Mary. And coming in, he said to her, "Greetings, favored one! The Lord is with you." But she was very perplexed at this statement, and kept pondering what kind of salutation this was. The angel said to her, "Do not be afraid, Mary; for you have found favor with God. And behold, you will conceive in your womb and bear a son, and you shall name Him Jesus. He will be great and will be called the Son of the Most High; and the Lord God will give Him the throne of His father David; and He will reign over the house of Jacob forever, and His kingdom will have no end* (NASB)(Luke 1:26–33).

The human birth of Jesus Christ has further implications for humanity. As Thomas Torrance pointed out, it "is upon Christ's unique birth once and for all that our birth depends and, in his birth, we are given to share."[7] This is very much at the heart of the ordinance of baptism. Indeed, in baptism we testify to the One we have been incorporated into, "the one who was born of the Spirit from above, whose birth was marked by miracle as the new beginning of mankind."[8]

The birth of Jesus Christ is essential in understanding the incarnate nature of His ministry, begun at His baptism. To be sure, the ministry of Jesus began with His baptism (Mark 1:1–15; Acts 1:21–22; 10:37). This is well attested to in the prophecy of Daniel 9:20–27. As already stated, the starting point of the prophetic time periods mentioned in Daniel is 457 B.C. This date coincides with the decree to the Israelites to return from their captivity and re-build the Sanctuary. The first period of time mentioned in seven weeks, which amounts to 49 years when the prophetic day for a year principle is applied (Num. 14:34; Ez. 4:5–6). Adding to this 62 week (or 434 prophetic years) brings the prophecy to "the Messiah the Prince" in 27 A.D. In that year Jesus begins His ministry at His baptism when the Holy Spirit descends and anoints Him (Luke 3:21–23). When Christ declared the "The time is fulfilled (Mk. 1:15)", He was referring to the fulfilment of Daniel's prophecy.

The virgin birth is well attested to by the early church. Tertullian, a Christian writer from Carthage, North Africa, emphasised the importance of the virgin birth in describing the two natures of Christ. In the virgin birth, one finds a union between humanity and the divine in one person. He wrote that the "ray of God, then,

---

7. Torrance, *Incarnation: The Person and Life of Christ*, 91.
8. Torrance, *Incarnation: The Person and Life of Christ*, 91.

as it was always foretold in ancient times, descended into a certain virgin. And He was made flesh in her womb. So, in His birth, God and man were united."[9] However, like many of the early writers, Tertullian cautions that to reject the virgin birth is to reject Jesus Christ. A merely human Jesus Christ is not able to offer salvation, and a wholly divine Messiah lacks any ability to be a representative of humanity. Therefore, as Tertullian stated, whoever "wishes to see Jesus, the Son of David, must believe in Him through the virgin's birth."[10] Irenaeus, the first century Bishop of Lyons, wrote scathingly about the Ebionites[11] for rejecting the virgin birth, clearly allocating them among the heretics. Indeed, the importance with which he held to the virgin birth is emphasised in his assertion that God will judge the Ebionites. "How will man escape from the birth that is subject to death, if it is not by means of a new birth, given in a wonderful and unexpected manner by God—that regeneration that flows from the virgin through faith?"[12]

Later, Apollinaris of Laodicea (c. 310-c.390), in an overreaction to Arius, would claim that Jesus was not fully human. This can be seen in a letter Apollinaris wrote to the bishops at Diocaesarea, in which he asserted that the "Word did not assume a 'changeable' human mind in the incarnation, which would have led to the Word being trapped in human sin."[13] Writing on the Mind of Christ, he stated:

> *We confess that the Word of God has not descended upon a holy man, which was what happened in the case of the prophets. Rather, the Word himself has become flesh without having assumed a human mind—that is, a changeable mind, which is enslaved in filthy thoughts—but which exists as an immutable and heavenly divine mind.*[14]

In response, Gregory of Nazianzus (329–389) wrote a vigorous letter confronting the central thesis of Apollinaris. Gregory primarily argued that the Apollinarian school denied the possibility of redemption. His argument forms the basis of the eastern church's concept of salvation: that which is not assumed cannot be saved. Biblically, this refers to Jesus' ability to be a complete representative for humanity, which leads to a totally sufficient atonement. That is, Christ being fully one of us was fully able to represent us on the cross as an offering for sin. His human resurrection from the grave also points the way to the possibility for all the redeemed to follow

---

9. Bercot, *A Dictionary of Early Christian Beliefs*, 671.
10. Bercot, *A Dictionary of Early Christian Beliefs*, 671.
11. The doctrines of this sect are said by Irenaeus to be like those of Cerinthus and Carpocrates. They denied the Divinity and the virginal birth of Christ; they clung to the observance of the Jewish Law; they regarded St. Paul as an apostate, and used only a Gospel according to St. Matthew (Adv. Haer., I, xxvi, 2; III, xxi, 2; IV, xxxiii, 4; V, i, 3). Catholic Encyclopedia at http://www.newadvent.org/cathen/05242c.htm.
12. Bercot, *A Dictionary of Early Christian Beliefs*, 670.
13. McGrath, *Historical Theology*, 53.
14. McGrath, *Historical Theology*, 53.

in a mass bodily resurrection from the dead at Christ's return. (Matt. 20:28; John 3:14–18; 12:27–33; Gal. 3:13; Heb. 2:14; 2 Cor. 5:21; Col. 2:13; 1 Cor. 15:20–23; 1 Pet. 2:24). Apollinarianism was finally settled at the Second Ecumenical Council held in Constantinople in 381. The council reaffirmed the full humanity of Jesus by concluding that His humanity lies at the heart of orthodox Christology.

The teaching that Apolinaris railed so heavily against, and which Gregory sought to correct, was the Arian Controversy. When the Bishop Alexander called upon a number of presbyters, especially Arius, to explain their interpretation of Proverbs 8:22–23, he set in motion one of the most controversial debates in Christian history. Arius believed that when Christ was "brought forth" it was at a moment in time when He was created. In a letter to Eusebius, Arius argued the point that, "before he was begotten or created or ordained or established, he did not exist." Therefore, he followed the belief that Christ had been created. As a consequence, the Father created the Son in order to work through Him, but He was not one with Him. However, the expression, "brought forth", carries the meaning that the Father began to direct and make use of the powerful creative work of the Son in the creation of the universe.[15] As Alister McGrath put it, "The term 'Son' is thus a metaphor, an honorific term intended to underscore the rank of the Son among other creatures."[16] Indeed, the Council of Nicea asserted, in contrast to Arius, that only the one who had created the universe could save it. To be sure, He who was "in the beginning" did not Himself have a beginning. Athanasius, representing the Alexandrian school, further argued "that created life should be founded in any except 'the Lord who is before the ages and through whom the ages came into existence, so that, since it was in him, we also might be able to inherit eternal life.'"[17] Arius, therefore, presented a description of Jesus Christ who could not be a Saviour. By contrast, the Jesus Athanasius knew could be nothing less than God. Like so many in the early church, the battle was for a biblical expression of the identity of Jesus Christ that stood in contrast to the philosophical orientation of the society in which the early Christians resided.

In the aftermath of the Reformation, the formulation of Hollaz dictated that the personal union of the two natures in the one hypostasis of Christ "is the conjunction of the two natures, divine and human, subsisting in the one hypostasis of the Son of God, bringing with it a mutual and indissoluble communion of both natures."[18] Therefore, Christ cannot be referred to as consisting of two essential parts, but "one person with two natures." At the incarnation, the divine nature was active in "assuming", in a passive way, human nature, "which did not have an existence of its own

---

15. Pelikan, *The Christian Tradition: Vol. 1*, 205.
16. McGrath, *Historical Theology*, 49.
17. Pelikan, *The Christian Tradition: Vol. 1*, 205.
18. Pelikan, *The Christian Tradition: Vol. 4*, 355.

before being assumed."[19] From this it could be concluded that worshipping Christ was not a form of idolatry, since the full divinity of Christ was present with His full humanity.

There are a number of implications that arise when considering the manner in which the two natures of Christ interact and associate with each other. The "Formula of Concord" draws out three distinctive areas of interest. The first is that any property that belongs to one of the natures is ascribed not only to that nature but also to the entire person. Consequently, Scripture can affirm that God has redeemed Christians with "His own blood", even though this blood was obviously from the human nature of Christ. It was not only the human nature of Christ that suffered and died, but the Son of God who "truly, really, and properly died." While secular historians may have described Christ as the crucified sage, it was the Christians who acknowledged that they worshipped the Son of God who had died for their sins. Indeed, without the full divinity of Christ the crucifixion has no effect. Secondly, the Protestant theology embedded in the "Formula of Concord" affirmed that the divine attributes of Christ, together with His power and authority, were fully communicated in Christ's human nature. Therefore, the "human nature of Christ had, moreover, been in possession of that majesty and omnipresence from the very moment of the incarnation." To be sure, Christ exercised authority in His earthly ministry on the basis of possessing the full nature of God. Therefore, His teaching carries divine authority, His character was of divine origin, and His practices displayed an approach to life in the direct image of God. The result is that Christians worship Christ, because He is fully God, incorporate His teachings into their belief systems, and desire a following after His character and practices. Thirdly, the works of Christ cannot be said to be limited to a single nature, but pertain to both. Indeed, the "union of the two natures in Christ occurred so that the work of redemption, atonement, and salvation might be accompanied in, with, and through both natures of Christ."[20] This secures for Christians the authoritative nature of Christ's teaching, the validity of His mission, the effectiveness of His death and the real possibility of the resurrection.

Having established the traditional opinion, it is none-the-less important to ask in what sense Jesus Christ was actually human.

The Book of Hebrews points to the true humanness of Jesus, who shared in the flesh and blood of humanity (2:14). As Stanley Grenz asserted, "traversing this route, we actually follow the lead of the New Testament writers themselves. For them, Jesus' historical life forms the foundation from which they draw conclusions concerning his fundamental humanness."[21] What the Gospels offer is the description of a person who experienced the common dimensions of life "as knowing human needs,

---

19. Pelikan, *The Christian Tradition: Vol. 4*, 355.
20. Pelikan, *The Christian Tradition: Vol. 4*, 358.
21. Grenz, *Theology for the Community of God*, 275.

undergoing trials and temptations, and being subjected to a variety of limitations."[22] Indeed, the humanity of Christ, as the One who is the Lord and in whom faith is given, is never questioned in the New Testament. Indeed, by contrast, it is emphasised. The Gospels allude to His physical needs of hunger and thirst (John 4:6–7); His need for personal support (Matthew 26:36–38); together with His desire to have His spiritual needs met (Mark 1:35). Jesus also needed to endure trials and temptations in His spiritual battle with Satan (Matt. 4:1–11; 16:22–23; 26:36–39). However, Jesus' struggle with temptation differs from ours in that He was not enticed into sin. And yet, in all other regards, He was very human. In the Gospel accounts, He is treated in a very human way. He interacted with people in spoken language and touch. He was known for His sense of humour and outrage at injustice and hypocrisy. Jesus worked within the framework of a teacher of parables, a sage, and as Josephus tells us, a doer of wonderful works.[23] In response He was lauded, criticised, plotted against and worshipped. He was referred to as a rabbi, yet not in the modern sense. The position of rabbi, in the formal sense of being a religious dignitary, did not develop until after the Gospel period.

As a Jew from Galilee, He was one characterized as a person before God. To be one before God does not amount to any physical or mental attributes. For the German Protestant, Otto Weber, it meant rather "to be the being before God who is ordained to be God's opposite in relationship, and whose existence takes place 'under the law', that is, in obedience given or refused."[24] In this regard Jesus is the ultimate partner. He is not just "a" person, but "the" person under the law. To be "under the law", means that Jesus was placed in the realm of the Old Testament law. Jesus' faithful obedience to the law is seen in His compliance to paying the temple tax (Ex. 30:13; Matt 17:24ff.) Matthew also shares with Mark and Luke the fact that Jesus sent the healed leper to the priest, in accordance with the legal regulations. "It is also remarkable that Jesus defends the disciples' breaking of the custom of ritual hand washing (which as such was not based in the Torah), but he does not participate in their act (Mark 7:1ff)." In a similar fashion, nowhere is Jesus seen attempting to change the dietary laws of Leviticus. Indeed, He clearly upholds them, as He does the Sabbath. Therefore, He is seen as submitting to what comes directly, or indirectly, from the law. Indeed, there is not a single passage which would suggest that Jesus found the will of God, to live His life and generally conduct Himself, other than in the will "the law and the prophets."[25] What Jesus does add to this, in particular circumstances, is prayer (Mk. 1:35; Lk. 5:16). However, the guidance He received in prayer in no way contradicted the law and the prophets. Indeed, Jesus

---

22. Grenz, *Theology for the Community of God*, 275.
23. Prosser, *Was Jesus Crucified?* 225.
24. Weber, *Foundations of Dogmatics: Vol. 2*, 50.
25. Weber, *Foundations of Dogmatics: Vol. 2*, 51.

clearly understood His mission, at its very core, to be a fulfilment of the law and the prophets culminating and finding ultimate expression, in His own life. Therefore, it is only *in Christ*, by way of a baptism of the Holy Spirit, that any person can hope to live prophetically under the terms of the law in obedience to God, as God intended. Consequently, the new community of Christians did not turn against the law, but committed itself to the One who fulfilled the law. In His struggle for the law, in contrast to a usurped or distorted law, He is obedient. Therefore, as Weber asserted, "Jesus' relation to the law is not that of one who knows better, nor that of the mere prophet, (nor primarily as an example) but that of the Fulfiller."[26] Consequently, in Jesus the law is transformed from a codex of norms, in which the person finds a protective wall against God's wrath, into the ways of a relationship in which God takes humanity for Himself and seeks for signs of loving faithfulness and the fullness of life in His Son. Clearly, the law continues in the Christian community as the structured and tangible manifestation of a heart turned from stone to flesh and from sin to salvation.

As one who had been baptized in the Holy Spirit, was in close communion with the Father, and with a clear sense of personal vocation, Jesus Christ constantly made those choices that were in direct correlation to the will of God. In this sense, we have a hope in Jesus Christ that the robe of righteousness, that He wove in His life, is able to be passed on to us who repent of sin and have saving faith. Jesus' sinlessness also opens up for believers the possibility of full obedience to God; although nowhere does Scripture cast sinless perfection as a pre-requisite for salvation. We find this most profoundly in the Gospel of Luke, which goes beyond Mark and Matthew, in its emphasis of Jesus as "a Spirit-filled man who was able to overcome temptation and live a victorious life."[27] In the Review and Herald, August 4, 1874, Ellen White described the identification that Jesus had in His humanity, an identification that had at its aim the uplifting of repentant humanity. She wrote that;

> *the humanity of Christ reached to the very depths of human wretchedness, and, identified itself with the weaknesses and necessities of fallen man, while his divine nature grasped the Eternal. His work in bearing the guilt of man's transgression was not to give him license to continue to violate the law of God, which made man a debtor to the law, which debt Christ was himself paying by his own suffering. The trials and sufferings of Christ were to impress man with a sense of his great sin in breaking the law of God, and to bring him to repentance and obedience to that law, and through obedience to acceptance with God. His righteousness he would impute to man, and thus raise him in moral value with God, so that his efforts to keep the divine law would be acceptable.*

---

26. Weber, *Foundations of Dogmatics: Vol. 2*, 52.
27. Moody, *The Word of Truth*, 417.

> *Christ's work was to reconcile man to God through his human nature, and God to man through his divine nature.*[28]

Ellen White described the incarnation of Christ as a mystery of godliness.[29] Indeed, "without the help of the Holy Spirit we cannot hope to comprehend this subject."[30] However, the nature and significance of the incarnation is clear in Mrs White's writings. Her kenotic theology is particularly evident when she described Christ as taking on human nature, "a nature inferior to His heavenly nature. Nothing so shows the wonderful condescension of God as this. He 'so loved the world that he gave his only begotten Son (John 3:16).'" Clearly, Christ's pre-existence is in view here.[31] Further, the incarnation was not an event in theory, but of literal fact. "He did in reality possess human nature."[32] In so doing, Christ took the part of every human being. He was the head of humanity, and yet totally divine. Ellen White's firm conviction regarding the humanity of Christ, as it is expressed in the two natures of Christ, is elegantly expressed in an article written for *The Signs of the Times*, June 9, 1898. "A Being divine and human, with His long human arm He could encircle humanity, while with His divine arm He could lay hold of the throne of the Infinite."[33] The link between human and divine is further enhanced in Christ as He ascended to Heaven. Indeed, the role of Christ's incarnation in the role of salvation is clearly outlined when she stated that, "Christ took with Him to the heavenly courts His glorified humanity. To those who receive Him, He gives power to become the sons of God, that at last God may receive them as His, to dwell with Him throughout eternity."[34]

---

28. White, *The Temptation of Christ*.
29. White, *Selected Messages: Book One, Review and Herald, 1958,* 246.
30. White, *Selected Messages: Book One,* 249.
31. But while God's Word speaks of the humanity of Christ when upon the earth, it also speaks decidedly regarding His pre-existence. White, *Selected Messages: Book One,* 247.
32. White, *Selected Messages: Book One,* 247.
33. White, *Selected Messages: Book One,* 252.
34. White, *Testimonies for The Church: Vol. 8,* 267–8.

CHAPTER 6
―――

THE DEITY OF JESUS CHRIST

THE NEW TESTAMENT STRONGLY ASSERTS the deity of Jesus Christ. Paul tells the Christians at Colossae: "For in him dwelleth all the fullness of the Godhead bodily (Colossians 2:9)." In his letter to Titus, Paul further declares Jesus Christ to be "the great God and our Saviour (Titus 2:13)." Indeed, with an apologetic tone, John asserts that "no man hath ascended up to heaven, but he that came down from heaven, even the Son of man which is in heaven (3:13)." Paul clearly weighs into gnostic scepticism when he states that while "(t)he first man is of the earth, earthy; the second man is the Lord from heaven (1 Cor. 15:47)." John, in his Gospel, begins with the assertion that Jesus is divine. To be sure, the whole gospel rests on the opening declaration that "(i)n the beginning was the Word, and the Word was with God, and the Word was God."

Given the weight of biblical evidence, the only conclusion that can be drawn is that Jesus Christ was fully God. Clearly, the early church had the strong conviction of the full deity of Nazarene teacher. In defence of this assertion, Jaroslav Pelikan referred to the oldest surviving sermon of the Christian church after the New Testament. It starts with the words: "Brethren, we ought so to think of Jesus Christ as of God, as of the judge of living and dead. And we ought not to belittle our salvation; for when we belittle him, we expect also to receive little."[1] The oldest surviving source from outside the church describes Christians meeting before sunrise, "singing a hymn to Christ as though to [a] god." Further, the prayer "Our Lord, come!" clearly indicates that the early believers had the conviction that Jesus Christ was God.[2] However, controversy regarding the nature of Christ continued until finally being settled at the First Ecumenical Council of Nicea in 325. For example, the Marcionites, quoting Romans 8:3, which describes Jesus as coming in the "likeness of sinful

---

1. Pelikan, *The Christian Tradition: Vol. 1*, 173.
2. Pelikan, *The Christian Tradition: Vol. 1*, 173.

THE DEITY OF JESUS CHRIST

flesh", protested against the notion of Jesus having a material body. The Gnostics asserted that His suffering was make-believe, while docetism carried the conviction that Christ's divinity came at the expense of His humanity. However, it was the Definition of Chalcedon that sought to settle this matter. Its opening remark clearly articulates its conclusion. "Following then, the holy fathers, we unite in teaching all men to confess the one and only Son, our Lord Jesus Christ. This self-same one is perfect both in deity and also in human-ness; this self-same one is also actually and actually man with a rational soul and a body."[3]

For the Reformers, the issue arose as the nature of Christ ascending into heaven as now both God and man. That is, they sought to investigate the nature of Christ's divinity after the incarnation and resurrection. It is one thing to be God and man on earth, but how does this work in heaven? Bullinger contended that "the body of Christ is in heaven in a state of glory."[4] The argument has good biblical grounding. Scripture clearly portrays Christ as having risen with a physical body. When they went to the tomb where He had been laid, they found that it was empty (Luke 24:23). Later, they met with Him and He taught them (Mark 16:9). Indeed, five hundred people were eyewitnesses to the resurrected Christ in physical form. "And that he was buried, and that he rose again the third day according to the scriptures: And that he was seen of Cephas, then of the twelve: After that, he was seen of above five hundred brethren at once; of whom the greater part remain unto this present, but some are fallen asleep (1 Corinthians 15:4–6)." The importance of the bodily resurrection of Christ is seen in His own careful instruction. "Look at my hands and my feet. It is I myself! Touch me and see; a ghost does not have flesh and bones, as you see I have (NIV) (Luke 24:39)." It is this bodily Christ that is then seen ascending into heaven (Acts 1:9). However, the resurrected body Christ is not corruptible, but perfect and eternal. It is this same body that will be the experience of all God's people who rise at Christ's return (1 Cor. 15:50; 2 Cor. 5:1–2; 2 Cor. 5:4; Phil 3:21).

Ellen White had a convinced and thoroughgoing belief in the divinity of Christ. In *The Desire of Ages* she wrote that, "Christ had actually come from God to a sinful world to save the fallen sons and daughters of Adam."[5] Indeed, the power He possessed for salvation could only come from His divinity. "Only He who is one with God could say, I have power to lay down My life, and I have power to take it again. In His divinity, Christ possessed the power to break the bonds of death."[6] Indeed, Mrs White sounded a distinctly orthodox note when she taught that Christ was divine before He became incarnate.

---

3. Leith (ed), *Creeds of the Church: A Reader in Christian Doctrine from The Bible to The Present*, 35.
4. Pelikan, *The Christian Tradition: Vol. 4*, 159.
5. White, *The Desire of Ages*, 507.
6. White, *The Desire of Ages*, 785.

According to Seventh-day Adventist academic, Erwin Gane, Ellen White categorically stated on a number of occasions that there never was a time when Christ did not exist. "He was not brought into existence by the Father either by a process of creation or of eternal generation. He has always been with the Father. He did not have a beginning."[7] In *Selected Messages* she stated that the life of Christ was His own, therefore His divinity was His own and constituted the nature of His being. It was unborrowed and underived.[8] In *Evangelism*, she pointed to the "eternal self-existent Son."[9] Again, in *Selected Messages*, Mrs White astutely alluded to the fact that as God's Word describes Christ's life upon the earth it also "decidedly regards His pre-existence." Indeed, "The Word existed as a divine being, even as the eternal Son of God, in union and oneness with His Father."[10] To be sure, "from eternity Christ has been man's Redeemer."[11] In addition, as divine, He continues to do a work of redemption as High Priest. "Jesus cares for each one as though there were not another individual on the face of the earth. As Deity He exerts mighty power in our behalf, while as our Elder Brother He feels all our woes."[12]

---

7. Gane, *The Arian or Anti-Trinitarian Views Presented in Seventh-day Adventist Literature and the Ellen G. White Answer.*

8. White, *Selected Message, Book One* 296. Citing *The Signs of the Times, April 8, 1897.*

9. White, *Evangelism*, 615. Citing *Manuscript 101, 1897.*

10. White, *Selected Messages, Book One*. Citing *Review and Herald, April 5, 1906.*

11. White, *Testimonies for the Church: Vol. 9*, 220.

12. White, *Testimonies for the Church: Vol. 5*, 346.

CHAPTER 7

THE SELF-AWARNESS OF JESUS

HAVING ESTABLISHED THE NATURE OF Jesus Christ as being both fully human and fully Divine, it is important to establish Jesus' own sense of self. Firstly, the biblical record is very clear that Jesus was very conscious of His relationship to the Father. This was not only seen in His use of *Abba* to describe the nature of God as "my Father", but also in His use of "Sonship". The revelation of Jesus as the "Son" who is in communion with "Abba, Father", describes "a relationship of communion in which revelation takes place so that the Son is able to reveal the Father."[1] Therefore, sonship for Jesus was more than a term that He used to describe his status or even his identity. It outlined the nature of His relationship to the Godhead, which, in His earthly ministry, was integral to His mission to reveal and to save.

SON OF MAN

The title "Son of Man" has its background in the books of Ezekiel and Daniel. Ezekiel is referred to as the Son of Man in reference to his humanness, as one who dwelt with the people of exile by the Chebar River. Indeed, "Ezekiel is called 'son of man' by God because he is identified as a representative of Israel, the people of God."[2] However, in Daniel (7:13f) the image is given of an apocalyptic and royal figure, quite clearly Jesus Christ, who has been given special recognition, as he enters into the presence of the Father to be given his new ministry during the Investigative Judgement. It is for this reason that by the time of the New Testament era, "Son of Man" is deliberately used as a Messianic title referring to Jesus. Given that Jesus was never challenged as to the meaning of this title, it can be safely assumed that the term had already developed during the pre-New Testament period as one which referred

---

1. Marshall, *Jesus The Saviour: Studies in New Testament Theology,* 155.
2. Aune, *Son of Man,* 574.

to the expectant Messiah. This sense of expectancy clearly derives from Daniels 70-week prophecy (Dan. 9:24–27) and was exacerbated by Roman occupation.

In the Gospels, the Son of Man sayings appear to reveal Jesus' real status as one who has authority. To be sure, the authority of Jesus, as the Son of Man, is proclaimed (2:10, 28), but denied by Jewish leaders. This leads to the Son of Man's suffering (8:32; 9:9,31; 10:33, 45; 14:21, 42), and final vindication (8:38; 13:26; 14:62). Further, the Son of Man is a title that clearly sees Jesus revealing Himself as the Messiah. This is particularly so in Mark 8:38. "Whosoever therefore shall be ashamed of me and of my words in this adulterous and sinful generation; of him also shall the Son of Man be ashamed, when he cometh in the glory of his Father with the holy angels."

In the Synoptic Gospels, the Son of Man is also seen as one who has authority over the Sabbath. "Therefore, the Son of Man is Lord also of the Sabbath (Mark 2:28. Also, Mt. 12:8; Lk. 6:5)." His lordship over the Sabbath points to His creation of it and therefore His pre-existence. The nature of His lordship is seen in the way in which He adhered to it as a commandment. Therefore, the keeping of the Sabbath is indicative of those who recognise the true lordship of the pre-existent creator, Jesus Christ; the one who Himself, demonstrated the nature of faithfulness to the Father in Obedience, by keeping the Sabbath. To be sure, Jesus challenged many traditional teachings and practices, but not this one. Indeed, Ellen White reminded us that "Christ, during His earthly ministry, emphasized the binding claims of the Sabbath; in all His teaching, He showed reverence for the institution He Himself had given."[3] It is significant that Jesus, as the promised end time apocalyptic Son of Man, gives such emphasis to the Sabbath as a sign of His lordship and therefore of fidelity among His followers. However, the keeping of the Sabbath is symptomatic of something far greater and deeper, and this is the forgiveness of sins. The authority of the Son of Man is that He has the power to forgive sins. "But I want you to know that the Son of Man has authority on earth to forgive sins." So he said to the paralyzed man, "Get up, take your mat and go home (NIV) (Mt 9:6)." Therefore, the title, Son of Man, was integral to Jesus' mission as the apocalyptic lord and saviour of the world, since without the forgiveness of sins there is no salvation and without lordship there is no ability to give it. Further, without the recognition of His lordship, there is no ability to receive salvation. That is, salvation is not efficacious.

MESSIAH-THE CHRIST

The ministry of Jesus rests upon his own self-conscious awareness that He Himself was the Christ. Indeed, there is no doubt in the Gospels that Jesus had a pronounced messianic consciousness. In this sense Jesus has an understanding of Himself that is essentially prophetic. He is the One who fulfils prophecy and He is one who acts in

---

3. White, *Prophets and Kings*, 183.

a prophetic capacity to bring into action what was prophesied about Him. However, past prophecy and present fulfilment is only part of the story. Jesus clearly comes both announcing the Kingdom of God and pointing towards the end of all things. In the ultimate Kingdom of God, where all sin has been destroyed, a people reside who have been regenerated by their union with the life of Christ by faith, which has made possible through His death and resurrection, but also His teaching. In His death, he pays for the sin of the world and bestows forgiveness and salvation upon those who accept it by way of repentance and faith. His resurrection provides the source of that animating power that enables, through the agency of the Holy Spirit, those who confess faith in Christ and are baptised into Him; to die to sin and to live in Him. Christ's teaching provides the shape in which this new life takes its form. That is, the teaching of Jesus Christ is both instructive and transformative. Those who are ready for the Kingdom, are ready in Christ. Therefore, Jesus is aware of His new and unique roll. He is not presented as a super rabbi, nor does He fit completely under that title. He came as an apocalyptic prophet, in the spirit of an already fully established Hebrew prophetic proclamation, calling people to a new life only made possible by a new birth, characterised by His own imputed righteousness.

The prophetic nature of Jesus' ministry is well outlined by N.T. Wright. Prophetically, Jesus looked forward to the execution of the justice of God when His judgement will come upon the earth, on the basis of a judgement that has been completed in heaven. His means was proclamation, but also with signs of power. It is for this reason that "Jesus himself, explaining the nature of His work, is portrayed using both Elijah and Elisha as models."[4] However, it is to God's own people that much of His attention is directed.

> *Like Ezekiel, Jesus predicts that the Temple will be abandoned by the Shekinah, left unprotected to its fate (Ezek. 10:1–5, 15–22; 11:22–3; cf. Mt. 23:38/ Lk. 13:35.) Consequently, like Jeremiah, Jesus constantly runs the risk of being called a traitor to Israel's national aspirations, while claiming at the same time that he nevertheless is the true spokesman for the covenant God (Jer. 7; Mt. 21:12–13/Mk. 11:15–19/Lk. 19:45–8).*[5]

There is also a connection to be made with Amos, who declared that the people of God are to be judged before the nations are (Amos 9:9). Therefore, any proclamation by the Church must be accompanied by constant renewal and reformation, since those who hold the message of the Gospel, and more precisely of the Gospel for the end times, have the greatest accountability.

---

4. Wright, *Jesus and the Victory of God*, 166.
5. Wright, *Jesus and the Victory of God*, 167.

FOUNDATIONS OF THEOLOGY

I AM

The biblical title, "I Am", is unique to the Bible and does not occur in classical literature. In the New Testament, it is a distinctive characteristic of John's Gospel. It is well established as God's personal name revealed to Moses in Exodus 3 :14. There are a number of ways in which "I Am" is used by Jesus. The most striking is found in Chapter 8, during a dispute with the Jewish authorities at the Temple. The accusation that Jesus is a Samaritan is only found here. It is not explained why; however, it can be surmised that the association of Jesus with heresy and magic is what is in mind. Jews regarded Samaritans as heretics for not worshipping in Jerusalem and they were commonly thought of as magicians. Therefore, Jesus, to them, is both a heretic and deceiver of the people. Later Justin "viewed (Samaritans) as demon possessed (*Apol.* 26:1,4-5), and Origen reported that the Jews regarded them as mad (*Contra Celsum.* 6.11).[6] Jesus responded by asserting that He is not demon possessed but does in fact honour the Father. He then made the provocative statement in verse 52, that if anyone keeps His word they shall not taste death. The corresponding charge of, as it where, "who do you think you are?" is that Jesus did not think of Himself as anything other than what the Father has declared. Indeed, the Father glorifies Him. However, it is the assertion that He has seen Abraham that baffles His antagonists. Jesus cannot be old enough to have seen Abraham. Yet this is the point. Jesus is not finite, but infinite. It is God the eternal they are addressing. This is clearly announced with Jesus' use of the well-known "I Am" title. This use of *ego eimi* is quite different from its use in vv. 24 and 28, where Jesus is simply saying, *I am he,* or *it's me*.[7]

There are seven "I Am" sayings. Firstly, "I am the bread of life (6:35, 48)." In this culture where bread was essential for life, Jesus is saying that He, Himself, is essential: "To come to him is to enter a really satisfying life, a life in which there is no longer a deep, unsatisfying longing (6:36). Moreover, the gift of life is at the cost of Jesus' death, for 'the bread that I will give is my flesh, for the life of the world (6:51).'"[8]

Jesus also refers to himself as the light of the world (8:12). In this way Jesus was revealing Himself as Divine, as He made connection with this significant metaphor of God. In *The Desire of Ages* Ellen White drew together this often-used symbol found in the Bible. Jesus described Himself as the Lord who has always been present in creation and with His people. "In the manifestation of God to His people, light had ever been a symbol of His presence. At the creative word in the beginning, light had shone out of darkness. Light had been enshrouded in the pillar of cloud by day and the pillar of fire by night, leading the vast armies of Israel. Light blazed with awful grandeur about the Lord on Mount Sinai. Light rested over the mercy seat in

---

6. Beasley-Murray, *36 Word Biblical Commentary: John,* 136.
7. Beasley-Murray, *36 Word Biblical Commentary: John,* 38.
8. Morris, *New Testament Theology,* 235.

THE SELF-AWARNESS OF JESUS

the Tabernacle. Light filled the temple of Solomon at its dedication. Light shone on the hills of Bethlehem when the angels brought the message of redemption to the watching shepherds."[9] In addition, Ellen White made a connection between Jesus' declaration that He is the light of the world with the prophetic expectation of the coming of the Messiah.

> *In the words, 'I am the light of the world,' Jesus declared Himself the Messiah. The aged Simeon, in the temple where Christ was now teaching, had spoken of Him as 'a light to lighten the Gentiles, and the glory of Thy people Israel (Luke 2:32).' In these words, He was applying to Him a prophecy familiar to all Israel. By the prophet Isaiah, the Holy Spirit had declared, 'It is too light a thing that Thou shouldest be My servant to raise up the tribes of Jacob, and to restore the preserved of Israel: I will also give Thee for a light to the Gentiles, that Thou mayest be My salvation unto the end of the earth. (Isa. 49:6, R.V.).' This prophecy was generally understood as spoken of the Messiah, and when Jesus said, 'I am the light of the world,' the people could not fail to recognize His claim to be the Promised One.*[10]

While declaring Himself to be the light of the world, Jesus, in fact, took it further by describing believers as the light in the world.

> *You are the light of the world. A town built on a hill cannot be hidden. Neither do people light a lamp and put it under a bowl. Instead they put it on its stand, and it gives light to everyone in the house. In the same way, let your light shine before others, that they may see your good deeds and glorify your Father in heaven.* (NIV)(Matt. 5:14–16).

In *Gospel Workers*, Ellen White reflected on this passage in the context of the whole biblical council of God.

> *In all ages, the people of God have been the light of the world. Joseph was a light in Egypt. He represented Jehovah in the midst of a nation of idolaters. While the Israelites were on the way from Egypt to the promised land, they were a light to the surrounding nations. Through them God was revealed to the world. Satan sought to extinguish their light; but by the power of God it was kept alive through successive generations while Israel maintained a national existence; and even during the captivity there were faithful witnesses for God. From Daniel and his companions, and Mordecai, a bright light shone amid the moral darkness of the kingly courts of Babylon. In holy vision, God revealed to Daniel light and truth that he had concealed from other men, and through his chosen servant this light has shone down through the ages, and will continue to shine to the end of time.*[11]

---

9. White, *The Desire of Ages*, 465.
10. White, *The Desire of Ages*, 466.
11. White, *Gospel Workers*, 433.

CHAPTER 8

THE TWO NATUES OF JESUS CHRIST

IN THE YEAR 451, THE Council of Chalcedon met and formulated the faith of the Church respecting the person of Christ, and declared Him

> to be acknowledged in two natures, inconfusedly, unchangeable, invisibly, inseparably; the distinction of the natures being in no wise taken away by the union, but rather the property of each nature being preserved, and concurring in one Person and One Subsistence, not parted or divided into two persons.[1]

The difficulty in comprehending this doctrine is expressed by Lois Berkhof, who asserted that the

> doctrine of the two natures in one person transcends human reason. It is the expression of a supersensible reality (beyond reason), and of an incomprehensible mystery, which has no analogy in the life of man as we know it, and finds no support in human reason, and therefore can only be accepted by faith on the authority of the Word of God. For that reason, it is doubly necessary to pay close attention to the teachings of Scripture on this point.[2]

Indeed, both natures are represented in Scripture as united in one person. A number of verses can provide a clear reference. In Romans, Paul wrote that Jesus Christ was born in the flesh and confirmed as the Son of God at His resurrection. "Concerning his Son Jesus Christ our Lord, which was made of the seed of David according to the flesh; and declared to be the Son of God with power, according to the spirit of holiness, by the resurrection from the dead." (Rom 1:3–4). To the believers in Galatia he referred to Christ as the Son of God who was born in the flesh of a woman. "But when the fullness of the time was come, God sent forth his Son, made of a woman, made under the law, to redeem them that were under the law, that we

---

1. Hoeksema, *An Exposition of The Heidelberg Catechism: Part 2*, 292.
2. Berkhof, *Systematic Theology*, 323.

might receive the adoption of sons (Gal 4:4–5)." To the Philippians, Paul emphasised the incarnation of God,

> *who, although He existed in the form of God, did not regard equality with God a thing to be grasped, but emptied Himself, taking the form of a bond-servant, and being made in the likeness of men. Being found in appearance as a man, He humbled Himself by becoming obedient to the point of death, even death on a cross. For this reason also, God highly exalted Him, and bestowed on Him the name which is above every name, so that at the name of Jesus* EVERY KNEE WILL BOW, *of those who are in heaven and on earth and under the earth, and that every tongue will confess that Jesus Christ is Lord, to the glory of God the Father.* (NASB) (Phil 2:6–11).

In several passages both natures are set forth as united. The Bible nowhere teaches that divinity is in the abstract, or some divine power, was united to, or manifested in, a human nature; but always that the divine nature, in the divine person of the Son of God, was united to the human nature, in the person of Jesus (John 1:14; Rom. 8:3; Gal. 4:4; 9:5; 1 Tim. 3:16; Heb. 2:11–14; 1 John 4:2–3).

During the Reformation, Protestant thinkers reopened the ancient question of the proper way of conceiving Christ's person. However, the Reformers were divided in their understanding of the patristic doctrine. Luther appealed to an analogy of iron and heat in order to understand the divine and human in Christ. Just as heat pervades an iron bar so also in the incarnation Jesus' divinity extends throughout his humanity. On this basis, Luther's followers supposed that the unity of the two natures in Jesus' personality requires a genuine communicating of the divine attributes in human nature. The human nature participates in the divine attributes, especially in the glory and majesty of the deity. Yet Jesus' humanity is not thereby lost, nor are human attributes transferred to his divine nature. One of the implications of this thesis is that the human nature of the resurrected Jesus participates in the omnipresence of the divine nature.

Similarly, Calvinists held to a hypostatic union of two natures that were mysteriously united into one person. Huldrych Zwingli stated:

> *We believe and teach that this Son of God, who is of God, so took to himself the nature of man that his divine nature was not destroyed or changed into that of man: but that each nature is present truly, properly and naturally: his divine nature has not in any way been diminished so as not to be truly, properly and naturally God. Nor has his human nature passed into the divine so that he is not truly, properly and naturally man, except in so far as he is without the propensity to sin.*[3]

In the sixteenth century, The Heidelberg Catechism declared:

---

3. Johnson and Leith, (eds), *Reformed Reader*, 203.

> *The union which exists between the two natures in Christ was made by the operation of the Holy Spirit in the very conception . . . It is called the hypostatical or personal union, because the two natures that are different are united in a mysterious manner in one person, while the essential properties of each nature are retained whole and entire . . . Christ is true God and man. (Lk. 1:35; Col. 2:9; John 1:14; Heb. 2:16; 1 Tim. 3:16).*[4]

In the 1940s, Lorraine Boettner sought to answer the question of how Christ, being the Son of God, become man. He referred to the Shorter Catechism: "Christ, the Son of God, became man, by taking to Himself a true body and a reasonable (that is, reasoning) soul, being conceived by the power of the Holy Ghost, in the womb of the virgin Mary, and born of her, yet without sin."[5] Donald Bloesch averred to Calvin, who compared the two natures of Christ to two eyes of a human person: "Each eye can have its vision separately; but when we are looking at everything . . . our vision, which in itself is divided, joins up and unites in order to give itself as a whole to the object that is put before it."[6] Bloesch himself drew on modern physics to state that just as light can have the characteristics of both waves and particles, so Jesus embodies both humanity and divinity in one person.[7] Furthermore, Stanley Grenz stated that central to a true understanding of Jesus Christ is that He is divine. Concurrently, in the form of the man from Nazareth, God himself encounters us.[8] Indeed, as John declares at the commencement of his Gospel, "the Word became flesh".

In the Old Testament the term for "word", *davar*, refers to what is revelatory, revealing the significance of an event or even the nature of God. Dynamically, the "word of God" stands for the creative power of God, such as God's wisdom in creation (Prov. 8:22–31), or even God's utterance as carrying power. The link between *davar* and *logos* is evident in the "creation" language of John 1, which is clearly reminiscent of the first chapter of Genesis. In recent times, Donald Bloesch sought to explain the link between the two natures and the incarnation. He contended that John speaks of the Word becoming flesh (1:14) and that Paul asserts that God was "born in human likeness" (Phil. 2:7). The Nicene Creed expresses the consensus of the early church that "God became man".

When the church affirms that God became man, it does not mean that God changed into a man, as in ancient mythology. The flesh was not "changed into the nature of Godhead nor was the ineffable nature of the Word of God transformed into the nature of flesh." Orthodox Christianity holds neither to an appearance of

---

4. Ursinus, The Commentary of Dr. Zacharias Ursinus on the Heidelberg Catechism, 209.
5. Boettner, *The Person of Christ*, 113.
6. Bloesch, *Jesus Christ*, 57.
7. Bloesch, *Jesus Christ*, 57.
8. S. Grenz, *Theology for the Community of God*, 262.

God in a man nor a metamorphosis of God into a man. As the Athanasian Creed puts it, He is one "not by conversion of the Godhead into flesh, but by taking of the manhood into God." In the words of Augustine, "Christ added to himself that which he was not; he did not lose what he was."[9] Therefore, divinity was not transmuted into bodily flesh but it assumed flesh while still remaining divine.

Beginning with the early church, the heresy of docetism threatened to undermine the established view of the two natures of Christ. This doctrine claimed that Jesus Christ only seemed to be human. Indeed, the word doceticism comes from the Greek *dokeo*, "to seem".[10] In response, the Gospels go to great lengths to assert the humanity of Christ. "The Word became flesh" in John's Gospel is seconded by a comprehensive genealogy in Matthew and Luke. To add to this the book of Hebrews carefully distinguishes the difference between the humanity of Jesus and His sinlessness. It was the sinless, yet human, Jesus, who provided salvation through His sacrifice on the cross. "Forasmuch then as the children are partakers of flesh and blood, He also Himself likewise took part of the same; that through death He might destroy him that had the power of death, that is, the devil. And deliver them who through fear of death were all their lifetime subject to bondage (Heb. 2:14)."

The other major theory the church rejected was the Monophysite Heresy. This argued that Jesus did not have two natures, but one. This single nature was neither truly divine nor truly human but a mixture of the two. It was called a "theanthropic" nature. The Monophysite Heresy involves either a deified human nature or a humanized divine nature. In contrast, R. C. Sproul believed that we must distinguish between the two natures without separating them. When Jesus hungers, for example, we see that as a manifestation of the human nature, not the divine. On the cross, Christ died as God-man. However, this is not to say that God died. And, though the two natures remain united after Christ's ascension, we must still distinguish the natures regarding the mode of His presence with us. Concerning His human nature, Christ is no longer present with us. However, in his divine nature, Christ is never absent from us.[11] Indeed, Ellen White stated that "When Christ was crucified, it was His human nature that died. Deity did not sink and die; that would have been impossible."[12]

Ellen White discussed the nature of Christ on numerous occasions. The humanity of Christ is clearly expressed in *Selected Messages*;

> the humanity of the Son of God . . . is the golden chain that binds our souls to Christ, and through Christ to God. This is our study. Christ was a real man; He gave proof of His humanity in becoming a man. Yet He was God in the flesh.

---

9. Bloesch, *Essentials of Evangelical Theology: Vol. 1*, 128.
10. Hinson, Caner, *The Popular Encyclopaedia of Apologetics*, 179.
11. Ferguson, *Encyclopaedia of Early Christianity: Vol. 1*, 777–8.
12. White, *Letter 280, Sept. 3, 1904*.

> *When we approach this subject, we would do well to heed the words spoken by Christ to Moses at the burning hush, 'Put off thy shoes from off thy feet, for the place whereon thou standest is holy ground' (Ex. 3:5).*[13]

The self-emptying of Christ, or kenotic theology, in which Christ, as God, humbled Himself in his descent to earth to take on human nature, is clearly outlined by Mrs White in her letter to brother and sister William L. H. Baker. In it she stated,

> *Christ's perfect humanity is the same that man may have through connection with Christ. As God, Christ could not be tempted any more than He was not tempted from His allegiance in heaven. But as Christ humbled Himself to the nature of man, He could be tempted. He had not taken on Him the nature of the angels, but humanity, perfectly identical with our own nature, except without a taint of sin.*[14]

Later in the letter, she clearly asserted that the divine nature of Christ was combined with His human nature. Indeed, she commended Jesus Christ, "the source of all heavenly grace."[15]

---

13. White, *Selected Messages: Vol. 1*, 244.
14. White, *Letter 8*, in *13 Manuscript Releases*, 18–20.
15. White, *Letter 8*, in *13 Manuscript Releases*, 18–20.

CHAPTER 9

THE HOLY SPIRIT

THE PERSON AND WORK OF the Holy Spirit finds precedence in the Old Testament, before flourishing in the New. In the Old Testament, the Spirit of the Lord is an expression of God's power, whereby He carries out many of His mighty deeds. As Mullins stated, in the Old Testament the "Spirit of God was God in action accomplishing an end."[1] The word "spirit", in both Hebrew (*ruarch*) and Greek (*pneuma*), stems from words denoting "wind" and "breath", which in ancient cultures are associated with unseen spiritual forces. The nature of this "breath" is seen in the derivation of the word denoting to "breath out violently". This does not describe the nature of God, but rather the unusual force or energy that one might experience in the impressive power of the wind (Ps. 107:25; 148:8). This is seen to find manifestation in the "dominating aspect of a person's disposition (Ex. 6:9; Nu. 5:14; 14:24), or most commonly in the ecstatic states of prophetic consciousness experienced in invasion by an external power (1 Sam. 10:6; 2 Chron. 24:20; Hos. 9:7)."[2] However, when discussing the activity of the Holy Spirit it is important to stipulate that we are not dealing with an impersonal force or power. "The Spirit of God was always thought of as having personal qualities and performing personal functions."[3] Indeed, when Jesus referred to the Holy Spirit, He described another Paraclete (advocate/helper). That is, the Spirit takes on a similar ministry to that of Jesus. "As Jesus had strengthened, comforted, guided them until now; so, this unseen Friend, this comforting Helper is now to be their companion guide. This is no impersonal influence or power; it is a personal presence."[4] These personal attributes are seen in a number of instances in the Bible. In 1 Corinthians 12:11,

---

1. Mullins, *The Christian Religion and its Doctrinal Expression*, 203.
2. Bromiley, *The International Standard Bible Encyclopedia: Vol. 2*, 730.
3. Conner, *Christian Doctrine*, 108.
4. Connor, *Christian Doctrine*, 109.

for example, the Spirit is described as distributing gifts according to His will. The personal attributes of the Spirit are also evident when He speaks to Phillip in Acts 8:29. "Then the Spirit said unto Philip, go near, and join thyself to this chariot." Further, Jesus used the personal pronoun to describe the teaching ministry of the Holy Spirit. When "the Spirit of truth, is come, He will guide you into all truth: for He shall not speak of Himself; but whatsoever He shall hear, that shall He speak: and He will shew you things to come (John 16:13)."

The ministry of the Holy Spirit is evident at creation. The Spirit is described as an energizing power in the primeval chaos. Indeed, one perceives the Spirit as "bringing beauty out of chaos (Gen. 1:2; Ps. 104:28-30; Job 26:3)". This is analogous to bringing new life into the experience of believers. To be sure, life is imparted to humanity through God's Spirit (Gen. 2:7).[5] According to Geoffrey Bromiley, the Holy Spirit described in the Old Testament is above all the "Spirit of Prophecy", considering that the most frequent manifestation of the Spirit's work is through the prophets. Therefore, one can delineate that in the Old Testament the primary role of the Spirit was to inspire the prophets (Num. 11:17; 1 Sam. 16:15; Mic. 3:8; Ezek. 2:2). However, the Spirit's ministry is not limited to the prophets (Ex. 31:3; Num. 27:18; Judg. 6:34; 1 Chron. 28:12). To be sure, the Holy Spirit is seen to be working among the people, which will culminate in a glorious conclusion that will see all of God's desires for His creation, primarily in the crown of His creation, human beings, reaching their fulfilment. Indeed, in Old Testament prophecy, a time is anticipated when God will pour out His Spirit (Joel 2:28ff; Isa. 11:1ff; Ezek. 36:14ff), and transform a people into a holy nation. They will be a people cleansed on the inside and endowed with new hearts. Outward obedience to the commands of God will be replaced with hearts that desire to do the Father's bidding. This new era, as depicted in Old Testament prophecy, will centre on a coming Messiah. Indeed, the Spirit will rest upon the Messiah (Isa.11:1ff; 42:1ff; 63:1ff) with manifestations which point to a new heaven and earth.[6]

In the New Testament, the person and work of the Holy Spirit plays a prominent part. Indeed, the incarnate life of the Son of God has its beginnings in the supernatural activity of the Holy Spirit (Matt. 1:18,20; Luke 1:35). The Holy Spirit is a central feature at Jesus' baptism. In fact, all three Synoptic Gospels report a manifestation of the Holy Spirit at this event (Mark 1:10; Matt. 3:16; Luke 3:22). John's account, similar to Luke's, contrasts the water baptism of John the Baptist, with the baptism of the Holy Spirit (1:32-34). The descent of the Holy Spirit upon Jesus at His baptism inaugurates His public ministry, but also carries with it a sign that Jesus was the bearer and dispenser of the Spirit's power. In addition, since the rabbis had announced that the Holy Spirit had departed Israel after the last of the minor prophets, the

5. Connor, *Christian Doctrine*, 109.
6. Caulley, *Holy Spirit*, 521-2.

baptism of Jesus announces the return of the Spirit's work amongst God's people.[7] This points to the ultimate conclusion that where God's people are present there will always be manifestations of the Holy Spirit; in the lives of individuals and in the life of the corporate church. Indeed, the church does not exist without the presence and work of the Holy Spirit. Manifestations of the Holy Spirit come in the form of hearts changed from abiding sin to repentance and life in the love of Christ, manifested in the fruit of the Spirit (2 Corinthians 5:17; Gal. 5:22; Eph. 5:9) the proclamation of the Gospel, and evangelism (Acts 13:4-5; 1 Cor. 2:4-5).

The early church wrote extensively in support of the divinity of the Holy Spirit. Athenagoras, a second century apologist, who had been a Greek philosopher before his conversion, wrote that the "Holy Spirit Himself, who operates in the prophets, we assert to be an effluence of God, flowing from Him, and returning back again like a beam of the sun."[8] Tertullian clearly placed the Holy Spirit within the godhead when he named Him to be "the third name in Divinity, and the third degree of Divine Majesty."[9]

During the Reformation, there was a recognition of the role of the Holy Spirit in the event of conversion. Martin Luther, seeking to emphasise grace and the sovereignty of God, stipulated that there were "only two efficient causes" of conversion. That is, "the Holy Spirit and the word of God as the Holy Spirit's instrument whereby He effects conversion."[10] By contrast, Philip Melanchthon sought to infuse the important place of the human will. In his theology of the conversion of the believer, Melanchthon saw the Holy Spirit as an essential part in a cooperating triad of "the word, the Holy Spirit, and the human will."[11]

Ellen White defined the Holy Spirit as a divine person, who is Christ's representative, a comforter, guide and teacher. The divinity of the Holy Spirit is well attested in her writings as she described the three holy dignitaries of heaven,[12] the three living persons of the heavenly trio,[13] the three persons of the Godhead[14] and the third person of the Godhead.[15] Further, as God, the Holy Spirit provides illumination, produces spiritual fruit in the form of gifts, and empowers believers. According to Ellen White, as the individual accepts the wooing of the Holy Spirit and finally surrenders to Jesus Christ, there is an ultimate acceptance of His work, which arises

7. Garrett, *Systematic Theology*, 147-8.
8. Bercot, *Dictionary of Early Christian beliefs*, 345.
9. Bercot, *Dictionary of Early Christian beliefs*, 345.
10. Pelikan, *The Christian Tradition: A History of the Development of Doctrine: Vol. 4*, 145.
11. Pelikan, *The Christian Tradition: Vol. 4*, 144.
12. *Seventh-day Adventist Bible Commentary*, Vol. 5, 1110.
13. White, *Evangelism*, 615.
14. White, *Evangelism*, 615.
15. White, *Evangelism*, 617, White, *Desire of Ages*, 671; White, *Councils on Health*, 222; White, *My Life Today*, 36.

out of repentance leading to faith.[16] She further sounds a biblical note when stating that without the Holy Spirit there can be no repentance.[17] In addition, Mrs. White claimed that part of the work of the Holy Spirit is to create an awareness of sin, which leads to the desire to turn to the righteousness of Christ in faith[18] and an opening of the mind to the truth.[19] This process of transformation is referred to as the baptism of the Holy Spirit. Therefore, in Ellen White's theology, the divinity of the Holy Spirit is affirmed, along with His indispensability in the process of conversion and subsequent Christian growth.

There are numerous occasions when Ellen White affirmed that all of God's people need to seek[20] and receive the baptism of the Holy Spirit.[21] In ministry, companies of gospel workers should pray for the baptism of the Holy Spirit[22] because it is what God's people need.[23] Then, from conversion, comes the constant working and regeneration of the Spirit.[24] Through the work of the Holy Spirit humanity is restored to the image of God[25] whereby he or she becomes a partaker of the divine nature.[26] Therefore, she asserted, it is through the Spirit that God minsters to humanity.[27] From the regeneration of the individual comes the Gospel mission of the individual in the context of the mission of the church. It is only through the working of the Holy Spirit that the Gospel can go forward.[28] Indeed, it is not possible for the Gospel work to be accomplished without the work of the Holy Spirit.[29]

Ellen White further averred that the Holy Spirit does the work of transforming the Christian character. He is essential to right thinking[30] as He communicates truth with power[31] and assists in resisting Satan's power.[32] Indeed, the Holy Spirit

---

16. White, *Fundamentals of Christian Education*, 435.
17. White, *Desire of Ages*, 175.
18. White, *Testimonies to Ministers and Gospel Workers*, 144.
19. White, *Evangelism*, 169.
20. White, *Councils on Health*, 548; White, *Fundamentals of Christian Education*, 240.
21. White, *Evangelism*, 369, 472, 558; White, *Fundamentals of Christian Education*, 532, 537; White, *My Life Today*, 49; White, *Testimonies: Vol. 8*, 110; White, *Testimonies to Ministers and Gospel Workers*, 168.
22. White, *Acts of the Apostles*, 50.
23. White, *Selected Messages: Vol. 1*, 411.
24. White, *Gospel Workers*, 286.
25. White, *Testimonies to Ministers and Gospel Workers*, 378.
26. White, *Desire of Ages*, 675.
27. White, *The Ministry of Healing*, 417; White, *My Life Today*, 48.
28. White, *Testimonies to Ministers and Gospel Workers*, 313.
29. White, *Gospel Workers*, 289; White, *Testimonies to Ministers and Gospel Workers*, 313.
30. White, *Patriarchs and Prophets*, 460.
31. White, *Medical Missionary*, 12.
32. White, *Desire of Ages*, 102.

transforms the human heart, providing the experience of new life.[33] In *Testimonies for the Church, Volume Five*, she wrote that believers must pray,

> *that the mighty energies of the Holy Spirit, with all their quickening, recuperative, and transforming power, may fall like an electric shock on the palsy-stricken soul, causing every nerve to thrill with new life, restoring the whole man from his dead, earthly, sensual state to spiritual soundness. You will thus become partakers of the divine nature.*[34]

To be sure, the whole person is restored from a dead, earthly, sensual state to spiritual soundness.[35] There is a provision to bear the fruit of the Holy Spirit, which is the result of conversion.[36] Indeed, those who are born again with renewed hearts, and are new creatures in Christ, bear the fruit of the Spirit.[37] Following, there is a consequential quickening of the soul for good,[38] as the seed of truth is germinated.[39] Sincere searchers for the truth are given the Holy Spirit to understand God's word,[40] and solve Scripture problems[41] and difficulties.[42] Indeed, the Holy Spirit gives guidance regarding personal difficulties[43] and empowers the believer to break through the powers of darkness.[44]

In addition to regeneration and illumination, the role of the Holy Spirit is to act as Christ's representative. This representation takes place within the church[45], in the midst of His people[46] so as to do, she asserted, a mighty work.

---

33. White, *Testimonies: Vol. 5*, 267.
34. White, *Testimonies: Vol. 5*, 267.
35. White, *Testimonies: Vol. 5*, 267.
36. White, *Desire of Ages*, 173.
37. White, *Steps to Christ*, 58; White, *Patriarchs and Prophets*, 372.
38. White, *Messages to Young People*, 55.
39. White, *Testimonies to Ministers and Gospel Workers*, 154.
40. White, *Great Controversy*, 526–7.
41. White, *Messages to Young People*, 259.
42. *Seventh-Day Adventist Bible Commentary: Vol. 7*, 919.
43. White, *Sons and Daughters of God*, 295.
44. White, *Councils to Teachers, Parents and Students*, 366.
45. White, *Testimonies to Ministers and Gospel Workers*, 15.
46. White, *Councils to Teachers, Parents and Students*, 418; White, *Fundamentals of Christian Education*, 363.

Chapter 10

THE DOCTRINE OF THE TRINITY (THE DIVINE TRIO)

IN ADDITION TO FIRMLY ESTABLISHING the biblical doctrine of the two natures of Christ, the early church also worked to affirm the biblical doctrine of the place of Christ within the Godhead. The doctrine of the Trinity developed as the consequence of the biblical search for the identity of Jesus Christ. The Patristics needed to respond to the question that if Jesus was of the same substance (*homoosios*) as God, then what was the nature of God, if God is said to be one God? Indeed, the more certain the early church became that Jesus was divine, the more pressure it came under to define how Jesus, as God, was related to God the Father. Further, if the New Testament witness points to the presence and activity of God in the life of Jesus Christ, by way of the working of the Holy Spirit,[1] what then must be said about the nature of the biblical God the Christians sought to worship, honour and proclaim?

The biblical vision is of a God who is sovereign, but not solitary. However, it cannot be said that God is simply a unity, for while being one, He is also a tri-unity, since the Godhead consists of three persons.

The debate surrounding the doctrine of the Trinity is that while it is definitely suggested in Scripture it is not clearly enunciated. However, this is not the case. The Bible consistently describes God as one, but it also describes each member of the Trio (Father, Son and Holy Spirit) as being God.

The oneness of God is the foundation of the ancient Hebrew faith and is found extensively throughout the Old Testament. This oneness is best attested to in the declaration of faith found in Deuteronomy 6:4. "Hear, O Israel: The Lord our God, the Lord is one!" The teaching on the oneness of God is also maintained in the New

---

1. McGrath, *Historical Theology*, 61.

THE DOCTRINE OF THE TRINITY (THE DIVINE TRIO)

Testament. In Paul's letter to the Ephesians he wrote that, "there is one body, and one Spirit, even as ye are called in one hope of your calling; one Lord, one faith, one baptism, one God and Father of all, who is above all, and through all, and in you all (4:4-6)." However, Scripture is equally clear that while God is one, God is also a plurality. One of the names used for God in the Old Testament, Elohim, is a plural form of the noun, El. There are a number of instances when God uses the plural form to describe Himself. The first attestation of this is found in Genesis 1:26. In His creation of humanity God declares: "And God said, let us make man in our image, after our likeness: and let them have dominion over the fish of the sea, and over the fowl of the air, and over the cattle, and over all the earth, and over every creeping thing that creepeth upon the earth."[2]

The case for the Trinity is at its strongest in the New Testament. Here it can be shown that the Father is God, (John 6:27; 20:17; 1 Cor. 8:6; Gal. 1:1; Eph. 4:6; Phil. 2:11; 1Pet. 1:2) the Son is God (Col. 1:17; John 1:1,3; John 5:27; John 17:5, 20:28; Matthew 9:4, 28:20; Heb. 1:3,8; Titus 2:13) and the Holy Spirit is God (John 3:5-6, 8; Acts 5:3-4; 1 Cor. 2:10, 6:11,19; Titus 3:5). Furthermore, the New Testament teaches that these three names are not synonymous, as with modalism, but speak of three distinct and equal Persons. In addition, there are a number of passages that portray a Trinitarian image of God. In 1 Corinthians 12: 4-6, Paul combined the three members of the Divine Trio in his discussion of spiritual gifts. "Now there are diversities of gifts, but the same Spirit. And there are differences of administrations, but the same Lord. And there are diversities of operations, but it is the same God which worketh all in all." That there was a consensus regarding the nature of the Trinity amongst the Apostles is seen in Peter's salutation in his first letter. "Peter, an apostle of Jesus Christ, to the strangers scattered throughout Pontus, Galatia, Cappadocia, Asia, and Bithynia, elect according to the foreknowledge of God the Father, through sanctification of the Spirit, unto obedience and sprinkling of the blood of Jesus Christ: Grace unto you, and peace, be multiplied (1:2)."

The early church's belief in the Trinity is well attested to by numerous citations. Athenagoras, the second century apologist, presented his thesis to the Emperors Marcus Aurelius and Commodus in around A.D. 177. In it he stated that,

> *Christians know God and His logos. They also know what type of oneness the Son has with the Father and what type of communion the Father has with the Son. Furthermore, they know what the Spirit is and what the unity is of these three: The Spirit, the Son, and the Father. They also know what distinction there is in unity (2:134).*[3]

---

2. See also: Gen. 3:22; 11:7; Isa 6:8.
3. Bercot, *Dictionary of Early Christian Beliefs*, 652.

Around the same time, Irenaeus described the Trinity in relation to each member's role and function. In this description, each member is part of the one God, yet undertaking different functions.

> *It is after the image and likeness of the uncreated God: The Father planning everything well and giving His commands, the Son carrying these into execution and performing the work of creating, and the Spirit nourishing and increasing.*[4]

Indeed, the dogma of the Trinity was the climax of the doctrinal development of the early church. In it was an affirmation of the monotheism that had already been established in the Hebrew Scriptures, which Christianity had claimed as its forebear. The dominant figure in the establishment of a Trinitarian doctrine at the core of Christian faith was Athanasius, "who became bishop of Alexandria and champion of orthodoxy in 328, three years after the Council of Nicea, and died in 373."[5]

It was Athanasius, at the Council of Nicea, who led the charge against Arius in affirming that Jesus Christ was of the same substance as the Father.

The Arian controversy began in Alexandria. Its bishop, Alexander, clashed over several issues with Arius, "who was one of the most prestigious and popular presbyters of the city." Despite the many issues that proved contentious, the coeternity of the Word of God with God, became the main point of contention. While Arius insisted that "there was when He was not", Alexander insisted that the Word existed eternally with the Father. In response, Arius accused Alexander of denying Christian monotheism, since he seemed to be inferring that there were two gods; one being God and the other the Word of God, Jesus Christ. Alexander retorted that Arius' proposal denied the divinity of Christ, whom the church worshipped. Following Arius, the church would therefore need to cease to worship Him, or recognize that it was worshipping a created being. The consequent dismissal of Arius led to protests in the street and the establishment of a pro-Arian alliance among the bishops of the eastern portion of the Empire.

In the twelfth century, Richard of St Victor wrote of relationships within the triune Godhead. In his *de Trinitate,* he concluded that if "there was only one person in the divinity, that one person would certainly not have anyone with whom he could share the riches of his greatness."[6] Therefore, Richard was able to propose that the nature of God's love, which constitutes the essence of His being, cannot exist other from the sharing of love among less than three persons.[7]

During the Reformation, Luther and Calvin both affirmed the orthodox creeds of the ancient church, asserting their beliefs in the doctrine of the Trinity as it had

---

4. Bercot, *Dictionary of Early Christian Beliefs,* 652.
5. Pelikan, *The Christian Tradition: A History of the Development of Doctrine: Vol. 1,* 173.
6. Ribaillier, *Richard de Saint Victor,* 110.
7. McGrath, *The Christian Theology Reader,* 111.

been formulated by the Council of Nicea. The issue, however, became a contentious topic when the antitrinitarian Unitarians pronounced their assertion that the doctrine was totally unscriptural. To be sure, they believed that the "entire method of Trinitarian exegesis was 'repugnant to Scripture'; in reality, it was 'an invention of Satan.'"[8]

In the twentieth-century, Friedrich Schleiermacher argued in favour of the doctrine of the Trinity by stipulating that redemption is not possible other than it is executed by a divine Christ. Further, redemption in the church today is not possible unless a divine Holy Spirit is imparting the life of Christ into the hearts of believers. "Unless the being of God in Christ is assumed, the idea of redemption could not be thus concentrated in His person. And unless there were such a union also in the common Spirit of the Church, the church could not thus be the bearer and perpetuator of the redemption through Christ."[9]

In the opening of his *Church Dogmatics*, Karl Barth discussed the doctrine of the Trinity. In contrast to Schleiermacher, who contended that the Trinity is the last word to be said about God, Barth asserted that the Trinity is the first word to be announced before revelation is even possible. Indeed, the starting point for Barth's discussion of the Trinity is not a doctrinal dissertation, but "the actuality of God's speaking and God's being heard. For how can God be heard, when sinful humanity is incapable of hearing the Word of God?"[10] Indeed, God can only be known in the love of Jesus Christ, through the agency of the transforming Holy Spirit, who directs the sinner to the throne of a gracious father.

Walter Thomas Conner contended that the "true method of interpreting the Christian facts must recognise two things: the unity of God and his trinity."[11] Indeed, within the unity of God is a trinity that amounts to the work of the Father, Son and Holy Spirit; each being the work of God. Therefore, the "work of Christ is the work of God. Christ is not a 'delegate' whom God sent, nor is the Holy Spirit an external agent sent by the Father and the Son. The work of Christ and of the Holy Spirit is as much the work of God as the work of the Father."[12] As a result, the work of each is inclusive of the work of the other rather than exclusive. When Christ performed His ministry, for example, He did so dependent on the authority of the Father and empowered by the Holy Spirit. The role of the Holy Spirit is to baptize the repentant into Christ and remind us of all those things that Christ taught. The doctrine of the Trinity enables Christians to name God, as Father, Son and Holy Spirit and also to identify His nature. The God of absolute power, who yields destructive force to the

---

8. Pelikan, *The Christian Tradition: A History of the Development of Doctrine: Vol. 4*, 328.
9. Schleiermacher, *The Christian Faith*, 116.
10. McGrath, *Christian Theology: An Introduction*, 261.
11. Conner, *Christian Doctrine*, 124.
12. Conner, *Christian Doctrine*, 125.

innocent and unsuspecting, is not a Trinitarian God, since it depicts a God apart from Jesus Christ. As Donald Bloesch reminded us, God is not simply a monarch, but a friend and saviour.[13]

In the Seventh-day Adventist Church the doctrine of the Trinity was established over time, largely due to the influence of Ellen White. Mrs White affirmed that there "are three living persons of the heavenly trio; in the name of these three great powers—the Father, the Son, and the Holy Spirit—those who receive Christ by living faith are baptized, and these powers will co-operate with the obedient subjects of heaven in their efforts to live the new life in Christ."[14] In *The Desire of Ages* she wrote that "sin could be resisted and overcome only through the mighty agency of the Third Person of the Godhead, who would come with no modified energy, but in the fullness of divine power".[15] She also referred to the "three highest powers in heaven," the "heavenly trio" and the "eternal heavenly dignitaries".[16] Further, in a letter Ellen White addressed to "My Brethren in America," dated February 6, 1896, she wrote that, "[e]vil had been accumulating for centuries, and could only be restrained and resisted by the mighty power of the Holy Spirit, the third person of the Godhead, who would come with no modified energy, but in the fullness of divine power."[17] As early as the 1850s Ellen White "reported visions that confirmed the individual personhood of Christ and the Father, and opposed views that tended to blur their real personality . . . By 1869, contrary to her anti-Trinitarian colleagues, she affirmed the eternal pre-existence of Christ and His complete equality with the Father."[18] Indeed, against Arianism, she wrote that Christ our Saviour, "was the brightness of His Father's glory and the express image of His person. He possessed divine majesty, perfection, and excellence. He was equal with God." Indeed, only one who was co-equal with the Father in every way, could make sufficient sacrifice to make atonement for the sin of the world.[19]

---

13. Bloesch, *Essentials of Evangelical Theology: Vol. 1*, 36.
14. White, *Manuscript 21, 1906*, 4.
15. White, *Desire of Ages*, 671.
16. Fortin and Moon, *The Ellen G. White Encyclopedia*, 844.
17. White, *Letter 8, 1896*.
18. Fortin and Moon, *The Ellen G. White Encyclopedia*, 844.
19. White, *Testimonies: Vol. 2*, 200.

Chapter 11

HUMANITY AND THE PROBLEM OF SIN

IN THE CREATION ACCOUNT, THE essence of humanity is seen to be derived from the creative will of God who moulded the first man from the "dust of the ground." God then "breathed into his nostrils the breath of life" and he "became a living being" (Gen. 1:20,24; 2:19). The result of the earth's elements, and the breath of life, is a living being, or soul. The soul, therefore, is the individual person, and describes this person in their individuality and personality. Consequently, the soul does not have a life of its own and does not continue to exist when life ceases. It is the spirit, the life-giving breath of God, that leaves the body at death and returns to God (Ecc. 12:7; Jm. 2:26).

A biblical theology affirms that humanity bears the image of God. Genesis 1:27 sets the impetus for the rest of Scripture when it declares that "God created man in his own image, in the image of God created he him; male and female created he them". Consequently, humanity is patterned after God. The nature of this pattern can be found in Colossians 3:10, which states that the Christian has "put on the new man, which is renewed in knowledge after the image of him that created him." The renewing of the mind to knowledge can be linked to rationality. Therefore, to bear the image of God is to possess the capacity to think rationally. However, Ephesians 4:24, which describes the Christian as created after God in "righteousness and true holiness", adds the dimension of the moral nature of humanity being in the image of God. Consequently, F. L. Forlines summed up the idea of rationality and morality with the word "person". Both God and humanity are personal. "The basic thrust of the idea of being created in the image of God is seen in the fact that man is a personal being. A person is one who thinks, feels and acts."[1] The picture of "God's person" was distorted after the first humans rebelled against God's command and fell into

---

1. Forlines, *Biblical Systematics: A Study of the Christian System of Life and Thought*, 109.

the consequences of estrangement from God, since rebellion against God's law is sin, and sin is roundly condemned by a just God.

Scripture depicts sin as deriving in heaven before entering the stage of human history in the event of the fall. While it was the first humans who introduced sin into the world, it was Lucifer who introduced sin into the universe. The War in Heaven, and ultimate expulsion of Lucifer with a third of the angels, changed the course of the cosmos forever (Rev. 7:7–14). The beings of Heaven, along with those of the universe, await the final stages of history with interest.

The most general word for sin in the Bible is *hamartia,* which in ancient literature describes an offence against morals, laws, people and gods. *Adikia* is a more specialized word; drawn from the legal world, it describes the opposite of righteousness. Therefore, *Adikia* denotes unrighteousness, injustice and unjust deeds. It has to do with unholy action; the sinful deeds that people perform. To be sure, in the New Testament *hamartia* is always used to describe people's sins, which are ultimately directed against God. Jesus also referred to sin in the context of action. In Mark 7:21–23 He states that it is that "For from within, out of the heart of men, proceed the evil thoughts, fornications, thefts, murders, adulteries, deeds of coveting and wickedness, as well as deceit, sensuality, envy, slander, pride and foolishness. All these evil things proceed from within and defile the man (NASB)." Indeed, the one who commits sin is a slave to sin (John 8:34) and such a slavery denies the omnipotence of God. Therefore, sin becomes habitual and central to a way of life and those who separate themselves from God in sin, separate themselves from God's presence (Matthew 7:23).

The apostle Paul also firmly believed that the act of sin is what leads to unrighteousness. In Ephesians 2:1–3, he wrote:

> As for you, you were dead in your transgressions and sins, in which you used to live when you followed the ways of this world and of the ruler of the kingdom of the air, the spirit who is now at work in those who are disobedient. All of us also lived among them at one time, gratifying the cravings of our flesh and following its desires and thoughts. Like the rest, we were by nature deserving of wrath (NIV).

However, he equally affirmed that the born-again Christian, empowered by the Holy Spirit, is to overcome sin under God's grace.

> *What shall we say then? Are we to continue in sin so that grace may increase? May it never be! How shall we who died to sin still live in it? Or do you not know that all of us who have been baptized into Christ Jesus have been baptized into His death? Therefore we have been buried with Him through baptism into death, so that as Christ was raised from the dead through the glory of the Father, so we too might walk in newness of life. For if we have become united with Him in the likeness of His death, certainly we shall also be in the likeness of*

HUMANITY AND THE PROBLEM OF SIN

His resurrection, knowing this, that our old self was crucified with Him, in order that our body of sin might be done away with, so that we would no longer be slaves to sin; for he who has died is freed from sin. (NASB) (Rom. 6:1–7).

By its very nature sin amounts to an act of wrongdoing against God, but is also to be understood as alienation from God. The prophets of the Old Testament believed sin to signify a rupture in the personal relationship between the Lord and humanity. God created humanity and endowed her with responsibility, however this trust was betrayed by the first couple (Gen. 3:1–7) and this rebellion echoes through the ages and sways the decisions of all humanity (Rom. 5:12). Consequently, the Bible affirms that sin is universal, for "All have sinned and fall short of the glory of God (Rom 3:23)."[2]

During the time of the early church, Tertullian (c 212) believed that every individual is born into original sin, which is cleansed at baptism. After baptism, there should be no sin found in the life of the Christian. "Every unrighteousness is sin. And there is a sin unto death. But we know that everyone who has been born of God does not sin . . . that is, the sin which is unto death. Therefore, there is no course left you but to either deny that adultery and fornication are mortal sins, or else acknowledge that they are irremissible (unpardonable)."[3]

By the time of the Reformation sin was described as idolatry. According to Martin Luther, "That to which your heart clings and entrusts itself is, I say, really your God." The Heidelberg Catechism (1645) states that sin is a transgression of the law or an action contrary to the divine law. It is an offence against God, which subjects the creature to God's eternal wrath, unless forgiveness is obtained. Of original sin, the catechism states that the whole human race, on account of the fall of our first parents, is in guilt. It includes an inclination of the heart for those things which the law of God forbids.[4]

In the modern era Reinhold Niebuhr declared: "The most classical definition of sin in the New Testament, that of St. Paul [is as follows] . . . The sin of man is that he seeks to make himself God."[5]

James Leo Garrett pointed to sin as covenant unfaithfulness. He averred to the Hebrew word, *para,* which means to "break off". In the New Testament, the concept of sin as covenant unfaithfulness is used by the word *asynthetous*. This is found in Romans 1:31, which has been translated "covenant breakers" (RSV), "faithless" (NIV) and "untrustworthy" (NRSV). Garrett believed that the translation "covenant breakers" seems to be accurate inasmuch as the word comes from *syntithemi*, "to join together, or covenant". Sin also refers to rebellious disobedience. The noun

---

2. Gunther, *Sin*, 573–583.
3. Bercot, *A Dictionary of Early Christian Beliefs,* 616–618.
4. Willard, *The Commentary of Dr. Zacharias Ursinus on The Heidelberg Catechism,* 36–56.
5. Bloesch, *Essentials of Evangelical Theology: Vol. 1,* 92—103.

apeitheia, meaning "disobedience", is used in Eph. 2:2c; Tit.1:6c and 3:3a, 1 Pet. 2:8b and 3:20a.⁶ Otto Weber, Professor of Reformed Theology at the University of Gottingen until his death in 1966, held that biblical and church doctrine dictates that the knowledge of sin is affected through the law of God. Further, Weber held that sin is personal. It is something about humanity. However, he incorrectly stated that it is neither a defect nor an attribute, or an act performed. It is the comprehensive qualification of humanity's being, in that it defines his or her direction.⁷ Millard Erickson, by contrast, is closer to the biblical notion of sin when he discussed terms that emphasize the character of sin in relation to personal responsibility. He assessed sin as "missing the mark", that is, a failure to hit the mark God has set, being His standard of perfect love and obedience to Him. Erickson believed that an individual misses the mark when he or she fails to love the brother or sister, since love of others follows love of God. Erickson also spoke of sin as transgressing the Lord's commands. For example, in Num. 14:41f, the people of Israel want to go up to the place which the Lord has promised, but Moses says, "Why are you disobeying the Lord's command? This will not succeed! Do not go up, because the Lord is not with you. You will be defeated by your enemies." Therefore, the people of Israel were not to transgress God's covenant or His commands. Erickson also discussed sin as rebellion, iniquity, treachery, perversion and abomination.⁸

Donald Bloesch wrote that the essence of sin is unbelief, which appears as both idolatry and hardness of heart. From the biblical perspective Bloesch held, in contrast to Weber, that sin is both an act and a state. It embodies both separation from God as well as a deliberate violation of His will. It entails both a state of alienation and a transgression of His law. Bloesch also pointed to the penalties for sin, including guilt, death, moral servitude and spiritual blindness. Indeed, humanity in sin forfeits happiness and becomes paralyzed by guilt and is captive to forces and powers beyond one's control. In regard to causes and effects of sin, Bloesch quoted Paul, who states: "Wherefore, as by one-man sin entered into the world, and death by sin; and so, death passed upon all men, for that all have sinned (Rom. 5:12)." However, humanity is not only to be characterized by physical death, but also an eternal death (that is, a destruction) that awaits the doomed sinner.⁹

Edgar Mullins (1860–1928), a Pietist, held that sin is humanity's personal opposition to a personal God. Guilt, therefore, takes the form of self-condemnation based on a sense of God's disapproval. However, Mullins, typical in Protestantism, misunderstood the role of the law. Guilt, for Mullins, is not so much a transgression against the law, as against the divine will, even though the law is an expression of

---

6. Garrett, *Systematic Theology: Biblical. Historical and Evangelical: Vol. 1*, 451–465.
7. Weber, *Foundations of Dogmatics: Vol. 1*, 580–618.
8. Erickson, *Christian Theology*, 583–598.
9. Bloesch, *Essentials of Evangelical Theology: Vol. 1*, 98.

the will of God. However, he did hold that the chief penalty of sin in the Scriptures is death, physical and spiritual. Death of the body is declared in Scripture to be the penalty of sin. Death has entered the world through sin (Rom 5:12), however spiritual death is the chief penalty of sin. That is, a loss of fellowship with God and of the blessedness which attends that fellowship.[10]

There has also been debate regarding the doctrine of original sin. Original sin is an important part of Reformed and Roman Catholic dogmatics. In these doctrines, all individuals are born sinful to the core. Within the Reformed school, original sin and total depravity provide a united description of the human condition before conversion. James Packer represents this theology when he stated that "sinfulness marks everyone from birth, and is there in the form of a motivationally twisted heart, prior to any actual sins . . . The assertion of original sin makes the point that we are not sinners because we sin, but rather we sin because we are sinners, born with a nature enslaved to sin."[11] Arminianism, however, sounds a more biblical note when it asserts that here is no such thing as original sin in this sense. One is a sinner because of the actual sins one commits. Therefore, Christ died, not for inherited sin, but for actual sins committed. This is expressed in the Waterland Confession (1580) (IV) and by F.L. Forlines, who stated that the "Bible knows of no imputation from one to another except in a manner that makes it so the action can in some sense be said to be the action of the person." Therefore, while born into sinful humanity, with a propensity for sin, condemnation is a consequence for the act, not the disposition to act because of a state of being. Consequently, an infant is guaranteed salvation since they are not capable of deciding to sin. Forlines referred to Matthew 18:10 to defend this position.[12] "Take heed that ye despise not one of these little ones; for I say unto you, that in heaven their angels do always behold the face of my Father which is in heaven".

The consequences of the sin of Adam has been widely debated. While Pelagians[13] and Socinians[14] maintain that Adam acted for himself alone; without any consequence on his posterity, a more scriptural approach is that Adam was a kind of natural representative of his posterity; so that the effects of his fall are visited upon his posterity but not the penal infliction for guilt. This is in the same sense in which children are compelled to suffer poverty or disgrace, by the crimes of their

---

10. Mullins, *The Christian Religion in Its Doctrinal Expression*, 281–84.

11. Packer, *Concise Theology*, 83.

12. Forlines, *Biblical Systematics*, 127, 172.

13. Pelagius was born c. 354, probably in Britain (Ireland). He was a monk and theologian who emphasised human effort in salvation. He denied the teaching of predestination and original sin. He was condemned as a heretic at a number of councils.

14. Faustus Socinus (1539–1604), wrote that Christ was divine by office, rather than by nature. Indeed, Christ was fully human, yet without sin. His life was an example of how to overcome sin. Salvation could come about through the study of Scripture.

parents, without suffering the penal consequences. That is, condemnatory guilt that causes a penalty only attaches to presumptuous sinning, which always occurs with the awakening of conscience. It is not supposed original or inherited sin that brings condemnation, but actual sin that arises from the will and intention to deliberately sin. Therefore, there is no implication that a person is condemned in their sinfulness upon birth. Indeed, biblical theology does not support the notion that an infant's nature is condemned by a wrathful God. Condemnation comes upon the act of sin (Isa. 59:2; Lk. 15:24; Rom. 5:12; Rom. 7:9, Col. 2:13), not in the state of being of a person, even though the act of sinning arises from that state. Sure enough, each inherits a sinful nature, but Scripture nowhere determines that a person inherits damnation. Consequently, children are in a state of grace until they arrive at such a point of deciding to deliberately sin and against God and deny His grace. (Deut. 24:16, 2 Kng. 14:6, 2 Chron. 25:4, Jer. 31:29–30, Eze. 18:2–4, Eze. 18:19–20).

James Arminius made the point that since all who have not committed a transgression are saved, then all infants are saved, since none have transgressed.[15] Indeed, when Adam sinned it was of his own person and free will. "There is no reason then why it was the will of God to impute this sin to infants, who are said to have sinned in Adam, before they had any personal existence, and therefore, before they could possibly sin at their own will and pleasure."[16] Before the fall, humanity thought, felt and acted in the likeness of God consciously and unconsciously. After the fall, this is no longer the case. However, while there is a distortion of the image of God in humanity there is not a demolition. After the fall, humanity still possesses the capacity for rationality and morality. Humanity is still personal, but God is not pleased since humanity possesses enough sin to mare the image originally bestowed. Besides, at the root of sin is not weakness, but rebellion. Indeed, in the biblical worldview being a member of a fallen race leads to the inevitability of sin, and in sin condemnation. But in the economy of God there is, accompanying this dim reality, a message of hope, that in spite of sin there is sufficient grace, in that redemption may come through Jesus Christ.

As a result of their rebellion against God, the first humans took the whole of humanity into a state of sin. Consequently, humanity owes God a debt that cannot be re-paid. As Geoffrey Bromiley expressed Barth's idea: "In his pride man incurs the guilt of resisting God, denying his glory, and disrupting his order."[17] Consequently, a unity arises between humanity and sin in which the law of sin is followed and guilt imputed. However, sin is an action emanating from a state of mind rather than an inherited state of being. Therefore, the severity of sin is seen in its consequences,

---

15. Arminius, Nichols, Bagnall, The Works of James Arminius, DD, Formerly Professor of Divinity in the University of Leyden, 287.

16. Arminius, Nichols, Bagnall, The Works of James Arminius, 288.

17. Bromiley, *Introduction to the Theology of Karl Barth*, 187.

through the form of sorrow, heartache and despair, and more particularly through God's revelation in the life and death of Jesus Christ.[18] John Banks correctly defined sin as lawlessness, since sin is a deviation from the law. [19] Mullins agreed that sin is lawlessness (1 John 3:4) but rightly pointed to the God who stands behind the law, since the law is an expression of God's character. Therefore, to rebel against the law is to rebel against God. The result, is that sin is "a breach of our personal relations with God."[20]

Ellen White rightly pointed to the plot of Satan to undermine the authority of God as being at the root of the problem. Driven by envy, he promotes disobedience as a primary means to fulfil his ambitions. In Patriarchs and Prophets, she wrote: "No longer free to stir up rebellion in heaven, Satan's enmity against God found a new field in plotting the ruin of the human race." Indeed, according to Mrs. White, Satan's work since the Garden of Eden has been "to destroy the moral image of God in man, by making void the divine law."[21] The consequence is humanity being formed, by personal choice and decision, into an image of his or her own moral deformity.[22] The hallmark of this deformity is a failure to keep the law.

> *In the happiness and peace of the holy pair in Eden he beheld a vision of the bliss that to him was forever lost. Moved by envy, he determined to incite them to disobedience, and bring upon them the guilt and penalty of sin. He would change their love to distrust and their songs of praise to reproaches against their Maker. Thus, he would not only plunge these innocent beings into the same misery which he was himself enduring, but would cast dishonor upon God, and cause grief in heaven.*[23]

Ontologically, sin leads to an inner discontentment, with self, others, and the world order, since humanity now fails to have the life for which it was created. In the early church Tertullian, a major figure in early Latin theology, believed the origin of discontent is to be found in the devil, since it was he who had been discontented with God.[24] However, there is not an obliteration of God's design for his creation. Indeed, humankind, even in its fallen state, is still capable of reflecting the glory of God and acting according to His will as it is reflected in the Law. Fallen humanity is still endowed with freedom and ability to choose for good or ill. For the Reformers, the image of God in humanity is defaced but not totally erased, otherwise humanity would cease to be human. Emil Brunner maintained that humanity's relation with

---

18. Bromiley, *Introduction to the Theology of Karl Barth*, 187.
19. Banks, *A Manuel of Christian Doctrine*, 106.
20. Mullins, *The Christian Religion*, 288.
21. White, *Review and Herald*, Jan. 26, 1897.
22. White, *Review and Herald*, Aug. 25, 1896.
23. White, *Patriarchs and Prophets*, 52.
24. McGrath, *Christian Theology: Introduction*, 212.

God is "not sundered by sin but perverted". Consequently, the person, while still being responsible before God, is no longer in "a state of being-in-love". Therefore, there is enough of the image of God to maintain human responsibility and the ability to choose for God.[25]

Donald Bloesch proposed that a knowledge of sin comes through both the law and the Gospel. To be sure, sin is a transgression of the law and a violation of God's love as revealed in Christ. "Through the Law alone we can arrive at a knowledge of our guilt, but we cannot have a true perception of our sin. We can be awakened to the burden of our guilt through the Law by itself, but we will not know the enormity of our sins until they are exposed in the light of the cross and resurrection of Jesus Christ."[26] Since sin is rebellion against God, particularly as He reveals His character in His law, ungodliness is an appropriate word to define its meaning (Romans 1:18), since sin amounts to a broken relationship with God, which leads to estrangement.[27] We see this particularly in Genesis 3:8, where we read that Adam and Eve "heard the voice of the Lord God walking in the garden in the cool of the day: and Adam and his wife hid themselves from the presence of the Lord God amongst the trees of the garden."

The hiddenness of humanity is well expressed in the Parable of the Prodigal Son (Luke 15). The son finds himself in a far country away from the influence, protection and love of his father. Having abandoned all that had been given into his possession he has a longing for what is unclean. He is without hope and seemingly his arduous and fruitless journey is about to come to an end. But then a miracle takes place; a spark of light ignites and brings hope to a cold and dark scene. It is not so much that the son crafts a cunning plan to return to his father as a servant to, at least, live out the rest of his life with food and shelter, but that the father waits in eager expectation and greets this wayward son with love, mercy and grace. Without this turn of repentant faith, and the love of the father, the son remains hidden from hope and estranged from God. To this extent, the father appears to be hidden to the son, since he has not come to a realization that the father waits for his return. Nor has the son in fact returned to experience the embrace of the father. Therefore, God is hidden so long as He remains unacknowledged.

The ultimate result of humanity's estrangement, due to waywardness, is condemnation by a just God. It is God who condemns (Job 10:2; Jer. 42:18; John 12:48) and His condemnation is deserved, since it is based on His justice. In addition to its being deserved it is also individual, since each is responsible for his, or her, self. The ones who sin are the ones who perish, since they bear their own guilt. "The

---

25. Brunner, *The Christian Doctrine of Creation and Redemption*, 109.
26. Bloesch, *Essentials of Evangelical Theology: Vol. 1*, 97.
27. Moody, *The Word of Truth*, 276.

righteousness of the righteous shall be upon himself, and the wickedness of the wicked shall be upon himself." (Ezekiel 18:20).

This individualism is evident in the doctrine of the Investigative Judgement (Dan. 8:14). In this continual event, beginning with the prophetic year of 1844 and concluding at the end of probation before the return of Christ (Dan. 12:1), individual responses to the Gospel, in the form of repentance and sustained faith, are recorded in the Book of Life (Revelation 20:11–15). Those lacking repentance and faith are recorded in the Book of Death (1 Peter 4:17; Ecclesiastes 12:14; Matthew 12:36, 37; 1 Corinthians 4:5; Isaiah 65:6, 7). What is required, therefore, is a discernment that chooses the light of the Gospel, as it is expressed in the law and manifested in the life of Christ. This life of Christ, as exemplified in Christian behavior, will be recorded in the Book of Remembrance (Mal. 3:16–17). This life is a discernment and awakening to a reality that is latent in fallen humanity and not totally eradicated. It is a hidden life created by God to do His will that is buried under the detritus of sin. However, this hidden person after God's own heart can only be revived and animated by the working of the Holy Spirit, who is charged with restoring that which was marred by sin. It is at the heart of God, therefore, to long for righteousness to be manifested in His much-loved creation. Consequently, God expresses an intense hate for sin in His decision to eradicate it, so that what He loves might be free to reflect His image. Indeed, Ellen White pointed to the justice of God as being an expression of His hatred for sin, since "offense against God's law, however minute, is set down in the reckoning, and when the sword of justice is taken in hand, it will do the work for impenitent transgressors that was done to the divine Sufferer. Justice will strike; for God's hatred of sin is intense and overwhelming."[28]

That spiritual death is a result of sin is evident in the Book of James, who states: "Then when lust has conceived, it gives birth to sin; and when sin is accomplished, it brings forth death. (NASB) (1:15)". However, the biblical account is clear that sin's consequences reach beyond spiritual death to include guilt, moral servitude, spiritual captivity, death and destruction. Humanity, in sin, forfeits the chance for happiness and becomes captive to powers that appear beyond their control. Each faces a future that is dire and foreboding. Judgement, then after judgement, destruction. "Sin carries death with it and calls for death (Wisdom of Solomon 1:11–16; Proverbs 8:36; John 8:24)."[29] Further, in Romans, "(w)herefore, as by one man sin entered into the world," declares the apostle, "and death by sin; and so death passed upon all men, for that all have sinned (Romans 5:12)." Therefore, Scripture stipulates that the ultimate consequence of sin is destruction (see also, Ps. 37:20; Matt. 10:28b; Rom. 6:23; Phil. 3:19; 2 Thess. 1:9; Jm. 4:12a). Those who reject salvation through Jesus Christ have their names entered in the Book of Death. If they are alive

---

28. White, Manuscript 58, 1897.
29. Bloesch, *Essential of Evangelical Theology: Vol. 1*, 98.

at Christ's return they are destroyed (Rev. 19:21), otherwise if they have already died when Christ returns, they are resurrected at the conclusion of the millennium and destroyed along with Satan (Rev. 20:5). Conversely, those whose names are found in the Book of Life receive redemption. Indeed, true biblical religion concerns itself with God's aim of the transformation of humanity. According to Ellen White, the "elevation and restoration of human nature is the purpose of Christ's incarnation (MH 180), sacrifice (RH, July 15, 1909) and sending of His Spirit (RH April 5, 1906). The effects of God's renewal of the person are found in a new character, displayed in the tenderness of sentiments (ST, Nov. 28, 1892), cheerfulness (MH 180), and change in cherished habits and practices. (PC 418)".[30] According to the Twenty-Fifth Fundamental Belief of the Seventh-day Adventist Church, God, who alone is immortal, will grant eternal life to His redeemed. Until that day death is an unconscious state for all people. When Christ, who is our life, appears, the resurrected righteous and the living righteous will be glorified and caught up to meet their Lord. The second resurrection, the resurrection of the unrighteous, will take place a thousand years later. (Rom. 6:23; 1 Tim. 6:15, 16; Eccl. 9:5, 6; Ps. 146:3, 4; John 11:11–14; Col. 3:4; 1 Cor. 15:51–54; 1 Thess. 4:13–17; John 5:28, 29; Rev. 20:1–10.)[31] In "The Acts of the Apostles" Ellen White discussed the state of the dead in her discussion of Paul's first epistle to the Thessalonian believers. In it "Paul endeavored to instruct them regarding the true state of the dead. He spoke of those who die as being asleep—in a state of unconsciousness:

> *I would not have you to be ignorant, brethren, concerning them which are asleep, that ye sorrow not, even as others which have no hope. For if we believe that Jesus died and rose again, even so them also which sleep in Jesus will God bring with Him . . . . For the Lord Himself shall descend from heaven with a shout, with the voice of the Archangel, and with the trump of God: and the dead in Christ shall rise first: then we which are alive and remain shall be caught up together with them in the clouds, to meet the Lord in the air: and so shall we ever be with the Lord.*[32]

---

30. Fortin and Moon, *The Ellen G. White Encyclopedia*, 885.
31. White, *Great Controversy*, 661.
32. White, *The Acts of the Apostles*, 257.

CHAPTER 12

JESUS CHRIST: SAVIOUR AND LORD

WHILE JESUS CHRIST STANDS AS the central figure of the Scriptures, salvation is its primary issue. Indeed, while Christ can be identified as the creator and Lord of all, His work is for the salvation of the universe. In this sense, the Lord's earthly mission can be divided into two parts. Firstly, His ministry demonstrated His authority over creation, sickness, and sin. He was also able to demonstrate His attributes of obedience, faithfulness and resistance to Satan and sin. These demonstrations, however, are without a point if they do not serve to give an authentication to His work. Therefore, secondly, Jesus' earthly ministry was to do the work that leads to salvation. Therefore, the basis of who Jesus is, gives authenticity to the accomplishment of what He does.

The mission of Jesus Christ is primarily concerned with bringing glory to God by doing the will of the Father. In His love, God the Father seeks to enter into an eternal relationship with as many people as will respond to His free invitation. As Jesus brings this about through His work, so does He accomplish it in His person. A saving relationship with God can only be bought about through the work of Christ. It is in Christ that the relationship takes its form and character, and is maintained. The task of salvation is to deal with the problem and issue that led to the need for salvation and the restoration of relationship between God and humanity. As sin alienates an unholy person from a pure and Holy God, so does the work of Christ cancel sin, build a bridge and restore relationship. "In Jesus Christ, the new relationship of man to God is established, the relationship which first reveals sin as what it is and which simultaneously overcomes it."[1] While for historical reasons, Justification by Faith has been the central argument for a Protestant presentation of the Gospel, reconciliation would seem to be more at the heart of a gospel soteriology. It is true that this is a difficult argument to make on the basis of a word study alone. A word

---

1. Weber, *Foundations of Dogmatics: Vol. 2*, 177.

study will not lead us to that conclusion. The word "reconciliation" does not occur that often in the New Testament. To be specific, we find the word "reconciliation" only in Romans 5:11; 11:15 and 2 Corinthians 5:18f. We can add to this the verb "to reconcile" and extend the list by three more verses. That is, Romans 5:10; 2 Corinthians 5:18f and, in another sense, 1 Corinthians 7:11. Yet to make the assertion that reconciliation is only a minor theme in the New Testament would be a mistake. Word studies are not the basis of theology. To be sure, a metaphor found in a parable, or a life lesson discovered in a narrative, usually does not have the word that lies at the centre of its meaning. Indeed, in the thematic sense, the idea of reconciliation permeates Scripture.

The concept of reconciliation in the Bible begins where the need to be reconciled first presents itself. To be reconciled is to be in conciliation in the first place. This is the experience of the first people, as they walked in the garden and conversed with God. Yet one day, after they had disobeyed Him, it is evident that shame and guilt had led them to be estranged from God.

> *They heard the sound of the LORD God walking in the garden in the cool of the day, and the man and his wife hid themselves from the presence of the LORD God among the trees of the garden. Then the LORD God called to the man, and said to him, "Where are you?" He said, "I heard the sound of You in the garden, and I was afraid because I was naked; so I hid myself." And He said, "Who told you that you were naked? Have you eaten from the tree of which I commanded you not to eat?" The man said, "The woman whom You gave to be with me, she gave me from the tree, and I ate." Then the LORD God said to the woman, "What is this you have done?" And the woman said, "The serpent deceived me, and I ate." The LORD God said to the serpent, "Because you have done this, Cursed are you more than all cattle, And more than every beast of the field; On your belly you will go, And dust you will eat All the days of your life; And I will put enmity Between you and the woman, And between your seed and her seed; He shall bruise you on the head, And you shall bruise him on the heel (NASB) (Gen. 3:8–15)."*

The path to reconciliation, as it is outlined in Scripture, amounts to a movement away from estrangement and into relationship characterized by love and acceptance. It is not a move away from the hate of God to the love of God, since hate is not an attribute of God, other than the hate of sin. The problem of sin relates to the need for justice, which is an attribute of God. Sin must be punished if God is to maintain integrity and uphold His attribute of justice. Therefore, the estrangement between humanity and God is characterized by condemnation for sin, which results in just punishment. Consequently, reconciliation must somehow overcome the condemnation of sin which leads to punishment and find a way to a pardon for sin. The Bible outlines a mechanism by which this takes place. Since punishment is cancelled, or expiated, after it has been paid for, the punishment of God must also be cancelled when paid. This too is a reflection of the justice of God. When payment is made for sin, reconciliation is achieved. The establishment of a law which, when broken, results in sin which must be paid for before there is reconciliation between parties, was referred to in the Ancient Near—East as a covenant.

CHAPTER 13

JESUS CHRIST: PROPHET, PRIEST AND KING

THE MINISTRY OF JESUS CHRIST has commonly been described utilizing the "threefold office", namely: Prophet, Priest and King. In theological literature, its origins can be traced to Eusebius of Caesarea (c 263—339). It was then used extensively by the Protestant Reformers. Jesus understood Himself to be a prophet, in what Dale Moody has referred to as Christ's "prophetic consciousness." This is most evident when Jesus referred to Himself as a prophet, when He lamented that a prophet is without honour among His own people (Mark 6:4; Matthew 13:57; Luke 4:24; John 4:44).

Many of Jesus' contemporaries also recognised Jesus to be fulfilling the role of a prophet, including the accounts of His own disciples. The Gospels emphasise that God sent Jesus in the same manner that God sent Moses. Both Jesus and Moses were known by their signs. Indeed, "the Gospel of Matthew draws numerous parallels between Jesus and Moses. Moses received the Torah, but Jesus gave the New Torah as it appears in the five teaching sections of Matthew's Gospel."[1] Jesus' message bears a striking similarity to the classical prophets. His teaching follows a prophetic form of speech, most noticeable in his pronouncements of both doom and deliverance, but also in his teaching in parables. The priestly ministry of Jesus is also well founded in Scripture. Jesus also made a number of prophetic predictions that came true, including the fate of Jerusalem and the Temple, his own death and the coming of the Holy Spirit (Matt. 16:21; Matt. 24:1-2; 34-35; Matt. 26:2; 11-13; 21-22; 31-32; 33-34; Lk. 21:20,24; Lk. 23:28-30; Jn. 2:18-22).

In the Old Testament, the Priests were set aside to offer sacrifices to God in a system designed to cleanse repentant hearts from sin in the form of a blood sacrifice

---

1. Moody, *The Word of Truth*, 368.

JESUS CHRIST: PROPHET, PRIEST AND KING

(Leviticus 1:5, 16:33; Numbers 1:53). In the New Testament Jesus Christ is seen to take upon Himself, as designated by the Father, the ultimate role of priest over the House of God. In this way type meets anti-type. Indeed, as Hebrews points out (10:21) and as Arminius alluded, Christ, as a minister in the Heavenly Sanctuary, has the authority to fully and successfully intercede for sinners, based on His efficacious sacrifice on the cross. To be sure,

> *Christ discharges the whole of this part of his function in heaven, before the face of the Divine Majesty; for there, also, is the royal seat and the throne of God, to which, when we are about to pray, we are commanded to lift up our eyes and our minds. But he executes this part of his office, not in anguish of spirit, or in a posture of humble genuflection, as though fallen down before the knees of the Father, but in the confidence of the shedding of his own blood, which, sprinkled as it is on his sacred body, he continually presents, as an object of sight before his Father, always turning it towards his sacred countenance. The entire efficacy of this function depends on the dignity and value of the blood effused and sprinkled over the body; for, by his blood shedding, he opened a passage for himself 'into the holiest, within the veil.' From which circumstance, we may with the greatest certainty conclude, that his prayers will never be rejected, and that whatever we shall ask in his name, will, in virtue of that intercession, be both heard and answered.*[2]

The activity of the priesthood is in the context of God's everlasting covenant. The covenant had been established as a bond in blood between God and His elect people (Deut. 29). The requirement of the covenant came in the form of the Commandments, which, if broken, needed to be atoned for (Exodus 24:8; Matt. 26:28; Heb. 9:20). Importantly, the environment in which these sacrifices were to be carried out was the sanctuary; a tabernacle, and then temple, where God resided among His people. This "Tent of Meeting" contained a Holy and Most Holy Place. The Most Holy Place was only to be entered by the High Priest and that only once a year (Lev. 23). It contained the Ark of the Covenant, holding within it the Ten Commandments, the moral and legal basis for the rule of God, the terms of the Covenant, and the standard of His justice (Exodus 30). The Most Holy Place was separated from the Holy place by a curtain. Therefore, it makes sense, that when the covenant was breached atonement would be made in front of it. Indeed, the priest would sprinkle blood before the curtain, to signify that a payment had been made to meet the terms of the covenant and therefore the just requirements of the law (Lev. 4:6–17). Over the course of a year, a stockpile of payments would accrue. Therefore, at the end of each year, on the Day of Atonement, the Sanctuary was cleansed. That is, having made reparation for sin as stipulated by the law throughout the year, in this two phase process, forgiveness was applied as the accumulation of payments was taken before

---

2. Arminius, *Orations of Arminius: Oration 1*.

the throne of God and made efficacious to those who came with repentant hearts (Lev. 16). In addition, the sin of the people was not only paid for but also eradicated and forgotten, since there ceases to be a record of it. Significantly, the sanctuary on earth was a copy of the sanctuary in heaven. While the High Priest fulfilled this role in the old Covenant, in the new covenant Jesus fulfils this role as the One who made an ultimate and final sacrifice for the sin of the world. Furthermore, in the Heavenly Sanctuary, He intercedes for sinners on the basis of His own perfect sacrifice, which is sufficient to cleanse the whole world, but is applied only to those who repent of sin and continue to put their faith in Jesus Christ (Heb. 4:14–16; Rom. 10:13; Acts 2:21).

The kingship of Jesus Christ is well attested to in Scripture. Prophecy concerning His kingship are found as early as the book of Genesis. "The sceptre shall not depart from Judah, nor a lawgiver from between his feet, until Shiloh come; and unto him *shall* the gathering of the people *be* (Gen. 49:10)." There is later elaboration by the prophet Isaiah before the exile;

> *For unto us a child is born, unto us a son is given: and the government shall be upon his shoulder: and his name shall be called Wonderful, Counsellor, The mighty God, The everlasting Father, The Prince of Peace. Of the increase of his government and peace there shall be no end, upon the throne of David, and upon his kingdom, to order it, and to establish it with judgment and with justice from henceforth even for ever. The zeal of the* LORD *of hosts will perform this* (Isaiah 9:6–7).

This theme is maintained during the exile by Ezekiel;

> *My servant David will be king over them, and they will all have one shepherd. They will follow my laws and be careful to keep my decrees. They will live in the land I gave to my servant Jacob, the land where your ancestors lived. They and their children and their children's children will live there forever, and David my servant will be their prince forever.* (NIV) (Ezekiel 37:24–25).

Among the minor prophets, Zechariah provides a precise identification of the coming king. "Rejoice greatly, O daughter of Zion; shout, O daughter of Jerusalem: behold, thy King cometh unto thee: he is just, and having salvation; lowly, and riding upon an ass, and upon a colt the foal of an ass (Zechariah 9:9–10)."

The authority of Jesus as king is outlined in a number of Gospel passages. Here, Christ is seen to found the kingdom of God; calls for obedience; speaks with authority; works miracles; establishes the ordinances; starts the church; conquers death; commissions the disciples; ascends to the right hand of God; sits in judgement; and promises to return as King over the whole earth.[3] The rule of Jesus Christ is further

---

3. Mullins, *The Christian Religion*, 204.

seen in His victory over the powers, "for by his cross and resurrection victory they have been dethroned (Mt 12:29; Mk 3:27; Lk 10:18; Col. 2:15)."[4]

The self-understanding of Jesus, as one who has authority to rule, is chiefly expressed in the title, *Son of Man*. Derived from the book of Daniel, it is clearly a messianic title that refers to His exaltation and rule.

> *I saw in the night visions, and, behold, one like the Son of man came with the clouds of heaven, and came to the Ancient of days, and they brought him near before him. And there was given him dominion, and glory, and a kingdom, that all people, nations, and languages, should serve him: his dominion is an everlasting dominion, which shall not pass away, and his kingdom that which shall not be destroyed* (Dan. 7:13–14).

Jesus refers to this theme in Matthew.

> *When the Son of Man comes in his glory, and all the angels with him, he will sit on his glorious throne. ³² All the nations will be gathered before him, and he will separate the people one from another as a shepherd separates the sheep from the goats. He will put the sheep on his right and the goats on his left. Then the King will say to those on his right, 'Come, you who are blessed by my Father; take your inheritance, the kingdom prepared for you since the creation of the world'* (NIV) (Mat. 25:31–34).

Indeed, kingship "is the chief concern when the Messiah is designated Son of Man."[5] It is a particular emphasis of the Gospel of Mark. As Dale Moody pointed out, the "kingly role of the Son of Man appears more frequently in Mark than in any other Gospel."[6] Associated with the kingship of Jesus Christ is His kingdom. Essentially, the kingdom of God is that which comes under His rule. Now we see this in part, since rebellion still holds sway and Satan is yet to be destroyed. However, the coming of the Son of Man, promised by Jesus, brings this duality to a close, as Christ will have dominion over all, without dissent. Therefore, it will be triumphant (Dan. 2:44; Rev. 20:13) and eternal (2 Pet. 1:11) and is to be characterised by joy (Psalm 46:4), peace (Isa. 11:6–9) and truth (Jn. 18:37). Significantly, the kingdom of God is transformative.

> *Say to them that are of a fearful heart, be strong, fear not: behold, your God will come with vengeance, even God with a recompense; he will come and save you. Then the eyes of the blind shall be opened, and the ears of the deaf shall be unstopped. Then shall the lame man leap as a hart, and the tongue of the dumb sing: for in the wilderness shall waters break out, and streams in the desert. And the parched ground shall become a pool, and the thirsty land springs of*

---

4. Bloesch, *Jesus Christ*, 212.
5. Moody, *The Word of Truth*, 381.
6. Moody, *The Word of Truth*, 382.

water: in the habitation of dragons, where each lay, shall be grass with reeds and rushes. And an highway shall be there, and a way, and it shall be called the way of holiness; the unclean shall not pass over it; but it shall be for those: the wayfaring men, though fools, shall not err therein. No lion shall be there, nor any ravenous beast shall go up thereon, it shall not be found there; but the redeemed shall walk there: And the ransomed of the Lord *shall return, and come to Zion with songs and everlasting joy upon their heads: they shall obtain joy and gladness, and sorrow and sighing shall flee away* (Isaiah 35:4–10).

CHAPTER 14
===

ATONEMENT

THE BACKGROUND TO THE ATONEMENT idea is well established in the Old Testament. The need for an atonement arises out of humanity's failed test of faithfulness in the Garden of Eden. This led humanity to immediately come under the condemnation of God. However, no sooner had God revealed His judgement for sin, of spiritual and physical death, that He revealed His promise of redemption in Genesis 3:15. Sometimes called the "proto-evangel", it is a vision of ultimate salvation in which Satan, the instigator of sin, is destroyed. God states that the "seed of the woman" will crush the head of the tempter. The motivation behind finding a solution to the dilemma of sin in the form of an atonement, is in the love of God. "For God so loved the world, that he gave his only begotten Son, that whosoever believeth in him should not perish, but have everlasting life (John 3:16)." Therefore, the atonement is an expression of God's love. As Conner contended, the "cross of Christ is the pledge of God's love for a sinful and ruined race. As such, the Cross represents an act of grace. It stands for God's gracious love going out to redeem."[1] Importantly, the anti-type of the cross has a type. It is for this reason that "ritual sacrifice came into the picture, for Cain and Abel offered sacrifices to God, apparently for the expiation of sin (Gen. 4:3–7)."[2] During the time of the patriarchs, sacrifice continued its central position. When Noah came out of the ark he built an alter and made a sacrifice to God. With the sacrifices of Abraham and his descendants comes the elaboration of the sacrificial system, with particular places being set apart for sacrifices.

> *Then he went up from there to Beersheba. The* LORD *appeared to him the same night and said,*

---

1. Conner, *Christian Doctrine*, 174.
2. Bromiley, *Atone, Atonement*, 353.

FOUNDATIONS OF THEOLOGY

> *"I am the God of your father Abraham;*
> *Do not fear, for I am with you.*
> *I will bless you, and multiply your descendants,*
> *For the sake of My servant Abraham."*
>
> *So he built an altar there and called upon the name of the* LORD, *and pitched his tent there; and there Isaac's servants dug a well.* (NASB) (Gen. 26:23–25).

The near sacrifice of Isaac by Abraham points to the vicarious meaning of the sacrifices, since a ram is provided as a substitute.

> *But the angel of the* LORD *called to him from heaven and said, "Abraham, Abraham!" And he said, "Here I am." He said, "Do not stretch out your hand against the lad, and do nothing to him; for now I know that you fear God, since you have not withheld your son, your only son, from Me." Then Abraham raised his eyes and looked, and behold, behind him a ram caught in the thicket by his horns; and Abraham went and took the ram and offered him up for a burnt offering in the place of his son.* (NASB) (Gen. 22:11–13).

However, it is with the exodus of the Hebrews out of Egypt that a much clearer revelation of the atonement develops. For Egypt's rebellion against the commands of God the eldest sons died; "only those protected by the blood of the Passover Lamb escaped. Thus, the heart of the Passover stands the idea of atonement through believing in the sacrifice. Release from Egypt was its fruit."[3]

This was something of a prelude to sacrificial system initiated through Moses on Mount Sinai, which introduced the concept to Israel that sin needed to be paid for. The law reflected the character of God and set the standard of righteousness that God required. Further, the sacrificial service provided a payment in blood. It was a substitutionary payment that stood in contrast to the Canaanite practice of offering human sacrifices. The penitent would lay hands on the animal sacrifice, transfer the guilt to the substitute, which was subsequently killed and burned. Importantly, its blood was taken to the tent of meeting where it was offered symbolically as a payment of life for the sin committed. In John's Gospel, Jesus describes Himself as the good shepherd who lays His life down for His sheep (10:11). Indeed, Christ offered Himself as a payment for sin that came in the form of a sacrifice, to atone for sin and initiate reconciliation between sinful humanity and God. As Donald Bloesch pointed out, "The sacrifice is performed not simply by Jesus as man but by the Son of God in the form of man. It is consequently a divine self-sacrifice: God not only demands but also makes the offering."[4]

---

3. Bromiley, *Atone, Atonement*, 353.
4. Bloesch, *Jesus is Victor! Karl Barth's Doctrine of Salvation*, 46.

ATONEMENT

In the New Testament, atonement is referred to as the eternal plan. In 2 Timothy 1:9-10 the eternal plan of salvation through Jesus Christ is outlined when Paul refers to Christ as One;

> (w)ho hath saved us, and called us with a holy calling, not according to our works, but according to his own purpose and grace, which was given us in Christ Jesus before the world began, but is now made manifest by the appearing of our Saviour Jesus Christ, who hath abolished death, and hath brought life and immortality to light through the gospel.

Also, in Ephesians 1:4, Paul states that "according as he hath chosen us in him before the foundation of the world, that we should be holy and without blame before him in love."

The idea of Christ's death gaining victory over sin, death and Satan through His cross and resurrection, is emphasized in the New Testament as well as the early church. "The theme of Christ the victor (Christus Victor) brought together a series of themes, centering on the idea of a decisive victory over forces of evil and oppression."[5] The Book of Hebrews (2:14-15) illustrates this when it states that "he also himself likewise took part of the same; that through death he might destroy him that had the power of death, that is, the devil; And deliver them who through fear of death were all their lifetime subject to bondage." In the early church Irenaeus picks up this theme when he asserted that "Christ fought and conquered . . . For He bound the strong man and set free the weak. He endowed His own handiwork with salvation, by destroying sin."[6]

Associated with the victory of Christ is the image of Christ's death as a ransom. McGrath stated that the word "ransom" suggests three related ideas. Firstly, liberation. A ransom is something which achieves freedom for a person who is held in captivity. Secondly, a payment. A ransom is a sum of money which is paid in order to achieve an individuals' liberation. Finally, there must be someone to whom the ransom is paid. A ransom is usually paid to an individual's captor, or his agent.[7] The difficulty with this analogy, however, is the necessity of God paying a ransom to Satan, who has humanity held captive. While Gregory the Great wrote extensively along these lines, there is nothing to warrant a biblical theology of such a theory. Both the Old and New Testaments point to God as the One who seeks reparation. In the Temple Sacrifices, a payment is made to God. It was the Lord who sat on His throne in the Most Holy Place, not Satan. It is God's law that has been violated and must have satisfaction. Therefore, while ransom payment is made to secure a release, the payment is made to God; and since sin is paid for, and death is overcome, Satan has no claim on the sinner, who is, by consequence, released from his power.

---

5. McGrath, *Christian Theology*, 345.
6. Bercot, *Dictionary of Early Christian Beliefs*, 43.
7. Bercot, *Dictionary of Early Christian Beliefs*, 43.

Therefore, it is God's ransom payment in Jesus Christ, and His receiving satisfaction in that payment, that is the basis of Christian victory for all who claim it. Satan's power is in his holding sinful humanity captive, who have not had satisfaction made for their sin through faith and life in Jesus Christ.

It was Tertullian who seems to have introduced the term "satisfaction" into theological language. According to Jaroslav Pelikan, "Tertullian's doctrine of 'Satisfaction' was a term borrowed from Roman private law were reparation was made necessary by sin. However, it was Hilary who applied this concept to the death of Christ."[8]

Hilary equated "satisfaction" with "sacrifice" by asserting that Christ's death on a cross was His "great act of reparation to God on behalf of sinners."[9] Anselm built upon this model when, in the eleventh century, he emphasized sinful humanity's debt to the honour or majesty of God. A payment must be made to expiate our sin before a just God. This payment is made by Jesus Christ on our behalf in the sacrifice of the shedding of His blood. As in the Temple sacrifice, this payment must be put before the law in the sanctuary, since sin is a violation that affronts God's moral character. The emphasis is on payment which makes restitution. There is no notion, contrary to latter developments in the Substitutionary Atonement Theory, of a reception of the wrath of God who kills in righteous anger. In the Temple sacrifices, which clearly point to the sacrifice of Christ, fire did not consume the sacrifice in an act of restorative justice. Rather, an offering is made to atone for sin; a payment which brings about reconciliation and the justification of the sinner. Consequently, biblically, Christ's death is not only a sacrificial payment which leads to forgiveness of sins, but also a ransom payment that releases us from the grasp of sin, death and Satan, to which we are held captive. Furthermore, Christ's death is victorious since it leads, through the resurrection, to an overcoming of death, which is the associate of sin; Both being the instruments by which Satan holds us in His grasp. What Christ did for us we could not do for ourselves. To that extent, therefore, Christ is our substitute.

In the early church, Origen asserted that it was not enough for Christ to be a "wise and perfect man," but that "by his death he had begun the overthrow of the devil's dominion over the whole earth.[10] As Mullins pointed out, "(w)e might think of him as our representative. But this is not an adequate conception. We did not appoint him. Man did not send him. He did not bear man's message to God, but God's message to man. Christ indeed becomes our representative after we believe in him, but prior to that our relation is one of antagonism. He is our representative only after

---

8. Pelikan, *The Christian Tradition: Vol. 1*, 147.
9. Pelikan, *The Christian Tradition: Vol. 1*, 147.
10. Pelikan, *The Christian Tradition: Vol. 1*, 149.

we approve his work and obey his gospel."[11] The Christian's hope is in asking Christ to be our representative and to believe that He will accomplish His task. As we appropriate in faith the benefits of His representative atoning sacrifice, the reign of sin and death is broken in His own death and resurrection. In this event, the benefits "of his obedience and conquest of death becomes ours by faith."[12]

The French Reformer, John Calvin, formed the basis of a contemporary understanding of satisfaction, which has been broadly embraced by evangelicalism. Calvin proposed that through the sacrificial death of Christ God's wrath is appeased, with this being the foundation of peace between God and the elect. This has led to the almost militant insistence by Calvinists that Christ's atonement is a propitiation for sin. That is, it turns away God's wrath. On the cross, according to this view, Christ died receiving a full blast of God's anger for sin upon His life. By contrast, Martin Luther, while at ease in using the language of satisfaction, emphasized the victory of Christ over His enemies. "Seeking to attack and conquer Christ . . . the enemies were themselves conquered instead: 'Thus in Christ all sin is conquered, killed, and buried, and righteousness remains the victor and the ruler eternally.' Death, too, was 'conquered and abolished,' and the ancestral curse pronounced on Adam and Eve must yield to the blessing of Christ."[13]

James Arminius explored further biblical perspectives when he stated that "God satisfies his love for the creature by forgiving sins, while at the same time satisfying his love for justice by inflicting the punishment for sin ("inflicting stripes") on his Son."[14] As God gave satisfaction to His love He also did so for His own justice. Arminius explained that God "rendered satisfaction to himself, and appeased himself in the Son of his love."[15] In addition, satisfaction is made to the law. The keeping of the law is the prerequisite for justification and all its benefits. Of course, since humanity cannot perform it, Arminius stressed, Christ the mediator must perform it on their behalf. Therefore, there is a "twofold satisfaction of the law: one, by which the obedience prescribed by the law is rendered; the other, by which the punishment imposed by the law on disobedience is suffered."[16]

Alister McGrath was right to assert that, the "New Testament, drawing on Old Testament imagery and expectations, presents Christ's death upon the cross as a sacrifice."[17] However, it is not a sacrifice of receiving God's wrath, but of payment for sin on humanity's behalf. It is in this sense that God's wrath for sin is satisfied and expiated, or cancelled. Indeed, one must not lose sight of the purpose of the

11. Mullins, *The Christian Religion*, 325.
12. Mullins, *The Christian Religion*, 325.
13. Mullins, *The Christian Religion*, 162.
14. Pinson, *The Nature of Atonement in The Theology of Jacobus Arminius*, 778.
15. Pinson, *The Nature of Atonement in The Theology of Jacobus Arminius*, 779.
16. Pinson, *The Nature of Atonement in The Theology of Jacobus Arminius*, 783.
17. McGrath, *Christian Theology*, 342.

atonement. As Barth put it, the cross is not so much the fulfilment of a legal contract, which calls for the shedding of innocent blood, but a "triumph of sovereign love over enmity and alienation."[18] The heart of atonement is the love of God, which has practical effect in reconciliation. The message of the cross is not limited to the satisfaction of the law, since it serves to go beyond the strict requirements of justice to distribute divine grace into the arena of human history. Christ's sacrifice seeks to disassemble humanity's propensity to independence and competition, and replace it with a new narrative of dependence upon Jesus Christ and inter-dependence within the Christian community.

Ellen White embraced both ransom and satisfaction theories. In the pamphlet "The Sufferings of Christ", she stated that at the cross Satan was defeated, "He knew that his kingdom was lost."[19] In the same pamphlet she outlined a case for the substitutionary atonement. Indeed, in *The Desire of Ages* she argued that Christ's substitutionary death is the means by which sinners can be justified by faith.[20] However, when Mrs. White stated that "the sword of justice was now to awake against His dear Son" and that "the Father's wrath was upon Him"[21], there is nothing to indicate anything other than that justice and wrath were placated by a payment for sin in the form of the blood of Jesus Christ. This is quite different from the popular notion that Christ died at the hand of God's wrath. Perhaps Ellen White's clearest statement on the topic is found in the *Review and Herald* of September 24, 1901. "He [the Father] planted the cross between heaven and earth, and when the Father beheld the sacrifice of His Son, He bowed before it in recognition of its perfection. 'It is enough,' He said. 'the atonement is complete.'"[22]

It is important to note that the work of atonement is Christ's work, on which the Christian depends. As Conner rightly asserted, "Our salvation was his achievement."[23] Jesus affirms this in Mark 10:45 by stating that the Son of Man came to give His life as a ransom for many. Paul elaborates in his comment to the Galatians when he stated that "Christ hath redeemed us from the curse of the law, being made a curse for us: for it is written, cursed is everyone that hangeth on a tree (3:13)." Hebrews 9:12 further directs the reader to the fact that it was Christ who obtained eternal redemption for all when He entered into the holy place.

In the Synoptic Gospels, there are two instances when Jesus speaks of His death and its significance. In Mark 10:45 He refers to the giving his life as a ransom for many. "For even the Son of man came not to be ministered unto, but to minister, and

---

18. Bloesch, *Jesus is Victor! Karl Barth's Doctrine of Salvation*, 46.
19. White, *The Sufferings of Christ*, 622.
20. White, *The Sufferings of Christ*, 622.
21. White, *The Sufferings of Christ*, 622.
22. White, *The Sufferings of Christ*, 623.
23. Conner, *Christian Doctrine*, 169.

to give his life a ransom for many." In Matthew 26:28 Jesus speaks of His blood shed for the remission of sins. Together, these verses imply the need for a payment. Yet it is the nature of the payment that is significant here. In the first, a purchase is made which securers a release of 'the many' back to their original owner. A release from captivity, in this case Satan and his realm of sin, must be initiated. In the second, an offense for sin is paid, resulting in absolution.

Ellen White held to a biblical and orthodox view of the atonement when she wrote that;

> (t)he sacrifice of Christ as atonement for sin is the great truth around which all other truths cluster. *In order to be rightly understood and appreciated, every truth in the Word of God, from Genesis to Revelation, must be studied in the light that streams from the cross of Calvary. I present before you the great, grand monument of mercy and regeneration, salvation and redemption, —the Son of God uplifted on the cross.* This is to be the foundation of every discourse *given by our ministers.*[24]

Indeed, according to Mrs. White, Christ gave up His life for the human race. This sacrifice was offered to give to all who accept Him as their Saviour, an entire transformation of character.[25] Therefore, the cross is essential and central to Christian life. With characteristic perception, she added that the "fact that the companions of Christ in His crucifixion were placed the one on His right hand and the other on His left is a significant one; His cross is placed in the very center of the world."[26] However, the significance of this sacrifice is ongoing and encompasses the basis and authority of Christ's continual work for the redemption of the world. "The wounded hands, the pierced side, the marred feet, plead eloquently for fallen man, whose redemption is purchased at such an infinite cost. Oh, matchless condescension! Neither time nor events can lessen the efficacy of the atoning sacrifice."[27]

---

24. White, *Gospel Workers*, 315.
25. White, *Manuscript 56, 1899*.
26. White, *Manuscript 52, 1897*.
27. White, *Testimonies for the Church: Vol. 4*, 124.

Chapter 15

ATONEMENT AND THE HEAVENLY SANCTUARY

The *Sanctuary Doctrine* is the earliest and most distintive teaching of Seventh-day Adventism. Indeed, this doctrine, and particularly a search for its meaning, gave birth to the movement. Not only was a long forgotten doctrine of Scripture renewed, but a method of biblical investigation emerged, based on a prophetic reading of Scripture and an illumination based on a fresh outpouring of the prophetic gift. It all began with a baptist lay preacher by the name of William Miller.

William Miller taught that Christ would return in 1844. This date, originally 1843[1], was derived from a careful reading of the prophecy of Daniel 8:14, "2300 days and the sanctuary shall be cleansed." Miller's calculations were based on the starting date of the 2300 day prophecy being 457 B.C., the year of the decree to return and rebuild Jerusalem (Dan. 9:25; Ezra 7:13, 20). The 2300 days becomes years, based on the 'day for a year' principal of biblical prophecy (Num. 14:34; Ez. 4:6). Further adding to the importance of this date is the fulfillment of the so called 70-week prophecy of Daniel 9. The calculations of this chapter point to the baptism of Jesus in 27 A.D (Dan. 9:25), the crucifixion of Jesus in 31 A.D (Dan. 9:26–27), and the stoning of Stephen to death in 34 A.D (Dan. 9:27), resulting in the Gospel going to the Gentiles. One of Miller's associates, Samuel Snow, concluded that the specific day would be October 22. This was the day of atonement (Yom Kippur) in the Karaite (original) Jewish calender for that year. Since Jesus did not return on that day it became known among the Advents as the *Great Disapointment*.

The day after the Great Disappointment of October 22 1844, Hiram Edson (1806–1882), one of the Millerite followers, was walking through cornfields near Port Gibson, on the way to encourage others who were feeling despondent and

---

1. Initially the year 0 was included. When this year was removed, since it is a point in timer and not a whole year, then an extra year is needed to make up 2300 years. Hence, 1843 becomes 1844.

ATONEMENT AND THE HEAVENLY SANCTUARY

discouraged, when he had a vision of Christ entering the Most Holy Place in the Heavenly Sanctuary. Following further Bible study of Daniel 8:14, and associated passages, with F.B. Hahn and O.R.L. Crosier, he became convinced that the date of October 22 1844 was correct, but that the event had been misinterpreted. The "sanctuary to be cleansed was the heavenly sanctuary, and not the earthly, as they had formerly believed."[2] Just two months later, in December of that same year, Ellen Harmon received her first vision that God had indeed provided guiding light. In the February of 1845, "she was shown in another vision that at the end of the 2300 days, the Father and Son moved to the Holy of Holies of the heavenly sanctuary, where Jesus was presently engaged in His high-priestly ministry."[3] She recalls,

> *I saw the Father rise from the throne, and in a flaming chariot go into the holy of holies within the veil, and sit down. Then Jesus rose up from the throne, and the most of those who were bowed down arose with Him. I did not see one ray of light pass from Jesus to the careless multitude after He arose, and they were left in perfect darkness. Those who arose when Jesus did, kept their eyes fixed on Him as He left the throne and led them out a little way. Then He raised His right arm, and we heard His lovely voice saying, 'Wait here; I am going to My Father to receive the kingdom; keep your garments spotless, and in a little while I will return from the wedding and receive you to Myself.' Then a cloudy chariot, with wheels like flaming fire, surrounded by angels, came to where Jesus was. He stepped into the chariot and was borne to the holiest, where the Father sat. There I beheld Jesus, a great High Priest, standing before the Father. On the hem of His garment was a bell and a pomegranate. Those who rose up with Jesus would send up their faith to Him in the holiest, and pray, 'My Father, give us Thy Spirit.' Then Jesus would breathe upon them the Holy Ghost. In that breath was light, power, and much love, joy, and peace.*[4]

I beheld till the thrones were cast down, and the Ancient of days did sit, whose garment was white as snow, and the hair of his head like the pure wool: his throne was like the fiery flame, and his wheels as burning fire. A fiery stream issued and came forth from before him: thousand thousands ministered unto him, and ten thousand times ten thousand stood before him: the judgment was set, and the books were opened. (Daniel 7:9–10)[5]

> *Thus, was presented to the prophet's vision the great and solemn day when the characters and the lives of men should pass in review before the Judge of all the earth, and to every man should be rendered 'according to his works.' The Ancient of days is God the Father. Says the psalmist, 'Before the mountains were brought forth, or ever thou hadst formed the earth and the world, even*

---

2. Davidson, *Doctrine of the Sanctuary*, 1131.
3. White, *Day Star*, March 1846. Also, *Early Writings*, 54–56.
4. White, *Early Writings*, 55.
5. White, *Great Controversy*, 479.

from everlasting to everlasting, thou art God.' [Psalm 90:2.] It is he, the source of all being, and the fountain of all law, that is to preside in the Judgment. And holy angels, as ministers and witnesses, in number 'ten thousand times ten thousand, and thousands of thousands,' attend this great tribunal. 'And, behold, one like the Son of man came with the clouds of heaven, and came to the Ancient of days, and they brought him near before him. And there was given him dominion, and glory, and a kingdom, that all people, nations, and languages, should serve him; his dominion is an everlasting dominion, which shall not pass away.' [Daniel 7:13, 14.] The coming of Christ here described is not his second coming to the earth. He comes to the Ancient of days in Heaven to receive dominion, and glory, and a kingdom, which will be given him at the close of his work as a mediator. It is this coming, and not his second advent to the earth, that was foretold in prophecy to take place at the termination of the 2300 days, in 1844. Attended by heavenly angels, our great High Priest enters the holy of holies, and there appears in the presence of God, to engage in the last acts of his ministration in behalf of man, —to perform the work of investigative Judgment, and to make an atonement for all who are shown to be entitled to its benefits.[6]

Indeed, Ellen White had been in eastern Maine only a short time when, at Exeter, she was given the significant vision she described in two early letters. One, dated February 15, 1846, was to Enoch Jacobs; the other, dated July 13, 1847, was to Joseph Bates. Of this vision, she wrote: "It was then I had a view of Jesus rising from His mediatorial throne and going to the Holiest as Bridegroom to receive His kingdom."[7]

In her ministry, she mentioned this vision from time to time, for it confirmed the results of Bible study "of which she knew nothing at the time" in western New York State by Hiram Edson and O.R.L. Crosier. In a letter to J. N. Loughborough, written August 24, 1874, she recounted:

Other passages in the books of Daniel and Revelation specifically applied to the beginning of the judgment are Daniel 8:14, 7:13, Revelation 14:7, and 11:19.[8] *The coming of the Lord to His temple as foretold in Malachi 3:1 and, in the parable of the ten virgins, the coming of the bridegroom to the marriage (Matthew 25:10), were also both understood to be descriptions of the same event.*[9]

This doctrine is a radical departure from common and widely held Christian theology, in that it stipulates when when Christ returns the judgement has already been completed. Further, it stipulates that while Christ died His atoning death for

---

6. White, *Great Controversy*, 479.
7. White, *Letter 3, 1847*.
8. White, *Great Controversy*, 424, 433.
9. *The Investigative Judgement in the Writings of Ellen G. White*, 4.8.

sinners, each sinner must repent and put their faith in Christ for their sins to be forgiven. It does so but drawing on the often quoted *Book of Life* and expounding, in a profound manner, the implications of the Book of Hebrew's description of a Temple in Heaven. This doctrine also provides a more comprehensive and satisfying application of the sanctuary service found in the Old Testament as it relates to its fruition in the New Testament. Indeed, the sanctuary service of the Hebrew Scriptures can not find application and full representation in the New Testament unless the sacrificial system, in which sin was atoned for, is seperated from the Day of Atonemnt, or Cleansing of the Sanctuary. To be sure, the day of Atonement fully and completely forshadows the Gospel in that it requires an afflication of the heart and an earnest committmeht to God.

CHAPTER 16

ELECTION AND PREDESTINATION

IN THE NEW TESTAMENT, EKLEKTOS, to chose or pick out, signifies to pick out or choose, from *lego*, to gather and to pick out. In the New Testament it is used of Christ, the chosen of God (Luke 23:35), of angels (1 Tim. 5:21), who were chosen as messengers, and believers (Matt 24:22, 24, 31; Mark 13:20, 22, 27; Luke 18:7; Rom 8:33; Col 3:12; 2 Tim 2:10; Titus 1:1; 1 Peter 1:1; 2:9). Also, *proorizo*, from which predestinate (AV) originates, means to determine beforehand, to mark out beforehand, to determine before, and foreordain (Rom 8:30; Eph 1:4).[1]

The theological discussion on election and predestination has generally been dominated by Calvinists, who have taken their lead from Augustine. According to Augustine, all have been stained by sin and deserve damnation. However, God, in His grace, has selected some to be saved and has chosen who will not be saved. This has been referred to by theologians as "double predestination". According to Augustine, there is an exact number of the saved and damned. Indeed, the "number is so certain that one can neither be added to them nor taken from them . . . that the number of the elect is certain and neither to be increased nor diminished."[2] The early reformer, John Wyclif (1331–84), progressed Augustine's doctrine in England. "Wyclif argued that the true Church is made up of those elected by God and is invisible, and that since it is God's choice which determines membership, no visible church or its officers can control entrance or can exclude from membership."[3] Though vigorously oppressed, Wyclif eventually became one of the champions of the English Reformation.

The Westminster Confession of Faith, representing the best of seventeenth century English Calvinist scholarship, states that those

---

1. Vine, *Expository Dictionary of New Testament Words*, 306 and 361.
2. Latourette, *A History of Christianity: Vol. 1*, 179.
3. Latourette, *A History of Christianity: Vol. 1*, 663.

ELECTION AND PREDESTINATION

of mankind that are predestined unto life, God, before the foundation of the world was laid, according to his eternal and immutable purpose, and the secret council and good pleasure of his will, hath chosen in Christ unto everlasting glory, out of his mere free grace and love, without any foresight of faith or good works, or perseverance in either of them, or any other thing in the creature, as conditions, or causes moving him thereunto; and all to the praise of his glorious grace (III/V).

Robert Shaw, reflecting on this, stated that "God made a choice of, and predestined, a certain and definite number of individuals to eternal life."[4] Representing the American Calvinist tradition is Louis Berkhof, who contended that Predestination includes two parts: election and reprobation. Berkhof held that election is an expression of God's sovereign will. It is unconditional and irresistible. Indeed, the fact that God chooses some and not others indicates that salvation is totally part of God's decision making. This is not unjust, claimed Berkhof, since justice would decree that none be saved, since all have sinned. By God's good grace a limited number are saved. Reprobation, on the other hand, amounts to God passing over others and punishing them in their sins. Berkhof appealed to this doctrine on the basis of logic. If God chooses some to eternal life then, logically, he surely passes over others.[5]

Contemporary Calvinism is well represented by the Anglican scholar, James Packer. Packer believed that predestination and election amount to the same thing. It defines God's choice of certain sinners for salvation and eternal life (Rom 8:29; Eph 1:4–5, 11). Indeed, only those chosen by God will come to faith because God chose them to make this decision.[6] Leon Morris, an Australian New Testament scholar in the Calvinist tradition, is of the opinion that Paul was insistent that the will of God is always done. This is seen in the following passages: Rom. 1:10; 12:2; 1 Cor. 1:1; 4:19; Eph. 1:1, 4–5, 11; Col. 1:1, 4:12; 1 Thess. 5:8. Morris believed that there is a strong argument for the classic Reformed doctrine of predestination in the opening chapter of Ephesians. There believers are said to have been chosen in Christ before the foundation of the world, according to the plan of God. Clearly Morris did not believe that any individual is free to put their faith in Christ. Those who are saved have been called to it. Morris also stipulated, on the basis of Ephesians 2:10, that people are predestined for ethical achievement.[7]

In contrast to Calvinism, a free-will Arminian theology has consistently maintained a biblical perspective. Free from the imposition of Augustinianism, James Arminius took the argument back to Jesus Christ by stating that "(t)he first absolute decree of God concerning the salvation of sinful man, is that by which he decreed

---

4. Shaw, *An Exposition of the Confession of Faith of The Westminster Assembly of Divines*, 48–52.
5. Berkhof, *Systematic Theology*, 109–125.
6. Packer, *Concise Theology*, 37–39.
7. Morris, *New Testament Theology*, 26–27.

to appoint his Son, Jesus Christ, for a Mediator, Redeemer, Saviour, Priest and King, who might destroy sin by his own death, might by his obedience obtain the salvation which had been lost, and might communicate it by his own virtue."[8]

The second aspect of Arminius' theology of predestination clearly outlines the conditions of repentance, faith and perseverance. In this, the theology of faith alone is put in its right context and given its full meaning. It is the decree of God "to receive into favor those who repent and believe, and, in Christ, for his sake and through Him, to effect the salvation of such penitents and believers as persevered to the end."[9] However, such conditions can not be seen as a work of any person. Indeed, Arminius' third aspect, or Divine decree, is that God puts in place the means by which the one might come to saving faith. That is, He put in place the "sufficient and efficacious manner" a means by which repentance and faith might be received and attained. Finally, Arminius stipulated that God has full foreknowledge of those who would, through grace, believe and by grace persevere, and those who would not.[10]

The Orthodox Creed (IX) of the General Baptists responds well to Morris's claim that Ephesians 1 speaks clearly of predestination of the individual. A closer examination will in fact clearly reveal that election is corporate. To be sure, *a people have been predestined to faith*. Indeed, the Confession speaks of being chosen in Jesus Christ. It's Christological focus is seen in the comment that Jesus Christ is the one whom God elected before the foundation of the world. It is Christ who is called God's elect. The creed further believes (X) that God did not only elect Christ but all those who come to put their faith in him. If any should be retrobate, it is of themselves.[11] The Arminian and Baptist document, The Standard Confession states (VIII):

> *That God hath even before the foundation of the world chosen (or elected) to eternal life, such as believe, and so are in Christ, John 3:16, Eph. 1:4, 2 Thes. 2:13. And in (IX), that 'men not considered simply as men, but ungodly men as such, who turn the grace of God unto wantonness, and deny the only Lord God, and our Lord Jesus Christ, Jude 4. God indeed sends a strong delusion to men, that they might be damned. In regard to the death of infants the confession follows the Arminian doctrine children dying in infancy, 'having not transgressed against the law of God in their own persons, are only subjected to the first death, which comes upon them by the sin of the first Adam; and not that any of them (dying in that estate) shall suffer for Adam's sins, eternal punishment in hell.*[12]

---

8. Arminius, *The Works of James Arminius: Vol. 1*, 222.
9. Arminius, *The Works of James Arminius: Vol. 1*, 223.
10. Arminius, *The Works of James Arminius: Vol. 1*, 223.
11. Lumpkin, *Baptist Confessions of Faith*, 302—304.
12. Lumpkin, *Baptist Confessions of Faith*, 227-228.

ELECTION AND PREDESTINATION

John Wesley's teaching on predestination is primarily based on Romans 8:29-30. Out of this text, Wesley pursued a doctrine of predestination that sustained grace-enabled freedom. Wesley held that God seeks that we choose him. Humanity has the free will to choice life or death, but can only choose life with the assistance of God. God offers grace to all those who will receive it. Further, he believed that God does will eternal life, but that this is in accordance with his foreknowledge. 1 Peter 1:2 is important to Wesley's argument here. For Wesley, those God predestined means those he foreknew would believe in him in response to his gracious invitation.[13]

Charles Finney, A North American Arminian revivalist, asserted that the biblical doctrine of election is not that some are chosen for salvation while others are not. Indeed, he was more concerned with asserting that God had predestined that the means of salvation be through sanctification. Predestination can also be defined by the assumption that foreknowledge and election are consistent with free agency. God foreknows those who will repent and embrace the gospel. It is these people who enjoy God's election. More importantly, God has forknowledge that they will meet the conditions of election. Indeed, God has foreknowledge of the entirety of their lives. Some are predestined to eternal life because it has been forseen that they will attain to repentance, faith and final perseverance.[14] In the twentieth-century Edgar Mullins contended that there is absolutely no barrier to the salvation of any, such us not being chosen, except the will. Christ died for all and is willing to receive all those who will come. Further, Mullins contended that God chooses some because he forsees their faith. He believed that in Romans 8:29-30, Paul drew together God's foreknowledge, his foreordination, his calling, his justification, and his final glorification in a single bond of spiritual unity.[15]

In the Twentieth Century, no one made a greater contribution to the doctrine of election than Karl Barth. Barth believed that election is primarily *election in Jesus Christ*. Christ is both electing God and elected man. As God, He decrees that there will be an elect people, as man He constitutes the embodiment of the elect. It is in this self-election that Christ elects his people. Barth's doctrine of election contains a number of distinguishable parts.

THE ELECTION OF JESUS CHRIST

Barth contended that Christ was elected on behalf of humanity, so that in him one may participate in this election by a decision of faith and obedience. Thomas Torrance took up this theme when he averred that

---

13. Oden, *John Wesley's Scriptural Christianity*, 261—262.
14. Finney, *Lectures on Systematic Theology*, 766-783.
15. Mullins, *The Christian Religion*, 338-358.

> (w)hatever we do, we cannot speak of election or a predestination behind the back of Jesus Christ, and so divide God's saving action in two, into election and into the work of Christ on the cross. God's eternal election is nothing else than God's eternal love incarnate in his beloved Son, so that in him we have election incarnate.[16]

THE ELECTION OF THE COMMUNITY

Barth deals with the election of the community on the basis of a totally Christological orientation. As Barth explained it, divine election is of Jesus Christ. This does not mean the election of individuals. God elects a community in Jesus Christ. Romans 9:1–5 forms Barth's biblical basis for his initial statements before providing an exposition of Romans 9–11 for the remainder of his argument. Therefore, those who freely decide to join the community of faith participate in the election of God. As God chose Israel, so does He now choose the church, a community of faith that exists in their corporate faith in Jesus Christ. To this extent, all redemption is co-redemption.

THE ELECTION OF THE INDIVIDUAL

Barth seeks to avoid individualism on the one hand, but also, on the other hand, any collectivism that cuts out or crushes the individual. Indeed, the one God, through the one Son elects the one person.

According to Barth, each individual *has already been elected in Jesus Christ*. However, the person only begins to live as elected in the event of faith by which they receive this promise of God. However, if one were not to receive it then they live as one rejected in spite of their election. This does not amount to universalism, a label often wrongly applied to Barth. Indeed, Barth rejected universalism. The rejected is the one who stands against God and is ungrateful. The weakness of Barth's argument at this point is that while rejecting universalism he avoids speaking of the consequences of rejecting God. One assumes he had planned to leave this matter to his final volume on eschatology which, sadly, he was unable to pursue.

Otto Weber (pronounced Vaber), strongly influenced by Barth, held to the corporate nature of election when he stated that God decided for people and that this electing takes place through the Son. Further to this, Weber contended that in Paul's doctrine of election the individual does not appear. Consequently, when Paul speaks of election he has the community in mind. The individual is elect as a member of the elect community. Therefore, the community of faith is not the sum of elect individuals, it is the elect of God, and those who join by faith, join the elect. According to Weber, wherever election is described in terms of the individual, or the collective

---

16. Torrence, *Atonement: The Person and Work of Christ*, 183.

ELECTION AND PREDESTINATION

of individuals, the community is deprived of its true nature. Weber also followed Barth in contending that all of humanity has been elected in Jesus Christ. However, the message of salvation does not reach all. Consequently, faith does not only come to those who have been elected, nor does it belong to those whose faith has been foreknown. It is nothing other than a response to divine election. Therefore, each person is responsible for their faith or unbelief. Consequently, within this broader view, one can still speak of being in Christ and outside of Christ. The person outside of Christ, in whom that person has been elected, is avoiding the faith they are called to embrace. Such a person is rejected by Jesus (John 12:48).[17]

Barth's doctrine of election has had an influence on some North American evangelicals. Here we mention the doctrine of election in the theology of James Daane, a theologian of the Reformed Church. Daane firstly dealt with the election of Israel. According to the Old Testament, Israel is God's chosen people. This fact throws some helpful light on the Bible's teaching about election. In the Old Testament God chose Abram. However, in choosing Abram God did not choose an individual. God's election of Abram included the election of his seed. The election of the nation flows from this. Indeed, the most distinctive thing that can be said about Israel is that they were a nation chosen by God (Psalm 147:20). Secondly, Daane discussed the election of Jesus Christ. Daane believed that the election of Jesus was both dependent upon the election of Israel and a fulfilment of it. Consequently, the goal of Israel's election was achieved, and totally fulfilled, in Jesus Christ. Daane admitted that the election of Jesus is seldom expressed in the Gospels, however it is inferred on many occasions. Daane noted the declaration from heaven at Jesus' baptism (Luke 3:22). The same affirmation was made on the Mount of Transfiguration. According to Luke, the affirmation spoke of Christ's election: "This is my Son, my chosen, listen to him (Luke 9:35)." Thirdly, Daane discussed the election of the church. God began Israel by choosing Abram and the church out of Christ. In fact Daane contended that the church would not exsist apart from its election. Therefore, the individual is elect due to his or her election in Jesus Christ, for those who are in Christ by faith are in Christ, the elect of God. Therefore, the individual Christian is elect because they share in the election of Jesus Christ. In effect, His election becomes theirs. This consequently spells the end to any individualistic doctrine of election. Daane followed by asserting that the truth of election is participation in Christ's election and this can only be spoken of in the language of faith and worship, proclamation and the summons to believe.[18]

According to Dale Moody, predestination in the New Testament can be observed as predestination *of* Christ and predestination *in* Christ. Christ's ministry was predested by God and those who are saved are predestined in Christ's

---

17. Weber, *Christian Dogmatics: Vol. 1*, 437–480.
18. Daane, *The Freedom of God*, 99–178.

predestination. In order to outline the second point, Moody used the illustration of flying in a plane. A plane might be predestined for another city. The call goes out for all those who want to board the plane. The destination of the plane, as they enter, becomes theirs. Therefore, the passengers who board the plane know where they are headed and are confident they will get there. However, this does not preclude free choice. At any time a passenger can choose to jump out.

Moody is also able to speak of double predestination. In 1 Peter 2:8, Moody contended that there are those who are predestined for salvation in accordance with their obedience and those who are predestined for damnation in accordance with their disobedience. Neither situation is predetermined by God. Each individual is free to choose either path.[19] Therefore, each person has a choice to make.

Robert Lee Shank sounded a similar note when he contended that in

> *Him who is the Elect from eternity is posited the gracious election of men ... In the realization of the kingdom purpose of God, the election is first of Christ and then of men in Him ... God affirms that, in the election, Christ Himself is the first object; and hence He is called the Elect, absolutely speaking,.. His brethren are elect in Him, Eph 1:4–6.*[20]

The Arminianism of Ellen White's theology is particularly evident in her doctrine of election, which is clearly conditional and based on a free assent to Christian faith and sanctity. In *Patriarchs and Prophets* she wrote that every

> *soul is elected who will work out his salvation with fear and trembling. He is elected who will put on the armour and fight the good fight of faith. He is elected who will watch unto prayer, who will search the Scriptures, and flee from temptation. He is elected who will have faith continually, and who will be obedient to every word that proceedeth out of the mouth of God. The provisions of redemption are free to all; the results of redemption will be enjoyed by those who have complied with the conditions.*[21]

To be sure, personal freedom is at the heart of a biblical understanding of predestination. God determining the salvation and damnation of individuals according to His divine will, contradicts His call to obedience and faithfulness. It also contradicts His loving intention for His creation to exercise personal choice. As E. J. Waggoner stipulated,

> *(f)reedom to do right implies freedom to do wrong. If a man were made so that he could not do wrong, he would have no freedom at all, not even to do right. He would be less than the brutes. There is no virtue in forced obedience, nor would there be any virtue in doing that which is right if it were impossible to*

---

19. Moody, *The Word of Truth*, 337–348.
20. Shank, *Elect in The Son*, 31.
21. White, *Patriarchs and Prophets*, 208.

ELECTION AND PREDESTINATION

do wrong. Moreover, there could be no pleasure or satisfaction in the professed friendship of two persons if one associated with the other just because he could not avoid it. The joy of the Lord in the companionship of his people is that they of their own free-will choose him above all others. And that which is the joy of the Lord is the joy of his people.[22]

Ellen White clearly sounds a biblical note when she referred to the evident theology of foreknowledge in the Book of Jeremiah. In her clear reading the text plainly states that "'whom he did foreknow, he also did predestinate to be conformed to the image of his Son, that he might be the first-born among many brethren.' God's thoughts toward men are thoughts of peace, and not of evil (Jeremiah 29:11). He ordains peace for us (Isaiah 26:12). We read nothing about men being foreordained to destruction; the only thing that God has predestinated is that men should be conformed to the image of His Son." Her Christological orientation is evident in her assertion that,

> *it is only in Christ that we become conformed to His image. It is in him that we come 'unto the measure of the stature of the fullness of Christ (Ephesians 4:13).' Therefore, it is that men are foreordained or predestinated only in Christ. The whole story is told in the following passage of Scripture:—'Blessed be the God and Father of our Lord Jesus Christ, who hath blessed us with all spiritual blessings in heavenly places in Christ; according as He hath chosen us in Him before the foundation of the world, that we should be holy and without blame before Him in love; having predestinated us unto the adoption of children by Jesus Christ to Himself, according to the good-pleasure of his will, to the praise of the glory of His grace, wherein He hath made us accepted in the Beloved (Ephesians 1:4).' Everything is in Christ. We receive all spiritual blessings in Him; we are chosen in Him unto holiness; in Him we are predestinated unto the adoption of children; in Him we are accepted; and in Him we have redemption through His blood. 'God hath not appointed us to wrath, but to obtain salvation by our Lord Jesus Christ. (1 Thessalonians 5:9).'*[23]

---

22. Waggoner, *The Signs of the Times*, Vol. 22, June 11, 1896.
23. White, *Foreknowledge and Foreordination*, 4.

Chapter 17

RECONCILIATION

The act of making atonement has as its aim the establishing of reconciliation between a holy God and sinful humanity. The need for reconciliation arises from being in conciliation in the first instance. Therefore, reconciliation, as the word implies, refers to the return of a previous state of existence. In the biblical narrative, this is seen in God's relationship with Adam and Eve and the Garden of Eden. The capitulation to sin brought about the fracturing of the relationship that needed to be reconciled. The securing of this reconciliation was foreshadowed in the antitypical sacrifices performed in the Sanctuary. The service of the Sanctuary was prepared by way of the teaching of Moses, as he had received it from God. The teaching gave the moral framework within the terms of covenant that put the service of the Sanctuary in its context. That is, God's love expressed in His law is offended by sin, which must be atoned for if sin is to be expiated. On the annual Day of Atonement this payment was made efficacious in the believer as they approached God with repentant hearts, for without repentance there is no forgiveness (2 Chron. 7:14;1 John 1:9). Ellen White pointed to this fundamental conditions of salvation when she wrote that "repentance towards God, because His law has been transgressed, and faith in Jesus Christ, are the only means whereby we may be elevated to purity of life and reconciliation with God."[1] However, this reconciliation, while being conditional, is wholly a work of God in the willing believer, who comes to God in faith, that the atoning blood of Christ is such a sufficient payment for sin as to cleans a sinner from sin, erase condemnation for sin, establish forgiveness of sin on God's part and initiate reconciliation.

In the New Testament, the path to full reconciliation with God begins with the teaching of Jesus, who reveals the nature of a holy God, the sinfulness of humanity, its subsequent alienation from its creator and, therefore, the need for reconciliation.

---

1. White, *Review and Herald*, March 4, 1875, 74.

RECONCILIATION

This reconciliation is brought about through the sacrificial payment of Jesus on the cross, a sacrifice that the sanctuary service pointed towards. However, while the payment is general and potentially for all, in contradistinction from universalism, each must claim the benefit personally if Christ's payment is to have effect. The personal application of Christ's atoning sacrifice to the repentant sinner advances the process of reconciliation, begun at the cross and finally completed at Christ's return, when the full benefits of Christ's atoning sacrifice result, by way of faith and perseverance, in effectual reconciliation. That is, not just reconciliation in theory, but in fact. This cannot be brought about until, as in the garden, full communion with God is re-established. According to Thomas Oden, reconciliation is at the heart of salvation, since salvation may be broadly summarized as follows: "In the justifying work of the Son, the obstacles of divine-human reconciliation are overcome. In the Spirit's regeneration of new life, grace to live by faith is actually being imparted and received (Luke 3:6; 2 Cor. 5:2)."[2]

---

2. Oden, *Life in the Spirit: Systematic Theology: Vol. 3*, 81.

CHAPTER 18
─────────

JUSTIFICATION

THE THEOLOGY OF JUSTIFICATION IS at the heart of Reformational Theology. The Pauline use of the word *dikaioun*, "to justify", begins with the *object* of justification as sinful, unrighteous, or ungodly, human beings (Rom 4:5b), while the *agent* of justification is the God of grace (Gal 3:8a; Rom 3:24; 8:30). The *ground* or *basis* of justification is the atoning death of Christ (Rom 3:24-25; 5:9a) which is merited to believers as satisfaction for sin on the *conditions* of repentance from sin and faith in Christ (Gal 2:16a; 3:8a, 24; Rom 3:26, 28). The *blessings* issuing from justification include "peace with God", "access" to God's "grace", joy, and hope (Rom 5:1-2). The *central meaning* of justification is to be accepted by God as righteous and to be declared as righteous.[1] However, justification by faith is not a mere change of legal status, but the result of the creative work of the Holy Spirit that is fundamentally ontological. Consequently, it is a mistake to isolate justification from sanctification. Both are part of a single act of God upon an individual and a faith community.

In the early church, justification was not a widely discussed issue, yet Clement of Rome (c 96) sounded a biblical note when he wrote that,

> (a)ll of these persons, therefore, were highly honoured, and were made great. This was not for their own sake, or for their own works, or the righteousness which they wrought, but through the operation of His will. And we, too, being called by His will in Christ Jesus, are not justified by ourselves. Nor are we justified by our own wisdom, understanding or godliness, or works that we have done in holiness of heart. Rather, we are justified by that faith through which, from the beginning, Almighty God has justified all men.[2]

---

1. Garrett, *Systematic Theology: Vol. 2*, 267–268.
2. Bercot, *Dictionary of Early Christian Beliefs*, 575.

JUSTIFICATION

By the time of the Reformation, however, the situation had drastically changed. In Europe, the dominant state Church assumed the role of redeeemer and sanctifier. A small biblical voice had been supressed for years, but this would soon change. It began with the personal transformation of a German monk who, while struggling to be free from the burdan of guilt, encountered the liberating truth of Romans 1:17. Martin Luther wrote in 1545, a year before his death, about his struggle with this verse.

> *I began to understand that 'righteousness of God' as that by which the righteous lives by the gift of God, namely by faith, and this sentence, 'the righteousness of God is revealed', to refer to a passive righteousness, by which the merciful God justifies us by faith, as it is written, 'The righteous lives by faith.' This immediately made me feel as though I had been born again, and as though I had entered through open gates into paradise itself.*[3]

His journey to the point of discovering the true biblical message of justification by faith had begun while in Rome, at "Pilate's Staircase".

> *Luther was one day devoutly climbing these steps, when suddenly a voice like thunder seemed to say to him, 'The just shall live by faith.' He sprung from his feet, and hastened from the place in shame and horror. That text never lost its power upon his soul. From that time he saw more clearly than ever before the fallacy of trusting to human works for salvation, and the necessity of constant faith in the merits of Christ.*[4]

The English Puritans maintained a theology of Justification by Faith in distinction from the Established Church. Thomas Watson stated that, "justification is the very hinge and pillar of Christianity. An error about justification is dangerous, like a defect in a foundation. Justification by Christ is a spring of the water of life." The ground of justification is the free grace of God "being justified freely by grace." Watson pointed to Ambrose, who expounded:

> *not of the grace wrought within us, but the free grace of God' . . . as a king freely pardons a delinquent. Justification is a mercy spun out of the bowels of free grace. God does not justify us because we are worthy, but by justifying us makes us worthy. The ground of our justification is Christ's satisfaction made to his Father. Christ, having made satisfaction for our fault, pronounces us righteous. 'It is a just thing for a creditor to discharge a debtor of the debt.'*[5]

In the twentieth century, justification by faith became the hallmark of conservative Protestantism. Adolph Schlatter (1852–1938), a German evangelical, declared

---

3. Luther, *Preface to the Latin Works (1545)*; D. Martin Luther's Werke: Kritische Gesamtausgabe. Vol. 54, 228.

4. White, *Great Controversy*, 125.

5. Watson, *A Body of Divinity*, 226–230.

that the proclamation of justification is at the same time a proclamation of life and God's love. Indeed, Paul describes the success of the cross by using a metaphor derived from Jesus Christ, that He redeemed us through His death. "We are justified through the redemption prepared for us by him; by his death, he paid the price by which he made us his own and bought us for himself (Rom 3:24; 1 Cor 6:20; 7:23; Eph 1:7; Col 1:14)." Schlatter further contended that because,

> *justification determines God's stance towards us, it arises through two processes: a revelatory act of God, and a process within the human being by which God's act touches and influences him. The practical application of the doctrine of justification depended completely on this formulation. Because we are justified in Christ, it is completely identical with the question of for whom Christ intercedes and against whom Christ turns, to whom he grants God's grace and whom he denies it. Concurring with all of Christendom, Paul answers this question by affirming that all who believe in the Christ are his. Man's justification thus occurs through God's sending of the Christ and by God's surrendering him to death, and further by man's believing in him (Rom 3:21–26; Gal 2:16–21).*

However, Schlatter by no means proposes any kind of synergism. "If a synergism arose from the fact that justification is based on Christ's death and man's faith, a synergism by which the working of righteousness was divided up between God and man, the doctrine of justification would be rendered impossible. But faith arises from what Christ is and does. It is based on Christ's conduct towards mankind." Consequently, faith is the right conduct toward the manifestation of God in Christ.[6]

Millard Erickson believed that in order to understand justification it is necessary to understand the biblical concept of righteousness, for justification is a restoration of the individual to a state of righteousness. Erickson followed the classical evangelical judicial route, in which justification is a legal exchange. In the New Testament, claimed Erickson, Justice demands that one be condemned; a judge who justifies or acquits the unrighteous is acting unrighteously. He proposed that in the New Testament justification is God's declaration by which, on the basis of the sufficiency of Christ's atoning death, He pronounces believers to have fulfilled all the requirements of the law that pertain to them. Erickson believed that justification by faith is a forensic act imputing the righteousness of Christ to the believer in such a way as to declare the person to be righteous, just as a judge acquits the accused.[7] In a similar vein, Edgar Mullins, a Pietist, believed that justification is a judicial act of God in which He declares the sinner to be free from condemnation, and restores him or her to divine favour. This takes place only when the sinner trusts in Christ. Mullins believed that to "justify" in the New Testament, does not mean to make just, but to pronounce or reckon just. However, God's declarative act is on condition of

---

6. Schlatter, *The Theology of the Apostles*, 228–240.
7. Erickson, *Christian Theology*, 968–972.

JUSTIFICATION

faith. To be sure, "(t)he Old Testament is quoted as proof of the fact that faith has always been the condition of justification . . . Abraham believed God, and it was reckoned unto him for righteousness (Rom 4:3; Gen 15:6)."[8]

The Australian New Testament scholar, Leon Morris, asserted that in Romans, "Paul is quite definite that 'no one will be justified in (God's) sight by works of law' (3:20; 4:2). Justification, on the contrary, is God's good gift: people are justified freely by his grace (3:24)." Several times Paul links justification with faith, making it quite clear that it is only by believing that anyone can appropriate the gift of God (3:26, 28, 30; 4:5; 5:1). Finally, Morris contended that the cross plays a necessary part in justification, for "we have now been justified by his blood (5:9)".[9]

In his discussion of the Doctrine of Justification, Donald Bloesch dealt with the possible difficulties posed by the Epistle of James who writes that "a man is justified by works and not by faith alone (James 2:24)." Bloesch firstly pointed to Luther, who "did not attempt any reconciliation and relegated James to the level of law, not Gospel." Consequently, Bloesch prefered Wesley's contention that James refers to a different kind of faith and a different kind of work to Paul's. "James is speaking of faith as intellectual assent, not faith as the commitment of the whole person to the living Christ (as in Paul). Moreover, he is referring not to the works of the law (which preoccupy Paul) but to the fruits of faith. Our justification is exhibited and carried forward by the practice of our faith, though its grounds or basis is in the free mercy of God." Bloesch also discussed the theology of Thomas Aquinas, who stressed salvation by grace. However, what is not so well known is that he held to justification by faith alone. Indeed, he saw "no hope of justification" in the precepts of the law "but in faith alone." With Paul, he held that "God saves man by faith without any preceding merits, *that no man may glory* in himself but refer all the glory to God." [10]

Bloesch reviewed the contribution of the Reformers by stating that the "Reformers intended not to denigrate good works but to give them a new motivation and purpose. We cannot make ouselves accepted by God by our works, but we can show forth our gratefulness for what God has done for us in his great work of salvation accomplished in Jesus Christ. Our works do not make us righteous, but they spring from the righteousness of Christ who dwells within us."[11] Indeed, the Christian is saved by faith alone, but faith does not remain alone. Further, Christians are not saved by works, but they are not saved without them. To be sure, Christ is not ultimately a lawyer or a court clerk who adminsiters transactions with a rubber stamp. He is a loving savour, who sacrificed his life for the ungodly and now seeks to work dynamically in the hearts of all His people; a great work of transformation.

---

8. Mullins, *The Christian Religion*, 389–401.
9. Morris, *The Epistle to The Romans*, 145.
10. Bloesch, *Essentials of Evangelical Theology: Vol. 2*, 194.
11. Bloesch, *Essentials of Evangelical Theology: Vol. 2*, 194.

The Pietists emphasised the place of the Christian life in a biblical theology of Justification by Faith. They believed that Christian practice is the cardinal evidence and consequence of a genuine faith. However, the Pietists also believed that a godly life does not itself result in the remission of sins, for this becomes a reality in a person's life only through faith. Bloesch further pointed to Wesley who, in 1740, described his doctrine as "the new path, of salvation by faith and works." Indeed, "Wesley's faith was synergistic, since in his view man's cooperation with saving grace is only possible on the basis of prevenient grace".[12] That is, the Christian, in a justified state of righteousness, lives the works of faith as a choice, but only because God in his grace provides the means through the work of His Holy Spirit.

Dale Moody, an Arminian, believed that biblical exegeses requires a translation of *dikaiosis* that denotes relationship rather than a legalistic declaration. Moody held that when it is "remembered that the most important New Testament writings on justification focus on the prophetic passages in Habakkuk 2:4, then a return to the Old Testament from Roman legalism seems 'justified!' "Behold, he whose soul is not upright in him shall fail, but the righteous shall live by his faith."

Moody believed that the confrontation between Paul and Peter in Antioch led to the most crucial clarification of justification through faith (Galatians 2:11-21).

> *The long defence of justification through faith that follows appeals to the experience of the Holy Spirit, received by faith and not by the works of the law (3:1-5), the example of Abraham in the Scriptures, who was reckoned righteous before the law was given (3:6-18), and the Christ event by which he was delivered from the bondage of sin into the freedom of faith (3:19-29).*

Clearly, Moody objected to the claim that justification is a legal term. Alternatively, he sought a discarding of the bondage of legalism for the dynamic view of righteousness as the obedience of faith.[13]

The Reformation placed justification by faith at the centre of Christian soteriology. Just as the Apostle Paul "maintains a universal sinfulness, and an atonement in Christ as the necessary ground of salvation, so does he set forth and maintain a justification by faith as the only mode of actual salvation."[14] As Donald Bloesch surmised, justification "is the act by which God declares the sinner righteous by virtue of faith in the perfect holiness of Jesus Christ, thereby restoring the sinner to the positive favour of God."[15] However, the declaration of righteousness is accompanied and followed by a continuing work of righteousness. We are not only declared righteous but made righteous; whereas the former is complete the later is incomplete until the full process of our salvation concludes. Indeed, both are

---

12. Bloesch, *Essentials of Evangelical Theology: Vol. 2*, 219.
13. Moody, *The Word of Truth*, 325–328.
14. Miley, *Systematic Theology: Vol. 1*, 308.
15. Bloesch, *Jesus Christ*, 177.

necessary for our salvation, for without imputed righteousness there is no justification at all. To be sure it "is not enough to believe in Christ; we also need to be engrafted into His righteousness."[16]

The precondition for justification is the acceptance of sin. Those who are justified by faith understand that once they were lost sinners. Those who will not receive Christ's forgiveness are those who believe that they can justify themselves. They remain within the confines of themselves and will not seek validity from another master. Natural instincts tell us that we must maintain mastery of ourselves, however those who acknowledge who Christ is for them, acknowledge that their trust is not accessible to ordinary human thought, it comes by way of a miracle. To be sure, our justification is totally a work of God.

In the legal sense, justification amounts to a declaration of one being just or righteous. However, the mistake should not be made that salvation is purely a legal process, since a purely legal analogy is devoid of any sense of a relationship. As Miley pointed out, forgiveness "really has no place in a strictly forensic justification."[17] Indeed, Miley proposed that the justification of a sinner is an act of God in the exercise of forgiveness based on the sufficiency of the atonement. From the basis of this forgiveness, and the subsequent absence of condemnation, comes an indwelling of Christ through the ministry of the Holy Spirit. The Christian is declared righteous, sure enough, however the "being Christian" comes about through imputed righteousness, in which Christ lays hold of the believer, and the believer, Christ. While justification and sanctification are two different aspects of salvation, they are inextricably linked. As Vincent Taylor has averred, righteousness "can no more be imputed to a sinner than bravery to a coward or wisdom to a fool." Indeed, while Christ's righteousness is alien, it is, essentially, imputed to the person of faith. This person is not only declared righteous, but they are made righteous. This righteousness, however, is not instantaneous. As Taylor has stated, in faith the person "possesses the germ or potency of righteousness."[18] However, it is not the faith that results in the fruit of this growth, rather it is in the object of the faith. Faith in itself does nothing, it is God who does all. Therefore, the Christian is not a mere acquitted person in the dock, but a child of God and an inheritor of the Kingdom. Indeed, as Moody pointed out, "a return to biblical exegesis requires a translation that denotes relationship rather than a legalistic declaration."[19] The nature of this relationship is expressed in a biblical concept of covenant, in which the faithfulness of God calls for the faithfulness of the believer that is evident in obedience to the stipulations of the covenant. That is,

---

16. Bloesch, *Jesus Christ*, 178.
17. Miley, *Systematic Theology: Vol. 1*, 309.
18. Taylor, *Forgiveness and Reconciliation*, 57.
19. Moody, *The Word of Truth*, 326.

obedience to the law correlates with a "yes" to God's call into covenant relationship. Indeed, the "yes" of the justified is an echo of the "yes" of Christ for them.

As already stated, the confrontation at Antioch between Paul and Peter led to a crucial clarification of justification through faith (Galatians 2:11–21). In this clarification Paul provides the meaning of justification through faith and the meaning of a covenant relationship with Christ. "I am crucified with Christ: nevertheless, I live; yet not I, but Christ liveth in me: and the life which I now live in the flesh I live by the faith of the Son of God, who loved me, and gave himself for me (Gal. 2:20)". The lengthy apologetics that follows looks to the experience of the Holy Spirit, which can only be received by faith, and never by the works of the law (3:1–5). However, faith cannot be described as a work, or some kind of possession of the Christian that can be used in some way to manipulate the divine will. Rather, faith is the outcome of Divine action. It is the willing assent to the command of God to capitulate to the wooing of the Spirit, who calls for love and obedience through Christ to the Father. Therefore, faith is not a mere acknowledgement, but rather a state of being that comes about through the renewing and salvific action of God. To illustrate, Paul provides the example of Abraham in his letter to the Galatians. Here, Abraham is described as being accounted righteous through his faith in God. Consequently, "(t)hat the blessing of Abraham might come on the Gentiles through Jesus Christ; that we might receive the promise of the Spirit through faith (3:14)." The doctrine of Justification is presented by Paul again in his letter to the Romans. "For I am not ashamed of the gospel of Christ: for it is the power of God unto salvation to everyone that believeth; to the Jew first, and also to the Greek. For therein is the righteousness of God revealed from faith to faith: as it is written, *the just shall live by faith*." The important implication here is that while justification is by faith alone, the faith professed leads to a faith lived. Faith leads to faith. Therefore, right relation with God is a continuous expression of trust and dependence, rather than a mere once-for-all legal transaction by which one is declared righteous.

The idea of justification by faith being a lived experience is further supported by the basis of justification, which is the death and resurrection of Jesus Christ. Just as Christ literally died and rose from the dead to embrace a new resurrection life, so the person transformed under God's grace by faith enters into a new lived experience in a state of righteousness. "But for us also, to whom it shall be imputed, if we believe in him that raised up Jesus our Lord from the dead; Who was delivered for our offences, and was raised again for our justification (Romans 4:24–25)."

Thomas Oden was right to connect justification with the nature of Christian existence, since justification is part of the experience of conversion through which the believer finds peace of conscience. Therefore, that justification is a legal transaction has been too heavily emphasized in Christian theology. More so, it is the culmination of a divine merciful action leading to the individual who trusts in Christ to be accounted righteous. Indeed, "Justification is the reversal of God's judgement against the sinner whereby the sinner is . . . restored to divine favour."[20] In this relational dynamic the Christian does not so much meet the judge who hands down a decision of the court, but rather a parent who reaches out in embrace a new child. Not so much a release from charges, but an empowering and enabling for Christian life. Here one is not set before a judge, but brought into the embrace of a loving Father who protects, loves and guides.

Protestant Christianity has often made the mistake of discussing justification in isolation from other dimensions of salvation. Yet rightly understood justification by faith cannot be separated from sanctification, since both are part of the new experience of the born-again believer and both are imputed by the work of the Holy Spirit. Indeed, both draw the believer into a relational paradigm with God that is factual, in terms of the status of the Christian, but most importantly, relational. As Oden put it, "Justification's nature is pardon, its condition is faith, its ground is the righteousness of God, and its fruit and evidences are good works."[21] However, while justification is a more concerned with a relationship with God than a legal transaction, God's law embodies the nature of that relationship, since the law is a reflection of God's character.

James Arminius declared, justification "is a justification by which a man, who is a sinner, yet a believer, being placed before the throne of grace which is erected in Christ Jesus the propitiation, is accounted and pronounced by God, the just and merciful Judge, righteous and worthy of the reward of righteousness, not in himself but in Christ, of grace, according to the gospel."[22] Indeed, there is a transformation in the believer from guilty to innocent. The law of God is at the centre of His activity of transformation, since perfect obedience to the law is the hallmark of the life of Christ that is imputed into the life of the believer. Therefore, while the Christian is justified by faith alone, faith does not remain alone. The consequence of justification is new life in Christ, which automatically leads to sanctification and entire sanctification, since, at the moment of faith, the Holy Spirit fills the life of the repentant faithful. After all, it is the perfect faith of Christ that is imputed, as a foreign righteousness, unmerited, into the life of the believer. Therefore, it is both forgiveness of sin *and the life of Christ* that is merited to the Christian on profession of faith. Consequently, what will ultimately be seen in the Christian's life is the perfect life of Christ.

A theology of justification assumes both its need and therefore a universal condition in humanity characterized by unrighteousness. In Ephesians 2:3 people are described as "by nature children of wrath." However, a nature is a disposition to act

---

20. Oden, *Life in the Spirit: Systematic Theology: Vol. 3*, 108.
21. Oden, *Life in the Spirit: Systematic Theology: Vol. 3*, 109.
22. Bangs, *Arminius: A Study in the Dutch Reformation*, 344.

in a certain way. It is the act that brings the wrath. This is further seen in the context of the passage. Clearly behavior, acts of unrighteousness in the flesh, is in view here. This point is reiterated by Paul in Romans 3:9–18. The standard to determine what is or is not righteousness is found in the law. Only perfect obedience to the law of God results in justification, since the law is the perfect reflection of the character of God. Since the law is not kept there is condemnation. However, the law also provides hope. The role of the law is to point the condemned to their sin, as it reveals the nature of sin. Because it reveals sin, it teaches the need for a saviour. In this sense, it directs the sinner to the Gospel. That is, the good news that Jesus Christ died as a payment for sin and justifies those who claim its forgiveness in faith. However, the law also serves to provide the path of righteousness. As Ellen White pointed out in *The Great Controversy*, when discussing the contribution of Wesley: "On the one hand, the law continually makes way for and points us to, the gospel; on the other, the gospel continually leads us to a more exact fulfilling of the law."[23] To be sure, Ellen White believed that justification amounted to a transformation of the individual, resulting in more than a change in status. Indeed, there is a reorientation of the individual toward conformity to the will of God. In this new condition, the believer no longer depends on themselves, in fact they realize that they are unable to. What is needed is a total surrender to Jesus Christ who, in the life of the believer, works a path to righteousness. This work, however, requires the willing submission of the believer.

> *As the penitent sinner, contrite before God, discerns Christ's atonement in his behalf and accepts this atonement as his only hope in this life and the future life, his sins are pardoned. This is justification by faith. Every believing soul is to conform his will entirely to God's will and keep in a state of repentance and contrition, exercising faith in the atoning merits of the Redeemer and advancing from strength to strength, from glory to glory.*[24]

In fact, Ellen White referred to the justified believer moving from being a rebel against God to being a loyal subject.[25] That being said, good works, traditionally seen by Reformed Protestants as extraneous to salvation, is seen by Mrs White to be from faith. Reflecting her Arminian and Wesleyan heritage, she declared that,

> *God's promises are all made upon conditions. If we do His will, if we walk in truth, then we may ask what we will, and it shall be done unto us. While we earnestly endeavor to be obedient, God will hear our petitions; but He will not bless us in disobedience. If we choose to disobey His commandments, we may cry, 'Faith, faith, only have faith,' and the response will come back from the sure Word of God, 'Faith without works is dead (James 2:20).' Such faith will only be as sounding brass and as a tinkling cymbal. In order to have the benefits of*

---

23. White, *Great Controversy*, 263.
24. White, *Faith and Works*, 103.
25. White, *Faith and Works*, 103.

JUSTIFICATION

God's grace we must do our part; we must faithfully work and bring forth fruits meet for repentance.[26]

Indeed, faith "is not an opiate, but a stimulant. Looking to Calvary will not quiet your soul into non-performance of duty, but will create faith that will work, purifying the soul from all selfishness."[27]

Otto Weber, a German Evangelical, has pointed out that there

> is no Evangelical confessional document which speaks of the involvement of 'good works', for the attainment of justification. But none of them seeks to imply that the justified person can be without 'good works.' Works cannot make a person into something which he or she is not already. But the person whom God has pronounced righteous then does in faith 'good works'. Both sides must be maintained in combination with each other.[28]

To be sure, the New Testament makes it clear that, while works do not procure salvation, God's work in the life of a Christian have as their aim, "good works". This led Paul to speak of the "work of faith" to the Thessalonians as he gave thanks for the fruit of their faith, which was evident in the community as a result of the power of God at work in their lives. "We give thanks to God always for you all, making mention of you in our prayers; Remembering without ceasing your work of faith, and labour of love, and patience of hope in our Lord Jesus Christ, in the sight of God and our Father (1 Thessalonians 1:2–3)." In his second letter to them he wrote: "Wherefore also we pray always for you, that our God would count you worthy of this calling, and fulfil all the good pleasure of his goodness, and the work of faith with power (2 Thessalonians 1:11)." To the Galatians he exhorted a doing of good to all. "As we have therefore opportunity, let us do good unto all men, especially unto them who are of the household of faith (Gal, 6:10)." Indeed, the Reformation affirmed that justification concerns the whole person. Luther clearly established this in his "Lectures on Romans". There he asserted that the activity of a person, their good works, is the fruit of justification (Gal. 5:22f; Eph. 5:9; Rom. 6:22; Phil. 1:11). This is not to say that saving faith will automatically lead to righteous works. To be sure, as an assent to faith is a conscious act of the will, so is the will to cooperate with God's will, and to align oneself with His character, by obeying the commandments (John 14:15–23) and keeping in step with the Spirit (Gal. 5:25). Therefore, the act of having faith and living in obedience is both a total act of God in grace, and an absolute commitment and resolution of the believer. With only God's grace, one has automated Christians lacking any free will or accountability. With only obedience, salvation is a legalistic prescription separate from a need for the Holy Spirit. Therefore, good works are the

---

26. White, *Faith and Works*, 47.
27. White, *Review and Herald*, Jan. 24, 1893.
28. Weber, *Foundations of Dogmatics: Vol. 2*, 321.

fruit of faith, but not the automatic product; neither can they be equated with it. As Weber put it, "Justification is a completed reality; good works are a reality to be carried out on the basis of that complete action."[29] It is for this reason that in the New Testament the law still remains valid.

In his letter to the Romans Paul excludes all "boasting" (Rom. 3:27), but he does not exclude the law (Rom 3:31). Nor does he seek to replace the law with love, which he referred to as an expression of the law (Rom 13:10). The new creature in Jesus Christ must operate with more than just a general impression or a flow of feelings. The new life has a new modus operandi, and the law is its way. Scriptural faith amounts to a personal faith-relationship with Christ. In this way faith, as discussed by Paul, is to be understood of as amounting to more than an attitude, and more even than a selfish relationship. It is of self-surrender and self-committal to Jesus Christ. Just as the person of Christ cannot be separated from His work, neither can the redemptive work of Christ be separated from His lordship. Therefore, justification can only be truly understood as it is embodied, lived out and expressed as the life of Jesus Christ in the life of the believer. Therefore, the efficacy of justification cannot primarily be in the faith of the believer, but in the person and work of Jesus Christ; both being imputed to the believer. This is what Luther referred to as alien righteousness. The believer receives the life of Christ and that life indwells, leads, shapes and guides. Faith cannot be defined as a work, and it cannot be claimed by the believer as an achievement deserving of the reward of eternal life. Faith is not the Christian's; it is the result of God's work. One does not get Christ by faith and attain His benefits. Rather, Christ is given. The righteousness of Christ comes to the believer in the shape of faith. Faith is an outworking of what that presence looks like. Therefore, it is Christ who saves, and it is a salvation by God's grace. The "yes" that is proclaimed in faith is a response to the "yes" of God for all people. When the Word is proclaimed that "yes" is immediate and a decision is required. The decision of faith is a submission to the call of God. It is an assent to what God seeks to do in us, and who He seeks to be for us.

Faith, therefore, is more than a decision, but a seizing hold of Christ and an attestation to the new faith of Christ within us. In this way faith, rather than being a work, or something in the possession of the believer, "denotes disavowal of one's own performance or will-to-be-right as well as trust in grace alone. This faith is possible only as a response to the divine word of forgiveness. Word and faith are thus in mutual relation, in which the Word always has pre-eminence."[30] In this way, the faith of God for the person, and the corresponding faith of that person for salvation, is a single action resulting in a new life lived for Jesus Christ.

---

29. Weber, *Foundations of Dogmatics: Vol. 2*, 323.
30. Lohse, *Martin Luther's Theology: Its Historical and Systematic Development*, 261.

JUSTIFICATION

Ellen White was adamant that justification is wholly a work of Christ. Just as it can be discerned in Scripture that repentance is essential to forgiveness and justification, so it also needs to be asserted that true repentance can only come from the inspiration of Christ who draws the sinner out of rebellion. Indeed, no one can repent and make themselves worthy of the blessing of justification. "The Lord Jesus is constantly seeking to impress the sinner's mind and attract him to behold Himself, the Lamb of God, which taketh away the sins of the world. We cannot take a step toward spiritual life save as Jesus draws and strengthens the soul, and leads us to experience the repentance which needeth not to be repented of."[31] Therefore justification is a free gift from God given in grace.[32] It amounts to imputed righteousness received through faith.[33] However, dependence on Christ does not amount to an unconditional election. "While the sinner cannot save himself, he still has something to do to secure salvation. 'Him that cometh to me,' says Christ, 'I will in no wise cast out (John 6:37).' But we must come to Him; and when we repent of our sins, we must believe that He accepts and pardons us."[34] Therefore, the conditions of justification are repentance and faith,[35] together with continual assent to the way of Christ.[36] Further, the doctrine of justification by faith is closely associated with the third angel's message. Indeed, Ellen White stated that justification by faith is "the third angel's message in verity."[37] The third angel calls all to worship God, keep the commandments and have the testimony of Jesus.

---

31. White, *Selected Messages: Book One*, Review and Herald, 390–391.
32. White, *Selected Messages: Book One*, Review and Herald, 372.
33. White, *Selected Messages: Book One*, Review and Herald, 360.
34. White, *Patriarchs and Prophets*, 168 431.
35. White, *Selected Messages: Book One*, 389.
36. White, *Selected Messages: Book One*, 366.
37. White, *The Review* and Herald, April 1, 1890. In White, *Selected Messages: Book One*, 372.

CHAPTER 19

SANCTIFICATION

IN THE NEW TESTAMENT, FAITH is discussed in the context of a Hebrew worldview. It is an understanding that encapsulates trust that is expressed as both a belief and an action. For this reason, sanctification always accompanies justification, since faith in Christ assumes life in Christ. While justification is by faith alone, faith cannot be understood as existing alone. Indeed, the biblical concept of faith, rooted in Ancient Near-Eastern concepts, embraces the identity of the whole person. This is primarily witnessed by a conviction expressed in a lifestyle. It is for this reason that a biblical faith is as deeply concerned with human behaviour as it is with a personal faith in God. If concepts of Christianity, and an individualised spirituality, are all that the Christian possesses, then they have embraced only a partial understanding of biblical faith that was never envisaged by the biblical authors. The Bible knows of no such dualism. To be sure, Christians today who have reduced Christianity down to belief alone, with the rhetoric that all that matters is what's in the heart, have submitted to western concepts of reality that are rooted in ancient paganism. Indeed, while good works cannot save us, we are not saved without good works.[1] The inter-relation between these two aspects of salvation is seen in the work of Jesus Christ, whose faith was expressed in faithfulness. While in justification the righteousness of Christ is imputed, sanctification infuses righteousness: which leads to a Christian living in step with the Spirit (Gal. 5:25) and bearing His fruit (Gal. 5:22).

Both justification and sanctification are a result of God's grace. They are empowered by His love and received both passively, as the life is opened to the grace of God, and actively, as the believer constantly cooperates with the will of God in Jesus Christ. Therefore, faith can never be possessed and owned as a personal item, let alone championed as a decisive accomplishment. It is not a ticket to heaven or

---

1. White, *Testimonies for the Church: Vol. 3*, 526.

an investment that guarantees a dividend. Faith is not a work. It is the evidence of a surrender to the indwelling of Jesus Christ, through His Holy Spirit. It is on the merits of this encounter, which has imputed an alien righteousness, that Christians are presented as righteous before the Father. It is only in this way that salvation is a gift of God, and not of ourselves (Ephesians 2:8–9).

Faith amounts to an abiding trust in God that binds the person with God in a covenant of love. Indeed, the root Indo-European word for faith also gives rise to *fiancé, fidelity* and *confidant*. This binding with the life of Christ fits well with the Hebrew worldview of a unity of body and mind. Conversely, the separation of belief from action is rooted in an ancient Greek, and therefore pagan, perspective of the separation of the material world from the spiritual. Consequently, Christian life should include praise, but also sabbath keeping, a call to right moral conduct, modest dress and a diet that separates right from wrong. In this holistic paradigm, for example, the Christian does not only think right from wrong and clean from unclean, but lives it as well. Therefore, both justification and sanctification are part of the imputation of the life of Christ in the believer. For this reason, faith in Christ, described in terms of both justification and sanctification, is transformational. From a life characterised by Satan's rebelliousness (as it is expressed in lawlessness, selfishness and the sour fruits of ego, hate, jealousy, power and oppression) to a life imbued with the fruits of the Spirit (known by love, obedience, grace and service).

The New Testament uses the word *hagiasmos* to describe sanctification. It's meaning refers to one who is separated, or set apart, for God as an act of consecration, (1 Cor. 1:30; 2 Thess 2:13; 1 Peter 1:2) but also, and importantly, to describe the course of life befitting those so separated. (1 Thess 4:3, 4,7; Rom 6:19, 22; 1 Tim 2:15; Heb 12:14). Therefore, sanctification is not merely a state of being, but a condition of life by means of God's work. Yet, while justification is imputed, sanctification is infused. The verb *hagiazein* means "to make holy" or "to sanctify". Paul stated in 1 Cor. 1:30 that Christ has become our sanctification. In 1 Cor. 1:2; 6:11, he uses the verb *hagiazein* to refer to the past event of sanctification, but elsewhere refers to the eschatological sanctification of believers or of the church (1 Thess 5:23; Eph 5:26).[2] Therefore, sanctification is to be seen across a spectrum of time, having been accomplished in Christ at His first coming, but completed in believers at His second.

In puritan England, Thomas Watson wrote that sanctification refers to a consecration and a setting apart for a holy use. That is, sanctified individuals are separated from the world and set apart for God's service. Watson further believed that sanctification amounted to a holiness of the heart that is made after God's own heart. Indeed, a sanctified person bears the image of God. This is made possible since sanctification is a supernatural event; it is divinely infused (Lev. 21:8). Watson believed that sanctification is necessary because firstly, God has called us to it (1 Thess 4:7).

---

2. Vines, *Expository Dictionary of New Testament Words*, 999; Garrett, *Systematic Theology*, 356.

Secondly, without sanctification there is no evidence of our justification (1 Cor 6:2). Thirdly, sanctification is the believer's title to the new covenant. The tenure of the covenant is that God will be our God. But who is interested in the covenant, and may plead the benefit of it? Sanctified persons only. "A new heart will I give you, and I will put my Spirit in you, and I will be your God (Exodus 36:26)." Fourthly, there is no going to heaven without sanctification (Heb 12:14). God is holy and he will not suffer "with plague-sores" to stand before him. Only a holy heart can see God in all his glory. Finally, without sanctification we cannot give evidence of our calling (2 Thess. 2:13). Indeed, sanctification is the evidence, claimed Watson, of the believer's election.[3]

Watson also discussed the signs of sanctification. Firstly, believers remember the time when they were unsanctified (Titus 3:3). Secondly, the indwelling of the Spirit. The Spirit dwells in the believer as guide and comforter. God's Spirit further dwells in believers, causing them to "mint holy thoughts" and to be inclined to do good. Thirdly, there is an antipathy against sin. A sanctified person hates sin. Fourthly, there is a spiritual performance of duties that comes from the new heart out of the principle of love. Fifthly, there is a well-ordered life (1 Pet 1:15). Finally, a steadfast resolution to never part with holiness. He quotes Job as saying: "My integrity I will hold fast, and not let it go." Job 27:6.[4]

John Wesley taught that Methodists were not only called upon to teach holiness, but also to live the holy life. Wesley believed that sanctification was realized through the circumcision of the heart. He taught this by way of his exposition of Romans 2:28–29. "A man is not a Jew if he is only one outwardly, nor is circumcision merely outward and physical. No, a man is a Jew if he is one inwardly; and circumcision is circumcision of the heart, by the Spirit, not by the written code." The circumcision of the heart, taught Wesley, can be defined

> as that habitual disposition of soul to walk by faith in the way of holiness. It implies so trusting in the coming righteousness of Christ as to be renewed in the spirit of our minds that the body, as temple of the Spirit, manifests the holiness of God fully and without blemish. It implies being cleansed from sin, from corruption of both flesh and spirit, and in consequence being drawn toward those virtues that were in Christ Jesus. Only by complete trust in the atoning work is one enabled to fulfil the command to be perfect as our Father in heaven is perfect.[5]

Edgar Mullins put it that the word "sanctify" has the meaning of being set apart to God's service, belonging to God, as well as becoming inwardly holy. Mullins alluded to Paul's writings, where there are frequent exhortations to consecration

---

3. Watson, *A Body of Divinity*, 240–250.
4. Watson, *A Body of Divinity*, 240–250.
5. Oden, *John Wesley's Scriptural Christianity*, 311–334.

SANCTIFICATION

or sanctification. Indeed, in Romans 12:1 Christians are enjoined to present their bodies as "living sacrifices to God". Along with this one is to be "transformed" in mind. Christians must think of themselves as dead to sin and alive to God (Rom 6:1–12).[6] According to Mullins, sanctification amounts to the attainment of moral character. In justification, our faith is reckoned to us for righteousness, but this is not the attainment of righteousness by us. In regeneration, a new moral disposition is imparted to us by the action of God's Spirit. In sanctification, we work out what God has wrought in us. We respond to that which is reckoned to us and react to that which is imparted to us. By repeated acts of our own wills, by repeated acts of holy choice, by successive victories, we are enabled by God's grace to achieve the ideal. Thus, our salvation is both a gift and a task. Indeed, Jesus calls upon one to "strive" and to "enter in" (Luke 13:24) and Paul exhorts Christians to fight the good fight (1 Tim 6:12).[7]

Donald Bloesch believed that the call to holiness resounds through Scripture. "God declares his children righteous and holy through faith (Gen 15:6). To be righteous means to stand in right relationship with God; to be holy connotes separateness as well as ethical purity. We are made righteous in order to pursue holiness (Col 1:21–22)."[8] Bloesch taught that Scripture does not speak of self-sanctification, but it does teach that the believer is active in realizing the fruits of their sanctification. The sanctification that comes by faith is a result of the substitutionary work of Christ, "but the righteousness of daily living is conditional upon our cooperation with the Holy Spirit." Bloesch believed that it is not enough to believe in the light since one must also walk in the light (1 John 1:6,7; Eph 5:8). He pointed to Martin Luther, who taught that the work of purification is a life-long process, completed only at death. Bloesch also believed that Luther expressed the paradox of the Christian way of life: "He is perfectly whole in hope, while he is in fact a sinner, but he has already begun to be actually righteous, and he always seeks to become more so, always knowing himself to be unrighteous." Bloesch also discussed Luther's repudiation of works-righteousness, but never good works. Indeed, Luther held out a note of victory for the Christian despite the continuing presence of sin.[9]

Dale Moody correctly wrote that perfect sanctification is good to pursue, but that self-righteousness is certain to accompany any claims that it has been achieved. Moody emphasised that sanctification is past, present and future. These three tenses are used to describe possessive, progressive and perfected sanctification.

> *In Pauline thought it is possible to say that Christ is our sanctification from the very beginning of the Christian life (1 Cor 1:30). This includes all who belong to*

---

6. Mullins, *The Christian Religion*, 418.
7. Mullins, *The Christian Religion*, 417–423.
8. Bloesch, *Essentials of Evangelical Theology: Vol. 1*, 32.
9. Bloesch, *Essentials of Evangelical Theology: Vol. 1*, 32.

> *the temple of God, the church (1 Cor 3:16f; 2 Cor 6:14–17:1) ... sanctification is progressive from the beginning of the holy life of a saint to the completion of sanctification at the resurrection of the dead.*[10]

Millard Erickson believed that sanctification amounts to the continuing work of God in the life of a Christian. The result of this work is to make the believer holy. To be "holy", stated Erickson, is to bear an actual likeness to God. In this process, the person's moral condition is conformed with the person's legal standing before God. In sanctification, the Holy Spirit applies to the Christian's life, the work done by Jesus Christ. The new believer is born again in Jesus Christ and continues to grow in Him. Erickson emphasised that sanctification is a supernatural work that is done by God and is not something that we do ourselves. He quoted Paul as saying: "May the God of peace himself sanctify you wholly; and may your spirit and soul and body be kept sound and blameless at the coming of our Lord Jesus Christ (1 Thess 5:23; see also Eph 5:26; Titus 2:14; Heb 13:20–21)."[11]

Stanley Grenz wrote that the saving work of the Holy Spirit does not end at conversion. The event of salvation is only the beginning of the process of transformation into Christ's likeness, which continues in the Christian all their days. Grenz believed that the word, sanctification, is related to holiness, which he understood as meaning to be separated and therefore "sacred". Therefore, sanctification is a process whereby someone is holy by being set apart. Grenz believed that God's work of sanctification in the believer not only arises out of his or her own holiness, but also from the purpose God has in calling a people to be His very own. We belong to God because He has chosen us and we have our existence in order to honour God and serve His purposes in the world (Eph 1:11–12). Therefore, Grenz stipulated that there are two aspects to sanctification. The first is *positional* and the second *conditional*. Positional sanctification has to do with our standing before God. It relates to our "position" before God on the basis of our new standing in Christ. "Positional sanctification, therefore, is an objective reality, a standing in righteousness which is ours solely by virtue of the grace of God extended to us in Christ and which the Holy Spirit applies to our lives. We receive this reality solely by faith."[12] Conditional sanctification, by contrast, refers to one's spiritual condition. This includes the morality of our lives, our character and our conduct. "Make every effort ... to be holy; without holiness, no one will see the Lord (Heb 12:14)". Grenz further stipulated that the goal of the Holy Spirit in sanctification is to foster Christ-likeness (Eph 4:14). However, when did Grenz believe that the Christian attains to this? Grenz betrays his Reformed influences when he contended that the believer never fully attains to this in their

---

10. Moody, *Word of Truth*, 323.
11. Erickson, *Introducing Christian Doctrine*, 313–315.
12. Grenz, *Theology for The Community of God*, 443.

lifetime. Consequently, he stated that the goal of our sanctification, entire sinlessness, is never realized until the day of our final glorification in heaven.[13]

Adolf Schlatter contended that Paul uses the term sanctification to designate what believers receive through Christ. "Their union with God separates them from what is profaned or stained and provides them with a share in God's integrity, purity, and majesty." Further, sanctification is brought about by God reconciling the community of Christ with Himself. Also, he used the metaphor of a "seal" to demonstrate that the community is "God's possession through Christ (2 Cor 1:22; Eph 1:13; 4:30; 2 Tim 2:19)."[14]

F.L. Forlines asserted that sanctification means to make holy, however holiness amounts to more than morality; it also speaks of our relationship with God. Therefore, the primary meaning of sanctification is to be dedicated to God. "It also involves the experience of growth. It begins at conversion (2 Cor 5:17) and progresses through the rest of life (2 Pet 3:18). Sanctification is finally completed at the resurrection."[15]

Therefore, while justification is a status, sanctification is a process with a goal in mind. Consequently, sanctification and holiness are closely linked. While holiness is a moral condition, sanctification is the gracious work of God that results in a state of holiness. Therefore, without sanctification there is no possibility of holiness. That God is holy necessitates the essentiality of holiness in the Christian, since regeneration brings the individual back to their true nature in the image of God. However, there are significant differences. As John Miley righty alluded, "divine holiness is an eternal possession, while Christian holiness is always an attainment. The latter fact gives propriety to the use of the word sanctification, which means a holiness wrought in us by a gracious work of God."[16]

There is both an outward and inward dimension to holiness. Outwardly, a Christian is seen to display characteristics of the inward sanctifying work of God. Progressively, language, behaviour, associations, recreation, appearance and the use of time and resources undertake a transformation. The Christian learns, as a cooperative agent in the renewing power of God, to "keep in step with the Spirit (Gal. 5:25)" and to bear his fruit in relationships and ministry (Matt. 3:23; Jn. 15:16; Gal. 5:22–23). The purity of God begins to be reflected, albeit in struggle with sin. In this way, we can speak of the Christian nature, and indeed a culture, which is sustained and nurtured in the community of faith. However, the outward forms of holiness can easily be fabricated and sustained as an "act", either in part or in whole. To be sure, maintaining outward forms and fostering civil constraint, for the purposes of

---

13. Grenz, *Theology for The Community of God*, 440–446.
14. Schlatter, *The Theology of the Apostles*, 248.
15. Forlines, *Biblical systematics*, 182.
16. Miley, *Systematic Theology: Vol. 2*, 355.

order and normality, are essential traits of a good society. However, the person of faith in Christ, who is born again in the Spirit of God, opens their life to an inward renewal, which does not bear artificial fruit, but fruit from God that is good for the tasting, is lasting, and partners with God's sanctifying work in the world (Jn. 15:16; Mk. 7:20–23). Together with the work of the Holy Spirit in the believer's life comes a deeper moral sense and a maturity that exhibits moral good. To do what is morally good requires the removal of the corruption that comes from sin. This is only possible through an interior purification that comes from an infilling of the Holy Spirit and a commitment to repentance.

Repentance is essential to sanctification since, as the word implies (*metanoia*) there must be a turning away from sin and a turning toward God. The presence of the Spirit of God brings a dislike for sin and a desire to pursue the work and life of God. This is from God in grace, but also, by consequence, necessitates a willing and cooperative spirit. Therefore, there is an essential link between sanctification and regeneration. As Miley pointed out, "regeneration is of the nature of sanctification; and whatever be the work of sanctification, as distinctively held, it cannot be different in kind."[17] Indeed, the imputation of the righteousness of Christ begins at regeneration and continues through sanctification to holiness. The completion of this work has been referred to as entire sanctification. However, this should not be confused with perfection.

The one who is entirely sanctified is perfect, as God is perfect (Matthew 5:28). Theologically, perfection is a term initiated by John Wesley and broadly used in Methodist theology, but is widely misunderstood. Wesley was often asked to drop the word, since it led to a considerable amount of misunderstanding and contention. He repeatedly refused, since it was a word used in the Bible (Matt. 5:48; Jm 1:4; 1 Jn 4:12; Heb. 10:14). The key to understanding a Methodist use of the word is in determining how it is defined and not in the word itself. Wesley's qualified understanding of perfection refers to a freedom from intentional sin, but not from mistakes. Further, he saw perfection as an aspiration, and a possibility under God's grace, but never claimed it himself.

The Bible does not speak of a physically perfect person before the return of Jesus Christ, but it does discuss the possibility of moral perfection in Jesus Christ before that time. Although, while being a possibility, it is not a condition of salvation, but denotes the earnest desire to grow in Christ by the one who is born again of the Spirit. In Wesleyanism, perfection is a state of the heart, rather than the fact of being a perfect person in life and thought. As the twentieth-century Wesleyan, Thomas Oden, asserted, "(e)ven where information is wrongly processed, the heart may remain pure, and every act spring from love."[18] A person can be wrong, but still filled

---

17. Miley, *Systematic Theology: Vol. 2*, 355.
18. Oden, *Life in The Spirit—Systematic Theology: Vol. 3*, 232.

SANCTIFICATION

with a sincerity and pureness of purpose that comes from the perfect love of God. An apt description would describe a perfect heart for God, rather than for sin. To be sure, active rebelliousness, in which disobedience is preferred to holiness, and there is a conscious choice to sin, stand in contradistinction to a Methodist understanding of perfection. It was the psalmist who made a distinction between willed sin and hidden sins. "Who can understand his errors? Cleanse thou me from secret faults. Keep back thy servant also from presumptuous sins; let them not have dominion over me: then shall I be upright, and I shall be innocent from the great transgression (Psalm 19:12-13)." In these terms, perfection is not sinlessness. As Wesley alluded, one "may be filled with the love of God and still remain liable to involuntary or unconscious or unavoidable transgressions."[19] Indeed, perfection has to do with living in the full love of God which reflects His character, and so, by consequence, His law (Psalms 145:17; 119:172; 1 Peter 1:16; Romans 7:12).

The first type of perfection mentioned has to do with wholeness, completeness and maturity in God and, most fully, in Jesus Christ. As Thomas Oden has noted: of "the various Hebrew words sometimes translated "perfect" or "blameless" (*shalem, tamim*), it is usually contextually clear that the individuals referred to are not wholly without sin (Hezekiah, 2 Kings 20:3; David, Pss. 37:37; 101:2). When the Old Testament spoke of the upright man such as Noah or Job as "perfect (Gen. 6:9; Job 1:1,8), this did not imply moral sinlessness but complete sincerity of trust in God."[20]

The New Testament continues with a similar theme. There is no claim in the New Testament that the old nature of sin is eradicated upon profession of faith. By contrast, sufficient grace is given so that sin is overcome through a process of daily consecration.

> *The world, the flesh, and the adversary are not eradicated in this present age, though their power is being overthrown. The world continues, temptation continues, the flesh exerts its power, the devil rails, but amid all these challenging conditions, the Spirit works to enable fully adequate responses in each circumstance and growth toward an ever-larger pattern of full responsiveness.*[21]

In his first letter, John puts forward the challenge that "whoever is born of God doth not commit sin (1 John 3:1-10)." Indeed, the verb *katarizō* implies completeness, "as if something is rightly adjusted and completely fitted to its purpose (2 Cor. 13:9; Eph. 4:12; 1 Thess. 3:10)."[22] It is brought about by a full surrender to the gracious work of the Holy Spirit, who is to be given the full credit for equipping and preparing God's people for works of service (Jn. 10:10). In a similar fashion the verb *teleioō* suggests a completion that brings something to its intended goal. It is

---

19. Wesley, *A Plain Account of Christian Perfection*, 67.
20. Oden, *Life in The Spirit—Systematic Theology: Vol. 3*, 227.
21. Oden, *Life in The Spirit—Systematic Theology: Vol. 3*, 234.
22. Oden, *Life in The Spirit—Systematic Theology: Vol. 3*, 234.

a fitting conclusion. (1 Cor. 2:6; Eph. 4:13; Phil. 3:15; Col. 3:14; 4:12). God's people are called on to grow to the maturity of their faith, to attain to full measure of the presence of the Holy Spirit in a human life, to reach the goal of their lives, which is wholeness in Jesus Christ. They do this through patience (James 1:4), love (1 John 4:17, 18), holiness (2 Cor. 7:1), and suffering (Rom. 5:3–5). To be sure, those who reach to this kind of perfection are those in which grace is working optimally in their lives by responding to God's sanctifying grace in full cooperation and sacrificial submission. They are those "who are thoroughly cleansed from sin by faith and wholly consecrated to God". This is not to say, however, that complete perfection, without sin, is not possible. If it was impossible, then God would be incapable of doing what he most longs for and is therefore somehow limited in His power. Importantly, however, perfection has nothing to do with human capability; but is rather a reflection of the sufficiency of the Holy Spirit to totally transform. There is nothing philosophically or rationally impossible about an all-powerful God imparting grace to the extent that sin is totally overcome. Consequently, there is certainly nothing intrinsically impossible about aiming to love God fully and totally in such a way as all our thoughts, words and actions are governed by pure love.[23] Such have the mind in them that was also in Christ Jesus (Phil. 2:5). Significantly, before Christ's return, our struggle with sin remains. Never-the-less, God's grace is sufficient to sustain us, as forgiveness is integral to the gospel.

Due to the influence of Reformed Calvinism in modern theology, which emphasises free grace without condition or consequence, the perfection of the believer is commonly viewed as an impossibility and therefore an unworthy aspiration. Yet this, based on scriptural evidence, limits God's vision and gives hope to the power of sin, rather than the possibilities that come through the victory of God's grace. It envisions men and women as mere receptors of a divine decision that leaves them as only spectators after the event of election, rather than free covenant partners in God's redemptive mission through His people.

There is no overcoming, in the earthly life, the struggle with temptation or sin, nor the consequences of living in a sinful world. As Oden observed, "(i)f the complete eradication of all possibility of sin were God's way of dealing with our fallen nature, then there would be little point in talking further of the continuing work of the Spirit. Rather, both Paul and John teach that the sin nature continues after faith begins, yet the indwelling Spirit empowers the new person of faith sufficiently in each circumstance.[24] Indeed, the "tendency to sin does not destroy free will or the moral culpability of sin, nor does it imply that what God has commanded is formally impossible."[25]

---

23. Oden, *Life in The Spirit—Systematic Theology: Vol. 3*, 228.
24. Oden, *Life in The Spirit—Systematic Theology: Vol. 3*, 234.
25. Oden, *Life in The Spirit—Systematic Theology: Vol. 3*, 228.

Therefore, humanly speaking, sin is inevitable, so grace is essential to overcome sin. The point of both saving and sanctifying grace is to overcome the guilt of sin and its consequences. God is able, and so is the grace filled person who avails themselves of the miracles of God.

Secondly, there is a final sanctification, in which the Christian is not only perfect in the context of sinful humanity, or morally perfect in total sincerity, but completely perfect, without even inadvertent and unintentional sin. There is certainly complete perfection in heaven that is classified as glorification, but also among those who have been sealed in their faith and endure suffering to the point of complete love. Paul draws this out in his vision of the church in Ephesians. Here he calls for the people to engage in ministry, both for the present, and with their ultimate state in mind when Christ returns. Paul clearly outlines the means of attaining this through ministry, and the ultimate goal, which is perfection. Such a situation: "the unity of the faith" in a state of the "fullness of Christ" ultimately describes a perfect state. Indeed, the "perfect person".

> *And he gave some to be apostles; and some, prophets; and some, evangelists; and some, pastors and teachers; For the perfecting of the saints, for the work of the ministry, for the edifying of the body of Christ: Till we all come in the unity of the faith, and of the knowledge of the Son of God, unto a perfect man, unto the measure of the stature of the fullness of Christ* (Eph. 4:13).

Following the Arminian fusion of justification and sanctification, Ellen White followed the pattern of asserting a conditional justification that is given evidence in a holy life in full surrender to Jesus Christ. In her reflection on the biblical model, the individual must take personal responsibility to co-operate with the wooing of the Holy Spirit as a faithful covenant partner. In this way, the believer comes to faith as a free agent, and must persevere in faith through the equipping of the Holy Spirit. Consequently, once saved, once not always saved, since freedom presumes the ability to quench the Holy Spirit and forsake salvation through Christ alone. This conditional situation is seen when she asserted that while

> *God can be just, and yet justify the sinner through the merits of Christ, no man can cover his soul with the garments of Christ's righteousness while practicing known sins or neglecting known duties. God requires the entire surrender of the heart, before justification can take place; and in order for man to retain justification, there must be continual obedience, through active, living faith that works by love and purifies the soul. James writes of Abraham and says, '(w)as not Abraham our father justified by works, when he had offered Isaac his son upon the altar? Seest thou how faith wrought with his works, and by works was faith made perfect? And the scripture was fulfilled which saith, Abraham believed God, and it was imputed unto him for righteousness: and he was called the Friend of God. Ye see then how that by works a man is justified, and not by*

FOUNDATIONS OF THEOLOGY

> *faith only' (James 2:21–24). In order for man to be justified by faith, faith must reach a point where it will control the affections and impulses of the heart; and it is by obedience that faith itself is made perfect.*[26]

Indeed, "God's forgiveness is not merely a judicial act by which He sets us free from condemnation. It is not only forgiveness for sin but reclaiming from sin. It is the outflow of redeeming love that transforms the heart. David had the true conception of forgiveness when he prayed, 'Create in me a clean heart, O God; and renew a right spirit within me.' Psalm 51:10."[27]

For Ellen White, being a Christian amounted to more than a declaration of faith, in and of itself. It amounts to being joined with Christ. This can only come about through the agency of the Holy Spirit.

> *The religion that comes from God is the only religion that will lead to God. In order to serve Him aright, we must be born of the divine Spirit. This will purify the heart and renew the mind, giving us a new capacity for knowing and loving God. It will give us a willing obedience to all His requirements. This is true worship. It is the fruit of the working of the Holy Spirit.*[28]

There appears to be a clear distinction here between the common Christian ascertain for a declaration of faith, and a conviction of faith that embraces the whole person. To be sure, she stated that the

> *greatest deception of the human mind in Christ's day was that a mere assent to the truth constitutes righteousness. In all human experience a theoretical knowledge of the truth has been proved to be insufficient for the saving of the soul. It does not bring forth the fruit of righteousness... The Pharisees claimed to be children of Abraham, and boasted of their possession of the oracles of God; yet these advantages did not preserve them from selfishness, malignity, greed for gain, and the basest hypocrisy.*[29]

As a consequence, sanctification is seen as the evidential wing of a truly justified believer. Therefore, according to Ellen White, the "faith that justifies always produces first, true repentance, and then good works, which are the fruit of faith. There is no saving faith that does not produce good fruit."[30] A necessary accompaniment with sanctification is obedience, which is at the heart of this good fruit born of the Spirit. For Ellen White, obedience is a necessary component of saving faith. Indeed in "setting aside the law of God, men know not what they are doing. God's law is the transcript of His character. It embodies the principles of His kingdom. He

---

26. White, *Faith and Works*, 100.
27. White, *Thoughts from The Mount of Blessing*, 114; White, *The Faith I live By*, 129.
28. White, *Desire of Ages*, 189. White, *My Life Today*, 46.I
29. White, *Desire of Ages*, 309.
30. White. *Selected Messages: Book 3*, 195.

SANCTIFICATION

who refuses to accept these principles is placing himself outside the channel where God's blessings flow."[31] This obedience, however, is never to be seen as a work that leads to salvation. Ellen White was very clear that true faith rests solely upon Christ. However, this utter surrender to Christ as the realisation of all our insufficiencies, a total consecration of Heart, depending totally on the righteousness of Christ, will "be manifested by obedience to all the requirements of God." To be sure, the

> *proud heart strives to earn salvation; but both our title to heaven and our fitness for it are found in the righteousness of Christ. The Lord can do nothing toward the recovery of man until, convinced of his own weakness, and stripped of all self-sufficiency, he yields himself to the control of God. Then he can receive the gift that God is wanting to bestow. From the soul that feels the need, nothing is withheld. He has unrestricted access to Him in whom all fullness dwells.*[32]

Further, "the Scriptures declare that by works is faith made perfect; and that, without the works of obedience, faith is dead (James 2:22). "He that professes to know God, and keep not His commandments, is a liar, and the truth is not in him (1 John 2:4)."[33] Consequently, a declaration of faith is a shallow edifice if the heart has not been changed and the believer has not been transformed by the renewing work of the Holy Spirit.

> *Nicodemus had come to the Lord thinking to enter into a discussion with him, but Jesus laid bare the foundation principles of truth. He said to Nicodemus, it is not theoretical knowledge you need so much as spiritual regeneration. You need not to have your curiosity satisfied, but to have a new heart. You must receive a new life from above before you can appreciate heavenly things.*[34]

While the doctrine of sanctification is firmly established in Scripture, its theological resurgence occurred in Germany during the seventeenth century. While strands of "Pietism" had been present in Protestantism for some time, it was in the ministry of Philipp Jakob Spener (1635–1705) that a movement was born.

Spener was raised in Alsace to an aristocratic Lutheran family. He studied theology at Strassburg (1651–59), and after gaining his doctorate became a pastor in Frankfurt am Main at age 31, in 1663, and then Frankfort in 1666. Concerned with reforming Lutheranism, he established his "colleges of piety". His aim was to encourage personal spiritual growth through Bible study and prayer. "Spener was intent upon moral and spiritual reformation."[35] He stressed genuine conversion and the cultivation of the Christian life, by way of preaching the necessity of new birth,

---

31. White, *Christ Object Lessons*, 305.
32. White, *Desire of Ages*, 300.
33. White, *Patriarchs and Prophets*, 73.
34. White, *Patriarchs and Prophets*, 172.
35. Latourette, *A History of Christianity: Vol.. 2*, 895.

FOUNDATIONS OF THEOLOGY

followed by a personal and warm Christian experience.[36] The born-again Christian life of virtue was of particular concern. For this reason, he advocated a self-discipline, which included abstinence from cards, dancing, the theatre, and moderation in food, drink and dress.[37] This was in contrast to what he saw as the rigidity of the church coupled with a lack of moral discipline among the clergy. "In 1675, five years after beginning this experiment, he published his 'Pia desideria', where he outlined a program for the development of piety. This became the fundamental charter of Pietism."[38] In it, Spener emphasized the priesthood of all believers, by suggesting less emphasis on the difference between the laity and clergy. Most particularly, among the laity, he advocated a more intense life of devotion and study. Importantly, the word of God must be spread by way of preaching the entire Bible. Believers should meet together in small groups for Bible study, teaching, pastoral care and encouragement in the holy life. The cause of Pietism in the following generation was taken up by one of Spener's godchildren, Count Nikolaus Ludwig von Zinzendorf (1700–1760).

"Zinzendorf was born in Dresden, on May 26, 1700."[39] After studying at the university of Halle, Zinzendorf married and entered the service of the court of Dresden.[40] It was at this placement that he met a group of Moravians who would change his life. These Hussites (Jan Hus, c. 1369–1415) had been forced to leave Moravia (now part of the Czech Republic) because of persecution. Zinzendorf offered them asylum. "There they founded the community of Herrnhut, which so attracted Zinzendorf's interest that he resigned his post at Dresden and joined it."[41] To Zinzendorf, the Herrnhut society was a body of the soldiers of Christ, a new Protestant monasticism placed under strict supervision. "Children were brought up away from their parents (and the) . . . community even attempted to regulate choices in marriage."[42] The stage was set for the emergence of a new denomination, a kind of revival of the ancient *Unitas Fratrum*. However, Zinzendorf had no such aspiration. Alternatively, he sought to keep the society as a movement within the Lutheran state church. To him, the society was a witness to true "heart-religion", with its emphasis on a warm spiritual life and missionary zeal.[43] Zinzendorf assisted in organizing missionaries to depart from the Herrnhut community to various mission fields. These included the Caribbean, Africa, India, South America and North America. The ministry of the Moravians was taken up by John Wesley.

36. Latourette, *A History of Christianity: Vol. 2*, 895.
37. Latourette, *A History of Christianity: Vol. 2*, 895.
38. González, *The Story of Christianity: Vol. 2*, 205.
39. Walker, Norris, Lotz, Handy, *A History of the Christian Church*, 592.
40. González, *The Story of Christianity: Vol. 2*, 208.
41. González, *The Story of Christianity: Vol. 2*, 208.
42. Walker, et. al. *A History of the Christian Church*, 593.
43. Walker, et. al. *A History of the Christian Church*, 594.

SANCTIFICATION

It was in late 1735 through early 1736, that a Moravian contingent of missionaries was sailing to Georgia, in the American colonies, to preach to the Indians. John Wesley was also on board with a similar mission in mind. He too desired to preach to the Indigenous Americans, but it would be in his capacity as a pastor in Savannah. During the crossing, the weather created a quite dangerous situation that put the entire ship in serious trouble. "The mainmast split, and panic would have overwhelmed the crew, had it not been for the unbelievable calm of the Moravians, who sang throughout the ordeal. Meanwhile, Wesley, who was also chaplain of the vessel, came to the bitter realization that he was more concerned about himself than about his fellow travellers."[44] On January 25, 1736, Wesley recorded in his diary.

> *At seven I went to the Germans. I had long before observed the great seriousness of their behaviour. Of their humility, they had given a continual proof, by performing those servile offices for the other passengers, which none of the English would undertake; for which they desired, and would receive no pay, saying, "it was good for their proud hearts," and "their loving Saviour had done more for them." And every day had given them occasion of showing a meekness which no injury could move. If they were pushed, struck, or thrown down, they rose again and went away; but no complaint was found in their mouth. There was now an opportunity of trying whether they were delivered from the Spirit of fear, as well as from that of pride, anger, and revenge. In the midst of the psalm wherewith their service began, the sea broke over, split the main-sail in pieces, covered the ship, and poured in between the decks, as if the great deep had already swallowed us up. A terrible screaming began among the English. The Germans calmly sung on. I asked one of them afterwards, 'Was you not afraid?' He answered, 'I thank God, no.' I asked, 'But were not your women and children afraid?' He replied, mildly, 'No; our women and children are not afraid to die.' From them I went to their crying, trembling neighbours, and pointed out to them the difference in the hour of trial, between him that feareth God, and him that feareth him not. At twelve the wind fell. This was the most glorious day which I have hitherto seen.*[45]

His time in Georgia was not a success. On his return to London Wesley contacted the Moravians and came under the mentorship of Peter Boehler. Convinced that he did not possess saving faith, Wesley, under Boehler's advise, continued to preach until on May 24, 1738, he had an experience that changed his life. In his *Journal*, May 24, 1798, he records:

> *In the evening, I went very unwillingly to a society in Aldersgate Street, where one was reading Luther's preface to The Epistle to the Romans. About a quarter before nine, while He was describing the change which God works in the heart*

---

44. González, *The Story of Christianity: Vol. 2*, 209.
45. Wesley, *Journal, January 25, 1736*.

> *through faith in Christ, I felt my heart strangely warmed. I felt I did trust in Christ, Christ alone for salvation: And an assurance was given me, that he had taken away my sins, even mine, and saved me from the law of sin and death.*[46]

Ellen White's theology of sanctification is clearly a reflection of her Methodist upbringing. Born at Gorham, Main, November 26, 1827 to Robert and Eunice Harmon, Ellen was raised in a household committed to the teaching of the Methodist Episcopal Church. In that church, her parents laboured for the conversion of sinners, and the building of the cause of God, for a period of forty years.[47] As in any Wesleyan theological system, Ellen White's inspired writings contain an abundance of teaching on sanctification far exceeding her contribution to justification by faith. In *The Great Controversy,* she defined Bible sanctification in terms of the followers of Christ becoming like Him—"by the grace of God to form characters in harmony with the principles of His holy law." Importantly, this "work can be accomplished only through faith in Christ, by the power of the indwelling Spirit of God."[48] In the work of sanctification the individual must rely on Christ.[49] However, God's sanctifying work will be accomplished only through constant conflict with self. Indeed, the "struggle for conquest over self, for holiness and heaven, is a lifelong struggle. However, without continual effort and constant activity there can be no advancement in the divine life, no attainment of the victor's crown." To be sure, "Paul's sanctification was a result of a constant conflict with self. He said: 'I die daily.' 1 Corinthians 15:31."[50] It involves the whole person and amounts to fullness of life in Jesus Christ in which the character is perfected. However, she warned against fanaticism; what she refers to as extreme sanctification. In this belief the individual cannot sin, and are ready for translation. In contrast to this pretentious arrogance,[51] Ellen White defined sanctification as continual growth in grace. It is not the work of a moment, an hour, or a day. To be sure, the

> *Christian life is constantly on an upward march. Jesus sits as a refiner and purifier of His people; and when His image is perfectly reflected in them, they are perfect and holy, and prepared for translation. A great work is required of the Christian. We are exhorted to cleanse ourselves from all filthiness of the flesh and spirit, perfecting holiness in the fear of God. Here we see where the great labor rests. There is a constant work for the Christian. Every branch in*

---

46. Wesley, Journal, May 24, 1738.
47. White, *Life Sketches of Ellen White,* 17.
48. White, *Great Controversy,* 469.
49. White, *Testimonies: Vol. 5,* 472.
50. White, "God leads His people on step by step. The Christian life is a battle and a march. In this warfare, there is no release; the effort must be continuous and persevering. It is by unceasing endeavor that we maintain the victory over the temptations of Satan . . . No one will be born upward without stern, persevering effort in his own behalf." *Testimonies Vol. 8,* 313.
51. White, *Life Sketches of Ellen White,* 133–134.

SANCTIFICATION

the parent vine must derive life and strength from that vine, in order to yield fruit.[52]

However, those "who are really seeking to perfect Christian character will never indulge the thought that they are sinless. Their lives may be irreproachable, they may be living representatives of the truth which they have accepted; but the more they discipline their minds to dwell upon the character of Christ, and the nearer they approach to His divine image, the more clearly they will discern its spotless perfection, and the more deeply will they feel their own defects."[53] Indeed, sanctification amounts to a daily conformity to the will of God,[54] and of the daily dying to self.[55] Sanctification seeks harmony with God,[56] which is brought about by way of the implanting of Christ's nature in humanity.[57] Sanctification arises by way of a truth received in the heart and practically carried out in life[58] and working out of the principle of love.[59] Importantly, from the sanctifying work of the Holy Spirit in sanctification comes the fruit of the Spirit, which arises from a high regard for the law of God.[60] In this regard, the keeping of the Sabbath is a sign of God's sanctifying work. Ellen White's conviction was that "the observance of the true Sabbath is to be the sign that distinguishes those who serve God from those who serve Him not."[61] Temperance is also an essential indication of God's sanctifying work in the life of the Christian, since "God requires that His people shall be temperate in all things. Unless they practice temperance, they will not, cannot, be sanctified through the truth."[62] Temperance includes an abstinence from alcohol (Prov. 20:1; Lk 21:34; Eph. 5:18), tobacco and unclean foods (Lev. 11; Isa. 22:12–13). Indeed, the sanctified life seeks for a healthy lifestyle (1 Thess. 4:4; 2 Tim. 1:14; 1 Cor 6:15–20).

Ultimately, Sanctification regards the work of the Holy Spirit, who infuses the life of Christ into the life of a Christian (Gal. 3:27). Sanctification embodies the consequences of repentance. That is, a turning away from sin, seen in a life independent of God, and a turning towards God, seen in a life committed to Jesus Christ and living in His equipping as He dwells in the life of His followers. For this reason, a study of the life of Jesus, His way and His teaching, is essential. Whoever claims to be

---

52. White, *Testimonies: Vol. 1*, 340.
53. White, *The Sanctified Life*, 7.
54. White, *Testimonies: Vol. 4*, 299.
55. White, *Testimonies: Vol. 4*, 299.
56. White, *Testimonies: Vol. 6*, 350.
57. White, *Christ Object Lessons*, 384.
58. White, *Testimonies: Vol. 1*, 339–40.
59. White, *Acts of the Apostles*, 560.
60. White, *Great Controversy*, 478.
61. White, *Testimonies: Vol. 7*, 108.
62. White, *Colporteur Ministry*, 132.

a follower of Jesus must live with the heartfelt desire to possess the kind of faithfulness, holiness and obedience that Jesus had (1 Jn. 2:6).

CHAPTER 20

GLORIFICATION

GLORIFICATION DESCRIBES THE GLORY OF God, as it comes to be found in the believer at the final stage of the Christian journey of transformation. In the New Testament, the word *glory* is a translation of the Greek, *doxa*. The word is found predominately in Paul's letters (Romans, 1 and 2 Corinthians), but is also found in Peter's two letters, John's Gospel, Revelation, and Luke's Gospel. Associated with the ultimate glorification of believers is an anticipatory daily giving glory to God. In the New Testament this is reflected in the exhortation for all Christians "to give God glory" (Luke 17:18; Acts 12:23; Rom. 4:20; Rev. 4:9; 11:13, and to live "to the glory of God" (1 Cor. 10:31). Of importance to our discussion is the assertion that believers share in God's glory (Jn. 7:39; 12:16), since any glorification in the believer is a reflection of the glory of God. More particularly, believers have the hope that ultimately, at the end of all things, they will reflect God's glory completely (Rom. 8:17; 1 Cor. 2:7; 2 Cor. 4:17; Phil. 3:21; 1 Thess, 2:12; Heb. 2:10; 1 Pet. 5:1). Indeed, the Christian is motivated to persevere by the hope of glory (Col. 1:27).[1]

The glory of God is such that it is represented in the believers, in so much as they will be fully and completely glorified. This transformative power is operative among believers (2 Cor. 3:18; Rom 8:30) "through the resurrection of Christ and our fellowship with him, who is 'the first fruits of those who have fallen asleep' (1 Cor. 15:20)."[2] Indeed, glorification is closely linked with sanctification (2 Cor. 3:17-18). The Holy Spirit is vital and essential to the process, enabling believers in Christ "to keep Christ before them and grow up into Him in all things (2 Cor. 3:19; Eph. 4:15). Meanwhile, the Christ who indwells the believer by the Spirit constitutes the hope of glory (Col. 1:27)."[3] Importantly, the hope of glory is a present reality for believers,

---

1. Aalen, *Glory*, 46.
2. Aalen, *Glory*, 48.
3. Harrison, *Glory*, 481.

but is yet to be realised. Indeed, the eschatological goal of glory is a popular theme in the New Testament. This future glory is contrasted with the current travail of the human condition (Rom. 8:18; 2 Cor. 4:17; 1 Pet. 5:10). To be sure, a "mark of the finality of this future blessing is the possession of the resurrection body that is portrayed in terms of glory (1 Cor. 15:43; Phil. 3:21). The reward for faithful service will be the unfading crown of glory (1 Pet. 5:4)."[4] That glorification is the final process in the line of salvation is attested in Scripture. In Mark's Gospel, Jesus refers to this when He promised that an ultimate experience for believers would come gradually, starting with the stalk, developing into the head and then, finally, the full kernel in the head (4:28). Thomas Oden has summed this up well with the assertion that the

> *converting-saving grace of God is often found to work especially in crisis moments or personal reversal, which are then followed by a continuing work of grace that develops over time. We have been saved from the penalty of sin in justification; we are being saved from the power of sin in sanctification; and we shall be saved finally from the presence of sin in glorification.*[5]

Ellen White referred to the glorification of the remnant just before the second advent of Christ. She saw in vision the triumph of the 144,000, whose "faces were lighted up with the glory of God."[6] Their countenances were lighted up with the glory of God; and they shone with the glory, as did the face of Moses when he came from Mount Sinai.[7] Indeed, at Christ's return the living righteous are changed for all eternity. At the voice of God, they will be glorified and made immortal.[8]

---

4. Harrison, *Glory*, 481.
5. Oden, *Like in the Spirit*, 84.
6. White, *Early Writings*, 37.
7. White, *Life Sketches*, 102.
8. White, *Great Controversy*, 645.

Chapter 21

PACIFISM

THE BIBLICAL ORIGINS OF PACIFISM have their roots in the Old Testament, Gospels and Epistles. The sixth commandment, "Thou shalt not kill (Ex. 20:13)", had its place in God's law from the very beginning. In Matthew's Gospel Jesus taught,

> *You have heard that it was said, 'An eye for an eye, and a tooth for a tooth.' But I say to you, do not resist an evil person; but whoever slaps you on your right cheek, turn the other to him also. If anyone wants to sue you and take your shirt, let him have your [b]coat also. Whoever forces you to go one mile, go with him two. Give to him who asks of you, and do not turn away from him who wants to borrow from you.*
>
> *You have heard that it was said, 'YOU SHALL LOVE YOUR NEIGHBOR and hate your enemy.' But I say to you, love your enemies and pray for those who persecute you, so that you may be sons of your Father who is in heaven; for He causes His sun to rise on the evil and the good, and sends rain on the righteous and the unrighteous. For if you love those who love you, what reward do you have? Do not even the tax collectors do the same?* (NASB) (Matthew 5:38–46).

Paul also addressed this issue in his letter to the Romans.

> *Never take your own revenge, beloved, but leave room for the wrath of God, for it is written, "Vengeance is Mine, I will repay," says the Lord. "But if your enemy is hungry, feed him, and if he is thirsty, give him a drink; for in so doing you will heap burning coals on his head." Do not be overcome by evil, but overcome evil with good.* (NASB) (Rom. 12:19–21).

Peter's testimony for non-resistance is expressed when he stated that if, "when ye do well, and suffer for it, ye take it patiently, this is acceptable with God . . . Christ also suffered for us, leaving us an example, that ye should follow his steps . . . when he

FOUNDATIONS OF THEOLOGY

was reviled, reviled not again; when he suffered, he threatened not; but committed himself to him that judgeth righteously (1 Peter 2:20–23)."

The early church supported a pacifistic stance. Athenagoras, a Christian apologist and philosopher from the second century, stated: "We have learned not to return blow for blow, nor to go to law with those who plunder and rob us. Not only that, but to those who strike us on the side of the face, we have learned to offer the other side also."[1] Earlier, Clement of Alexandria stipulated that "Christians are not allowed to use violence to correct the delinquencies of sins."[2] Indeed, in pacifism's favour is its dominance within the early church. Consequently, it stands squarely within the Christian tradition and has a theological and biblical basis solidly grounded in the Gospels and early years of the church. Indeed, "Pacifists appeal to the authority of the Bible, using specific texts such as the Decalogue and the Sermon on the Mount." Furthermore, pacifism "finds support in broader biblical injunctions such as the call to express God's love to all persons or to witness to the presence of the kingdom of God on earth."[3] However, by Constantine the situation had dramatically changed. Under Constantine, who understood the interests of the empire and Christianity as being synonymous, Christian soldiers were common. Indeed, during the reign of Theodosius II (408 A.D—450 A.D.) only Christian's could serve as soldiers.[4]

During the Middle Ages a number of sectarian groups, notably the Waldensians, and also the Hussites under Peter Chelciky, kept alive the pacifist vision. In general, the Reformers adopted the just war theory that had been developed by Augustine centuries earlier. However, the Anabaptists stood out as an exception. Indeed, pacifism "emerged as the dominant position of the Anabaptists, who rejected not only the sword of war but also refused to engage in political life."[5] Contemporary Anabaptists, such as the Mennonites, actively pursue a pacifist agenda. The "Anabaptist Core Convictions" published by the Network Steering Group stated that, "Peace is at the heart of the gospel. As followers of Jesus in a divided and violent world, we are committed to finding non-violent alternatives and to learning how to make peace between individuals, within and among churches, in society, and between nations."[6]

With deep connection with the Anabaptists and Waldensians, Seventh-day Adventism stands in the pacifist tradition. This is clearly evident in Ellen White's exhortation that "God's people . . . cannot engage in this perplexing war, for it is opposed to every principle of their faith. In the army, they cannot obey the truth and at the same time obey the requirements of their officers."[7] Indeed, the impetus to form

1. Bercot, *A Dictionary of Early Christian Beliefs*, 474.
2. Bercot, *A Dictionary of Early Christian Beliefs*, 474.
3. Weaver, *Pacifism*, 813.
4. Weaver, *Pacifism*, 815.
5. Weaver, *Pacifism*, 814.
6. *Anabaptism Today*, 30 (Summer 2002), 33.
7. White, *Testimonies for the Church: Vol. 1*, 357–361.

PACIFISM

the Seventh-day Adventist Church as a distinct denomination arose from a need for organisation. Only an organised entity could form representation for its members during the American Civil War. Prior to this representation individual Seventh-day Adventists needed to pay reparation for being conscientious objectors. However, the new organised church changed all that. The church was able to gain the same rights as Quakers and Mennonites. Indeed, "skilful lobbying of the government allowed for the church to attain conscientious objection status."[8] Many early Adventists were influenced by the New England Christian non-resistance movement led by the abolitionist, William Lloyd Garrison. "They regarded scripturally grounded pacifism as part of that radical faith that set them apart from the large majority of Americans. Christian non-resistance had been espoused by the Millerite Adventist reformer Joshua V. Himes, as well as William Miller himself."[9] As a consequence of the church's stance, "John N. Andrews was authorized by the General Conference Committee to go to Washington and seek governmental recognition for the non-combatant position held by Seventh-day Adventists."[10]

> *Andrews' petition, presented to James B. Fry, the Provost Marshal General, described Seventh-day Adventists as "a people unanimously loyal and antislavery, who because of their views of the ten commandments and of the teaching of the New Testament cannot engage in bloodshed." General Fry responded favorably to the petition, and issued an exemption that gave Adventists the option of either accepting assignment to hospital duty or care of freedmen or paying the $300 communication fee.*[11]

Ultimately, the Seventh-day day Adventist Church "made formal its commitment to pacifism in a resolution voted by the General Conference session of 1865."[12]

In the modern era, Kauffmann, et.al, has pointed out that when "Christ sent out His Disciples He did not arm them with swords and spears and other instruments of destruction, but He sent them forth 'as sheep in the midst of wolves' (Matt.10:16). They went forth, did a mighty work, even the devils being subject to them."[13] Further,

> *John Howard Yoder emphasizes in his significant writings on pacifism that the cross has made a difference. Christ has come into the world to redeem all people and has acted for the sake of every person on the globe. We cannot kill a person for whom he died and rob him or her of the privilege of knowing the fullness of*

---

8. Chung, *Rise of the Remnant: The Formation of the Seventh-day Adventist Church from the Era of Slavery and the Civil War*, California State University, Fullerton, ProQuest Dissertations Publishing, 2005.
9. Morgan, *Following the Prince of Peace in a Time of War*, Adventist Review, June 12, 2007.
10. Morgan, *Following the Prince of Peace in a Time of War*.
11. Morgan, *Following the Prince of Peace in a Time of War*.
12. Morgan, *Following the Prince of Peace in a Time of War*.
13. Kaffman, *Doctrines of the Bible: A Brief Discussion of the Teaching of God's Word*, 510.

life that Jesus Christ offers. This calls us to express a pacifist position not by a negative but a positive stance. Ours is to be an active penetration into society with the redeeming love of God. Above everything else, we want our fellow men to become our brothers in Christ. When Jesus stated that the first commandment is to love God and that the second is just like it (to love your neighbor as yourself), he was asking that we bring to bear on the life of our neighbor that which we find most important in our own relationship with God.[14]

Therefore, when a Christian engages in war, he or she is abdicating their responsibility from the higher calling to live and give witness to the Gospel of Jesus Christ.

---

14. Augsburger, *Christian Pacifism*, in *Intervarsity,* May, 07, 2004.

CHAPTER 22

THE CHURCH

It is the Greek, *ekklesia*, that has been translated as assembly, meeting, congregation, or church. In classical literature, the word *ekklesia* was used for summoning the assembly to gather, from *kaleo*—to call. Members of a city, or polis, would assemble to make important decisions, suggest changes in the law and debate other important matters. An ekklesia, therefore, would have a particular purpose. Therefore, when Paul referred to the Christian church, he had in mind an assembly of people that have been called for the purpose to live in Christ together and proclaim Jesus Christ as saviour and lord. The criteria for calling into the church is repentance and faith. It is those who individually have been saved through faith that are gathered to constitute the church together (Rom 8:29f). For this reason, Paul can speak of the *kletoi*, the called, when he means the Christian community (e.g. Rom 1:6f; 1 Cor. 1:2).[1] Indeed, God calls a people through faith in Christ to live as His community on earth, proclaiming His Gospel and living as witnesses to the transforming holiness of God. To be sure, it is in the gathering of a people in relationship with one another that God's life in His people is most readily manifested.

In the Old Testament, two Hebrew nouns are used to describe the Israelite assembly: *qahal* and *edah*. Modern scholars have sought to differentiate the meanings of these two Hebrew words, but there seems to be no unambiguous consensus. George Johnston seemed to hold that *edah* referred to the congregation as an "organic unity", whereas *qahal* referred to it as assembled. For Robert Kicklighter, Jr., *qahal* referred to "the people of Israel, either as gathered in assembly or as constituting an organized community," and *edah* to "the whole congregation of Israel, assembled or unassembled, the society itself." However, whichever interpretation is preferred, there appears to be a biblical differentiation between the complete people

---

1. Coenen, *Church,* 298.

of God, and the people of God gathered in assembly for worship or as an organized community.

In the Greek "Septuagint" the noun *ekklesia* is used 96 times. Usually it is a translation of *qahal*, which is used 120 times in the Old Testament. *Ekklesia* is never used to translate *edah*. The usual translation for *edah* is synagogue, and synagogue is sometimes the translation of *qahal*. In the New Testament the single word, *ekklesia*, gives clarity to the concept of the church not found in the Old Testament. Indeed, the concept of the church in the New Testament is "expressed chiefly by the uses of the Greek noun *ekklesia* as its identifying term."[2] Therefore, in the New Testament, it is the gathered and organized assembly which is seen to be, unambiguously, the true people of God. Each gathering is the full and complete church.

In the New Testament, a number of metaphors are used to describe the people of God. The church as a living, organic organized and interrelated entity is evident in the metaphor of a body. The Apostle Paul in his first letter to the Corinthians, and in his letter to the Ephesians, referred to "the one body" (1 Cor. 12:13; Eph. 2:16; 4:4), and "the body of Christ" (1 Cor. 12:27; Eph. 4:12). To the Romans he sought to emphasize that there is only "one body in Christ" (Rom 12:5), which elsewhere he refers to as "his body"; that is, a church that belongs to Christ (Eph. 1:23; 5:23, 30; Col. 1:24). Therefore, the body of Christ was closely associated with its "members" (1 Cor. 12:12, 27; Rom 12:5; Eph. 5:30), which has Christ as its head (Eph. 1:22; 5:23; Col. 1:18a). The implications for this are quite clear. The church can never understand itself to be autonomous and self-directing, but always under the authority of Jesus Christ who reveals Himself in His Word. Further, the church is a community of inter-relationships, in which its people are bound by their common life in Christ, existing as a single entity and exercising their powers, given by the Spirit as He wills, for the common good.

The New Testament also describes the church as the People of God. Peter, appropriating language from Exod. 19:5, identified Christians as "a people belonging to God" ... "Once" they "were not a people, but now" they "are the people of God" (*laos theou*) (1 Pet. 2:9a, 10a). The New Testament church is also described as the Light of the World, Sons of Light, and illuminators in the World. These closely related usages focus on Christians as being collectively *light*. Jesus' disciples, as citizens of the kingdom of God, are to shine as a light placed on a lamp stand so that because of their good works other human beings may glorify God the Father (Matt 5:14–16). In the parable of the crafty steward "the sons of the world" are said to be "more shrewd in dealing with their own generation than the sons of light" (Luke 16:8, RSV). The "children of God" are to "shine like stars in a dark world" (NEB) amid "a crooked and perverse generation" (Phil. 2:15, RSV).

---

2. Garrett, *Systematic Theology: Biblical, Historical, and Evangelical*, 458–9.

The church's intimate relationship with Christ is depicted in the image of the church being the Bride of Christ in 2 Cor. 11:2. "For I am jealous over you with godly jealousy: for I have espoused you to one husband, that I may present you as a chaste virgin to Christ." Revelation utilizes this theme to describe the final state of God's people. "And I John saw the holy city, new Jerusalem, coming down from God out of heaven, prepared as a bride adorned for her husband (21:2)."

THE CHURCH AND THE KINGDOM OF GOD

In the New Testament, the word *basileia* is usually translated as "kingdom". It signifies the "being", "nature" and "state" of the king. Consequently, one speaks of the king's "dignity" or "power". It amounts to the rule of God, either over a literal and physical kingdom, or in the lives of His people. The New Testament points to the rule of Christ in the lives of all those who have confessed their faith in Jesus Christ. This is essential to salvation; since Christ must not only be our saviour but also our lord. The object of God's rule is the redemption of people and their deliverance from the powers of evil. (1 Cor. 15:23–28). Indeed, the

> *kingdom of God is the redemptive rule of God in Christ defeating Satan and the powers of evil and delivering (people) from the sway of evil . . . Entrance into the kingdom of Christ means deliverance from the power of darkness (Col. 1:13) and is accomplished by the new birth (John 3:3,5).*[3]

Therefore, Christ drew His listeners to the coming reality of the Kingdom of God, but also to the need to submit to the rule of God in the here and now.

The future reality of a coming kingdom is recorded in Luke 21:31. "So likewise ye, when ye see these things come to pass, know ye that the kingdom of God is nigh at hand." However, the present reality of the kingdom was also taught by Jesus. Once, having been asked by the Pharisees when the kingdom of God would come, Jesus replied, "The Kingdom of God does not come with your careful observation, nor will people say, 'Here it is,' or 'There it is,' because the kingdom of God is within you." (Lk. 17:21) In the early church Tertullian (c. 207) pointed to the reality of the Kingdom evident in the commandment keeping people of God. "He says, 'The kingdom of God comes not with observation. Neither do they say, Look here! Or, look there! For, behold, the kingdom of God is within you.' Now, who will not interpret these words "within you" to mean in your hand, within your power? That is, if you hear and do the commandment of God."[4] However, James Leo Garrett has noted that the

> *kingdom of God was not a prominent theme for the Church Fathers, but when mentioned in the pre-Constantinian age, it tended to be associated with the*

---

3. Ladd, *Kingdom of Christ, God, Heaven*, 608.
4. Bercot, *A Dictionary of Early Christian Beliefs*, 387.

> *future millennial reign. Irenaeus used the term 'the times of the kingdom' as a synonym for the millennium, and Tertullian wrote both of 'a kingdom promised to us upon the earth, although before heaven, only in another state of existence' and of removal to 'that kingdom of heaven'. On the other hand, for Augustine of Hippo the 'present' or 'militant' kingdom of God is to be identified with 'the Church'.*[5]

In the same way, during the time of the Protestant Reformation, the kingdom of God was not a major theme. Nevertheless,

> *Martin Bucer produced a major treatise, On the Kingdom of Christ (1550), addressed to the young king of England, Edward VI, for the purpose of advising him how to introduce the Protestant Reformation in England: The Kingdom of our Savior Jesus Christ is that administration and care of the eternal life of God's elect, by which this very Lord and King of heaven by his doctrine and discipline, administered by suitable ministers chosen for this very purpose, gathers to himself his elect, those dispersed throughout the world who are his but whom he nonetheless will to be subject to the powers of the world. He incorporated them into himself and his Church and so governs them in it that purged more fully day by day from sins, they live well and happily both here and in the time to come. Martin Bucer's (1491–1551) doctrine of the kingdom was not essentially eschatological. He assumed that the kingdom is presently realized but did not connect the kingdom directly to the public ministry of Jesus. In his view both the church and civil government are instruments of the kingdom; they differ as to means employed but not as to ultimate purpose.*[6]

Martin Luther, however, reflected on a dual understanding of the kingdom when he depicts it as being a real coming reality, but also that which may dwell in the heart. "The kingdom of God comes indeed of itself, without our prayer; but we pray in this petition that it may come also to us . . . When our heavenly Father gives us his Holy Spirit, so that by his grace we believe his holy Word, and live a godly life here in time, and hereafter in eternity."[7]

Stanley Grenz believed that "the major source for the Christian conception of the divine kingdom lies in the teaching of Jesus himself . . . In fact, according to Mark, Jesus' message centred around the proclamation of God's rule (Mk 1:15)." Jesus sometimes suggested that the kingdom is a present reality (Luke 17:20), present because the prophetic time is fulfilled. "Now after that John was put in prison, Jesus came into Galilee, preaching the gospel of the kingdom of God, and saying, the time is fulfilled, and the kingdom of God is at hand: repent ye, and believe the gospel (Mk 1:14–15)."

---

5. Garrett. *Systematic Theology: Biblical, Historical, and Evangelical: Vol. 2*, 733–34.
6. Garrett. *Systematic Theology: Vol. 2*, 733–34.
7. Weber, *Foundations of Dogmatics: Vol. 2*, 679.

Grenz further stipulated that

> (b)ecause God created everything, God possesses the right to rule over all creation. Consequently, the entire universe is the kingdom of God or the realm of God's dominion de jure. In principle, the entire universe constitutes the realm over which God exercises kingship. According to the biblical drama, however, what is true de jure is not yet fully true de facto. God has given humans the privilege and responsibility of acknowledging his rule. In our sin, however, we have rejected the kingship of the Creator. Thereby we have erected an enclave of rebellion in which another –Satan—appears to reign.

Therefore, one can assert that the kingdom of God is both present and future, both of which encompass living under the will of God (Matt. 6:10; 7:21–23), as a consequence of a radical decision (Matt. 13:44–46) to enter into "the already inaugurated explosion of God's power in the world."[8] The reality of experiencing this kingdom is temporarily marred by sin, yet the coming of Christ will see the end of all that inhibits the full manifestation of the rule of God. What is known in part now, will then be known fully (1 Cor. 13:9).

James Leo Garrett believed that the "importance of the kingdom of God for both testaments can hardly be overstated. It is a 'theme' that is 'central not only to the faith of Israel but also to the Gospel." In regard to the Old Testament, Garrett spoke of a "representative kingdom". 'Yahweh's kingdom was represented in and through Saul and his successors in the Israelite monarchy. Resistance to representative kingship during the era of the judges was evidenced by Gideon's declaration of reluctance. Gideon said to them, 'I will not rule over you, and my son will not rule over you; the Lord will rule over you.' (Jdgs. 8:23) (NRSV)

> The representative kingship was extended by the revelation through Nathan the prophet that Yahweh would establish forever the kingdom of David's offspring (2Sam. 7:11b-16; also 1 Chr. 17:10b-14). Solomon, that offspring, if obedient to Yahweh, would "sit on the throne of the kingdom of the Lord over Israel" "forever" (1 Chr. 28:5,7) (NASV). Seemingly it was this type of representative kingship about which Jesus' disciples inquired after his resurrection and prior to his ascension (Acts 1:6).[9]

There are different approaches that have been taken in regard to how the church, or churches, ought to be related to the kingdom of God. For some, what we see as the church can be equated with the kingdom of God. "This interpretation has assumed various forms . . . Emil Brunner of the Reformed tradition and William Robinson, of the Disciples heritage, have also equated church and kingdom in a manner similar to the seventeenth-century English confessions." By contrast Dale

---

8. Grenz, *Theology for the Community of God*, 472–476.
9. Garrett, *Systematic Theology: Biblical, Historical, and Evangelical: Vol. 2*, 726–729.

FOUNDATIONS OF THEOLOGY

Moody, a Baptist Arminian and Pre-millenialist, gives more weight to the future reality of the kingdom: "Although the kingdom of God is present in a hidden way known only to faith, the evidence for the visible realization of God's kingdom in the future seems overwhelming. The kingdom of God is near, but it is not already here in the sense anticipated by the writers of the Old Testament and the New."[10] The signs of the kingdom point to Zion's future glory, now seen in the fulfilment of prophecy, manifestations of healing and the conversion of sinners to repentance.[11]

Moody found support for his theology in the Gospels.

> *The Christology of John's Gospel [for example] is dominated by the signs and sayings related to the glory of God. Men must here and now be 'born from above' if they expect to 'see the kingdom of God' and 'to enter the kingdom of God' when it comes (John 3:3, 5). The kingdom of Christ does not belong to this world (kosmos, John 18:36), yet glimpses of His glory are seen in all His miraculous signs. This may well be designated the theme of John: And the Word became flesh and dwelt among us, full of grace and truth; we have beheld his glory, glory as of the only Son from the Father (1:14).*[12]

Otto Weber, Professor of Reformed Theology at the University of Gottingen until his death in 1966, believed that the notion of the kingdom of God is at the center of eschatology. "The Kingdom of God stands at the center of all Christian expectation and it comprehends everything which must be said about it in detail. (Rom. 14:17; 1 Cor. 4:20; 6:9f; 15:50; Col. 4:11; Eph. 5:5; 1 Thess. 2:12; 2 Thess. 1:5; Col. 1:13; 2 Tim. 4:18; Rev. 11:15; 12:10ff)." Weber sought to emphasize the glory of God rather than the new status of the community and its individuals. For Weber, it was not so much what Christians gain that should be their focus, but the glory of God, who will be seen to be just and faithful.[13]

According to Ellen White, the kingdom of God is an everlasting kingdom that "shall stand forever."[14] Importantly, however, Ellen White emphasised the characteristics of the kingdom in the life of Christians. This is evident when she wrote that the

> *works of Christ not only declared Him to be the Messiah, but showed in what manner His kingdom was to be established. To John was opened the same truth that had come to Elijah in the desert, when 'a great and strong wind rent the mountains, and brake in pieces the rocks before the Lord; but the Lord was not in the wind: and after the wind an earthquake; but the Lord was not in the earthquake: and after the earthquake a fire; but the Lord was not in the*

---

10. Moody, *The Word of Truth: A Summary of Christian Doctrine Based on Biblical Revelation*, 518.
11. Moody, *The Word of Truth*, 518.
12. Moody, *The Word of Truth*, 518–520.
13. Weber, *Foundations of Dogmatics: Vol. 2*, 675–6.
14. White, *The Kingdom of God*, 5.2.

fire:' and after the fire, God spoke to the prophet by a still, small voice (1 Kings 19:11-12). So, Jesus was to do His work, not by the overturning of thrones and kingdoms, not with pomp and outward display, but through speaking to the hearts of men by a life of mercy and self-sacrifice.[15]

Further to this, Ellen White contended that the "kingdom of God comes not with outward show. It comes through the gentleness of the inspiration of His word, through the inward working of His Spirit, the fellowship of the soul with Him who is its life. The greatest manifestation of its power is seen in human nature brought to the perfection of the character of Christ."[16] The apparent tension between the kingdom that is yet to come and that which already dwells in the hearts of believers, is resolved by her use of the terms "kingdom of grace" and "kingdom of glory". The kingdom of grace already resides among the people of God, yet they wait for the coming kingdom of glory.[17]

THE MARKS (OR NOTES) OF THE CHURCH

Over the years a number of opinions have been given in regard to the number and nature of the marks of the church. Lois Berkhof pointed out that "Reformed theologians differed as to the number of the marks of the Church. Some spoke of one, the preaching of the pure doctrine of the Gospel [such as Beza]; others, of two, the pure preaching of the word and the right administration of the sacraments [Calvin, Bullinger] and still others added to these a third, the faithful exercise of discipline."[18] Alister McGrath contended that a

> *central theme of ecclesiology relates to the four 'notes' or 'marks' of the church— that is to say, the four defining characteristics of the Christian church, as stated in the creeds of Christendom. These creeds affirm belief in 'one holy catholic and apostolic church.' The four adjectives included in this phrase – 'one,' 'holy', 'catholic' and 'apostolic'—have come to be known as the 'notes' or 'marks' of the church, and have been of importance to ecclesiological discussion since the fourth century.*[19]

"One" -The unity of the church is vitally important. Two episodes in church history are especially important to this topic:

> *The first relates to North Africa in the third century, when division within the church became a potentially destructive issue. The Decian persecution (250-1)*

---

15. White, *Ministry of Healing*, 36.1.
16. White, *Ministry of Healing*, 36.2.
17. Donkor, in *The Ellen White Encyclopedia*, 919.
18. Berkhof, *Systematic Theology*, 576.
19. McGrath, *Christian Theology: An Introduction*, 417.

> led to many Christians lapsing or abandoning their faith in the face of persecution. Division arose immediately over how these individuals should be treated: Did such a lapse mark the end of their faith, or could they be reconciled to the church by penance? Opinions differed sharply, and serious disagreement and tension resulted . . . In his "On the Unity of the Catholic Church (251)", written in direct response to the crisis . . . Cyprian of Carthage insisted upon the absolute unity of the church, comparing it to the 'seamless robe of Christ', which could not be divided because it had been woven from the top throughout . . . Cyprian concluded that there was no salvation outside the one true church. This resulted in the Catholic church proclaiming itself as the dispenser of salvation. This is, through the sacramental life of the church salvation was assured. Therefore, to leave the church, or be excommunicated from it, was to lose salvation. However, the sixteenth-century Reformation also witnessed controversy over this issue. How, it was asked, could the reformers justify forming breakaway churches, and thus compromising the unity of the church?

In response, the Reformers argued that the medieval church had become so corrupted that it could no longer be regarded as a church.[20]

According to John Banks, unity must be outward and visible, having its grounding in the Word. Church unity, the church as "one", is spoken about in the Lord's priestly, or great, prayer of John 17.[21] "Neither pray I for these alone, but for them also which shall believe in me through their word. (John 17:20)." In regard to this passage, George Beasley-Murray wrote: "By contrast (to the unity of the Qumran Community) the unity of Christian believers, for which this prayer is made, is more radical and fundamental: it is rooted in the being of God, revealed in Christ, and in the redemptive action of God in Christ. The prayer 'that they may be one' accordingly is defined as 'that they may be in us.'"[22]

Thomas Oden pointed to a number of biblical passages that refer to Christ's founding of one church. (John 10:16; 21:15; Heb. 3:6; 10:21; Eph. 5:27; Rom. 12:4,5). "In ascribing unity to the church, we mean that all the members of the church constitute one body, having one head, one origin, one faith, one baptism. They are united by their bond to the one living Lord (Eph. 4:2–15; 1 Cor. 1:10; Gal 1:6–8)" . . .)" Oden contended that the

> principle texts on unity of the church are from Paul: 'Make every effort to keep the unity of the Spirit through the bond of peace. There is one body and one Spirit—just as you were called to one hope when you were called—one Lord, one faith, one baptism; one God and Father of all' (Eph. 4:3,4). 'From him the whole body, joined and held together by every supporting ligament, grows and builds itself up in love, as each part does its work' (Eph. 4:16). 'Because there is

20. McGrath, *Christian Theology: An Introduction*, 418–19.
21. Banks, *A Manuel of Christian Doctrine*, 234.
22. Beasley-Murray, *John: 36 Word Biblical Commentary*, 302.

one loaf, we, who are many, are one body, for we all partake of the one loaf' (1 Cor. 10:17)." To be sure, the "New Testament does not hesitate to speak of the churches in the plural form (1 Cor. 16:19; Gal. 1:2; 1 Thess. 2:14; Rev. 1:11), all local churches are extensions and expressions of the one body unified in its head Jesus Christ and enlivened by the indwelling Spirit.

Indeed, the "Spirit sustains the unity of the church by enjoying and enabling centered variety, not uniformity, and by seeking and praying for reconciliation."[23] Donald Bloesch stated: "There can be only one true church—that which was founded by the Lord Jesus Christ and made viable and visible by the outpouring of the Holy Spirit." He also stipulated that the "unity of the church is to be found not in its rights or creeds but in its obedience to Jesus Christ, its one head and Lord." Bloesch also quotes P.T. Forsyth, who "contended that the unity of the church lies 'not in itself but in its message, in the unity of the Gospel that made the Church.'"[24]

In regard to church unity, Ellen White wrote that

God is leading out a people to stand in perfect unity upon the platform of eternal truth. Christ gave Himself to the world, 'that He might purify unto Himself a peculiar people, zealous of good works.' This refining process is designed to purge the church from all unrighteousness and the spirit of discord and contention, that they may build up instead of tearing down, and concentrate their energies on the great work before them. God designs that His people should all come into the unity of faith . . . . [25]

"Holy"—"As the body of Christ, the church is necessarily holy, yet its holiness is enmeshed in continuing human imperfection and finitude until the end of history." Christ "loved the church and gave himself up for her to make her holy, cleansing her by the washing with water through the word, and to present her to himself as a radiant church, without stain or wrinkle or any other kind of blemish, but holy and blameless.' (Eph. 5:25f)."

Oden asked,

What makes the church holy?" "The church is holy because her Lord is holy (1 Cor. 1:30), and her task is to fashion her members after her Lord . . . the church is holy because she is sanctified by Christ through his passion, teaching, prayer, and sacraments . . . Seventeenth-century Lutheran John Gerhard reasoned textually about the church's holiness in this way: "The Church is said to be holy, from 1 Cor. 14:33; Rev. 11:2, because Christ its Head is holy, Heb. 7:26, who makes the Church partaker of His holiness, John 17:19; because it is called by a holy calling and separated from the world, 2 Tim. 1:9; because the Word of God, committed to it, is holy, Rom. 3:2, because the Holy Ghost in this

---

23. Oden, *Life in the Spirit: Systematic Theology: Vol. 3*, 304–308.
24. Bloesch, *The Church*, 100.
25. White, *Manuscript Releases*, 311, 9.3; 10.2.

> *assembly sanctifies believers by applying to them, through faith, Christ's holiness . . . awakening in them the desire of perfect holiness.*[26]

Otto Weber's contention was that the church is holy by virtue of being sanctified. The church is "sanctified" by what it receives: The Word (John 15:3; Eph. 5:26, baptism (Eph. 5:26), the Lord's Supper (1 Cor. 11:27ff), the gift of the Spirit, the self-giving of Jesus Christ (1 Cor. 1:30).

Furthermore, the church can only be "regarded as legitimate for the faith that responds to its proclamation, and that faith is not directed toward it but to Jesus Christ."[27]

Bloesch stipulated that the

> *church is holy because it is marked off from the world by the interior illumination and cleansing work of the Holy Spirit. Its holiness is anchored in its Lord." "Luther considered the church holy 'even where fantastical spirits do reign, if only they deny not Word and Sacraments. For where these are denied, there cannot be the Church.' Calvin perceived holiness as a dynamic interplay between Christ and his people, who are led by his Spirit toward a deeper measure of holiness. 'The church is holy . . . in the sense that it is daily advancing and is not yet perfect: it makes progress from day to day but has not reached its goal of holiness.'*[28]

"Universal"—The term 'universal' comes from the Greek phrase *kath' holou* ('referring to the whole'). In general, Greek words adapted into Latin. Therefore, universal came to be spoken of in the Latin, *catholicus*. The sense of the word is retained in the English phrase "catholic taste", meaning "wide-ranging taste".

McGrath has pointed out that the term "catholic", as applied to the church, went through three stages of meaning. The universal and all-embracing church, which underlies and undergirds individual local churches. [It pointed] to the fact that a local church was the representative of the universal church. There is a connection here between unity and catholicity. That is, unity in the church which is orthodox in its theology. The term is now strongly prescriptive and polemical. "Catholicism" is now contrasted with "schism" and "heresy". A church which extends throughout the world. Therefore, today, the term possesses a geographical concept originally absent.[29]

Otto Weber has contended that while the

> *catholicity of the Community is not expressed in the New Testament with that term . . . it is clearly intended in Ephesians 1:23 and . . . Matthew 28:19. The*

---

26. Oden, *Life in the Spirit: Systematic Theology: Vol. 3*, 316.
27. Weber, *Foundations of Dogmatics: Vol. 2*, 513.
28. Bloesch, *The Church*, 101.
29. McGrath, *Christian Theology: An Introduction*, 424–25.

first expression of it is found in the fact that the Church as the Community of Jesus Christ is always 'ecumenical'. This has a twofold meaning. First of all, it refers to the crossing over of the boundaries set up in the various ecclesiastical traditions... Then it refers to the crossing over of national and social boundaries—universality as the internationality of the Church.[30]

Weber observed that in regard to the second, some Protestant groups have had difficulty.[31] Yet, the true catholicity of the church is ultimately found in God's remnant church who "keep the commandments of God and have the testimony of Jesus (Rev. 12:17)." While the people of God might be found throughout different religious bodies at present, these will "come out of Babylon (Rev. 18:4)" and embrace the truth of the Advent Message. Therefore, at the end, God's Sabbath keeping people will go through to the end with the Three Angels Message. As Gerhard Pfandl has described it,

As Adventists we proclaim the Ten Commandments, including the Sabbath; and we believe that as a church we have the testimony of Jesus, that is, that God manifested Himself in the life and work of Ellen G. White. Thus, the Seventh-day Adventist Church is a church prophetically foreseen, not just one church among many. God has called this church into existence for a very specific purpose: to proclaim the Three Angels' Messages (Rev 14:6–13).[32]

Ellen White described it well when she wrote that,

to come out of Babylon is to be converted to the true scriptural doctrine of the personal coming and kingdom of Christ; to receive the truth on this subject with all readiness of mind, as you find it plainly written out on the pages of the Bible: to love Christ's appearing, and rejoice in it, and fully and faithfully to avow to the world your unshrinking belief in God's word touching this momentous subject, and to do all in your power to open the eyes of others, and influence them to a similar course, that they may be ready to meet their Lord.[33]

"Apostolic"—The basic sense of this term refers to "originating with the Apostles" or "having a direct link with the Apostles". McGrath has noted that "(i)t is a reminder that the church is founded on the apostolic witness and testimony." The assertion that the church is apostolic affirms the "continuity between the church and Christ through the Apostles whom he appointed, and the continuing evangelistic and missionary tasks of the church."[34] Oden averred that the "church is apostolic insofar as it retains, guards, and faithfully transmits its apostolic mission. Those sent

---

30. Weber, *Foundations of Dogmatics: Vol. 2*, 563.
31. Weber, *Foundations of Dogmatics: Vol. 2*, 563.
32. Pfandl, *The Remnant Church*, 224.
33. White, *The Second Advent of Christ*, 2.
34. McGrath, *Christian Theology: An Introduction*, 426.

by the Son are the apostolate. As Christ was sent by the Father, the apostles were sent, empowered by the Spirit, and the continuing apostolate is still being sent." Indeed, "said Jesus to them again, peace be unto you: as my Father hath sent me, even so send I you." (John 20:21).

> The church does not merely have but is a mission, the historical embodiment of the mission of the Son through the Spirit. The church does not elicit mission, but rather mission elicits, awakens, and empowers the church. [The great mission of God] embraces all that the church is and does in its life in the world. This called out community has a key role to play in the emerging reign of God (Matt 13; 2 Tim 1:1–14; Heb. 12:22–28).

Furthermore, Oden claimed that "Apostolicity remains a defining mark of the church or each generation." This entails the faithful proclamation of the Word.[35]

THE MISSION OF THE CHURCH

In Matthew 28:18—20,

> Jesus came and spake unto them, saying, all power is given unto me in heaven and in earth. Go ye therefore, and teach all nations, baptizing them in the name of the Father, and of the Son, and of the Holy Ghost: Teaching them to observe all things whatsoever I have commanded you: and, lo, I am with you always, even unto the end of the world. Amen.

The basis of the commission is the authority of Jesus who has power to send and equip with power. The emphasis, therefore, is not in the going, but the authority and power of Jesus, who works through disciples to teach and baptise. The consequent vision of this passage, therefore, is an observant life based on the teaching and example of Jesus Christ. The commission contains one finite verb in the imperative, "make disciples".[36] The imperative is used to express various kinds of commands. It is also an action, which may come about by an exercise of the will.[37] It can therefore be concluded that Christians, gathered together in the power of Jesus Christ to proclaim Him, and live in and for Him, are to be actively endeavouring to make disciples. The emphasis is on the living Jesus Christ in the lives of His people, transforming them and then, through them, carrying the witness and message which leads to God transforming others.

---

35. Oden, *Life in the Spirit: Systematic Theology: Vol. 3*, 349–52.
36. Garrett, Systematic *Theology: Biblical, Historical, and Evangelical, Vol. 2*, 490.
37. Brooks, Winbery, *Syntax of New Testament Greek*, 114.

CHAPTER 23

THE HISTORY OF THE CHURCH AND ITS THEOLOGICAL DEVELOPMENT

THE EARLY CHURCH

THE EARLY CHURCH WAS HIGHLY aware of the importance of the message that it bore, but equally aware of the power it had been granted to it to deliver the message. Theirs was not a battle of words only, but of powers and principalities. Justin Martyr (c 160) clearly described the evangelistic impulse of the early Christians. Mission was a task that embodied the nature of the church. They had a message that was not only contained in inspired words, but also embodied in their transformed lives. Therefore, they were aware of the importance of their mission, the message they were entrusted with and the means for fulfilling their commission. Justin wrote: "From Jerusalem, twelve men went out into the world. These were uneducated and of no ability in speaking. But by the power of God, they proclaimed to every race of men that they were sent by Christ to teach the Word of God to everyone."[1] Indeed, they were sent by Christ with a message and a task to teach the Word of God and to baptize. They did so by God's grace, with the promise of His presence and with his equipping. Therefore, it was expected of new converts that they would not only know Christ in an intimate and transformative way, but that their lives would be changed in such a way as to result in obedience to the commandments. This is possible due to the transformative work of the Holy Spirit in the lives of the Christian community.

> *And Jesus came and spoke to them, saying, 'All authority has been given to Me in heaven and on earth. Go therefore and make disciples of all the nations,*

---

1. Hill, *Journal of the Evangelical Theological Society*, 101–19.

> *baptizing them in the name of the Father and of the Son and of the Holy Spirit, teaching them to observe all things that I have commanded you; and lo, I am with you always, even to the end of the age.' Amen* (Matthew 28:18–20).

Irenaeus was also highly aware of the church's dependency on the gracious work of the Holy Spirit with and through them, and of the importance of proclaiming the message that they had been entrusted with. He wrote in

c.180: "After our Lord rose from the dead, the apostles were empowered from on high when the Holy Spirit came down. They were completely filled and had perfect knowledge. They departed to the ends of the earth, preaching with glad tidings of the good things sent from God to us."[2] Irenaeus recognized the essentiality of the empowering of the Holy Spirit. He saw the result as an infilling, leading to a perfect (mature) knowledge of the Word. Having been equipped by the Spirit, and with maturity, they went out and proclaimed. Similarly, Augustine avouched that the Christian community had an obligation to bring people to Christ and build them up in their faith. He also averred that Christians should

> *infuse the secular order with Christian values so that the heads of state might give indirect support to the church in its heavenly mission. He concluded that the pagan states had been ruined because of the worship of false gods and that idolatry contains the seeds of social anarchy. The mission of the church is to instil true piety, which is the genuine worship of the true God and which is also the foundation for personal and social righteousness. Without justice, he believed, there can be no society, but without piety there can be no justice.*[3]

The Patristics had a clear understanding of the nature of the church as being one, holy, universal and apostolic. The doctrinal unity of the church was seen as essential as contrasts were established between truth and error. Importantly, the doctrinal correctness of the church was contrasted with the Gnostics. For this reason, heresy and schism were closely aligned, since both violated the unity of the church.[4] However, this unity came at a cost. The divergence of the church from its Gospel foundations soon became evident when unity was assigned to the authority of the bishop and the authority of the church's tradition.[5] It was Cyprian, in the second century, in his *Unity of the Church*, who gave primacy to Peter as the prerequisite for unity among the bishops, and therefore the church.[6] Indeed, for Cyprian, there was no salvation outside the church. To be sure, the elevation of the church as an institution resulted in it being understood as the "means of grace". For this reason, the church and its sacraments became synonymous. In Origen's (185–232)

---

2. Bercot, *Dictionary of Early Christian Beliefs*, 260.
3. Bloesch. *Essential of Evangelical Theology: Vol. 2*, 158.
4. Pelikan, *The Christian Tradition: Vol. 1*, 159.
5. Latourette, *A History of Christianity: Vol. 1*, 132.
6. Pelikan, *The Christian Tradition: Vol. 1*, 159.

teaching, for example, the Eucharist was "a certain holy body which sanctifies those who partake of it with a pure intention."[7] Therefore, the catholicity of the church had more to do with control than universality. To be sure, it emerged in response to the threat of heresy, but the result was far from the biblical model. As Kenneth Scott Latourette contended, the "popularity of Gnosticism, the teaching of Marcion, and the Montanist movement forced others who regarded themselves as Christians to develop a tighter organization and to give added attention to the clarification and formulation of their beliefs."[8]

While the initial intentions were to preserve the purity of the Gospel, the result was a church concerned with itself, and especially its power. Consequently, what finally emerged was not a unified body of believers, but a unified organization. Those who were in unity were those who believed the church's doctrines. Further, was the contention that only those who stood under the church's doctrinal umbrella were acceptable to God. In Jaroslav Pelikan's breviloquent, this

> *church was the repository of truth, the dispenser of grace, the guarantee of salvation, the matrix of acceptable worship. Only here did God accept sacrifices, only here was there confident intercession for those who were in error, only here were good works fruitful, only here did the powerful bond of love hold men together, and 'only from the catholic church does truth shine forth.'*[9]

The apostolic nature of the early church was essential for the perpetuity of the Gospel message. While apostolic authority later became associated with papal succession[10] it was initially grounded in the authority of Christ. Indeed, for Origen, "the words of Christ did not include only the words which he spoke while he was in the flesh, for Christ had also been the Word of God active in Moses and the prophets."[11] By consequence, the words of the Old Testament could be read as prophecies about Christ. Secondly, the "continuity in the apostolic tradition was the continuity of the apostles with one another as the faithful messengers of Christ."[12] As a result, the New Testament witness must be seen as of the Holy Spirit and inspired.

It is interesting to note that the earliest Christians did not consider themselves to be part of a new religion. They still saw themselves as Jews; Jews who had not abandoned their faith but had remained Jews in a new Messianic age which had finally arrived. "They differed from their fellow-countrymen by their faith that in Jesus of Nazareth the Messiah of the nation's expectation had now come."[13] Their

---

7. Pelikan, *The Christian Tradition: Vol. 1*, 156.
8. Latourette, *A History of Christianity: Vol. 1*, 129.
9. Pelikan, *The Christian Tradition: Vol. 1*, 334.
10. Pelikan, *The Christian Tradition: Vol. 1*, 131.
11. Pelikan, *The Christian Tradition: Vol. 1*, 110.
12. Pelikan, *The Christian Tradition: Vol. 1*, 112.
13. Chadwick, *The Pelican History of the Church: The Early Church*, 9.

Jewish roots, emanating out of their long standing immersion in the Hebrew Scriptures, explains why Christians in Jerusalem continued to keep the Sabbath and meet at the Temple. Yet, to the observance of the Sabbath was added the observance of the first day of the week. On this day Christians celebrated the resurrection of Jesus. It was during Constantine's reign that the biblical Sabbath was erased and replaced with Sunday worship only.

The Book of Acts outlines the integration of both Jews and Gentiles into a new Israel based on a common faith in Jesus Christ. This new entity became spiritual Israel. Here, the people of God are referred to as a tree, with gentiles of faith are described as being grafted in and those of Israel who had rejected Jesus Christ as being cut off (Romans 11:17).

The early communion services centered on the joy that Christ's death had bought and the liberation that ensues from victory. They were very much aware that the new Messianic age had dawned. Therefore, Communion was celebrated "with glad and generous hearts (Acts 2:46)". There were times set aside for the sorrow of one's sins on two weekly days of fasting. This was a practise borrowed from Judaism, which advocated fasting on Mondays and Thursdays. The early Christians fasted on Wednesdays and Fridays. It may have been that these two days were chosen in commemoration of the betrayal and crucifixion.[14]

Along with vibrant and Spirit filled communities, it was the evangelism that characterized the nature of the new community. Phillip Scheepers rightly contended that, "Acts leaves the reader with the inescapable impression that the preaching of the Gospel was right at the centre of how the early Christians understood themselves and their role in the world."[15]

Authority was primarily vested in the twelve. Of the apostles, Peter and John seem to have a greater authority than the others. Acts gives several indications of this, as does Paul who refers to them as the "pillars" in Galatians 2:9. However, the third "pillar" was not one of the twelve but James, the brother of the Lord. Paul informs us in 1 Corinthians 15:7 that the risen Jesus had appeared to James, who soon became the leader of the church in Jerusalem. Raoul Dederen, former Dean at Andrews University, importantly pointed to the Christological foundations of the early church's leadership.

> *The apostles were the twelve appointed by Jesus Himself (Matt. 10:1–4), Matthias replacing Judas, and Paul being added later (Gal. 1:11–24). Paul's claim to apostleship was that he had been called by Christ Himself on the road to Damascus. As the commissioned witnesses to the word of Jesus, crucified and risen, theirs was a unique position of authority. Their authority was not their own, an authority under their control, but a mediated authority. It was Christ's*

---

14. Webster, *Practical Christian Spirituality*, 8.
15. Scheepers, *Acts and the Mission of the Church*, 91.

> *authority mediated through them. Their proclamation and interpretation of Christ was not an intrusion upon God's revelation in Christ but very much part of it. They were not correctors, but conveyors of it.* [16]

Dederen further points to the importance of the Holy Spirit's equipping (Matt. 28:18-20; John 20:21-23). Of significance was what he referred to as "inspiration remembrance", in which they recalled the life and teaching of Jesus.[17]

PERSECUTION IN THE EARLY CHURCH

Despite the early growth of the Jewish Christian Church in Jerusalem, persecution changed everything. As Emeka Ekeke, of the University of Calabar, Nigeria, averred,

> *The Romans tolerated religious beliefs, ... [however] ... new and innovative teachings were regarded with distrust and Christianity was contrary to Roman toleration. Therefore, the Roman distaste for Christianity arose in a large part from its sense that it was not in line with ancient customs and that it was inappropriate for society.*[18]

In Palestine, Herod Agrippa, the grandson of Herod the Great, ordered the death of James the brother of John. When this action was well received by his subjects, Herod had Peter arrested. However, he later escaped. In A.D. 62 James, the brother of Jesus, was killed by orders of the High Priest, even against the advice of some of the Pharisees.[19] Soon after the leaders of the Jerusalem Church decided to move to Pella, a city beyond the Jordan, which had a mostly Gentile population. It would seem that they moved not only because of the persecution but also because of growing Roman suspicion as to the exact nature of the new religious sect. By this time Simeon, another relative of Jesus, had succeeded James as leader of the church. However Roman suspicions grew and Simeon was also eventually killed by the Romans. By A.D. 70, the year of the Temple's destruction, the ancient church, made up of both Jew and Gentile, had found itself in increasing isolation.

According to Acts, Christians were scattered throughout Judea and Samaria (8:1), were visited by Peter in Lydda, Sharon, and Joppa (9:32-42). Later Christians were scattered as far as Damascus, Phoenicia, Cyprus and Antioch (11:19).[20] We are also told in Acts that Paul took the Gospel to several cities in Asia Minor, to Greece and Rome. Others were involved in these regions and cities. Barnabas and Mark went to Cyprus, Apollos preached in Ephesus and Corinth. Countless others, whose

---

16. Dederen, *The Church: Authority and Unity*, 2-3.
17. Dederen, *The Church: Authority and Unity*, 2-3.
18. Ekeke, *Persecution and Martyrdom of Christians in the Roman Empire from AD 54-100: A Lesson for the 21st Century Church*, 176,
19. González, *The Story of Christianity: Vol. 1*, 21.
20. González, *The Story of Christianity: Vol. 1*, 23.

names we do not know, went from place to place spreading the Gospel of Christ.[21] Most of the many nameless Christians who took the Gospel to the various parts of the Roman Empire were merchants, slaves, and others who travelled for various reasons. Their travel provided many opportunities for the expansion of the Church. Yet conflict with the state became the Christian's day to day experience.

The early Christians were initially regarded by Jews as a heretical sect within Judaism. Jews believed that they were under the authority of the Empire because they had not been faithful enough to God. This meant that these heretical groups were the cause of their problems. This was a significant factor contributing to the Jewish persecution of Christians. But there were other issues that contributed to the early conflicts between Jews and Christians. Luke reveals a rampant jealousy of the success of the Gospel among the cities and towns. Opposition was first recorded in Pisidian Antioch (Acts 13:14–16; 42–43). Indeed, "Pisidian Antioch (*Colonia Caesarea Antiocheia*) is the first city in Asia Minor for which Christian missionary work and Jewish opposition is reported in the New Testament."[22] In addition, many Jews objected to the teachings of Christianity. This is certainly evident in Iconium (Acts 14:1–6). The impetus for their anger and subsequent accusations appears to have resulted from the successful conversion to Christianity from among those who had heard the Gospel as it had been preached in the Synagogue.[23] There also seems to have been an abhorance to the attempted connections that the Christians where seeking to make with traditional Judaism. This is apparent in Acts 21:27–28, where Luke reports that Paul's arrest in the Jerusalem Temple was caused by "Jews from Asia". It was this group who reportedly "had seen Paul in the city in the company of Trophimus from Ephesus and, when they saw Paul in the temple, assumed that he had brought a Gentile into the temple and thus violated the prohibition for non-Jews to enter the temple beyond the Court of the Gentiles."[24]

The result of this Jewish Christian conflict originally led the Romans to think of it as a conflict among Jews (Acts 18:14–15). For this reason they mainly left them alone, unless it was to intervene in order to break them up. A good example of this surrounds the policy of Emperor Claudius to expel Jews from Rome in around A.D. 51. Acts 18:2 mentions this without explanation. However Suetonius, a Roman historian, claims that it was a result of disorderly conduct, "because of Chrestus". Most historians agree that this is a reference to Christus, or Christ. As Christians gained more converts among Gentiles, the distinction between Jews and Christians become

---

21. González, *The Story of Christianity: Vol. 1*, 25.
22. Schnabel, *Jewish Opposition to Christians in Asia Minor in the First Century*, 234–5.
23. Schnabel, *Jewish Opposition to Christians in Asia Minor in the First Century*, 235.
24. Schnabel, *Jewish Opposition to Christians in Asia Minor in the First Century*, 239.

evident. It is also true that as Jewish nationalism and rebellion against Rome grew, Gentile Christians wanted to distance themselves from the Jewish population.[25]

Ten years after Nero's accession to the throne, in A.D. 54, he had become unpopular and despised because of his lust for pleasure and dreams of grandeur. The rumour soon began to circulate that he was mad. On June 18 A.D. 64, fire broke out in Rome and destroyed ten of the fourteen sections of the city.[26] The Roman historian Tacitus, who may well have been there at the time, was inclined to believe that the fire had started in an oil warehouse. However, the rumours were rife and pointed squarely at the "mad" Nero who supposedly set out to destroy Rome so that he could rebuilt it according to one of his grand plans. In order to deal with the runours, Tacitus records that Nero blamed the Christians. While Tacitus does not condone Nero's action, he does describe Christians as being hated for their sordid abominations, evil superstitions and hatred of humankind. It is not clear what Tacitus is referring to in all of this, however it is worth remembering that Christians abstained from many important social activities—such as theatre and sports—because they were intertwined with pagan worship.[27] Indeed, by this time the rumour had spread that Christians practiced incest and cannibalism at the nocternal meetings.[28] In A.D. 68 Nero was deposed by rebellion and killed himself. The persecution ceased for a while. Eventually Vespian gained control of the government. During his reign, and that of his son Titus, Christians were generally ignored. Indeed, there are no records of Martyrdoms under Vespasian.[29] The situation appeared to remain the same under Titus.[30] However, the persecution of Christians resumed under the rule of Domition (81–96), who followed Titus. Domition wanted to restore Roman traditions, which explains why Christians were again targeted.[31] The charge that was often brought against Christians was atheism, since they worshipped an invisible God (Revelation 2:10). Domitian styled himself as 'Master and God', and suspected treachery against those who "looked askance at his cult".[32] Like Nero, Domition was seen as a tyrant and eventually murdered. While it is true that recent scholarship has sought to rehabilitate Domitian, it is important to maintain persepective and balance. As Moore and McCormack have rightly noted,

> (e)valuating the character of either the man or his administration however, must involve more than counting the numbers actually murdered and whether

---

25. González, *The Story of Christianity: Vol. 1*, 32.
26. Dando-Collins, *The Great Fire of Rome: The fall of the Emperor Nero and His City*, 2.
27. González, *The Story of Christianity: Vol. 1*, 34–35.
28. Chadwick, *The Pelican History of the Church—The Early Church*, 26.
29. Canfield, *The Early Persecutions of the Christians*, 71.
30. Canfield, *The Early Persecutions of the Christians*, 72.
31. Domitian also made new strict laws against Judaism.
32. Chadwick, *The Pelican History of the Church: The Early Church*, 26.

> *Domitian had a lucid mind and displayed excellent administration skills. Those who have sought to rehabilitate Domitian have only succeeded in demonstrating that he was one of the best administrators who ever governed the empire. What they have failed to do, is to demonstrate that Domitian could very well have been both an able administrator and a tyrannical despot -like Stalin and Hitler. A further examination of the man will reveal another side of Domitian.*[33]

Indeed, the ancient historians who were closest to the events must be given credence and seen as generally reliable and accurate. As Moore and McCormack have stated, "(t)he attempt to rehabilitate the character of Domitian through an unreasonable questioning of the reliability of the ancient sources is unsatisfactory. There is a consistent picture of Domitian that runs throughout the standard sources that cannot be ignored or minimized."[34] Clearly Domitian, while gaining the reputation of an excellent administrator, can also be seen, by Suetonius's account of him at least, to have been particularly brutal in justice, even according to the standards of his day.

After the murder of Domition, Christians were afforded a few years of relative peace. Marcus Aurelius became emperor in A.D. 161 and reigned until 180. He was seen to be one of the enlightened minds of his age. He wrote a number of *Meditations*. However this did not prevent him from persecuting Christians, who he believed undermined the structure of society.[35] He wrote that Christians were obstinate and the cause of a string of invasions, floods, epidemics and other disasters. Christians, in their rebellion, had brought the wrath of the gods upon the Empire. One of the most informative documents concerning this action concerns the martyrdom of the widow Felicitas and her seven sons. Refusing to relent under threat they were sent to various parts of Rome and executed—probably to appease various gods.[36]

BATTLES FROM SOCIETY AND FROM WITHIN

In the early years, Christianity spread primarily among the lower stratus of society. A pagan writer, Celsus, complained that Christians were ignorant people who did not teach in schools or open forums, but in kitchens, shops and tanneries. While there were a few exceptions, (such as Justin, Clement and Origen) Celsus was right. Indeed, Christians were generally regarded as a despicable rabble. The Christians of the first three centuries belonged to the lower echelons of society. However it is true to say that many among them were astute and understood their faith well. A comparison of their writings with some of their more cultured brethren does not always favour the latter. For example, the active, sovereign, and just God who is depicted

---

33. Moore, McCormack, *Domitian (Part i)*, 19.
34. Chadwick, *The Pelican History of the Church: The Early Church*, 27.
35. Latourette, *A History of Christianity: Vol. 1*, 86.
36. Hoever, *Lives of the Saints, For Every Day of the Year*, 261–262.

in much of the common Christian's writings is closer to the character of God than the distant one depicted by Clement of Alexandria. While the great apologists made every effort to prove to the authorities that their faith was not opposed to imperial policies, there are indications that some common Christians were well aware that there was an unavoidable clash between the goals of the Empire and God.

The theological turbulence of the early church was seen in Tertullian of Carthage (c.160—c.225). Tertullian, born around 150 A.D. was a native of the North African city of Carthage.[37] He spent most of his life there, however it was in Rome that he converted to Christianity.[38] When he returned to Carthage he wrote a number of treatises in defence of the orthodoxy against the heresies. He defended the unity of the Old and New Testaments against Marcion, who had argued that they related to different gods. Tertullian stated that "Marcion used the knife, not the pen, massacring scripture to suit his own material."[39]

In response to Marcion, Tertullian defended the doctrine of the Trinity. He wanted to show that the "threeness" (he was the first to use the Latin, *trinitas*) of God is not contradictory to God's essential oneness and unity. The key to his teaching is summed up in the words *substantia* (substance) and *persona* (person). Each member of the Trinity has a different role, yet all are united in the same substance. They are distinct from each other, but not separated. The Trinity is one substance in three persons. He used this term in a relational way. The Father cannot be the Father without the Son, and the Son cannot be the Son without the Father. While the two are distinct they are inseparable. The same applies to the Spirit. This was different from the Monarchians who blurred distinctions between the members of the Trinity. To them God was a divine monad with no distinctions within the unity of God's own self.

Tertullian may have been a lawyer, or had been trained in rhetoric, since his writings bear the stamp of a legal mind. For example, in his *On the Witness of the Soul* he places the human soul on the witness stand for questioning. The conclusion is that the soul is "by nature Christian" and that its persistant rejection of Christianity is due to obstinancy and blindness. He also argued that once one had found the truth of Christianity one should abandon any further search for truth. Indeed, Christians who continue to search for truth lack faith. He wrote in his *Prescription against Heretics*: "You are to seek until you find, and once you have found, you are to believe. Thereafter, all you have to do is to hold to what you have believed. Besides this, you are to believe that there is nothing further to be believed, nor anything else

---

37. Shelley, *Church History in Plain Language*, 48.
38. McGrath, *Historical Theology: An Introduction to the History of Christian Thought*, 25–26.
39. Davidson, *The Old Testament in The Church?* 120.

FOUNDATIONS OF THEOLOGY

to be sought."[40] He believed, alternatively, that Christians should look deeper into their own faith.

However, anything that goes beyond the accepted body of doctrine, as well as anything coming from other sources, is to be rejected. This is particularly true of pagan philosophy. Indeed, he argued that heresies derive many of their leading ideas from secular philosophy. Tertullian argued that philosophy was pagan in its outlook, and its use in theology could lead to heresy in the church. In his *On the Rule of the Heretics,* he set up a contrast between Athens and Jerusalem, symbolising the tension between pagan philosophy and the revelation of the Christian faith. He concluded: "I have no use for a stoic, Platonic or dialectic Christianity. After Jesus we have no need of speculation... When we come to belief we have no need of anything else."[41] He defined heresies as "human and demonic doctrines" opposed to the divine truth of the faith. He saw them as engineered by human wisdom. Ironically, however, he paved the way for futrure heresy and deviations from a biblical faith.[42]

Indeed, Tertullian laid considerable emphasis upon the role of tradition and apostolic succession in the defining of Christian theology. He understood orthodoxy as being dependent upon historical continuity with the apostles, something the heretics could not do. The apostles were taught by Christ, taught everything necessary and handed it down to the churches. While there are evident strengths in an apostolic theology resting on the teaching of the apostles, the traditional trajectory emphasised by Tertullian paved the way for a theology resting on the authority of church tradition, rather than apostolic tradition.[43]

Never-the-less, Tertullian had his strengths, particularly when he wrote against idolatry in the work, *On Idolatry.* The early Christians lived in an explicitly pagan society. Indeed, paganism was the official state religion and it was very much a religion of idolatry. Tertullian saw idolatry as the chief sin. He opened his argument with the claim that idolatry holds a pivotal position as "the principal charge against the human race, the world's deepest guilt, and the all-inclusive cause of judgement."[44] Therefore, every offender commits idolatry, for what he does belongs to the owners of idols. One of the ramifications is that idolatry makers must renounce their trade. Indirectly, other trades must be weary. This may include builders, plasterers and decorators. Astrology and magic also come under condemnation. Tertullian also raises the question of public education. He notes that schoolmasters must "praise the gods of the heathen" and "keep their feasts and celebrations". Yet Tertullian believed that study in pagan schools need not be condemned. However, "it is more allowable

40. González, *The Story of Christianity: Vol. 1,* 75.

41. Platinga, *The Twin Pillars of Christian Scholarship,* 141.

42. McGrath, *Historical Theology: An Introduction to the History of Christian Thought,* 90.

43. McGrath, *Historical Theology,* 43.

44. Mbanisi, *Baptism and the Ideal of Unity and Universality of the Church in St. Augustine's Ecclesiology: An Exposition of His Theology of Baptism in the Light of Donatist Controversy,* 71.

for Christians to learn letters than to teach them."[45] He also takes a more lenient view of family ceremonies. These may carry with them "a whiff of idolatry". Even if an offering is made, attendance can be allowed so long as the Christian does not make an offering. The same applies to slaves with their masters and clients with their patrons. Further, he rejected military service for there is no compatibility between the oath to serve God and the oath to serve man.[46]

In A.D. 207 Tertullian's staunch orthodoxy was all to change. His mix of truth and error, and willingness to make compromises, finally took its toll. In that year he joined the Montanist movement.

Montanism was named after its founder, Montanus, who had been a pagan priest until his conversion to Christianity in A.D. 155. Some time later he began prophesying, claiming that he had been possessed by the Holy Spirit. Soon after two woman, Priscilla and Maximilla, also began prophesying. None of this was of any great concern to the church. What was of serious concern was the Montanist's claim that their movement was the beginning of the new age. The rest of the church believed that the new age had come with the resurrection of Jesus and the giving of the Holy Spirit at Pentecost.[47] The tendencies to mix truth with error are also seen in the contribution of Iranaeus

Iranaeus was a native of Asia Minor where he was born around A.D. 130 and died in about 200. He was a disciple of Polycarp of Smyrna (who died as a martyr and claimed to have been taught by John). Iranaeus was an ardent admirer of his old master whom he would refer to in his writing as the "old man". Later he migrated to Lyons in southern France (then called South Gaul). In Lyons, Irenaeus was made a presbyter, but while away in Rome persecution broke out (A.D.177) in Lyons and nearby Vienne. Bishop Photinus died, which susequently led to Iranaeus, on his return, being elected bishop of Lyons. He was a pastor first and lacked any interest in philosophical speculation or unsolved mysteries. He sought first to lead his flock in Christian life and faith. Consequently, his writings sought to refute heresy and instruct believers.[48] Only two of his works remain.

i) *Demonstration of the Apostolic Faith*, which contains instruction in Christian doctrine; and ii) *Five Books Against the Heresies*, which is a refute of Gnosticism.[49]

Iranaeus perceived of himself as a shepherd and saw God as above all a shepherd. He understood God to be a loving being who created the world and humankind out of a desire to have a creation to love and to lead, like a shepherd loves and leads the flock. History is seen in terms of the divine shepherd who leads creation to its

---

45. Tertullian, *On Idolatry*, 93.
46. See *Ante-Nicene Fathers: Vol. 3*.
47. González, *Historical Theology*, 76.
48. McGrath, *Historical Theology*, 25.
49. McGrath, *Historical Theology*, 41.

final goal. Humanity was created to be free and responsible. That is, free to increasingly be conformed to the divine will and nature—resulting in an ever-increasing communion with God. He believed in the importance of angels to this process. To be sure, angels exist temporarily as tutors who guide believers through the steps of life. Eventually, Christians will surpass the communion that angels presently enjoy. However, humans must also be instructed by the "two hands" of God: the Word and the Holy Spirit. By these two hands humans receive instruction and growth. The goal of instruction and growth is to reach "divinization". That is, to be like the Divine. Indeed, the Christian, as a new creation in the image of Christ, forms for Irenaeus an essential part of salvation. The image is of believers existing "with Christ". Therefore, redemption has as its goal "the union and communion of God and man". The incarnation makes this plain. It is a twofold movement of descent and ascent. "Bringing God down to man by the Spirit, and again raising man to God by his incarnation."[50] One of the angels, Satan, was jealous of humans, and attempted to thwart the plan by leading Adam and Eve into sin. This has resulted in the incarnation taking on the purpose of being a remedy for sin, and a means of defeating Satan. Jesus is the "second Adam" and because in his life, death and resurrection a new humanity has been created. Jesus corrected what was twisted by sin. He also defeated Satan who leads us into a new freedom. Further, Jesus Christ is the head of the church, which is his body, and this body is nourished through worship—particularly communion—and is joined to the head in such a way that it is already receiving the first benefits of Christ's victory. In Christ's resurrection, the final resurrection has dawned, and all who take part in the body will partake of it.[51]

Iranaeus was the first to develop the "rule of truth (or faith)" which proposed the holding to the tradition of faith protected by bishops and presbyters. This was designed to be a weapon against Gnosticism and Marcionism. Against Gnosticism, Irenaeus argues that the gospel came from the apostles both orally and in writing. These "first preached it abroad, and then later by the will of God handed it down to us in writings, to be the foundation and pillar of our faith."[52] While being practical and expedient at the time, this shift towards tradition ultimately led to the compromise and distortion of the New Testament Gospel.

During the first few centuries of the Christian Church, the New Testament scripture was still in the process of collection. Therefore, Irenaeus placed a lot of significance was given to the perpetuation of the oral witness as well as the written word. Tradition progressively came to hold more authority. Increasingly, Gnostics were opposed for not agreeing with either scripture or tradition. Indeed, scripture

---

50. Richardson, *Early Christian Fathers*, 386.
51. Ferguson, *Irenaeus*, 569.
52. Richardson, *Library of Christian Classics: Early Christian Fathers*, 370.

THE HISTORY OF THE CHURCH AND ITS THEOLOGICAL DEVELOPMENT

and tradition came to be understood as two forms of the apostolic teachings and both as needing to be safe guarded by the apostle's successors.

The apostle John played a special role for Irenaeus, primarily because his gospel is a direct refutation of Gnosticism. John 1 proclaims a true incarnation. Gnostics try to evade this. For them, Christ always had to be "without flesh and free from suffering." John, however, says simply in 1:14: "The Word was made flesh." By relating the witness of John the Baptist to that of Elijah, John also shows that the Word is that of the God who is the Fashioner of this world. Two planks in the Gnostic program are confronted in a single stroke.

Irenaeus also gave a greater place to the Spirit than did his predecessors. He strongly affirmed God as one but also recognises distinctions between Father, Son and Spirit. For Iranaeus, God is known in history through the Son and the Spirit. By stressing the Father as the One who is above all, the Word as through all, and the Spirit in all, Iranaeus led some to draw the conclusion that the Son and the Spirit are subordinate to the Father. However his contribution is his economic trinitarianism. He described how God was disclosed in history and how the three members of the Godhead may be described as distinct and equally divine.[53]

THE CHALLENGES OF SOCIETY

God's people have never been disconnected from the world around them. Most of the first Christians were first-century Jews. This is how they heard and received the message. Indeed, the Jews of the first-century were Jews of the Roman Empire. Most cultivated Greeks and Romans expressed a negative attitude towards Jews. They had customs that seemed strange to the Greek standards and were resented for their privileges (exemption from military service, Sabbath laws) and their efforts to advance in politics. In turn Jews experienced the impact of Greek culture. They responded in a variety of ways, from reactionism to all out embrace. Some turned to their own traditions and customs with a fiercer and more uncompromising loyalty than before. Others assimilated. The saying, "when in Rome do as the Romans do", comes from Rabbi Meir.[54] However, generally speaking, a number of fundamental observances were always kept. Even when much else might be given up, the Sabbath, circumcision, and the law, were emphasised.

The relationship between Judaism and Christianity is simply expressed in Acts 7, which describes the death of Stephen and fulfilled the 70 week prophecy of Daniel 9. The experts in the Jewish Scriptures, the Scribes and Pharisees, believed the Old Testament presented the law of God for his special people, the Jews. The law

---

53. González, *Historical Theology: An Introduction to the History of Christian Thought*, 68–71. See also McGrath, *Historical Theology: An Introduction to the History of Christian Theology*, 41–42.

54. Furguson, *Backgrounds of Early Christianity*, 429.

began with the Ten Commandments but it went on to cover every detail, action and thought in life. The law prescribed every move in worship and every step in piety.

Stephen, however, disagreed with them, and boldly told them so. Actually, God gave the law to point to the coming Messiah, who would fulfil all righteousness for all people. Stephen told them that Jesus was the promised Messiah. They responded by having Stephen killed. The death of Stephen was undoubtedly one of the crucial events in the life of the early church, and its effects were soon felt not only in Jerusalem but throughout the rest of Palestine, and ultimately the whole Empire. One of the immediate consequences was a widespread persecution of the Christians in Jerusalem. Persecution inevitably lead to the dispersal of Christians from Jerusalem itself, especially those who were most sympathetic to the message of Stephen. Caesarea, Antioch and Damascus all witnessed an influx of Christians. However, they were not just the first Christian refugees, but also the first Christian missionaries.

During the early years of the church, for the main part, Christianity developed in the context of ancient paganism. Most of the early Roman deities had no personality and are best characterised by the word *numen*, that is, a divine power or influence with no sense of personality. Another Latin word for them is *genius*, the spirit of a place. From the late third century B.C. there began an identification of Roman with Greek deities. There was a common belief in the ancient world that the gods needed food and drink sacrificed to them. This was particularly true in Rome. Sacrifice was thought to increase the deities supply of *numen*, which would be used up in helping people. There were a variety of calendar ceremonies that were performed by the state. Indeed, the connection of state and official religion can also be seen in the *Pomerium*, the sacred boundary of Rome. Only authorised cults could be practised within it. Therefore, religion was heavily regulated by the state.

Roman religion was quite legalistic. Certain ceremonies had to be done with precison, following minute prescriptions as they were recited from a book. The Greeks made their sacrifices with uncovered heads, but the Romans covered theirs (1 Cor. 11:4–5). There was a practical and legal reason for this: to the Roman, mind omens meant nothing if they could not be seen. So the priest was veiled from seeing anything out of the side of his eyes so that he could look only upon what he was doing. In time, however, Greek practice came to dominate. Even during the empire the essential spirit of religion was Greek. Rome's greatest contribution was creating security and uniting the people in one state. Rome had little of its own in the way of religion, so it filled the missing space with Greek content. Listed here are some of the prevailing features:

1. Greco-Roman paganism was nonexclusive. Giving of one's devotion to a deity did not exclude other deities. Therefore, the exclusive demands made by Jews and Christians were scandalous.

2. In time, people became more interested in divine deeds and power than with the divine personalities. Power was undefined, wonderful, and marvellous, and its manifestations were deserving of worship and worth trying to explain and control.

3. The demons of ancient Greco-Roman religion did not have the negative connotations they do today. Unlucky happenings were attributed to intermediary beings or forces.

4. The power of fate was also a strong feature. It was sometimes worshipped as a deity. Many of the dominant deities, such as Asclepius, Isis and Sarapis, claimed power over fate. The belief in fate was linked to the influence of the stars, so astrology came to prominence.

5. Magic was another popular expression of human relations with the powers of the universe. There was no distinction between magic and the spirit of a religion. Superstitions, sorcery, use of amulets, the magical power of statues, formulas for healing and cursing, and private divination were all on the increase in late antiquity.

6. The corporate nature of religion was not lost in the Hellenistic-Roman periods. The cult was an official act of society.

7. Morality was not closely associated with religion. There were some exemptions, but for the most part codes of conduct were derived from customs or the ethical teachings of the philosophical schools.

Therefore, the early church existed within an antagonistic worldview with which the Gospel message was in direct variance. Consequently, it was not only seen as new, but also, counter-cultural, anti-social and dangerous to the status quo that had kept society stable for so long.

THE THREAT OF THE GNOSTICS

A major threat to the orthodoxy of the early church was the infiltration of gnosticism. During the early years of the church the foundations of orthodoxy were defended and established. Of all the movements that sought to undermine this process none was as dangerous, nor as close to victory, as gnosticism. It was not a well-defined group, nor was it well organised. It existed outside the church and within it. It drew its ideas from a number of sources and took on a variety of forms. Its cultural and social setting seems to have been the urban world in which Jewish religious texts and symbols were drawn into syncretism. Many notions were drawn from Hellenistic religions. In Gnostic thought influences are found from pagan mythology, astrology, magic, Middle Platonism and Merkava (or chariot) Judaism. The name "gnostic" comes from the Greek *gnosis*, which means "knowledge". It is a good name to describe their most basic feature. They believed that they possessed a special mystical knowledge, reserved only for those with true understanding.[55]

Indeed, "Gnosticism may be defined as a system which taught the cosmic redemption of the spirit through knowledge."[56] This special knowledge was the secret key to salvation. Because the knowledge is secret and mystical a lot of its literature is in riddles, obscure, complex and mystifying. The main sources for our understanding of gnosticism has long been a small amount of material written by them and a large amount quoted from them by opponents. However, in 1945 all this changed when a small library of thirteen codices was discovered at Nag Hammadi in Egypt.[57] They contain 48 short pieces in Coptic, including *The Gospel of Truth*, *The Gospel of Thomas* and the *Epistle to Rheginos*. They believed that matter was evil, or in fact unreal. A human being was in fact an eternal spirit (or part of one) that had become imprisoned in a body. This made the human body a prison that misguides us as to our true nature. Therefore, it is evil and an obstacle to salvation. The Gnostics final goal was to escape from this body and the whole material world in which we, as eternal spirits, exist in exile. This image of exile is crucial to Gnostics. How did this situation come into being?

The Gnostics believed that all reality was originally spiritual. The supreme being had no intention of creating a material world. At creation, the world only had spiritual beings, or "eons". They could not agree on the exact number, some suggested 365. One of these eons fell into error by attempting to know the unknowable Father and created the material world. According to one system this was wisdom (one of the eons) making something by herself and ending up having an "abortion". This resulted in the material world. But since this world was made by a spiritual being, there are still "sparks" or "bits" of spirit in it. It is these that have been imprisoned in human bodies and must be liberated through gnosis. However, not everyone is capable of this knowledge. The result was a dual world of light and dark. The divine world was called "the fullness" and the material world was sometimes called "the Void".

According to the Gnostics, liberation could be achieved through the arrival of a special messenger who must come to wake us from our "dream". Our spirits are "asleep" in our bodies and must be woken up and liberated. The way of liberation is to break through the heavenly spheres, each ruled by an evil spirit. The only way we can do this is to have the secret knowledge. The heavenly messenger gives the knowledge, this is the message. For Christian Gnostics, the messenger is Christ. Because

---

55. Chadwick, *The Pelican History of the Church: The Early Church*, 35.
56. Pelikan, *The Emergence of Catholic Tradition (100–600)*, 82.
57. See B. Layton, The Gnostic Scriptures, M. Franzmann, *Jesus in the Nag Hammadi Writings*, 1996.

there were Gnostic they did not believe that Christ had a real body, many denied the birth of Jesus, which would have put him under the material realm. This aspect of gnosticism is called "docetism"—derived from the Greek—"to seem". Their views of the body meant that some Gnostics were extreme ascetics or libertines. They also denied the doctrines of creation, incarnation and resurrection.[58]

THE EMPIRE BEFORE CONSTANTINE'S CONVERSION

By the end of the fourth century the Roman Empire was in serious decline. There were several reasons for the fading of her glory. Barbarians beyond the border were getting increasingly restless, and their incursions into the Empire were getting more daring. There was also a serious economic crisis and the ancient classical traditions were generally forgotten. A traditional Roman like Decius understood the decline of the Empire to have resulted from the people abandoning the ancient gods. The gods were provoked to displeasure because of the citizen's neglect. However, restoration to the former glory of the Empire could only be achieved by a restoration of the ancient religion. Rome was at stake. To refuse was treason.

Decius was aware that the persecution of Christians in the past had led to the growth of the movement. Therefore, initially, he did not want to make martyrs and so withheld from the persecution of Christians. This began to change, however, when he decreed that worship of the gods was mandatory. Following the decree, everyone had to offer a sacrifice to the gods and burn incense before the statue of Decius.[59]

Christians responded to the decree in a variety of ways. Some obeyed it and others refused to comply until pressured. A number obtained fraudulent certificates, while others simply refused. During this period few were executed for refusing. What the authorities did was to arrest Christians and then, through a combination of promises, threats, and torture, try to force them to abandon their faith. The effect on the church was a separation between apostates and confessors.

Decius' persecution was brief. His policies were set aside when Gallus succeeded him in A.D. 251. Six years later Valerian, a former companion of Decius, began a new persecution. However, he fell prisoner to the Persians and the church enjoyed a time of relative peace.[60] In 284 A.D. Dioclectian succeeded to the imperial throne. He came from Dalmatia and had humble origins before coming to prominence in the army and rising to imperial rank. After becoming emperor his first step was to appoint, in 285, a second emperor to share his authority and supervise the western portion of the empire—Maximian. Diocletian then made two junior emperors, called "Caesars" who would succeed himself and Maximian, the two "Augusti". To

---

58. McGrath, *Historical Theology*, 40–41. González, *Historical Theology*, 58–66.
59. Latourette, *A History of Christianity: Vol. 1: Beginnings to 1500*, 87–88.
60. González, *Historical Theology*, 88.

himself he selected Galerius and to Maximian he selected Constantius I, father of Constantine the Great. Diocletian also doubled the number of provinces and then grouped these new provinces into larger administrative areas called "dioceses", each of which was put under a "vicar".

Diocletian, despite his reforms, was a traditional follower of the gods. Indeed, he believed that the fate of Rome depended on its alliance with them. Christians began, once again, to be the reason behind the woes of the empire. When he enquired of the oracle of Apollo at Miletus about what course of action to take, the answer was not favourable to Christians. Beginning in February 303, persecution began. Churches were destroyed, sacred books were confiscated and clergy were imprisoned and forced to offer sacrifices. Some were martyred, many suffered and many lapsed.[61]

However, a major change in the relationship between emperor and church was to occur under the reign of Constantine. So significant were the circumstances of Constantine's reign that the church was to change its status in the empire and ultimately its character. From a persecuted minority it became the established majority. However, what might be called the true church, faithful to the purity of the Gospel message, was soon to become a church in the wilderness.[62]

CONSTANTINES CONVERSION

Constantine's father, Constantius Chlorus, had been one of Diocletian's augusti. When he died the troops refused to obey Galerius and proclaimed the popular Constantine as their augustus. After the death of Galarius the Empire was divided up between Licinius, Maximinus Daia, Constantine and Maxentius. Soon Constantine manoeuvred for ultimate power. He gathered his armies in Gaul, crossed the Alps and marched on Rome, Maxentius' capital, and won control. According to Eusebius, Constantine, before going to battle with Maxentius, saw a vision in the sky of a cross with the words, "in this you shall conquer". It is impossible to verify this but the fact remains that Constantine ordered that his soldiers should use on their shield and on their standard a symbol that looked like the superimposition of the Greek letters *chi* and *rho*. Since these are the first two letters of the name, "Christ", this could well have been a Christian symbol. Although eventually Christians saw this to be the moment of Constantine's conversion, historians point out that he continued for some time after to worship the Unquonquered Sun.[63]

In reality, his "conversion" was a slow process that did not come to fruition until just before his death. It was only on his deathbed that he was baptised. Ironically,

---

61. González, *Historical Theology*, 102–104.
62. Chadwick, *The Pelican History of the Church: The Early Church*, 124.
63. González, *Historical Theology*, 107.

however, is that despite the results of the Council of Nicea refuting Arianism, Constantine was himself finally baptised by an Arian, Eusebius of Nicomedia.[64]

After defeating Maxentius, Constantine became master of the western half of the Empire. Eventually Licinius defeated Maximinus, which left the Empire divided between Licinius, who ruled in the east, and Constantine who ruled in the west (Italy, Western Europe and North Africa). Eventually Licinius was murdered and Constantine came to rule as Emperor of both east and west until his death in 337 A.D.

Constantine's conversion has been the subject of a lot of debate. Some have wanted to show that his conversion was the goal towards which the history of the church and the Empire had always been moving. Others have claimed that the emperor's conversion was simply a matter of a shrewd politician taking advantage of the religious situation. Whichever position is adopted, it is certainly true that, prior to Constantine, the church was composed of convinced believers. After his transition to Christianity came a growth in political ambition, religious disinterest and a church half-rooted in paganism. "This threatened to produce not only shallowness and permeation by pagan superstitions, but also the secularization and misuse of religion for political purposes."[65]

Unlike other converts to Christianity, Constantine never placed himself under the direction of Christian teachers or bishops. He reserved the right to determine his own religious practices, and even to intervene in the life of the church, since he considered himself to be the "bishop of bishops". However, after his conversion he repeatedly took part in pagan rites. This ambiguous situation continued until his final hour. So why did Constantine have "this thing" with Christianity since the days of the battle of Rome?

Constantine was most probably a sincere believer in the power of Christ. But he did not understand this power in the same way that a genuine Christian would. The emperor saw the Christian God as a powerful being who would support him as long as he favoured the faithful. Therefore, when Constantine passed laws in favour of Christianity, when he had churches built, or had land returned to them, he was not seeking the goodwill of the Christians, but the goodwill of their God. This interpretation is supported by Constantine's own writings, which reveal a sincere man who had a meagre grasp of the Christian faith. To this extent, it is right to refer to the nominal conversion of Constantine.[66]

Constantine worshipped other gods, notably the god of his father, the Unconquered Sun. It would seem that Constantine thought of this god and the Christian God as being compatible—perhaps two views of the same Supreme Deity. During his

---

64. Drake, *The Impact of Constantine on Christianity*, 132.
65. Shelley, *Church History in Plain Language*, 110.
66. White, *Great Controversy*, 49–50.

reign he favoured Christianity and yet the official religion of the Empire remained paganism, with him as High Priest. On coins minted as late as 320 A.D. the names and symbols of the gods can be found on them, as well as the Christian symbol he had used to conquer Rome.

Constantine's gradual turn to Christianity, and final conversion, can be seen in a number of ways. In 324 A.D. he decreed that all soldiers are to worship the Supreme God on the first day of the week. This was the day that Christians celebrated the resurrection of their Lord. But it was also the day of the Unconquering Sun. None-the-less, he also had a conceren for the church's teaching. A year later Constantime called a great assembly of bishops for the Council of Nicea. However, the founding of Constantinople demonstrated a decisive shift. The plan was designed to diminish the power of the ancient aristocratic families of Rome, who were mostly pagan. He raided pagan temples for statues and other objects to embellish the new capital. This was a blow to paganism, which lost the gods who served as objects of local devotion. This was contrasted with the building of new sumptuous churches. Perhaps the greatest irony in the story of Constantine is that despite his support of Christianity, and final conversion, his three sons agreed with the Senate that he be declared a god.[67]

THE IMPACT OF CONSTANTINE

Constantine's impact on the life of the church is still felt today.

Indeed, during his thirty year reign "more change took place in the status, structure, and beliefs of the Christian Church than during any previous period of its history."[68] The most immediate consequence of Constantine's conversion was the cessation of persecution. Most significant was the so called "Edict of Milan", which legalized Christianity and returned property taken during Diocletian's persecution. There were a variety of responses to Constantine's "conversion". Many Christians sought to show that Constantine was chosen by God to bring the history of both church and Empire to its culmination, where both were joined. Others took the opposite interpretation. For them, the fact that the emperors declared themselves Christian, and that for this reason people were flocking to the church, was not a blessing, but rather a great apostasy. Some of these withdrew to the desert to lead lives of meditation and asceticism. Indeed, the fourth century witnessed a massive exodus of devoted Christians to the deserts of Egypt and Syria. Most church leaders saw the new circumstances as offering unexpected opportunities, but also great dangers. As a result they affirmed their loyalty to the emperor and engaged in important theological debates. Constantine's conversion had a considerable impact on

67. White, *Great Controversy*, 120–123.
68. Drake, *The Impact of Constantine on Christianity*, 111.

Christian worship. Until his time, Christian worship had been fairly simple. At first believers gathered in homes. Then they gathered in cemeteries, such as the Roman catacombs. By the third century there were whole buildings set aside for worship. The oldest church that has been discovered is that of Dura-Europos, which dates from about A.D. 250. It is a fairly small room decorated with murals. However after Constantine's conversion Christian worship began to be influenced by imperial protocol. Incense, which was used as a sign of respect for the emperor, began to appear in services. Officiating ministers, who had worn ordinary clothes, began dressing in more luxurious garments. The service began with processionals, choirs were developed and congregations began to have a less active role. By the second century it became the custom to celebrate communion at the burial place of a martyr on the anniversary of the martyr's death. Churches were eventually built on those places. They became holy cites and worship was seen as particularly valid if it was undertaken in one of these places. Martyr's bodies, or part of the body, were unearthed and placed under altars. Eventually the relics of saints were said to have miraculous powers. Constantine's mother, Empress Helena, visited the Holy Land where she claimed to have found the cross. She distributed parts of it all around the Empire. The elaborate churches that Constantine built have mainly been destroyed, however those that followed in this tradition still remain today. Originally the baptistery building was separate from the church. This was usually round or polygonal, and was large enough to accommodate several dozen people. In its centre was the baptismal pool, into which one descended by a series of steps. Here baptism was celebrated, normally by immersion or pouring. This continued at least until the ninth century. Baptism by dabbing water on the head had developed long before that but initially was only administered in extreme conditions of poor health, deathbed baptisms, or at times when there was a scarcity of water. It was in the colder areas of western Europe, in the ninth century, that this alternate form of baptism was more common. In Italy, baptism by immersion continued until the thirteenth century.[69]

MISSION AND EXPANSION: THE CHURCH IN DARKNESS

The dramatic religious and political turning points that occurred between 311–324 A.D. meant that the church's missionary task encountered new possibilities that had seemed impossible only years earlier. However, there were a number of difficulties that accompanied these changes of events. Many converted to Christianity because it had been made the state religion. Some would have seen their conversion as an opportunity to advance their prospects in the Empire. There were also forced conversions.

---

69. Drake, *The Impact of Constantine on Christianity*, 124–128.

FOUNDATIONS OF THEOLOGY

Nevertheless, the outcome of the church's missionary expansion, lasting for more than a century, was clear: around the middle of the fifth century the people of the Roman Empire professed and felt themselves to be Christians, except for a few pagan remnants, Jews, and some German tribes.[70]

THE RISE OF SCHOLASTICISM

The thirteenth century was marked by a rise in papal power, the birth of the mendicant orders, and the apex of *scholasticism*. This was a name given to a theology that developed in the cathedral schools of theology and which had a characteristic methodology. Its early roots grew in monasteries, but in the twelfth century cathedral schools became the centres of theological activity, only to be replaced, early in the thirteenth century, by universities. This was another consequence of the growth of cities. It had a clear system that attempted to synthesize ideas expressed in classical Roman and Greek writings, in Christian Scripture, as well as those from the patristic fathers and other Christian writings preceding the medieval period. This often led to theology seeking to express its faith through reason. In many instances, apparently contradictory viewpoints were offered in order to show how they possibly could be synthesized through reasonable interpretation.

As a result of these developments reason assumed an important role in theology, not as an antithesis of faith, but as its supplement. Therefore, the scholastics made a systematic attempt to map out the field of theology as a science and in doing so developed new treatises on matters that had previously belonged to preaching. They borrowed freely from the philosophy of Aristotle.

The primary methods of teaching were the *lectio* (lecture) and the *disputatio* (formal debate), which consisted largely in the presentation and analysis of syllogisms. Although there was fairly general agreement as to method and aim, Scholastics did not always agree among themselves on points of doctrine. Consequently, distinct schools of theology emerged, the most influential being those of the Franciscan Duns Scotus, in which the world reflected the reason of its creator. Also, Thomas Aquinas, a Dominican, for whom faith required natural reason.

The most important forerunner to scholasticism was Anslem of Canterbury (1033–1109). He was born of a noble family at Aosta, in Italy, and joined the monastery of Bec, in Normandy, in 1060. In 1093, after serving in turn as prior (1063–78) and abbot (1078–93) at Bec, Anslem was called to England to succeed Lanfranc as Archbishop of Canterbury.[71]

---

70. See Baus, Beck, Hermann, J. Vogt, *The Imperial Church from Constantine to the Early Middle Ages*.

71. Norris, *The Later Middle Ages*, 325.

In the best tradition of Benedictine monasticism, Anselm held that learning should serve the ends of the religious life. He always proceeded as one who already possessed faith and sought understanding, hence he championed the concept of "faith seeking understanding". Anselm's significance for the development of scholasticism lies in his desire to apply reason to questions of faith. What he sought was not so much to prove something which he did not believe without such proof, but rather to understand more deeply what he already believed. This is seen in the way he dealt with the existence of God, and the motive for the incarnation. Anselm believed in the existence of God but sought to more fully understand what that existence meant. It was for this reason that he developed, in the *Proslogion*, what has come to be called "the ontological argument for the existence of God." In it, Anselm defined God as "the being than which non-greater can be conceived." God must therefore exist in reality as well as thought, "for if he existed in thought only, a yet greater being, existing in reality as well as in thought, could be conceived, which is impossible by definition."[72]

In his *Why God became Man*, Anselm explored the reason for the incarnation, and offered an answer that would eventually become standard in western theology. The importance of a crime is measured in terms of the one against whom it is committed. Therefore, a crime against God, sin, is infinite in its import. But, on the other hand, only a human can offer satisfaction for human sin. This is obviously impossible, for human beings are finite, and cannot offer the infinite satisfaction required by the majesty of God. For this reason, there is need for a divine-human, God incarnate, who through his suffering and death offers satisfaction for the sins of all humankind. "No one but God can make satisfaction." Man ought to make it. Therefore, "(i)t is thus necessary for a God-man to make it."[73] Why the Son should be incarnate, and not the Father or the Spirit, depends on congruity. It is not fitting that there be a heavenly Son and a different earthly Son, but it is supremely fitting that pardon should be through Christ when the offence is specifically against him as the true likeness of God.

Since sin against Christ's person "is incommensurate with every other conceivable sin" his death "outweighs all the sins of men."[74] Christ's self-offering constitutes a payment to God, partly because it is an example of perfect obedience, but chiefly because, in honouring the Trinity, it merits a recompense. The great reason why humanity's salvation follows from Christ's death is that Christ, not needing the recompense, both can and does pass it on to those for whose salvation he became human.[75]

---

72. Norris, *The Later Middle Ages*, 326.
73. Bromiley, *Historical Theology: An Introduction*, 178.
74. Bromiley, *Historical Theology: An Introduction*, 179.
75. McGrath, *Historical Theology*, 113–114. Latourette, *A History of Christianity*; Vol. 1, 499–502.

FOUNDATIONS OF THEOLOGY
THOMAS AQUINAS

Thomas Aquinas was born in about 1224 in the outskirts of Naples to an aristocratic family. All his brothers and sisters went on to occupy places of distinction in Italian society. His parents intended that he become a priest and at five years old placed him in the abbey of Monte Cassino, where he began his education. In 1229, at fourteen, he began studies at the University of Naples where he first encountered Aristotelian philosophy. In 1244, he decided to become a Dominican. His family tried to dissuade him—locking him up for a year—however he eventually escaped to enter the novitiate in this new—socially unfashionable—religious order. He received his training at the university, first at the *stadium generale* at Naples and then at Paris, then Cologne, under the well-known theologian, Albert Magnus, and finally at Paris again. Once he completed his training he worked as a theologian at the University of Paris (1256–1259; 1268–1272), or in University-like settings in Dominican houses of study back in Italy (1259–1268; 1272–1273).[76]

Aquinas' literary output was massive. His two most well-known publications are the *Summa Contra Gentiles* and the *Summa Theologica*. He died in 1274 when he was fifty years old. At the heart of his work is the relationship between faith and reason and his arguments for the existence of God is particularly significant. Aquinas represents the pinnacle of catholic scholasticism. In a penetrating fashion, he synthesized Aristotle and Christianity into a form that eventually produced what the Roman Catholic Church would regard as its "standard formulation of theology."[77]

According to Thomas Aquinas, some truths are within the reach of reason, and others beyond it. Philosophy only deals with the first. However, theology is not limited to the latter. The reason for this is that there are truths that reason can prove, but which are necessary for salvation. Since God does not limit salvation to those who are intellectually gifted, all truth necessary for salvation can be revealed. Indeed, "the existence of God can be demonstrated on the basis of the knowledge which we obtain through our senses and our reason."[78] For example, it is impossible to be saved without believing that God exists. For that reason, God reveals this truth. However, this does not mean that the existence of God is a truth that is beyond the scope of reason. Therefore, reason can prove what faith accepts. Further, rational enquiry helps in better understanding that which we accept by faith. This is the purpose of Thomas' "Five Ways", or arguments, for the existence of God. They are: efficient cause, the nature of possibility and necessity, the relative degrees and the supreme degree of truth, goodness and nobility, and the intellectual governance of things. Each of them starts from the world as it is known through the senses, before showing that such a world requires the existence of God. Thomas claimed, on the basis of

---

76. Wawrykow, *The Westminster Handbook to Thomas Aquinas*, viii.
77. Latourette, *A History of Christianity: Vol. 1*, 509.
78. Latourette, *A History of Christianity: Vol. 1*, 511.

Romans 1:20, that God can be demonstrated from his effects. This does not rule out faith, for natural reason affirms only the preambles to the articles of faith. While the effects are not proportionate to the cause, they show that the cause exists.

By the time the mediaeval church had run its course, the time for renewal was desperately needed.

THE BEGINNING OF REFORM

John Wycliffe (1330–1384) has come to be known as the *Morning Star* of the Reformation. He was born in the north of Yorkshire, on the banks of the Tees, in about 1324. He graduated from Oxford University in 1340[79] and spent most of his career there. Wycliffe became famous for his unflinching logic and received a doctorate in theology. In 1371 he left the university to become a diplomat. However, it is his contribution to the teaching of the church, and as a anticipator of the Reformation, that constituted his greatest gift. The context of his ministry provides the reason for his evident passion to see reform in the church. The morals of the clergy deserves important consideration. In addition to Bishop Burnell having five sons, monks and friars were noted for their panchant for good food and bad women. Nuns were known to attend services with their dogs on a leash and priests raced through their prayers to such an extent that they were referred to as graspers, leapers, galoppers, and mumblers. What was of greater concern, however, was the church's growing wealth. The clergy, by way of a considerable representation in the Upper House of Parliament, ensured that while they payed a tithe, they were exempt from tax. Further, it was evident that the income of the English Church, resulting from their considerable tenancies, amounted to large amounts of money being sent out of England directly to the Pope. "It was estimated that more English money went to the Pope than to the state or the King."[80] In response, Wycliff's work denied the validity of clerical ownership of land and property as well as papal jurisdiction over temporal affairs. His doctrine of dominion declared that all people are the tenants of God and only the righteous, as God's true stewards, ought to have political authority, because they alone have the moral right to rule and hold possession. The wicked, on the other hand, even if they are nobles, kings or popes, have no such right. These views led to condemnation by a series of papal bulls issued in 1377. However, this opposition drove Wycliffe to more radical views.[81] He rejected all ceremony and organisation not mentioned in the Bible, condemned transubstantiation, renounced the sacramental power of the priesthood, and denied the efficacy of the Mass. He came to agree with Augustine that the church is the predestined body of true

---

79. Murray, *The Life of John Wycliffe*, 16.
80. Durant, *The Story of Civilization: The Reformation: Vol. 6*, 27–28.
81. Latourette, *A History of Christianity: Vol. 1*, 663.

believers and that salvation comes through divine grace rather than through people's efforts to save themselves. However, he is best known for instigating a translation of the Vulgate into English. According to Wycliffe's doctrine of dominion, Christians are directly responsible to God. Therefore, in order to know and obey God's law it is necessary for them to read the Bible. For Wycliffe, the Scriptures were the only standard of faith and source of authority. He died of a stroke in 1384.

The followers of Wycliffe were the Lollards, who were made up of scholars from Oxford, the lesser gentry and the poor from both rural and urban areas. Their message led to their persecution, which some believe was effective in destroying the movement by the end of the fifteenth century.

While the movement came to an end in England their ideas spread to Bohemia through Czech students who attended Oxford. In Prague, John Hus (Jan Huss) adopted his teachings and the Hussites kept them alive for many years.[82]

JAN HUSS (1372–1415)

Jan Huss was born in Husinecz, Southern Bohemia, in about 1373. He died at the stake at Constance on July 15, 1415.[83] He became rector of the university of Prague in 1402. From that prestigious position, and from the pulpit of the nearby chapel of Bethlehem, he advocated a reformation similar to what the conciliarists of his time were proposing. Initially, he had no intention of altering the traditional doctrines of the church, but only of restoring Christian life, and particularly the life of the clergy. In 1398 he joined the arts faculty as a lecturer. He also took priestly vows. When Wycliffe's ideas arrived at the university they brought with them a great deal of controversy. The university was divided between Germans and Czechs, and soon that division was reflected in attitudes to Wycliffe's works. The Czechs accepted it and the Germans rejected it. Some of the Germans rejected Wycliffe, claiming that he was not orthodox. This put the Czechs in the difficult position of defending the teaching of a man whose orthodoxy had come into question. Eventually the king of Bohemia supported the Czech party and the Germans withdrew from the university to form one at Leipzig.

Huss became more influenced by Wycliffe, particularly those teachings dealing with the spirituality of the church. By 1407 Hus was clearly identified with the reformists. As a consequence, in 1409, Pope Alexander V empowered the Archbishop of Prague to root out heresy in his diocese. When the Archbishop asked Huss to stop preaching, he refused and was excommunicated in 1410. When Huss continued to attack the papal politics of the Great Schism and the sale of indulgences, rioting erupted in Prague against the church hierarchy. With no support from the king, and

---

82. González, *Historical Theology*, 346–348.
83. Gillett, *The Life and Times and John Huss*, 43.

the pope threatening to place Prague under interdict, Huss left the city in 1412 to live in southern Bohemia.

In 1414, with a promise of safe conduct issued by Emperor Sigmund, Jan Huss travelled to the Council of Constance. The great council promised to be the dawn of a new age for the church, and therefore Huss could not refuse. Upon arriving, however, it was clear that John XXIII[84] wanted to try him, apart from the council. Consequently, he was imprisoned and placed on trial for heresy. The emperor protested against this violation of safe conduct. But, when he realised that Huss's cause was not popular and that he would be seen to be supporting a heretic, he withdrew his protest and washed his hands of the whole affair. He refused to admit that the charges against him were true unless proven so by Scripture. Finally, convinced that he would not receive a fair hearing, he declared: "I appeal to Jesus Christ, the only judge who is almighty and completely just. In his hands I place my case, since he will judge each, not on the basis of false witnesses and erring councils, but of truth and justice."[85] On July 6, 1415, he was taken to the Cathedral, dressed in priestly garments, which were then torn from him. His head was shaved and a paper crown was placed on his head with demons on it. On his way to the stake he was led past a fire that burned his books. When he was tied to the stake he refused to recant and prayed aloud: "Lord Jesus, it is for Thee that I patiently endure this cruel death. I pray Thee to have mercy on my enemies."[86] His ashes were gathered and thrown into the lake.

Huss's sermons attacked clerical abuses, especially the high living and immorality of the clergy. His theology was a mixture of evangelical and traditional Roman Catholic doctrines. He taught against the veneration of the pope by stressing a strong Christocentric faith. He believed only Christ could forgive sins and expected a coming day of judgement. However, he still believed in purgatory. His understanding of communion came to be similar to Luther's consubstantiation. He emphasised the preaching of the Word of God to bring about moral and spiritual change. He believed in the priesthood of all believers. Importantly, like Wycliffe, he encouraged the reading of the Word of God and revised a Czech translation of the Bible.

There were other significant voices at this time. There were a number of late medieval theologians who stressed the importance of faith, not only as belief, but also as trust. Notable among them was Thomas a Kempis (1379-1471). He was a German monk and spiritual writer. In 1399 Thomas entered the monastery at Agnietenberg, which was Augustinian. He spent most of his life at Mount Saint Agnes, where he was ordained a priest and served as superior and director of novices.[87]

---

84. Baldassarre Cossa (c. 1370-1419) stood in opposition to Gregory XII during the Western Schism (1378-1417).

85. González, *Historical Theology: An Introduction to the History of Christian Thought*, 419.

86. Dever, Duncan, Mohler, Mahaney, *Preaching the Cross*, 151.

87. González, *Historical Theology*, 348-351.

FOUNDATIONS OF THEOLOGY

THE RENAISSANCE

The very name "Renaissance", or rebirth, describes an historical period which looked back to antiquity for inspiration. It was a time of great creativity in art, architecture, science and literature. During this period, from around 1300–1600, the printing press and the the telescope were invented. Explorers spread out across the globe, beautiful buildings were erected and literature and theatre flourished.[88] Those who first used this term called the thousand years since the fall of Rome the "Middle Ages", because they saw in them little more than a negative intermission between classical antiquity and their own time. In calling the best medieval art "Gothic", they showed the same prejudice, for the word itself meant that this art was the work of barbaric Goths. Likewise, in giving the name of the "Renaissance" to the intellectual and artistic movement that sprang up in Italy and spread to the rest of western Europe in the fourteenth and fifteenth centuries, they vented their prejudice against centuries immediately preceding them and claimed that what was taking place was a glorious rebirth of forgotten antiquity. Indeed, in its early stages, the Renaissance was primarily a literary movement that took as its guide the classics of ancient Greece and Rome. In its infancy it was an Italian movement, with Florence taking the lead.[89]

While the Renaissance did draw heavily from antiquity, the truth of it was that the movement also drew from the centuries immediately preceding it. Its art had deep roots in Gothic art and architecture; its attitude towards the world was inspired as much by St. Francis as by Cicero; and its literature was deeply influenced by medieval songs. However, many of its main figures believed that the immediate past, and perhaps even their present, was a period of decadence when compared with classical antiquityand therefore made every effort to promote a rebirth of ancient civilisation.

Another word associated with this time is "humanism". This is the same name given to the tendency to place humans at the centre of the universe and to make them the measure of all things. However 'humanism' is also the study of the humanities—what we might call today the "liberal arts". Consequently, many people of this period referred to themselves as "humanists" because they studied the liberal arts, or humanities. It is also true that many of them were "humanists" because their study of classical antiquity produced in them a sense of awe before human creativity. Humanism was initiated by secular scholars, rather than by scholar-clerics who had dominated medieval intellectual life and had developed scholastic philosophy. The fall of Constantinople in 1453 provided Humanism with a major boost, for many of its scholars fled to Italy, bringing with them important books and manuscripts and the tradition of Greek scholarship.

---

88. Elliott, *The Renaissance in Europe*, 4.
89. Estep, *Renaissance and Reformation*, 20.

From Italy, the humanist spirit and the Renaissance it engendered, spread north to all parts of Europe, aided by the invention of the printing press, which allowed literacy and the availability of classic texts to grow. Foremost among northern Humanists was Desoderous Erasmus (1466–1536), whose *Praise of Folly* (1509) epitomised the moral essence of humanism in its insistence on heartfelt goodness as opposed to formalistic piety. Although a sincere Catholic, he argued for liberalising the narrow constraints of Catholic worship, defended the use of vernacular in the Mass, and condemned the pope for abandoning his flock. The goal in his writings was to promote a meaningful reform of the church based on reason and Scripture.

In England, the most influential humanists were John Colet (1466–1519) and Thomas More (1478–1535). Colet sought to combine scholarship with piety to produce a balanced and harmonious Christian life. He stood for the simple exegesis of Scripture. More, in his *Utopia*, proposed a new social order in which reason, tolerance and co-operation would replace power, prestige and wealth as motivating forces.

It was in art that the spirit of the Renaissance achieved its sharpest formulation. Art came to be seen as a branch of knowledge, valuable in its own right and capable of providing people with images of God and his creations. In the hands of men like Leonardo da Vinci it was even a science, a means of exploring nature and a record of discoveries. Other well known names include Botticelli, Raphael, Donatello, and Michelangelo.

The Renaissance reached its height (the High Renaissance) during the first three decades of the sixteenth century. The glow of the High Renaissance was brightest in Rome where a number of artists, including Raphael and Michelangelo, amazed the world with their mightiest creations of classical-Christian beauty.[90] However, the religious quest found a deeper and far more extensive treatment in the Northern European Renaissance.

The Northern European Renaissance can be observed as possessing a deep religious quest not found in its Italian counterpart. A significant reason for the difference can be found in the impressive influence of the Brethren of the Common Life, a semi-monastic group of laypersons who produced such classics as Thomas a Kempis' *Imitation of Christ*, and the anonymous, *Theologica Germanica*.[91]

---

90. González, *Historical Theology*, 365–370.
91. Estep, *Renaissance and Reformation*, 45.

Chapter 24

THE REFORMATION

THE GERMAN REFORMATION—MARTIN LUTHER

At the close of the middle ages, the advocates of Reform had great hopes that the "dark ages" would close with it. The printing press, coupled with the flourishing of scholarship and the revival of classical literature, art and architecture, gave hope to the dawning of a new age of ideas that were open to fresh thinking, based on the resurrected wisdom of the ages. Corruption and the Great Schism, together with the failure of the Conciliar Movement, encouraged a surge of activity to bring about moral and ecclesiastical renewal. Reform was needed, since the papacy had become, in the spirit of the Renaissance, another wordly Italian court. The consequence was both a moral and spiritual deterioration.

> *The increased centralization of the administration of the Church in Rome created a bureaucracy where ecclesiastical offices could be bought by the highest bidder, indeed, often by the two highest bidders, with resulting lawsuits before ecclesiastical courts between the two men involved and new income for the papal treasury. In Rome, it was said, everything could be bought from top to bottom.*[1]

The humanists, led by Erasmus, were able to create an atmosphere of reform. Indeed, reform seemed ready to break out. However, it was the Protestant Reformation that changed everything. While humanism sought to clarify some aspects of Christian theology that might have gone astray, the Reformation radically shifted the fundamentals of its foundations.

---

1. Hillerbrand, *The Reformation: A Narrative History Related by Contemporary Observers and Participants*, 19.

THE REFORMATION

Ellen White rightly contended that Martin Luther was "foremost among those who were called to lead the church from the darkness of popery into the light of a pure faith."[2] His impact can largely be attributed to the kind of forthright passion that accompanied every new conviction he embraced. However, Huss had also possessed a passionate conviction. What Huss lacked was a changing society, growing tired of the old order and needing to accommodate the rising middle-classes who were eager to find their place in the new order. In addition, and of significant importance, is that Luther, unlike Huss, possessed the means to transmit his ideas. The printing press gave his writings a widespread audience, particularly among a growing literate society, spurred on by the literary revival of the Renaissance. Indeed, by the time of Luther's Reformation the number of universities had risen to 70 and a printing press existed in over two hundred cities and towns. By Luther's death, in 1546, about a million copies of the Bible, in whole or in part, had been printed and distributed.[3]

A conservative estimate of literacy, suggests that 30 percent of the urban population could read by the commencement of the the sixteenth century. However, the spread of new ideas was not limited to this literate minority. As Lindberg revealed, "those who could read passed ideas on to those who could not."[4] Therefore, while Wyclif's ideas spread very slowly through hand-written copies, Luther's blanketed Europe within months. Added to these important historical circumstances was a growing German nationalism which pitted Luther's eventual following against the heavy taxing and corrupt Roman hierarchy. Indeed, González encapulated this well when he wrote that, "(o)n studying Luther's life and work, one thing is clear: the much needed Reformation took place, not because Luther decided that it would be so, but rather because the time was ripe for it, and because the Reformer and many others with him were ready to fulfil their historical responsibility."[5]

Luther was born on November 10, in 1483, in Eisleben, Germany, the eldest of seven children. All the known children received the names of saints. Martin, Barbara, who died when Martin was thirty-six, Dorothy, Margaret and Jacob.[6] His father, Hans Luther, had been a miner and then the owner of several foundries. Martin Luther, despite quite humble origins, became an astute and hard working academic. Luther's father, who never had any schooling himself, "was concerned that his gifted son receive a good education."[7] At the right age the young Luther was sent to Latin school "where he industriously and quickly learned the Ten Commandments,

---

2. White, *Great Controversy*, 120.
3. Lindberg, *The European Reformations*, 35.
4. Lindberg, *The European Reformations*, 34.
5. González, *Historical Theology: An Introduction to the History of Christian Thought*, 15.
6. Hendrix, *Martin Luther: Visionary Reformer*, 20.
7. Lohse, Harrisville *Martin Luther's Theology: Its Historical and Systematic Development*, 29.

the Catechism, the Lord's Prayer, grammar, and Christian hymns."[8] At the age of fourteen he was sent to school at Magdeburg and then a year later to Eisenach. In his own words, Luther reflected on his origins and the unlikely course his life was to take. "I am the son of a peasant. My great-grandfather, grandfather and father were peasants. As he [Philipp Melanchthon] said, I should have been a superintendent, a bailiff or the like in the village, a servant with authority over a few. Then my father moved to Mansfield, where he became a mining operator. This is where I come from."[9] Further, Luther's childhood was not happy; described as one accompanied by grinding poverty. Indeed, Luther often recalled the hard struggles of his parents.[10] Further, his parents were extremely severe and many years later he spoke bitterly of some of the punishments he suffered. Luther later recalled how his mother had beat him until his hands bled, for stealing a nut. His father had whipped him for playing a joke on someone.[11] The brutality of his childhood brougfht lasting consequences. Indeed, throughout his life Luther had periods of depression and anxiety.[12] Finally, in 1505, when he was almost twenty-two years old, Luther joined the Augustinian monastery at Erfurt. There are a number of reasons leading to this decision. In a thunderstorm he promised St Anne, patron saint of the miners, that he would become a monk if he survived, overwhelmed by the fear of death and hell.[13] Ultimately, however, Luther was led to the monastery by a concern for his own salvation. The concern for damnation or salvation, and the purpose of life in this world being to prepare for the next, was very much the worldview in which he lived. Therefore, fulfilling his vow made passionately in the storm, Luther entered the monastery of the Augustine Friars at Erfurt on St Alexius's day, July 17, 1505.[14] To be sure, he "entered the monastery as a faithful child of the church, with the firm purpose of making use of the means of salvation offered by that church, of which the surest was the monastic life of renunciation."[15]

Luther began his monastic life well. He was at peace with God. However feelings of terror began to frequently grip him, for he felt unworthy of God's love, and he was not convinced that he was doing enough to be saved. For several years he was a disappointed, tortured soul.[16] Good works and the sacrament of penance were supposed to be enough for the young monk to feel justified before God. But they

---

8. Mathesius, *Historien*, 1, in Hillerbrand, *The Reformation: A Narrative History Related by Contemporary Observers and Participants*, 22.

9. M. Luther, *WA, TR* 5, No. 6250, in Hillerbrand, 22.

10. T.M. Lindsay, *History of the Reformation: Vol. 1*, 194.

11. Somerville, *Martin Luther: Father of the Reformation*, 16.

12. González, *Historical Theology*, 15.

13. González, *Historical Theology*, 16.

14. Gelzer, *The Life of Martin Luther and the Reformation in Germany*, 30.

15. González, Historical *Theology*, 16.

16. Latourette, *A History of Christianity*, Vol. 2, 705.

were not. He was more aware of his sinfulness and the sway of sin over his life. He repeatedly punished his body, as recommended by the great teachers of monasticism and he went to confession as often as he could. But this did not lesson his fear of damnation. He was fearful of forgetting to confess a certain sin and therefore remaining unforgiven. Indeed, he would later recall the extent of his piety. "I was indeed a pious monk and kept the rules of my order so strictly that I can say: If ever a monk gained heaven through monkery, it should have been I . . . I would have martryred myself to death with fasting, praying, reading, and other good works had I remained a monk much longer."[17] Consequently he would spend hours examining his thoughts and actions. He grew anxious and desperate. He sought answers in mysticism, but soon this path became another blind alley. The mystics stated that all one had to do was love God—the rest would follow. This suited Luther for a while, since it meant that he did not have to keep a strict account of his sins. However, he found that loving God was not easy. His past caught up with him and he could not envisage a God of love, but only of hate. His superior, who was also his confessor, made the decision to order Luther to become a teacher, in the belief that this would set him on a more constructive path. Luther was instructed, against his wishes, to prepare to teach Scripture at the new University of Wittenberg. By this time he had received, in 1512, on the 18th and 19th of October, a doctorate in theology. He was ready to commence his teaching career.[18]

In 1513 Luther began to prepare his lectures on the Psalms. He interpreted them Christologically. When the Psalm spoke of the first person, Luther took this to be Christ speaking about himself. Therefore, in the Book of Psalms, Luther saw Christ undergoing trials similar to his own. This was the beginning of his great discovery which probably came in 1515, when Luther began to lecture on the Epistle to the Romans. "He later declared that it was in the first chapter of the epistle that he found the solution to his difficulties."[19] The precise time is undetermined, but the phrase, "the just shall live by faith", brought him the illumination he craved for.[20] Indeed, to begin with he struggled with a particular word in the first chapter: righteousness. He hated the word, because the doctors of the church had taught that it was out of the righteousness of God that sinners are punished. In late medieval theology insecurity and uncertainty pervaded the concept of salvation. To be sure, one "of the key scholastic ideas that led to this uncertainty about salvation was expressed in the phrase *facere quod in se est*: do what lies within you; do your very best. That is, striving to love God to the best of one's ability—however weak that might be—will prompt

---

17. Luther, *Die Kleine Antwor auf Herzog Georg Nahestes Buch, 1533*. WA 38, 143, in Hillerbrand, p. 24.
18. H. Gelzer, *The Life of Martin Luther and the Reformation in Germany*, 40.
19. González, *Historical Theology*, 19.
20. Latourette, *A History of Christianity: Vol. 2*, 706.

God to reward one's efforts with the grace to do even better."[21] This "mathematics of salvation" mirrored early capitalism's principle that work merits reward. This was a particular challenge to Luther, since, despite his pius endeavours as a monk, he still felt that he was a sinner before God. He later recalled that a "furious battled raged within my perplexed conscience, but meanwhile I was knocking at the door of this particular Pauline passage, earnestly seeking to know the mind of the great Apostle."[22] He wondered how the message, "the righteousness (that is, the justice) of God is revealed" could be good news, since it was this justice that Luther had found so unbearable? The answer to the puzzle was Luther's conclusion that the justice of God did not refer to his punishment, but rather, the "righteousness of God" is that which is given to those who live by faith. It is given, not because they are righteous, nor because they fulfil the demands of divine justice, but simply because God wishes to give it.[23] Therefore, faith is not to be earnt for reward. Rather, both faith and justification are the work of God, a free gift to sinners. Later Luther recalled that he meditated on the significance of the words, "the righteous shall live by faith".

> *Then, finally, God had mercy on me, and I began to understand that the righteousness of God is that gift of God by which a righteous man lives, namely, faith, and that this sentence—The righteousness of God is revealed in the Gospel – is passive, indicating that the merciful God justifies us by faith . . . Now I felt as though I had been reborn altogether and had entered paradise.*[24]

As a result of this discovery, Luther stated in his preface to the *Latin Writings*: "I felt that I had been born anew and that the gates of heaven had been opened. The whole Scripture gained a new meaning. And from that point on the phrase *the justice of God* no longer filled me with hatred, but rather became unspeakably sweet by virtue of a great love."[25]

Luther's great discovery did not lead him to protest against the church. On the contrary, Luther continued teaching, although there are indications that he taught what he had learnt. Very quietly Luther eventually brought most of his colleagues at Wittenberg to his way of thinking. When he became convinced that he must challenge traditional views he composed ninety-seven theses to be debated in an academic setting.[26] To Luther's surprise few people were interested. In response, Luther wrote another set of theses, with no expectation that they would have any greater affect than the first set. However, the result was such a stir that eventually the whole of Christian Europe came to feel the effects. The reason for this very different

21. Lindberg, *The European Reformations*, 58.
22. M. Luther, *WA, TR 2, 2255A*, in Hillerbrand, 25.
23. Lindsay, *History of the Reformation: Vol. 1*, 445.
24. M. Luther, *WA 54, 183f*, in Hillerbrand, p. 27.
25. González, *Historical Theology*, 19–20.
26. González, *Historical Theology*, 20.

response was that this second set, now commonly known as Luther's "Ninety-five Theses", attacked the sale of indulgences and its theology. Luther was mostly unaware that he was attacking plans for profit made by some very powerful lords and prelates,[27] however it was this issue that focused the spot-light on him and that led him to become a centre of controversy.[28]

The sale of indulgences, that had prompted Luther's protest, were authorised by Pope Leo X and involved the economic and political ambitions of the powerful house of Hohenzollern. Leo authorized one of the members of this house, Albrecht of Brandenburg, to announce the sale of indulgences on condition that half the proceeds were sent to papal accounts. Albert was seeking to purchase the important archbishopric of Mainz for the sum of ten thousand ducats and one of Leo's dreams was to finish building the great Basilica of Saint Peter. The man put in charge of selling indulgences was the Dominican John Tetzel, who made outrageous claims about the wares he was selling.[29] "As Tetzel entered town, a messenger went before him, announcing, 'the grace of God and of the holy father is at your gates.'"[30] His activity enraged Luther, who determined to "put a hole in his drum."[31] Tetzel and his preachers were heard announcing that the indulgences they were selling made the sinner "cleaner then when coming out of baptism" and "cleaner than Adam before the fall", and that "the cross of the selling of indulgences has as much power as the cross of Christ." Those buying indulgences for a loved one who had passed away did so with the reassuring jingle: "as soon as the coin in the coffer rings, the soul from purgatory springs."[32] These claims aroused a lot of opposition. It was at this point that Luther nailed his famous Ninety-five Theses (in Latin) to the door of the castle church in Wittenberg. Luther published his theses on the eve of All Saints, about twelve years after entering the monastery. The impact of this publication was such that the date, October 31,1517, is usually given for the beginning of the Protestant Reformation.[33]

It was common place to post points for debate and discussion and the cathedral door doubled as a kind of notice board to facilitate exactly this. Translated into German from the original Latin they were printed into thousands of copies and distributed throughout Germany.[34] However, more significantly, Luther posted them to Albrecht, the archbishop of Mainz, with the naïve thought that this would expose Testzel. "The document was sent to Rome. The result was an explosion that startled

27. González, *Historical Theology*, 20.
28. Latourette, *A History of Christianity*, Vol. 2, 708.
29. González, *Historical Theology*, 20–21.
30. White, *Great Controversy*, 127.
31. Gelzer, The Life of Martin Luther and the Reformation in Germany, 43.
32. González, *Historical Theology*, 20–21.
33. González, *Historical Theology*, 22.
34. Somerville, *Martin Luther: Father of the Reformation*, 12.

and freightened Luther as much as anyone else. Luther had unknowingly touched some very sensitive nerves concerning papal authority and far-reaching political and ecclesiastical intrigue."[35] Indeed, the controversy over indulgences signaled the end of the medieval church.[36]

Following this publication, Luther wrote and distributed an extensive explanation clarifying what he had meant by each proposition. The pope's response was to ask the Augustinian order to deal with the matter. They called Luther to their next chapter meeting of the order, in Heidelberg. He went fearing he would be pronounced a heretic. However, he was surprised to find that many of his fellow friars favoured his teachings, and that some of the younger ones were even enthusiastic about them.[37] Eventually, Luther returned to Wittenberg, strengthened by the support of his order. The pope then took a different path.[38] The Diet of the Empire—the assembly of the princes and nobles—was scheduled to meet in Augsburg. The pope sent Cardinal Cajetan to find money to support a campaign against the Turks and to meet with Luther and obtain a recantation. If Luther refused he was to be sent to Rome as a prisoner.[39]

The meeting between Luther and Cajetan was unsuccessful. Cajetan refused to debate the issues and simply sought a decanting of everything.[40] In response to Cajetan's petition for a recantation, Luther responded that he was not conscious of having said anything contrary to Holy Scripture, the church fathers, or papal decretals or their correct meaning. Indeed, Luther asserted that all that he had done had been "sensible, true, and catholic."[41] When Luther discovered that Cajetan was armed with the authority of the pope to arrest him, he secretly left Augsburg at night and returned to Wittenberg where he issued an appeal to the general council.[42] During all this time Luther had benefited from the protection of Frederick the Wise, Elector of Saxony and therefore Lord of Wittenberg. Frederick protected Luther, not because he followed his teaching, but because he believed Luther had the right to be heard. Frederick had founded Wittenberg University and was aware of the situation leading to Jan Huss's death. This was a situation he did not want repeated.[43]

Meanwhile, Luther's associate, Dr. Andreas Bondenstein von Karlstadt (c1480-1541), had been challenged to a debate in Leipzig by Johann Eck (1486-1543), the prominent Ingolstadt theologian. Luther finally entered the debate, on 4 July 1519.

---

35. Lindberg, *The European Reformations*, 72.
36. Elton, Reformation Europe 1517-1559, in *Blackwell Classic Histories of Europe*, 1.
37. González, *Historical Theology*, 23.
38. González, *Historical Theology*, 23.
39. González, *Historical Theology*, 24.
40. González, *Historical Theology*, 24.
41. Luther, *Acta Augustana, 1518 (WA 2, 7-9)*, in Hillerbrand, 64.
42. González, *Historical Theology*, 24.
43. González, *Historical Theology*, 24.

THE REFORMATION

His knowledge of Scripture was evidently superior, however Eck's knowledge of cannon law and medieval theology was used by Eck to present Luther as a Hussite and a heretic. The debate lasted three weeks and ended up one of the most important steps on the road to the Reformation.[44]

Following this landmark debate, Luther produced a large volume of material. They consisted of three treatises published in 1520. By this time he was convinced that the pope was the Anti-Christ. One of his works, entitled *Address to the Christian Nobility of the German Nation*,[45] was an appeal to the princes of the Empire against the unjust dominion of the pope. Three walls needed to be broken down. They were: 1). The church is superior to the state. 2). The pope alone can interpret Scripture. 3). The pope alone has the right to summon councils. Luther also denounced celibacy, monasticism, and ritualism, by maintaining that Scripture had the final authority.

Another lengthier discourse, also published in 1520, was the *Babylonian Captivity of the Church*.[46] Unlike the previous work, it was written in Latin and addressed to academics. Primarily, it was a theological attack against the sacramental system of the Roman church. He denied the necessity of the priesthood and recognised only two sacraments, the Lord's Supper and baptism. He stated that baptism was the beginning and course of the Christian life.

In November, 1520, Luther wrote his third treatise, *On the Freedom of a Christian*. In it, he set forth what he called the true doctrine of salvation and of the Gospel. In its few pages he discussed the concept of faith, which alone—without works—justifies, frees, and through Christ, brings salvation. He also defined his view of Christian love, which, along with faith, is the fulfilment of God's commandments and the manifestation of Christian freedom.

In January, 1521, the newly elected Emperor Charles V met with his imperial diet in Worms. There he stood before the most powerful leaders of the Holy Roman Empire.[47] On the agenda was Luther and his teachings. Subsequently, he was summoned to the diet to answer charges of heresy and treason. The city was packed with masses of people, eager to see the new emperor and to get a glimpse of the now-famous Martin Luther, who had so boldly defied the pope. Luther was asked if he had published the books and pamphlets before him on a table and if he would recant what was in them. He answered "yes" to the first question and sought twenty-four hours to consider the second. The following day, and in a lengthy speech, Luther saw no reason to withdraw his writings, although he did admit that in some instances, regarding attacks on individuals, he may have been overly harsh. However, he did not consider himself a saint. When Luther had finished his speech, the imperial

---

44. González, *Historical Theology*, 26.
45. See M. Luther, *To the Christian Nobility of the German Nation—1520*.
46. Luther, *The Babylonian Captivity of The Church—1520*.
47. Somerville, *Martin Luther: Father of the Reformation*.

spokesman arose and chastised him for speaking in such a manner, instead of answering the question. He then ordered a simple response. Luther's response became the battle cry of the Reformation.

My conscience is a prisoner of God's Word. I cannot and will not recant, for to disobey one's conscience is neither just nor safe. God help me. Amen.[48]

LUTHER'S THEOLOGY OF THE WORD OF GOD

Luther sought to make the Word of God the starting point and the final authority for his theology. In response to questions that Cajetan had raised with Luther in 1518 regarding indulgences, "Luther appealed to the authority of Scripture and declared on the basis of Galatians 1:8 that 'the pope was not above but under the Word of God.'" Indeed, by the time Luther had famously spoken at Worms in 1521 "he had elevated scripture above other authorities as supreme in the church.[49] However, Luther did not confine the Word of God to the Bible. Primarily, the Word of God was none other than God. This is supported by the first verses of the Gospel of John, where it is written that "in the beginning was the Word . . . " Therefore the Bible itself states that the Word of God is the Son, the Word who was made flesh and dwelt among us. Therefore those who read the Bible and do not find Jesus in it, have not encountered the Word of God. Consequently Luther proclaimed that the book of James was "pure straw" because he could not find the gospel in it. The book of Revelation also caused him difficulty. Indeed, Luther maintained that final authority was not with the church, or the Bible, but with Jesus Christ, who had made both the church and the Bible.[50]

THE PRIESTHOOD OF ALL BELIEVERS

In Luther's *Address to the Christian Nobility* (1520), he maintained that the right to interpret scripture was in the hands of believers, who shared a spiritual priesthood. In contrast to the papal elite, or "Romanists" as he called them, Luther stipulated that all Christians form the "spiritual estate". However, this right to interpret scripture was not a private venture but was the responsibility of the Christian community. To support his conviction, Luther translated the New Testament into German (1522) so that scripture could be "more accessible to all believers and enable them to exercise the power which their common priesthood entitled them."[51] In terms of the knowledge of God, Luther maintained that God's highest self-disclosure takes place in the

---

48. González, *Historical Theology*, 28.
49. González, *Historical Theology*, 28.
50. González, *Historical Theology*, 29–30.
51. Hendrix, *Luther*, 46–47.

cross of Christ. There God is seen in weakness, in suffering, as a stumbling block. Indeed, God acts in a radically different way than people would expect. At the cross, God destroys all preconceived notions of divine glory. When we know God in the cross, we must set aside our previous knowledge of God, that is, all that we thought we knew by means of reason or of the inner voice of conscience. What we now know of God is very different from that other assumed knowledge of a theology of glory.[52] In addition, God reveals Himself in both the law and the Gospel. For Luther the two are inseparable, since at the hearing of the Gospel there is an awareness of sin that the law points to. However, on reception of the Gospel's word of pardon, the character of the law changes. "What earlier seemed an unbearable weight now becomes bearable and sweet."[53] In a sermon on John 1:17 Luther stated: "At an earlier time there was no pleasure in the law for me. But now I find that the law is good and tasty, that it has been given to me that I might live, and now I find my pleasure in it."[54] Therefore, Luther "certainly advocated the preaching and teaching of the law."[55] This is clearly in contrast to the teaching of Johann Agricola, an Antinomian, who taught that the saving nature of faith negated any need for law. Luther responded against his teaching with a treatise, "Against the Antinomians" and remained adament in his rejection of Agricola's theology.[56]

CALVIN'S REFORMATION

Bloesch contested that while John Calvin (Jean Cauvin) had a passion to build a holy community in this world, he also emphasised the spiritual mission of the church. "The pastor must always remember why he has been ordained, that he is the ambassador of God to declare the forgiveness of sins through Jesus Christ, 'that he is sent to procure the salvation of souls.' This missionary mandate of the church, however, is not just the prerogative of the clerics, but of all members of the body of Christ."[57] Thomas Torrance put his finger on Calvin's missionary impetus when he stated that those "who do not endeavour to bring their neighbours and unbelievers to the way of salvation plainly show that they make no account of God's honour, and that they try to diminish the mighty power of His empire."[58]

John Calvin was born in the small town of Noyan, a town of Picardy 60 miles northwest of Paris, in France, on July 27, 1509.[59] His father, Gerard Calvin, was

52. González, *Historical Theology,* 31–32.
53. González, *Historical Theology,* 32.
54. González, *Historical Theology,* 32.
55. Hendrix, *Luther,* 53.
56. Traver, *Agricola, Johann (1494–1566),* 5.
57. Bloesch, *Essentials of Evangelical Theology: Vol. 2,* 159.
58. Bloesch, *Essentials of Evangelical Theology: Vol. 2,* 159.
59. Beza, *Life of Calvin,* lix–lxi (CR 49m 121–2).

FOUNDATIONS OF THEOLOGY

part of the rising middle class of Noyon, and served as secretary to the bishop and procurator of the cathedral chapter.[60] His mother died four or five years after his birth and he was soon after sent to a neighbouring noble family, the Montmors, where he received his earliest education. "At fourteen, Calvin set out for Paris where he engaged in general studies at the College de la Marche and then theological studies at the College de Montaigu where Erasmus and Rabelais had preceded him and Loyala was to follow."[61] In 1528 he received a degree of Master of Arts and his father decided that his son should abandon theology and study law.[62] He subsequently moved from Paris to Orleans, and then Bourges, where he completed his law degree in 1532.[63] After his father's death, however, he appeared to return to his first passion of theology.

It is not known how Calvin came to break with Rome or the exact date on which this took place. In contrast to Luther, Calvin did not write much about the inner state of the soul. However it appears that significant factors included his own reading of Scripture together with his reading of Luther and early church history. Indeed, Calvin described his conversion "in terms similar to Luther's experience of liberation by the mercy of God from the burdens of the confessional piety of achievement."[64] Consequently, it appears that since he returned in 1534 to Noyon, and gave up the ecclesiastical posts his father had secured for him,[65] that Calvin, some time in 1533, underwent some kind of conversion experience. Although there are no signs of a deep struggle for righteousness, as with Luther, it seems that Calvin did receive a total conviction of God's omnipotence. "Like everything about Calvin, his conversion (so far as we can tell) was sober, clear-cut, psychologically almost uninteresting, but its manner accounts in great part for his ultimate success."[66] Unaffected by emotion, will-power, dicipline and order were his key watch words. It made him an astute and careful leader as well as an author of detail and systematic precision. These attributes were to flourish in his Genevan exile.

In the following year (January 5), as a result of the policies of Francis I, Calvin went into exile in Switzerland. At this time he did not seek to become a leader of the Reformation, but preferred a quiet environment where he could study Scripture and write about his faith. His main project was a short summary of the Christian faith from a Protestant viewpoint. Until then most Protestant literature had dealt exclusively with the points at issue and had said little about other basic doctrines, such as the Trinity and the incarnation. Calvin proposed to fill this vacuum with a

60. González, *Historical Theology*, 61.
61. Lindberg, *The European Reformations*, 235.
62. González, *Historical Theology*, 62.
63. Lindberg, *The European Reformations*, 235.
64. Lindberg, *The European Reformations*, 237.
65. González, *Historical Theology*, 63.
66. Elston, *Reformation Europe 1517–1559*, 149.

THE REFORMATION

short manual that he called the *Institutes of the Christian Religion.* The first volume appeared in 1536 and was a book of 516 pages. It was small in format so that it would fit easily into the wide pockets worn at the time. Importantly, it included a summary of the Protestant position regarding the "false sacraments" of Rome, and Christian freedom. The book enjoyed immediate success. The first edition, in Latin, was sold out in nine months. "From that point on Calvin worked on successive editions of the *Institutes,* and these grew in volume through the years."[67]

Another edition of the *Institutes* appeared in Strasbourg, also in Latin, in 1539. In 1541 he published in Geneva, the first French edition. From that point on all editions came out in both Latin and French: 1543, 1545, 1550, 1551, 1559, and 1560.[68] As Olsen has put it, the *Institutes* "became *the* textbook for Reformed theology for centuries and is still published, analysed, interpreted and debated."[69] The last two editions constitute the definitive text. The entire works show a profound knowledge, not only of Scripture, but also of ancient Christian literature, particularly the works of Augustine and the theological controversies of the sixteenth century.[70] There was a twofold purpose for Calvin writing the *Institutes.* Firstly, his publication was to serve as an *apologia* for his faith, a definitive doctrinal outline that represented the beliefs of the evangelicals. Secondly, Calvin saught to legitimize evangelicalism as fitting comfortably within Christendom. Indeed, evangelicalism was not a dangerous sect, but an expression of faith adhering to the main tenants of Christianity. "The presupposition to Calvin's argument is that the religion of the state was the Christian religion and that the Christian religion was the adherence to the Nicaeno-Constantinopolitan Creed."[71] His claim, however, was not that there could be more than one Christian church in the state, but that the Evangelicals were the true heirs of the early church and therefore the true holy, catholic and apostolic church on which France was legally established.[72]

After a short visit to Ferrara, and another to France, Calvin decided to settle in Strasbourg, where the Protestant cause was victorious and theological activity was high. However, the direct route to Strasbourg was closed by military operations, which meant that Calvin was redirected to make a detour through Geneva.[73] Only months earlier Geneva had been declared a Protestant city. Calvin arrived at Geneva in 1536 with the firm intention of stopping for no more than one day. However, someone told William Farel, leader of the Bern missionaries to Geneva, that the author of the *Institutes* was in town. Farel met with Calvin and presented

67. González, *Historical Theology,* 63.
68. González, *Historical Theology,* 64.
69. Olsen, *The Story of Christian Theology—Twenty Centuries of Tradition and Reform,* 408.
70. González, *Historical Theology,* 64.
71. Parker, *John Calvin: A biography,* 53.
72. Parker, *John Calvin: A biography,* 54.
73. González, *Historical Theology,* 64.

him with several reasons why he was needed in Geneva. Calvin refused, to which Farel responded with a dire threat: "May God condemn your repose, and the calm you seek for study, if before such great need you withdraw, and refuse your succour and help."[74] Calvin later reflected that "these words shocked and broke me, and I desisted from the journey I had begun."[75]

By the 1530s the episcopal city of Geneva had a mixed set of jurisdictions. Its bishops had previously ruled it. However, the dukes of Savoy expanded their power and like most of Switzerland, the townspeople had a share in government. By the time Calvin arrived the bishop of Geneva's power had been weakened. For all practical purposes, Geneva was now governed by a series of municipal councils: the Little Council (a twenty-five man board of elected members); a Council of Sixty; and an aristocratic Council of Two Hundred and a General Elected Council. However, the future of the city, now in the hands of its people, took a decisive decision. "On 25 May, 1536, a general assembly of the citizens voted to 'live by the gospel'. Geneza had become by constitution an evangelical city."[76]

Farel, who until then had been the leader of the Protestant cause, gladly became Calvin's main collaborator and supporter. A three-pronged campaign to reform religious worship, articulate a clear-cut and meaningful doctrinal basis for the church and clean up the moral life of the city, was launched in November 1536. Under the watchful eyes of Calvin and Farel, the remnants of Catholic ritual were eliminated and the Mass was replaced with simple services of prayers, sermons and psalms sung to homey melodies. Two months later Calvin submitted his reform program in the form of *Articles Concerning the Government of the Church,* also a *Confession of Faith and a Catechism,* which was abstracted from his *Institutes.*[77] He proposed to make the Confession mandatory for all citizens of Geneva by public profession of oath. He also insisted that the church have the right to examine the worthiness of its members and to discipline impenitent sinners. After considerable discussion and hesitation the councils accepted the plan. However, the middle class of Geneva protested against the extent of Calvin's reform and began to dissent. Indeed, Calvin's attempt to reform and regulate the lives of the Genevans met with opposition. Disorder and violence resulted. Indeed, there was so much dissention that the magistrates began to reneg on some points in the program and by July they rejected Calvin's plan for church discipline, fearing it would challenge their own authority. In response, Calvin locked horns with the council. He demanded that church authority only should determine the prerequisites and conditions of church fellowship and that the means of spiritual discipline should be exercised by the church. However, the council believed

---

74. González, *Historical Theology,* 65.
75. González, *Historical Theology,* 65.
76. Parker, *John Calvin: A biography,* 79.
77. Wright, *Calvin's Role in Church History,* 284.

that this was their domain. In response, Calvin believed that he had the right to excommunicate them. The gulf widened after February 1538 when several of Calvin's opponents were elected to the Little Council. A crisis developed when the Council of Two Hundred decided that the Lord's Supper should be celebrated with unleavened bread. Calvin protested and was banned from preaching. Riots and demonstrations ensued. On Easter morning, 1538, Calvin defied the ban and preached at Saint Peter's. In the sermon he denounced the council's action and refused to distribute the sacrament to anyone. Ultimately, Calvin was banned from the city. However, undeterred, he saw this as a God given opportunity to return to writing and scholarship. He therefore completed his journey to Strasbourg. There, Martin Bucer, the leader of the Reformation in Strasbourg, insisted that Calvin should be their pastor. There among French exiles he produced a French liturgy, as well as French translations of several psalms and hymns. He produced his second edition of the *Institutes* and married Idelette de Bure. They lived happily together until her death in 1549. The three years that Calvin spent in Strasbourg, from 1538 to 1541, were probably the happiest of his life. However, he regretted not being able to complete his work in Geneva. Consequently, when the situation changed, a new government invited him to return.

Calvin returned to Geneva in 1541. One of his first concerns was the preparation of a series of Ecclesiastical Ordinances[78] that the government approved with some modifications. However, tensions between the two persisted for the next twelve years. By 1553 Calvin's political position was precarious. It was then that the process against Michael Servetus took place.[79] Servetus was a Spanish physician of great note. He was also a theologian who wrote a number of treaties in which he argued that the union of church and state after Constantine's conversion was an apostasy and that the Council of Nicea, in its definition of the Trinity, had offended God. He had only recently escaped from the prisons of the Catholic Inquisition in France, where he was being tried for heresy. On passing through Geneva he was recognised and arrested. Calvin prepared a list of thirty-eight accusations against him. Some of Calvin's opponents took up Servetus' cause, arguing that he had been accused of heresy by Catholics and therefore an ally. However, Protestants also considered Servetus a heretic. Consequently, he was burned to death—although Calvin had argued in favour of a less cruel death by beheading.[80]

Servetus' death was severely criticized, especially by Sebastian Castello[81], whom Calvin had earlier expelled from Geneva for having interpreted the Song of Songs as a poem of erotic love. This episode came to symbolise a view of Calvin as

---

78. Calvin, "Ordonnances Ecclesiastiques: CR 38, 5ff, in Hilerbrand, p. 194.
79. See R. Lovci, *Michael Servetus: Heretic or Saint: The Life and Death of a Renaissance Man.*
80. González, *Historical Theology*, 67.
81. See J.E. Manross, *Sebastian Castello: Apostle of Tolerance in the Sixteenth Century.*

a rigid dogmatist. However, we do well to keep in mind that at this time all over Europe both Protestant and Catholics were acting in similar fashion against those considered to be heretics.[82]

After the execution of Servetus, Calvin's authority had no rival. This was especially true since the theologians of all other Protestant cantons had supported him, while his opponents had found themselves in the difficult position of defending a heretic who had been condemned by both Catholics and Protestants. In 1559 Calvin saw the fulfilment of one of his dreams by seeing the opening of the Genevan Academy, under the direction of Theodore Beza, who succeeded him as theological leader of the city. Calvin died in May 27, 1564.[83]

Calvin taught that through the fall all humankind became corrupt and spiritually deformed, leading to mortals being perverse and worthless in the sight of God. The Mosaic Law, as Luther had taught, is a mirror of sin, revealing the total depravity of humanity. But the law also manifested that God had not abandoned humanity. God provided a mediator and the only mediator possible between God and humanity is the God/man, Jesus Christ. It was his atoning death on the cross that made reconciliation possible. Therefore, through the redemptive grace of Christ, and the gift of faith received from the Holy Spirit, comes spiritual union with Christ. This union brings about a regeneration, or sanctification, and the believer is "born again", becoming a new creature in Christ and the inheritor of salvation. This results not from any human merit or effort but from faith in Christ. However, the justifying grace of Christ is not for everyone.

Calvin affirmed that only those who God preelects are saved. In his 1537 *Catechism*, Calvin explained that the

> seed of the Word of God takes root and grows fruitful only in those whom the Lord, by his eternal election, has predestined to be his children and heirs of the heavenly kingdom. To all the others who, by the same council of God before the constitution of the world, are reprobate, the clear and evident preaching of the truth can be nothing else but an odour of death in death.[84]

Therefore, God's Word only germinates in the elect, those he has already chosen for salvation even before their creation; only on them does Christ's redemption have any effect. The rest are predestined for perdition. One is either predestined for life or death. Further, God's will cannot be thwarted or questioned.

For Calvin, the invisible church of God consisted of the elect of all times and places, known only to God. But besides the invisible congregation there exists an outward church, the visible community of Christian believers grouped together for worship and communion. This visible church is composed of the gathered elect, but

---

82. González, *Historical Theology*, 67.
83. González, *Historical Theology*, 68.
84. McKim, *Readings in Calvin's Theology*, 163.

may also shelter some reprobates. According to Calvin, a true Christian church exists where the pure word of God is preached and believed and where the sacraments are administered according to the institution of Christ. Its members are those who profess Christ by confession, example, and participation in the sacraments.

The purpose and function of the church, in addition to providing fellowship, orderly discipline, and effective charity, is to give corrupt and fallen humanity an external aid by which faith may be engendered and grow. Indeed, Calvin, following Cyprian, asserted that "for those to whom he is father the church may also be mother."[85] Through the preaching of the word, faith is awakened in those to whom this gift is given, and by the administration of the sacraments spiritual life is communicated to the elect, thereby promoting their sanctification.

Calvin defined a sacrament as a testimony of an external sign confirming God's grace toward us. He recognised only two sacraments, baptism and the Lord's Supper. Baptism is a sign of the remission of sins. It is also an evidence of faith and the means to profess Christ through membership and fellowship in the church. The Lord's Supper is a confirmation of God's grace. Calvin rejected transubstantiation, disagreed with Luther's concept of the real presence and strongly opposed Zwingli's symbolism. Calvin believed that Christ was "truly and efficaciously" present in the Lord's Supper, but in a spiritual sense, and through the mysterious intervention of the Holy Spirit, the communicant partakes spiritually of Christ's body. "There is no body or blood in the sacrifice because Christ is in heaven, but to the believer Christ is spiritually present, having chosen the measns of bread and wine in the communion to infuse grace into the redeemed soul."[86] This means that the presence is not merely symbolic, nor communion a mere devotional exercise; rather, there is in it a true divine action for those who partake. On the one hand this does not mean that the body of Christ descends from heaven, nor is it present on many altars at the same time, as Luther claimed. Rather, in the act of communion, by the power of the Holy Spirit, believers are taken to heaven and share with Christ in a foretaste of the heavenly banquet. Indeed, Calvin's doctrine of communion came to be his distinguishing feature at the time. It was in the following century that predestination came to be seen as the hallmark of Calvinism, since Luther affirmed this doctrine as well.

THE THEOLOGICAL METHOD OF THE REFORMERS

Even before they began using the label "Protestant" as a contrast to "Roman Catholic", the Reformers distanced themselves from their opponents by using the term "evangelical". Why did they use this term? The standard Protestant historiography asserts that the Reformation was about the rediscovery of the biblical gospel, which

---

85. Calvin, *Institutes of the Christian Religion: Book IV*, 265.
86. Elston, *Reformation Europe*, 154.

had been lost in the Middle Ages. More specifically the Reformers emphasised anew the gospel as the good news of justification by grace through faith alone (*sola fide*). It has been noted that this doctrine became "the heart and essence of Luther's theological contribution."[87]

Luther was convinced that the doctrine of justification stood at the centre of soteriology and that soteriology stood at the centre of theology. Therefore, in Luther's thinking about the doctrine of justification is not that it is one doctrine among others, but rather that it is the basic and chief article of faith on which all else stands or falls. All other doctrine depends on this one foundational doctrine. It was a theological focus that amounted to a brilliant exposition of the doctrine of justification by faith. Its limitations are seen in the inadequate manner in which Luther tackles the doctrine of sanctification. However, one must consider the context in which Luther's theology took shape and the momentous task he had in combating a range of doctrinal issues that he felt compelled to confront. Simply put, one person can do so much within a lifetime. Luther himself admitted to his students that he also was constrained by the influences of the past and that it would be up to future generations to shed more light on the truth.

Luther's rediscovery of the gospel of justification by faith gave rise to a second theological focus, namely *Sola Scriptura*. This is a significant work in and of itself and is fundamental to the beginning of the Reformation. Indeed, one might say that the Reformation began when Luther entered the University of Erfurt in the January of 1501. Since it was at this time that Luther's exploration, that later led to the rediscovery of biblical truth, began. Nonetheless, his internal battle that led to a refreshed and accurate insight into the theology of justification by faith, became a component in his method that he used in the construction of his theological propositions and arguments. However, Luther's intent was not to devise a new theology of the Bible. Rather, his purpose was to undercut the Roman Catholic position which endowed the Pope, and Church Councils, with ultimate authority, and thereby effectively set the church above the Bible. This accounts for his particular emphasis and the orientation of his life's work and explains adequately any deficiencies that appeared in other areas of his theology. Indeed, Luther claimed that Scripture must take priority over the Church. Therefore, Luther declared: "The Scripture is the womb from which are born theological truth and the church."[88] Consequently, the theology of Martin Luther was *a theology of the Word of God*.

The theme of the church is found in the writings of Heinrich Bullinger, who opened the fifth and final decade of his historical sermons on the church.

> *The first of these, entitled 'The Holy Catholic Church', begins with a definition. After considering the various terms for 'the church'—'ecclesia' 'synagogue', and*

---

87. Grenz, *Renewing the Center: Evangelical Theology in a Post-Theological Era*, 34.
88. Rogers, McKim, *The Authority and Interpretation of the Bible: An Historical Approach*, 73.

> *'kuriake'—he describes the church as 'the whole company and multitude of the faithful . . . [in] heaven and . . . upon earth, where it doth agree plainly in unity of faith or true doctrine, and in the lawful partaking of the sacraments . . . joined and united together as it were in one house and fellowship.' It is called catholic or universal because it embraces believers 'in all places and times' (including the Old Testament saints), with no distinction of 'region, nation, or kindred', of 'condition, age, sex, or kind'. 'All the faithful are citizens and members of this church'.*[89]

Bullinger divided the church into two parts. Firstly, triumphant;

> *The church triumphant is 'that great company of holy spirits in heaven . . . triumphing truly through the blood of Jesus Christ' . . . To this fellowship we belong, 'for we are companions and fellow-heirs with the saints from Adam unto the end of all worlds.*

Secondly, Militant.

> *Between the church triumphant and the church on earth Bullinger sees no church expectant, for the Reformation doctrine of justification leaves no place for purgatory. Hence the second part of the church is the church militant, a congregation of men upon the earth, professing the name and religion of Christ, continually fighting in the world in spiritual warfare.*[90]

Further light was shed in the free theology of Jacobus Arminius, who successfully countered the Augustinian influence on the Magisterial Reformation by denouncing pre-determined salvation, unconditional election, the total depravity of humanity and the perseverance in faith of all Christians. In line with biblical theology, he clearly articulated justification by faith, but equally perused the importance of a dynamic Christian life. Consequently, Arminius understood the church to be "a company of persons called out from a state of natural life and of sin, by God and Christ, through the Spirit of both, to a supernatural life to be spent according to God and Christ in the knowledge and worship of both."[91] Those who profess faith in Christ become members of His church.

The doctrine of the church appears in numerous confessional statements. The Heidelberg Catechism describes the Church as

> *that assembly, or congregation of men, chosen of God from everlasting to eternal life, which the Son of God, from the beginning to the end of the world, gathers, defends and preserves to himself, by his Spirit and word, out of the*

---

89. Bromiley, *Historical Theology: An Introduction*, 259.
90. Bromiley, *Historical Theology*, 260.
91. Bangs, *Arminius: A Study in the Dutch Reformation*, 333.

whole human race, agreeing in true faith, and which he will at length glorify with eternal life and glory.[92]

The Westminster Confession of Faith states that the "catholic or universal Church, which is invisible, consists of the whole number of the elect that have been, are, or shall be, gathered into one, under Christ and head thereof; and is the spouse, the body, the fullness of Him that filleth all in all." Chapter XXV, Section I.

> *The visible Church, which is also catholic or universal, under the gospel . . . consists of all those throughout the world that profess the true religion (1 Cor. 1:2, Rom 15:9–12), together with their children (1 Cor. 7:14; Acts 2:39; Rom. 11:16); and is the kingdom of the Lord Jesus Christ, the house and family of God, out of which there is no ordinary possibility of salvation (Acts 2:47). Chapter XXV, Section II.*[93]

In the Articles of Religion of the Wesleyan Church it states:

> *We believe that the Christian church is the entire body of believers in Jesus Christ, who is the founder and only Head of the Church. The church includes both those believers who have gone to be with the Lord and those who remain on the earth, having renounced the world, the flesh, and the devil, and having dedicated themselves to the work which Christ committed unto His church until He comes.*[94]

In the twentieth-century Karl Barth affirmed a strong link between the institution of the church and the agency of the Holy Spirit.

> *Woe to us, where we think we can speak of the Church without establishing it wholly on the work of the Holy Spirit . . . I believe in the Holy Spirit, and therefore also in the existence of the Church, of the congregations . . . The Christian congregation arises and exists neither by nature nor by historical human decision, but as a divine convocation. Those called together by the work of the Holy Spirit assemble at the summons of their King.*[95]

---

92. Ursinus, *The Commentary of Dr. Zacharius Ursinus on the Heidelberg Catechism*, 286.
93. Shaw, *An Exposition of the Confession of Faith*, 258–9.
94. *Articles of Religion of the Wesleyan Church.*
95. Barth, *Dogmatics in Outline*, 142.

CHAPTER 25

THE RADICAL REFORMATION— THE ANABASPTISTS

ARISING FIRST IN ZURICH AFTER Zwingli had introduced his reforms, the Anabaptists, or re-baptisers, insisted that only those making a personal and public confession of faith should be baptized. They contended that Zwingli had not been faithful to his own reforming principles. While he had promoted the authority of the Bible alone, he maintained unbiblical practices. Conrad Grebel argued that these unbiblical practices included infant baptism, a close link between church and magistracy and the participation of Christians in warfare. According to McGrath, different Anabaptist groups held a number of beliefs in common. These included: "a general distrust in external authority; the rejection of infant baptism in favour of the baptism of adult believers; the common ownership of property; and an emphasis upon pacifism and non-resistance."[1] Indeed, the separation of church and state was their most radical endeavour. Many had as little to do with the state as possible, while some refused to cooperate altogether. Further, the doctrine of passive resistance was held by almost all of the early Anabaptists. However, due to the strong individuality of the Anabaptists, and the general complexity of the movememt, it is not possible to describe one form or expression of this movement. None-the-less, all of the "earlier Anabaptists believed that it was unchristian to return evil for evil, and that they should take the persecutions which came to them without attempting to retaliate."[2] Some Anabaptists withdrew from society and started separate communities uncontaminated by the world around them. Their worship was identified by its simplicity. "Some looked for the early end of history and the imminent visible return of Christ to set up his millennial reign."[3]

1. McGrath, *Historical Theology*, 162.
2. Lindsay, *A History of The Reformation: Vol. 2*, 438.
3. González, *Historical Theology: Vol. 2*, 779.

FOUNDATIONS OF THEOLOGY

In addition, their tendency was to austerity in morals and simplicity in food, dress and speech. Indeed, they emphasised the moral life, believing that while one was saved by faith alone, a genuine faith would issue in good works. "Even among their severe critics were those who admitted that they were honest, peaceable, temperate in eating and drinking, eschewed profanity and harsh language, and were upright, meek and free from covetousness and pride."[4]

The largest group on the continent to survive persecution were the Mennonites. Their name derives from Menno Simmons (1496–1561). Originally a catholic priest from the Low Countries, Simmons embraced the Reformation, but came to the conclusion, after a careful study of the Bible, that Luther, Zwingli and Calvin were wrong in practicing infant baptism. Therefore, on January 30, 1536, Menno Simmons "publicly renounced his Roman Catholic connexion and not long afterwards was baptised . . . (and was subsequently) . . . ordained as an Anabaptist minister."[5]

At their best, Anabaptists were Biblicists. In fact, they often took issue with other Reformers when they saw the need to be more faithful to the text. However, Anabaptists distinguished themselves from other Reformers primarily by way of their ecclesiology. "Believer baptism, a 'memorial' view of the Lords supper, and church discipline ('the ban') were tools used by the Anabaptists to form and maintain local churches consisting of professed believers."[6] Therefore, baptism was more than a profession of faith in a public space. By baptism, the believer came under the discipline of the biblical people of God. In this way, the door of entrance was closely watched so that a strong church could be maintained.[7]

Further, the Anabaptists linked their understanding of obedience to Scripture, and to personal piety. Indeed, "Christian behavior, motivated by love and obedience to biblical teaching (even to death), became a central tenet of Anabaptist discipleship."[8] In regard to worship, Anabaptists, along with the Magisterial Reformers, insisted that services be held in the language of the people. They objected to church festivals, to the blessing of buildings and to crosses and candles. Alternatively, they "met in each other's houses for public worship, which took the form of reading and commenting upon the Holy Scriptures."[9]

---

4. González, *Historical Theology: Vol. 2*, 779.

5. Latourette, *A History of Christianity: Vol. 1*, 784–785.

6. Patterson, "What Contemporary Baptists can Learn from Anabaptists", in M. Yarnell (ed), *The Anabaptists and Contemporary Baptists: Restoring New Testament Christianity, Essays in honour of Paige Patterson*, 13.

7. Little, *The Anabaptist View of the Church: A study in its Origins and Sectarian Protestantism*, 85.

8. Patterson, *What Contemporary Baptists can Learn from Anabaptists*, 13.

9. Lindsay, *A History of The Reformation: Vol. 2*, 433.

THE RADICAL REFORMATION—THE ANABASPTISTS

Radical for their day, the Anabaptists believed in the separation of church and state. They asserted that the church should be made up of those who had not been compelled or coerced by the state, but freely attended as an act of faith.

> With the exception of Balthasar Hubmaier (1482–1528) and the Anabaptist kingdom of Munster, most Anabaptists believed that civil authorities should not exercise authority over the church or over spiritual matters of individual conscience. Through their opposition to governmental control of religion and their willingness to suffer martyrdom for this belief, the 16th century Anabaptist eloquently advocated for a separation of church and state.[10]

Indeed, they sought to not only a separation of the institutional church, but also individual Christians, from the political world.[11] This separation also included strongly held pacifist views. To be sure, the Anabaptist refusal to participate in war brought them considerable hostility. "The Anabaptists based their pacifism on Scripture, citing Matthew 26, where Jesus told Peter to put away his sword. Anabaptists interpreted Jesus' words to mean that Christians should not necessarily defend against attacks of external foes."[12]

In regard to communion and baptism, Anabaptists preferred the term "ordinances". They held to the symbolic representation of the elements espoused by Zwingli. "In addition to baptism and the Lord's Supper some Dutch Mennonites practiced foot washing in conjunction with the Lord's Supper, in imitation of Jesus washing his disciple's feet at the last supper (John 13). Dirk Philips named foot washing as the third ordinance established by Christ for the true church."[13] Through this ordinance believers where to experience inner renewal through an act of deliberate humiliation and servanthood. Later, Ulli Ammann, founder of the Amish, maintained foot washing as a distinctive practice of his group. Today, they remain the only Anabaptist division to practice foot washing.[14] The Anabaptist conviction was that the new creation's coming involved a radical turn from the "world" to Christ. Baptism was an expression of this turn that was both radical and public. Indeed, "Anabaptists argued that Scripture consistently presented water baptism as the initial, public, outward expression of the new birth, or of inward Spiritual baptism, or of participation in Jesus' death and resurrection (esp. Rom. 6:3–11; Col. 2:11–13; 1 Peter 3:21)."[15]

---

10. D.B. Kraybill, *Concise Encyclopedia of Amish, Brethren, Hutterites, and Mennonites*, 45.
11. Hamburger, *Separation of Church and State*, 349.
12. Yarnell, *The Anabaptists and Contemporary Baptists: Restoring New Testament Christianity*, 71.
13. Lehner, Muller, Roeber, *The Oxford Handbook of Early Modern Theology, 1600–1800*, 382.
14. Lehner, Muller, Roeber, *The Oxford Handbook of Early Modern Theology, 1600–1800*, 382.
15. Finger, *A Contemporary Anabaptist Theology: Biblical, Historical, Constructive*, 169.

Furthermore, sixteenth-century Anabaptists, who shared with the most radical Reformers the belief that the true church had fallen during the patristic age, committed themselves to the church as restored. They gathered upon personal profession of faith in Jesus Christ, symbolized by the covenant sign of believer's baptism—a church separated from government and worldly society, living under its discipline, suffering persecution, and seeking to fulfil the Great Commission.[16] To be sure, as Luther predicted, continued study into the Word of God would produce more and more new light, which continued to be shed on those who pursued a rigorous and Spirit led study of the Bible.

---

16. J. L. Garrett, *Systematic Theology: Vol. 2*, 474.

CHAPTER 26

REVIVAL MOVEMENTS

BETWEEN 1750 AND 1815 PROTESTANT Christianity experienced a number of revivals that, to this day, define the theology and culture of the evangelical movement. These revivals, characterised as "The Great Awakenings" and "Evangelical Revivals", were not confined to any one branch of Protestantism, but cut across denominational and confessional lines. The roots of these movements lie with the Pietist movement of Germany in the seventeenth century. A significant figure in this movement was Philipp Jakob Spener (1635–1705), who was born and raised in Alsace, to an aristocratic family of deep Lutheran convictions. He received a doctorate in theology and became a pastor in Frankfurt. There, he founded groups for Bible study and devotion that he called "colleges of piety". In 1675, five years after beginning this ministry, he wrote his *Pia desideria (Heartfelt Desires for God Pleasing Reform of the True Evangelicals)*[1], which outlined a program for the development of piety. His book became the fundamental charter of Pietism. The work emphasised the priesthood of all believers, which should result, wrote Spener, in a common responsibility of all Christians. Its intention was that all Believers should display a more intense life of devotion and study. Further, the preacher's role was to lead the people to a greater obedience to the Word of God.

Pietism made an impact on Count Nikolaus Ludwig von Zinzendorf, a godchild of Spener. Zinzendorf studied law and entered the service of the court of Dresden. It was in Dresden that he first met a group of Moravians who would change the course of his life. They were Hussites, who had been forced to leave Moravia. Zinzendorf offered them land, where they founded the pietist community of Herrnhut.

In 1731, while in Denmark, Zinzendorf met a group of Eskimos who had been converted by a Lutheran missionary. This kindled in him a passion for mission that stayed with him for the rest of his life. Soon, the Herrnhut community burned with

---

1. Spener, *Pia Desidaria*.

the same zeal, and in 1732 its first missionaries left for the Caribbean. In a few years, there were Moravian missionaries in Africa, India and North and South America. The Moravians, officially called Unitas Fratrum, or Unity of Brethren, were the spiritual descendants of the Czech Reformer, Jan Hus. Forty-two years after his Martyrdom in 1415, in 1457, "some of his followers founded a church body consecrated to following Christ in simplicity and dedicated living."[2] The Awakening had begun.

At this time, during the eighteenth century, revivals occurred in Great Britain, in the form of the Evangelical Awakening and in North America (the Thirteen Colonies) in what would become known as the Great Awakening. In the Thirteen Colonies, its chief channels were the churches of the Reformed tradition. In Great Britain, revival was initially most prominent in the Church of England, but was also found in the Church of Scotland and in bodies dissenting from both, mostly Methodists, Congregationalists and Baptists. It later spread to the Reformed churches of Europe. In whatever country, or branch of Protestantism, the awakening appeared. It had distinctive features. It was characteristically Protestant and stressed the authority of the Scriptures, salvation by faith alone, and the priesthood of all believers. It made much of a personal religious experience, of a new birth through trust in Christ, commitment to Him, and faith in what God has done through him in the incarnation, the cross and the resurrection. The awakening was intensely missionary. It sought to win nominal Christians to the Gospel, as well as all non-Christians throughout the world. It endeavoured hopefully, in the words of the New Testament command, to "preach the Gospel to all the world" (Mk 16:15).

The awakening also gave rise to efforts to relieve suffering and to remedy collective evils. This included the promotion of such institutions as orphanages and hospitals and in enterprises such as nursing the sick and relieving famine. Other results arising included religious education in Sunday School, movements for the abolition of slavery, international peace, and temperance. The revival was by no means all from one source nor did it centre on any individual. However, John Wesley was a significant and dominant figure.

JOHN WESLEY

John Wesley (1703–1791) was the primary figure in the eighteenth-century Evangelical Revival and the founder of Methodism. He was born in Epworth, Lincolnshire, England, to Samuel and Susanna Wesley on the 17th of June 1703.[3] He was one of nineteen children. While his grandfathers were both Puritan Nonconformists, his parents returned to the Church of England. His father was a Church of England minister at Epworth (1697–1735) and Wroot (1725–35). John was educated at

2. Nouse, *Moravian Musical Origins*, 17.
3. Southy, *The Life of Wesley; and the Rise and Progress of Methodism*, 12.

Charterhouse, a school for boys in London, before going on to read at Christ Church, Oxford. From there, he received the B.A. degree in 1724 and then his M.A. in 1727. He was a serious student in both logic and religion, however he did not experience his 'religion' until his conversion in 1725.[4] After that moment he dedicated himself to Christian ministry.

Wesley was ordained a deacon in the Church of England in 1725 and served as his father's curate at Wroot (1727-29).[5] He then returned to Oxford and became the leader of a small band of students, which had been organized earlier by his younger brother Charles. This band, called the "Holy Club", would later be called "Methodist" for their prescribed method of studying the Bible and for their rigid self-denial, which included numerous charitable works. In 1735, the year that Wesley began his journal, he went to Georgia as a missionary to the Indians. While this venture was largely unsuccessful, he served as a priest to the Georgia settlers. During a storm, while crossing over from England, Wesley was deeply impressed by a group of Moravians. Their faith in the face of death (the fear of dying had been with him from his youth) led to Wesley being drawn to their evangelical faith. Consequently, after a disastrous time in Georgia, Wesley returned to England in 1738 and sought out the Moravian Peter Bohler, who exhorted Wesley to trust Christ alone for salvation. What had previously been a "religious" conversion now became an "evangelical" conversion.

At a Moravian band meeting on Aldersgate Street on May 24, 1738, Wesley listened to a reading from Luther's preface to his commentary on Romans. As he heard this he felt his "heart strangely warmed". After a short journey to Germany, in order to visit the Moravian settlement of Herrnhut, he returned to England and with George Whitfield, a former member of the Holy Club, began preaching salvation by faith. This "new doctrine" was considered redundant by the sacramentalists in the Established Church, who thought that people were saved by virtue of their infant baptism (Baptismal Regeneration). They closed their doors to the Methodist's preaching, who in turn continued to preach in the open air.

In 1739 Wesley followed Whitfield to Bristol, where a revival broke out among the miners of Kingswood. At that moment, the genius of Wesley became most evident, as he began to organize new converts into Methodist "societies" and "bands" that sustained both them and the revival. The revival continued under Wesley's direct leadership for more than fifty years. In that time, he travelled 250,000 miles throughout England, Scotland, Wales and Ireland, preaching some 40,000 sermons.

His influence extended to America, after he had ordained several of his preachers to work there. Wesley literally established "the world as his parish" in order to

---

4. Southy, *The Life of Wesley; and the Rise and Progress of Methodism*, 30–32.
5. Southy, *The Life of Wesley; and the Rise and Progress of Methodism*, 43.

spread "scripture holiness throughout the land". However, he remained a member of Established Church all his life.[6]

WESLEY'S THEOLOGY

John Wesley was a free-will Arminian who denounced the predestinational theology of Calvinism, which taught that God predestines who will be saved and that once saved a Christian is always saved. Arminianism also eschews commonly held perceptions of original sin, stating that sin is an action, rather than a state of being. Further, Christ died for all, not just the elect, and individuals being wooed by the influencing grace of the Spirit must make the personal decision, based on their liberated wills, to follow Christ. Further, they must continue to exercise that will.

Under Moravian influences, Wesley reacted against what he saw as
"salvation by works", in favour of justification by faith experienced in a sudden conversion or "new birth". In his mature theology, however, salvation was seen as an extended process which he described in terms of repentance, faith and holiness: "The first . . . the porch of religion the next, the door; the third, religion itself."[7] He stressed the possibility of perfection in this life. This perfection would be in terms of an experience of freedom from conscious sin and an uninterrupted relationship of love towards God and humankind. Perfection should be pursued actively by all means of grace but could be given in a moment in response to faith. Wesley's perfectionist theology resulted in many pulpits being closed to him. In response, Wesley defended his position in a tract of 1759 entitled, "Thoughts on Christian Perfection". In it he reiterated his contention that sinlessness does not mean freedom from ignorance, infirmities or mistakes. Indeed, Wesley believed that "a person filled with the love of God is still liable to these involuntary transgressions. Such transgressions you may call sins, if you please: I do not."[8]

Although Wesley was not a systematic theologian, his theology can be described with reasonable clarity from the study of his published sermons, tracts and correspondence. In essence, Wesley's theology is closely related to the Reformation in that it affirms God's sovereign will to reverse our "sinful, devilish nature" by the work of the Holy Spirit; a process called "prevenient, justifying" and "sanctifying" grace (grace being nearly synonymous with the work of the Holy Spirit).

For Wesley, prevenient, or preventing, grace describes the universal work of
the Holy Spirit in the hearts and lives of people between conception and conversion. Original sin, according to Wesley, makes it necessary for the Holy Spirit to initiate the relationship between God and people. Bound by sin and death, people

---

6. Tuttle, *Wesley, John*, 1164.
7. Murphy, *Religious Bodies, 1936: Pt 1*. 1082.
8. Malony, *The Amazing John Wesley: An Unusual Look at an Uncommon Life*, 30.

experience the gentle wooing of the Holy Spirit until they finally understand the claims of the gospel upon their lives. This doctrine constitutes the heart of Wesley's Arminianism. Wesley further believed that justification and perfection could be lost and regained. His Arminianism, with its perfectionism and stress on the role of disciplined piety, exposed him to Calvinist charges that he was reverting to salvation by works.[9]

Justifying grace describes the work of the Holy Spirit at the moment of conversion. It works in the lives of those who say "yes" to the call of prevenient grace by placing their faith and trust in Jesus Christ. Wesley understood such conversion as two phases of one experience. The first phase—justification—includes the Spirit attributing, or imputing, to the believer the righteousness of Jesus Christ. The second phase—the new birth—includes the Spirit launching the process of sanctification or imparted righteousness. These two phases identify, in part, the Wesleyan distinctive.

Sanctifying grace describes the work of the Holy Spirit in the lives of believers between conversion and death. Faith in Christ saves us *from* destruction and sin and *for* heaven and righteousness. The process of sanctification culminates in an experience of "pure love", as one progresses to the place where love becomes devoid of self-interest. It is important to note that this perfection is not static but dynamic, always improvable. Indeed, for Wesley, released "by the Aldersgate experience from attempted works-righteousness, he retained the belief that sanctification is the goal of justification."[10] Although Wesley did speak of an instantaneous experience called "entire sanctification" subsequent to justification, his major emphasis was the continuous process of going on to perfection. The watchword of the revival became: "Go on to perfection: otherwise you cannot keep what you have". Although realising that the word *perfection* offended many people, he could not abandon it due to its place in Scripture. Firstly, Wesley understood that people are never perfect in knowledge. From this, he observed, that Christians make mistakes. No living person is infallible any more than they are omniscient. Secondly, Christians suffer from infirmities, not merely as physical defects but also as mental and social defects. Thirdly, Christians are not free from temptation. Some may feel tempted while others enjoy freedom for a time. But temptation will recur. Therefore, Wesley concluded that there is "no absolute perfection on earth . . . none which does not admit of a continual increase." For perfection, after all, is "only another term for holiness."[11] Therefore, Wesley's understanding of biblical perfection combined intent and desire for entire sanctification (perfection) that comes by way of the imputed and alien righteousness of Christ and, consequently, a continual growth in holiness. Important to this process is a subsequent outcome of the working of the Holy Spirit in the life of the Christian.

---

9. Olson, *Arminian Theology: Myths and Realities*, 26.
10. Bromiley, *Historical Theology*, 338.
11. Bromiley, *Historical Theology*, 339.

This is seen in a freedom from outward and intentional sin, for the young Christian, and the inward evil heart with its pride, self-will and anger, for the more mature. In this way, to be born again in Christ is to be freed from sin.

Wesley's early writings reveal that his aspirations toward holiness (sanctification) were driven by a desire for assurance that he was in a state of divine acceptance (justification). His Aldersgate experience convinced him that justification precedes and empowers sanctification, rather than being based upon it. Yet he was initially led to expect that justifying faith would bring instantaneous moral perfection. He soon came to question this expectation, and in 1741 he published a sermon "Christian Perfection" in order to answer criticisms of his early claims. He hoped to sort out the ambiguity by defining both the limits and the possibilities of human perfection on earth. Wesley insisted that our actions are not products of isolated decisions but flow from our inner affections, meaning desires or dispositions. As such, we can only hope for consistent outward holiness in actions if we possess the inward holiness of Christlike affections. Jonathan Edwards, a New England Congregationalist, also promoted an affectional model of Christian life, but he disagreed with Wesley on how a person obtains Christlike affections. Edwards believed that these affections were unilaterally infused by God and instantaneously complete. Wesley, believing that God's grace works cooperatively in salvation, argued that the affections arise in response to God's empowering impact on our lives. These affections strengthen into enduring "tempers", as we exercise them, or fade away, as we resist them. This conviction lies behind Wesley's repeated claims: firstly, that we are only able to love God and neighbour when we have first felt God's love for us; and secondly, that when we allow love of God and neighbour to flow, it produces "every Christian grace, every holy and happy temper. And from these springs uniform holiness of conversion."[12]

It would seem that Wesley developed the notion that perfection could be reached within this lifetime, however towards the end of his life he integrated this belief with his teaching on progressive perfection, or gradual growth. It is possible that a surge in apocalyptic expectation in the latter half of the 1750s played a role in this change. That is, an increase in concern for perfection before Christ's return. However, by around 1760 he began to question his own theology because he believed it might hinder Christians in their walk of faith. To counteract this possibility, he began emphasising the limits of deliverance from sin that comes with Christian perfection.

Wesley also knew that by the early 1760s there were some extreme developments in this theology. This is seen in two associates of Wesley, Thomas Maxfield and George Bell. Maxfield and Bell portrayed perfection as "angelic" or absolute, such that there was no need for growth after the event, or for the continuing atoning work of Christ. Controversy resulted, and Wesley responded by dismissing them

---

12. Markham, *Rewired: Exploring Religious Conversion*.

and integrating his emphasis on attaining Christian perfection in this life with his earlier stress on gradual growth.[13]

However, not all of Wesley's associates were convinced that he found the proper equilibrium. The most significant dissenter was his brother Charles.

Charles Wesley (1707—1788) refused to adopt the modified assumptions about entire sanctification that had made it possible for John to stress its present attainment. Indeed, in reaction to John's modifications and the subsequent perfectionist controversy, Charles moved toward a more exacting expectation of Christian perfection. Charles remained profoundly aware of imperfection. He became convinced that perfection could be attained only at death.[14] Indeed, Charles worried that urging novices on too fast caused pride and the loss of their real grace. As he expressed it in a 1762 hymn on Matthew 13:5:

> *Lord, give us wisdom to suspect*
> *The sudden growths of seeming grace,*
> *To prove them first, and then reject,*
> *Whose haste their shallowness betrays;*
> *Who instantaneously spring up,*
> *Their own great imperfection prove:*
> *They lack the toil of patient hope,*
> *They lack the root of humble love.*

JOHN WESLEY AND THE PRINTING PRESS

Throughout Wesley's ministry throughout England, Scotland and Ireland, he also found time to publish hundreds of books, tracts, pamphlets and a periodical, the *Arminian Magazine*. Approximately 500 titles are attributed to the two Wesley brothers, a large number penned by John.

The Methodists took constant criticism from people who believed false reports about their doctrines and practices. Wesley defended himself and his movement with the press, seeking both to dispel misunderstandings and to generate sympathy. *An Earnest Appeal to Men of Reason and Religion* (1743) and *A Farther Appeal to Men of Reason and Religion* (1745) are classic examples of Wesley's attempt to explain his message and Methodism's place in English life. Wesley's published *Journal*, which covers the period from 1735 to 1790, described his ideas and actions in forming the Methodist movement. Besides conversion, nothing was more important to Wesley than providing for believers "holiness of heart and life." Consequently, much of his writing aimed at nurturing Methodists in holy living.

---

13. Wood, *The Meaning of Pentecost in Early Methodism*, 45.
14. Hynson, *Through Faith to Understanding*, 16.

FOUNDATIONS OF THEOLOGY

Since Wesley was thoroughly persuaded that the Bible was the most important book Christians possessed, he published two major biblical commentaries. His *Explanatory Notes Upon the New Testament* was published in 1755. It contained not only comments on almost every verse in the New Testament, but Wesley's own translation of the biblical text from Greek into English.[15] His massive *Explanatory Notes Upon the Old Testament* followed in 1765–1766. Between 1749 and 1755, Wesley edited and issued *A Christian Library*, a 50-volume series that included selections from early church fathers, such as Clement and Polycarp, to writers of his own time. He believed that Christians would be instructed, inspired, and encouraged by reading the selections he had chosen.

Wesley regularly exhorted his readers to heed God's call to correct their lives, the church, and the nation, therefore fulfilling what Wesley saw as God's charge to the Methodists movement: "to reform the nation, particularly the Church; and to spread scriptural holiness over the land."[16] *Thoughts upon Slavery* (1774) condemned the practice and pleaded with those engaged in the slave trade to abandon it for the sake of God and those it exploited.[17] In 1746 he published a collection of 151 of his own sermons. In the preface to the first edition he stated that these sermons contained the substance of his preaching and teaching. They were theological tracts to be read and studied by his preachers and people as a guide for Methodist proclamation and living.

WESLEYANISM

The Wesleyan tradition's defence has normally exercised four basic proofs, known as the Wesleyan Quadrilateral. They are: Scripture, reason, tradition, and experience.[18]

In *Scripture*, Wesley insisted that Scripture is the first authority and contains the only measure whereby all other truth is tested. Delivered by divinely inspired men, it is a rule sufficient of itself.

In *Reason*, although Scripture is sufficient, Wesley wrote: "Now, of what excellent use is reason, if we would either understand ourselves, or explain to others, those living oracles."[19] He stated that without reason we cannot understand the essential truths of Scripture. Reason, however, is not a mere human invention. It must be assisted by the Holy Spirit if we are to understand the mysteries of God. With regard to justification by faith and sanctification, Wesley stated that although reason cannot produce faith, we can understand by reason the new birth, inward holiness

---

15. Sheehan, *The Enlightenment Bible: Translation, Scholarship, Culture*, 94.
16. Wesley, Whaling, *John and Charles Wesley: Selected Prayers, Hymns, Journal Notes, Sermons, Letters and Treaties*, 34.
17. Wesley, *Thoughts Upon Slavery*.
18. Thorsen, *The Wesleyan Quadrilateral*.
19. Wesley, Emory, Jackson, *The Works of the Rev. John Wesley: Sermons*, 128.

and outward holiness. Therefore, although reason cannot produce faith it shortens the leap.

In *Tradition,* Wesley (although other evidence is perhaps stronger) insisted: "Do not undervalue traditional evidence. Let it have its place and its due honour. It is highly serviceable in its kind, and in its degree."[20]

Experience, apart from Scripture, is the strongest proof of Christianity. Wesley wrote: "What the Scriptures promise, I enjoy."[21] Again, Wesley insists that we cannot have reasonable assurance of something unless we have experienced it personally. John Wesley was assured of both justification and sanctification because he had experienced it in his own life. What Christianity promised (considered as a doctrine) was accomplished in his soul. Although tradition establishes the evidence a long way off, experience makes it present to all persons. As for the proof of justification and sanctification, Wesley stated that Christianity is an experience of holiness and happiness, the image of God impressed on a created spirit, a fountain of peace and love springing up into everlasting life.

Christianity in the United States: Advance on the Frontier and the Great Awakenings.

During the nineteenth century, Christian organizations and communities sprang up on the rapidly moving frontier. In the early days of the frontier movement many who had had a church connexion before going West, made no effort to re-establish one in their new homes. There was a tendency to ignore Christian moral standards. Yet it was on the frontier that Christianity made some of its most striking advances, which were made through a variety of channels and agencies. One of the conditions was the rapid growth in the new regions. In 1783, when Great Britain formally recognized the independence of the United States, the western boundary was the Mississippi River. In 1818, joint occupancy with Great Britain of the Oregon County bought the United States to the Pacific. In 1819 Florida was purchased. In the 1840s, Texas was brought in and the war with Mexico and added the huge region of California, New Mexico and Arizona.

Many clergymen moved West and, without support from the East, took up farms, worked on the six days a week for a livelihood for themselves and their families, and preached on Sundays. Eventually voluntary gifts from the people in the churches made it possible for numbers of clergymen to give a larger proportion of their time to the church. "Revivals" continued. They had been a feature of much of Protestantism in the new country in the forms of the Great Awakenings. The "evangelicalism" which was already characteristic of American Protestantism and which had as its aim, winning all the population to Christian faith, stressed revivals as a normal way of attaining this goal. Baptists, Methodists, and the Disciples of Christ,

---

20. Wesley, Whaling *Selected Prayers, Hymns, Journal Notes, Sermons, Letters and Treaties,* 129.
21. Wesley, Emory, Jackson, *Works of John Wesley,* 761.

maintained their spectacular growth. State missionary societies were organized, chiefly by Congregationalists, but also by some other bodies. The American Bible Society, the American Tract Society and the American Sunday School Union, drew their support primarily from Congregationalists and Presbyterians, but from others as well. They covered both the frontier and the older sections of the country. Several times during the century, first in 1829, the American Bible Society attempted to put a copy of the Scriptures in every family in the United States, including both cities and frontier. Another channel through which Christianity spread on the frontier was educational institutions, planted under the auspices of the several denominations. In time, each of the major denominations had a chain of academies, colleges, and universities stretching across the country.

The eighteenth century brought to North America the Pietistic movement. From an early date, many in the North American colonies had felt that a personal religious experience was important for Christian life. Figures associated with the First Great Awakening (c. 1735–43) include Dutch Reformed clergyman Theodore Frelinghuysen and the Presbyterian Gilbert Tennent. However, the full blossoming of this conviction started to come to life when in 1734 the first signs of the First Great Awakening appeared in Northampton, Massachusetts.

The pastor around which the events of the Great Awakening occurred was Jonathan Edwards, a staunch Calvinist who had been trained at Yale (then the Collegiate School), he was convinced about the need for a personal experience of conversion. He had been preaching in Northampton for several years, with average results, when his preaching began to evoke a response that surprised him. His sermons were not exceptionally emotive, although they did underscore the need for an experience of conviction of sin and of divine forgiveness. In Edward's mind, there was no doubt about what, under God, led to the beginning of the Great Awakening. He later published five of his sermons that had sparked the original excitement. The sermons are carefully argued defences of various aspects of Calvinist doctrines related to salvation. Each concludes with an application, but they are mainly composed of theological arguments.

In 1734, people began responding to his sermons, some with emotional outbursts, but many with a remarkable change in their lives and with an increased attention to devotion. In a few months, the movement swept the area and reached into Connecticut. Soon it subsided and after three years its extraordinary signs had almost disappeared. But the memory remained. Shortly after, George Whitfield visited New England. His preaching led to many experiences of conversion as well as outward expressions of repentance and joy. Although Edwards was a Congregationalist he invited Whitfield, an Anglican, to preach in his church. This gave the awakening new impetus. People wept in repentance for their sins, some shouted for joy at having been pardoned and a few were so overwhelmed that they fainted.

REVIVAL MOVEMENTS

The manifestations of the Awakening led to accusations that its leaders were undermining the solemnity of worship and were substituting emotion for study and devotion. It must be said, however, that many of the leaders of the movement were not particularly emotive and many were scholars. This is seen in the sermons of Jonathan Edwards. They were not emotive, but careful expositions of profound theological matters. At first the movement was led by Congregationalists and Presbyterians, but soon Baptists and Methodists joined. Initially Baptists were opposed to the movement, finding it frivolous and superficial. However, the experience of conversion led many to doubt the validity of infant baptism. Many became Baptists. In fact, whole congregations did so. Baptists and Methodists spread rapidly as they moved with ecclesiological freedom into the western frontier.[22]

The Second Great Awakening (c 1795–1830) was more diffuse, with origins in the frontier west under the leadership of Methodist, Baptist and Presbyterian itinerants. The Second Great Awakening stimulated religious life on an unprecedented scale at the turn of the nineteenth century and beyond. It breathed new life into the denominations. Also, the soteriology of the Second Awakening moved away from the Calvinism of Edwards. While Edwards had stressed the inability of sinful people to save themselves, the frontier revivalists emphasised the ability, which God had bestowed on all people, to come to Christ.

The revivals of the Second Great Awakening broke out afresh with augmented fervour and swept various parts of the country. Preaching to those of low income and little education, the Baptists grew rapidly, notably in North Carolina, Virginia, and Kentucky. In Virginia, they were persecuted by the established church until in 1776 they gained religious liberty through the Virginia Bill of Rights, which was not made into legislation until 1785. This led to the further growth of the Baptists, who had a particular appeal to the masses. Their preachers, usually with little education, knew their audience and how to address them in a language that would hold their attention and bring conviction. They tended to be highly emotional. Their churches, simple democracies, fitted in with the temperament of the rural communities. These Baptists differed markedly to those of the establishment kind in the North, whose pastors were often educated in England. There, they founded Rhode Island College, which impacted upon denominational life there for some time. However, Baptists multiplied most especially in the South. Eventually prestigious institutions of academic learning included: The Southern Baptist Theological Seminary, in Louisville, Kentucky; Southwestern Seminary, in Texas; and Denver Seminary. However, growth was also shared with Methodists and new movements which thrived under the banner of Christians or Disciples of Christ.

Many of the new Christians became dissatisfied with the existing

---

22. Latourette, *A History of Christianity: Vol. 2*, 958–59.

denominations and sought to transcend them by simply calling themselves Christians or Disciples of Christ. They sought to return to the pristine and uncorrupted church of the New Testament. Independent of one another, these groups sprang up in several different parts of the country, but mainly on the frontier. Two of the main leaders were Barton Stone (1772–1844) and Alexander Campbell (1788–1866). The two met and came under the name of Reformers or Disciples. Former Presbyterians, they called for unity among Christians, embraced Arminianism, believer's baptism and opened the Lord's Supper to anyone with faith in Christ.

THE MILLERITE MOVEMENT—A PRELUDE TO SEVENTH-DAY ADVENTISM

The Millerite movement was a significant collective of people that arose during the nineteenth century awakenings. William Miller was born at Pittsfield, Massachusetts, on December 20, 1849 and died on December 20 at Low Hampton, New York. He was a Baptist farmer who held various positions in the community, including deputy sheriff and justice of the peace. He also served as a captain of the 30th Infantry in the war of 1812 between the United States and Great Britain conducted over Britain's violation of America's maritime right. After two years of Bible study, particularly the books of Daniel and Revelation, Miller made, in 1818, his central and defining text, Daniel 8:14, "Unto two thousand and three hundred days; then the sanctuary be cleansed." Seeking to further consolidate and verify his conclusion, he committed himself to a further five years of study. This time of study "left him fully convinced of the correctness of his position."[23] He concluded that the cleansing of the sanctuary was the cleansing of the earth, when Jesus returned. Miller came to the initial conclusion that Jesus would return in 1843. A later revision with his associates, however, saw the times revised to the spring of 1844, then the autumn, and finally, the movement embraced October 22 under the exhortation of Samuel Snow, as the Day of Atonement in 1844. Reluctant to preach the message, he concluded that he would only do so if asked. Soon after praying as much he was invited to preach at his local Baptist Church. Beginning in 1831 Miller's extensive ministry reached tens of thousands of people.

At first, Miller only preached in small towns. However, after a meeting with Joshua V. Himes (a New Connection minister), Miller had audiences in the larger cities that numbered in the thousands. It is estimated that between 50,000 to 100,000 people became Millerites, or "Adventists".[24]

October 22, 1844, came and went without apparent effect. Some put hope in a "tarrying time" of seven months and ten days (Hab. 2:3; Lev. 25:9). When this failed

---

23. White, *Great Controversy*, 330.
24. Gordon, *William Miller*, 469.

to eventuate, Miller expressed that he had "fixed his mind on another time, and that is today, until he comes."[25] Most left the movement in discouragement or disillusionment. Miller lived for a further five years. However, a small band of followers, intent on finding the meaning behind the verse that so clearly had pointed to this date, sought for answers in further Bible Study and prayer.

Following the vision of Hiram Edson, and the establishment of the Sanctuary Doctrine, a small group began to gain momentum under the passionate and inspired ministry of Ellen Harmon. Her first vision, of the Narrow Path, confirmed that a new movement had begun, and the conditions under which it would press forward until the end. After her marriage to James White, the two became a formidable ministry team, preaching and sharing the Advent message where God led them. They were supported in their ministry by a significant group of pioneers. Among their number was Rachel Oakes Preston (1809–1868), who had been a Seventh-day Baptist before joining the movement. While Ellen White initially rejected Preston's claims regarding the Sabbath, a subsequent vision confirmed the truth of the Seventh-day Sabbath. Extensive travel for the purposes of exhortation, correction and teaching, by the White's, built a loosely affiliated and scattered people into a formidable denomination by 1863.

Of William Miller, Ellen White later wrote: "I saw that William Miller erred as he was soon to enter the heavenly Canaan, in suffering his influence to go against the truth. Others led him to this; others must account for it. But angels watch the precious dust of this servant of God, and he will come forth at the sound of the last trump."[26]

---

25. Miller, *The Midnight Cry, Dec 5, 1844,* 179–80.
26. White, *Early Writings,* 258.

CHAPTER 27

THE PRACTICAL MARKS OF THE CHURCH

THE MARKS OF THE CHURCH "have to do with the activity of the church, the way it demonstrated its faith and witness in wider society." Donald Bloesch listed a number of practical marks mentioned by the Reformers, including the preaching of the Word, the right administration of the Sacraments, and church discipline. Bloesch also mentioned that in "Pietism the fellowship of love (the koinonia) was often cited as a mark of the church." He believed that the

> strength of Pietism lay in the fact that it gave the laity a role in determining the validity of the church's witness and rites. It is not simply the message we profess but the fruits we produce by living a Christian life that attest that apostolic reality of the church (Mt. 7:16-20; 12:33; Gal 5:22). Pietism also added the urgency of mission as a mark of the true church . . . The church does not fulfil its mandate until it acts to share the good news of Christ's redemption with the world outside its fellowship. John Chrysostom manifested this evangelical concern already in the fifth century: There is nothing colder than a Christian who in unconcerned about the salvation of others.[1]

Bloesch also pointed to Good Samaritan service, such as that advocated by William Booth, and the Anabaptist prime marks of "peace, suffering, spiritually faithful ministers and shepherds, and separation from sin." Prayer is also to be seen as a mark of the church. Indeed, "only a church fortified in prayer can be assured that its witness will bear fruit."[2]

---

1. Bloesch, *The Church,* 103–107.
2. Bloesch, *The Church,* 103–107.

THE PRACTICAL MARKS OF THE CHURCH

THE CHURCH AS A COMMUNITY

Stanley Grenz claimed that, fundamentally,

> *the church of Jesus Christ is neither a building nor an organization. Rather, it is a people, a special people, a people who see themselves standing in relationship to the God who saves them and to each other as those who share in this salvation. As the early church father Hippolytus declared, 'It is not a place that is called church, not a house made of stones and earth . . . It is the holy assembly of those who live in righteousness.'*[3]

Stated theologically, the church is a people in covenant. Grenz began his study of this assertion with an analysis of the Greek word: *ekklesia*. The New Testament writers commonly used the Greek word, *ekklesia*, in order to describe the church. This term arises from the Greek verb *kaleo* ('to call'), plus the preposition *ek* ('out of'). On this etymological basis, many theologians conclude that the idea of 'the called-out ones' inheres in the resulting noun *ekklesia*." Grenz further pointed out that the New Testament use of the word *ekklesia* provides an important link between the Christian church and Israel. "The Jewish scholars who translated the Hebrew Scriptures into Greek (the Septuagint) chose *ekklesia* to render the Hebrew word *qahal* ('assembly'), which the historical writers used to refer to Israel as the 'congregation' or 'assembly of the Lord'".[4] Alternatively, "*Qahal* can refer to the whole congregation of Israel, whether or not in actual assembly, or to a local assembly called to stand in the presence of God." Thomas Oden pointed to "one noteworthy difference that quickly emerged between *qahal* and *ekklesia*: the *qahal* was, strictly speaking, a calling forth of men only, the circumcised, while the *ekklesia* included woman, children, congregation."[5]

Grenz drew a link of continuity between the Hebrew nation and the New Israel in Jesus Christ. He believed that 1 Chron. 28:8 "may have formed the background for Jesus' promise that he would build his congregation." "Now therefore in the sight of all Israel the congregation of the Lord, and in the audience of our God, keep and seek for all the commandments of the Lord your God: that ye may possess this good land, and leave it for an inheritance for your children after you forever." He contended that Jesus referred to the foundation of the church when he stated: "And I say also unto thee, that thou art Peter, and upon this rock I will build my church; and the gates of hell shall not prevail against it." (Matt. 16:18). Importantly, the foundation of the church is Jesus Christ, and not Peter. Literally, Jesus is the rock, *petra*, and Peter is

---

3. Grenz, *Theology for The Community of God*, 464.
4. Grenz, *Theology for The Community of God*, 464.
5. Oden, *Life in The Spirit*, 265.

the pebble, *petros*. That is, Peter's faith and mission is important, but it is lesser to the greater and foundational importance of Jesus Christ.[6]

Further, Grenz concluded that the early Christians, in their choice of *ekklesia*, sought to "link themselves as followers of Jesus to what God had begun in the wilderness with the nation of Israel." Oden added, in relation to this verse, that "Jesus did not hesitate to describe the *ekklesia* as 'my church' in a highly personal sense—my own assembly, my own called out people, and myself personally as their cohesion." Oden believed that the "personal phrase 'my church' indicates that Jesus, according to Matthew, deliberately intended to form a continuing community of prayer, preaching, and discipline." This is primarily seen in the calling and training of disciples, for the purpose of perpetuating the message. "It is from Jesus' own carefully and accurately remembered personal phrase, 'my church'—spoken first in Aramaic and later in Greek—that the Greek term *ekklesia* came to have preeminence thereafter over all other terms used to described the community of faith. (Acts 5:11; 7:38, Rom. 16:5, 16; 1 Cor. 7:17; 11:16, Matt. 18:17)."[7]

However, while "the Old Testament formed the theological context, the linguistic significance of the New Testament's use of *ekklesia* arises out of its common use in the first-century Roman world. Ekklesia connoted an 'assembly', the citizens of a given community called together to tend to city affairs." This is referred to in the New Testament in Acts 19. "And certain of the chief of Asia, which where his friends, sent unto him, desiring him that he would not adventure himself into the theatre. Some therefore cried one thing, and some another: for the assembly was confused; and the more part knew not wherefore they were come together." (Acts 19:31–32)

Grenz further commented that the "early Christians found in this term a helpful means for expressing their self-consciousness. They saw themselves as a people called together by the proclamation of the gospel for the purpose of belonging to God through Christ."

> *The choice of ekklesia as the designation of the Christian community suggests that the New Testament believers viewed the church as neither an edifice nor an organization. They were a people—a people brought together by the Holy Spirit—a people bound to each other through Christ—hence, a people standing in covenant with God. Above all, they were God's people (2 Cor. 6:16).*[8]

---

6. Catholic scholars would assert that there is no difference between these two words. In so doing, they make Peter the foundation of the church and hand authority to the Pope. A valid question has to do with this word play (petros/petra) being in Greek, when Jesus most likely spoke in Aramaic. Clearly, the Greek word play reflects two different words in Aramiac (evna/kepha).

7. Oden, *Life in The Spirit*, 266.

8. Grenz, *Theology for The Community of God*, 464–465.

THE PRACTICAL MARKS OF THE CHURCH

THE CHURCH AS A FELLOWSHIP

The early church was distinguished by its sense of fellowship, which was derived from the believer's unity in Jesus Christ. "Acts 4:32ff gives a picture of the communal sharing of goods which was practiced for a time in the early church."

> *The idea of an earthly society grounded in human nature is foreign to Paul. For him koinonia refers strictly to the relation of faith to Christ: 'the fellowship of the Spirit' (1 Cor. 1:9), 'the fellowship of the Holy Spirit' (2 Cor. 13:13), 'fellowship in the gospel' (Phil. 1:5), 'fellowship of faith' (Phlm. 6) . . . Similarly, koinonia in 1 Cur 10:16 means 'participation' in . . . union with the exalted Christ. This fellowship with Christ comes about through the creative intervention of God. It happens through the transformation of man to the very roots of his being. It is birth into a new existence, and can be expressed by the contrast of life and death.' According to 2 Pet 1:4, believers are made 'partakers of the divine nature', 'through the knowledge of him who called us to his own glory and patient endurance . . . Participation in evil is rejected (Eph. 5:11; Rev. 18:4). But one can participate in suffering (Phil. 4:14) and the gospel and its hope (1 Cor. 9:23; Phil. 1:7).*[9]

In Tomas Oden's understanding: "Christ called a living human community to proclaim and become the kingdom of God. He came to inaugurate the kingdom of God through a continuing transgenerational human community." In this way, God's church meets the human need of His creation. That is, *koinonia*—fellowship, mutuality, community. "The church is a family set apart by God, belonging to a people set apart by God. Persons are social beings. Even God is not a lonely individual lacking sociality, being triune. God's plan includes and requires interpersonal testimony, interpersonal meeting, one-on-one passing on of the tradition of apostolic testimony." It is for this reason that people are not saved individually apart from the body of Christ. The apostle, Paul, alludes to this when he wrote to the Colossians that

> *their hearts might be comforted, being knit together in love, and unto all riches of the full assurance of understanding, to the acknowledgement of the mystery of God, and of the Father, and of Christ . . . And not holding the Head, from which all the body by joints and bands having nourishment ministered, and knit together, increaseth with the increase of God* (Col. 2:2, 19).

Thomas Oden also believed that "Ecclesiology reflects upon the Spirit's work in bringing communities into being in response to grace. The corporate organism through which God the Spirit provides for the administration of the means of grace is the church." Furthermore, Oden contended that in time *ekklesia* becomes *koinonia*.

---

9. Schattenmann, *Fellowship*, 641–644.

FOUNDATIONS OF THEOLOGY

> *Whether viewed locally or generally, the church is fellowship, a shared social process involving primary engagement of persons in the family of God. This runs against the premise that the church is essentially an impersonal, imposed, hierarchical organization of offices and officers. It is a primary community of persons that meet, being called and summoned by the gospel (Phil 2:1-2).*[10]

The community is a gathered community, called by God to join together so they can praise God and pray for the salvation of the world. (Hebrews 10:19-25).[11]

In addition, Oden made the observation that "Jesus did not leave behind him a set of formal written teachings signed 'Jesus' so much as a living community that remembered him as having met them personally." Indeed, Jesus works dynamically through His chosen instrument, the community of God, the Ekklesia. Therefore, to "belong to that community means to live life in Christ, to belong to his body, to be enlivened by his life, to live in union with this one who lived his human life in incomparable union with God."[12]

Ellen White wrote that those

> *who are of the household of faith should never neglect the assembling of themselves together; for this is God's appointed means of leading His children into unity, in order that in Christian love and fellowship they may help, strengthen, and encourage one another . . . . As brethren of our Lord, we are called with a holy calling to a holy, happy life. Having entered the narrow path of obedience, let us refresh our minds by communion with one another and with God. As we see the day of God approaching, let us meet often to study His Word and to exhort one another to be faithful unto the end. These earthly assemblies are God's appointed means by which we have opportunity to speak with one another and to gather all the help possible to prepare, in the right way, to receive in the heavenly assemblies the fulfilment of the pledges of our inheritance.*[13]

THE MINISTRY OF THE CHURCH

One Greek word serves as guide in helping to bring together the New Testament material on the ministry of the church: *charismata*. Charismata describes the gifts of the church. A succession of various passages gives a number of lists of a variety of gifts. A total of nine gifts are listed in 1 Cor. 12:8-10. "the utterance of wisdom", "the utterance of knowledge", "faith", "gifts of healing", "working of miracles", "prophecy", "discernment of spirits", "various kinds of tongues", "interpretation". A list of eight spiritual gifts soon follows in 1 Cor. 12:28-30. Dale Moody believed that the

---

10. Oden, *Life in The Spirit,* 280, 284.
11. Oden, *Life in The Spirit,* 280, 284.
12. Oden, *Life in The Spirit,* 283-4.
13. White, *Our High Calling,* 166.

THE PRACTICAL MARKS OF THE CHURCH

"numbering of the gifts would indicate that Paul has some rating of value in mind." "apostles", "prophets", "teachers", "deeds of power", "healing", "forms of assistance", "forms of leadership", "various kinds of tongues". "The seven gifts of Romans 12:6–8 include prophecy and teaching, but service, exhortation, liberality, ruling, and showing mercy are added." There are five gifts listed in Ephesians 4:11 and two new gifts: evangelists and pastors.[14]

Understanding the role of the Holy Spirit to the true nature of the ministry of the church is vital. It is by the equipping of the Spirit that gifts are bestowed, fellowship is entered into and the ministry of God's people takes place. Maldwyn Hughes, former principle of Wesley House, Cambridge, wrote in 1927 that the "most important point to be noted is that in the New Testament the essential qualification for the ministry is to be 'filled with the Spirit.'"[15]

Donald Bloesch averred that in "the original or Pauline communities of the church, ministry and charism were closely related; there were indeed as many ministries as charisms." He further contended that ministry and service for others are closely related. "If we take the ministry of Jesus as our paradigm we can see that ministry does not mean elevation over others but service to others—both spiritual and material. Jesus was sent by the Father in order to serve those in need. "I am among you as one who serves" (Lk. 22:27; Jn. 13:13–15). [In fact]: "Greatness in . . . ministry is accounted, not in outward rank, but in proportion to service" (Mt. 20:25–28; Mk. 10:42–45; Lk. 22:24–27).[16]

Millard Erickson discussed Christian's willingness to serve as one of the characters of the church. "Jesus stated that his purpose in coming was not to be served, but to serve (Matt 20:28). In becoming incarnate he took upon himself the form of a servant (Phil 2:7) . . . The church must display a similar willingness to serve. It has been placed in the world to serve its Lord and the world, not to be exalted and have its own needs and desires satisfied." Erickson believed that the second characteristic of the church should be adaptability. The Christian fellowship, as a corporate entity, needs to possess the ability to change in order to meet the missional needs of the surrounding society.

> *The church must also be versatile and flexible in adjusting its methods and procedures to the changing situations of the world in which it finds itself. It must go where needy persons are found, even if that means a geographical or cultural change. It must not cling to all its old ways. As the world to which it is trying to minister changes, the church will have to adopt its ministry accordingly, but without altering its basic direction.*[17]

---

14. Moody, *The Word of Truth*, 453–4.
15. Hughes, *Christian Foundations: An Introduction to Christian Doctrine*, 188.
16. Bloesch, *The Church*, 206–7.
17. Erickson, *Christian Theology*, 1077–8.

FOUNDATIONS OF THEOLOGY
THE AUTHORITY AND MISSION OF THE CHURCH

The authority of the early church rested upon the apostolic authority of Paul. Paul frequently alluded to his having received a divine commission for his apostleship to the Gentiles. In so doing, he outlines the Gospel message to which he had been called. (Gal. 1:16; Rom 1:5, 11:13-14; 15:15b-16; Eph. 3:8; Acts 9:15-16; 13:46-47; 22:14-15, 21; 26:16b-18). He spells this out clearly in his letter to the Galatians. "But when it pleased God, who separated me from my mother's womb, and called me by his grace, to reveal his Son in me, that I might preach him among the heathen (Gal. 1:16)." In his letter to the Romans, Paul introduced himself as one of the apostles who had "received grace and apostleship (Rom. 1:15)." Later in the letter he clarifies his specific calling as the apostle to the Gentiles (Rom. 11:13). However, it is in the Book of Acts that Paul most ardently outlines the legitimacy of his apostleship. Indeed, at his conversion on the road to Damascus Jesus had said to him,

> *But get up and stand on your feet; for this purpose I have appeared to you, to appoint you a minister and a witness not only to the things which you have [a]seen, but also to the things in which I will appear to you; rescuing you from the Jewish people and from the Gentiles, to whom I am sending you, to open their eyes so that they may turn from darkness to light and from the dominion of Satan to God, that they may receive forgiveness of sins and an inheritance among those who have been sanctified by faith in Me. (NASB) (Acts 26:16-18).*

Along with a strong conviction in the Gospel message to which he had been called to be an apostle, Paul also had the conviction that it was the responsibility of every Christian to be a missionary for the Gospel. Importantly, Paul appears to have had a mission strategy. James Leo Garrett outlined the following approach.

1. Paul preached the gospel to the Jews and then to the Gentiles.

2. Paul maintained a close contact with his home base, or sending church. "At the end of his first and second missionary journeys he returned to Antioch to report to the church there (Acts 14:26-28; 18:22c-23a)."

3. Paul concentrated his labors in four provinces of the Roman Empire (Galatia, Asia, Macedonia, and Achaia) and in the large cities within those provinces. "His aim was not simply to cover territory but to plant churches."

4. Paul baptized those who confessed faith in Jesus Christ, constituted churches, and instructed new converts.

5. Paul made good use of fellow workers. "Some twenty fellow workers are named in Acts and the Pauline epistles", not to mention a list of church members in Romans 16.

THE PRACTICAL MARKS OF THE CHURCH

6. Paul was willing to become all things to all people. (1 Cor. 9:22).[18]

"It is now commonly agreed that throughout the patristic, the medieval, the Reformation, and post-Reformation eras Christianity generally held that the apostles had in their time fulfilled the Great Commission and hence, even as their apostolic office had ceased, the obligation of the Great Commission had ceased." However, there were notable and important exceptions to this view. The Anabaptists, for example, believed that the Great Commission was the obligation of all Christians of all generations. This concept was further developed by the missionary movements of the eighteenth and nineteenth centuries. William Carey's (1761–1834) "An Enquiry into the Obligations of Christians to Use Means for the Conversion of the Heathen (1792)" argued that the Great Commission was an obligation applying to all Christians.[19] In the contemporary church, Donald Bloesch pointed out that "Jesus called his disciples to the work of mission and evangelism: 'The harvest is plentiful, but the laborers are few; pray therefore the Lord of the harvest to send out laborers into his harvest.' (Matt. 9:37, 38. Also note John 4:35)." The great commission, given by the risen Christ to the apostles, was the proclamation of the remission of sins through his death and resurrection: "Thus it is written, that the Christ should suffer and on the third day rise from the dead, and that repentance and forgiveness of sins should be preached in his name to all the nations, beginning from Jerusalem (Luke 24:46–47; see also Matt 28:28–19; Mk 16:15)." The commission had a practical effect on the organizational life of the church. "Because the apostles understood their mandate as the ministry of the Word, they appointed deacons to care for the material needs of the congregations so that they could devote all their time to the preaching of the Gospel (Acts 6:1–4)."[20]

In the twentieth-century the mission of the church has also been discussed by Dietrich Bonhoeffer (1906–45). In his "Life Together" he devoted a section to The Ministry of Proclaiming.

> *What we are concerned with here is the free communication of the Word from person to person, not by the ordained ministry which is bound to a particular office, time, and place. We are thinking of that unique situation in which one person bears witness in human words to another person, bespeaking the whole consolation of God, the admonition, the kindness, and the severity of God.*[21]

In regard to method, Bonhoeffer stated: "If it is not accompanied by worthy listening, how can it really be the right word for another person? . . . If it issues, not

---

18. Garrett. *Systematic Theology: Vol. 2*, 493–495.
19. Garrett. *Systematic Theology: Vol. 2*, 495–96.
20. Bloesch, *Essentials of Evangelical Theology: Vol. 2*, 157.
21. Bonhoeffer, *Life Together*, 80–82.

from a spirit of bearing and forbearing, but from impatience and the desire to force its acceptance, how can it be the liberating and healing word?"[22]

In his 1937 publication in German, *The Cost of Discipleship*, Bonhoeffer wrote on the work of a disciple.

> *All the activity of the disciples is subject to the clear precept of their Lord. They are not left free to choose their own methods or adopt their own conception of their task. Their work is to be Christ-work, and therefore they are absolutely dependent on the will of Jesus. Happy are they whose duty is fixed by such a precept, and who are therefore free from the tyranny of their own ideas and calculations. In his very first word Jesus lays down a limitation of their work.*[23]

They were to go where they were sent. The work was God's not theirs. Bonhoeffer brought his discussion to an exposition of Matthew 10:11–15. He noted that the disciples work must begin with those who warmly welcome the disciples and the gospel message. These people will support the work with their prayer.

Time is precious. The proclamation of the message is essential. It is simple. The Word must go out that people must be summoned to repentance and faith. Bonhoeffer made the challenging point that "since the cause brooks no delay there is no need for them to enter into any further discussion to clear the ground or to persuade their hearers. The King stands at the door, and he may come at any moment."[24]

More recently, Donald Bloesch warned that in

> *a climate of religious pluralism and syncretism it is incumbent on the church to emphasize the uniqueness and finality of Jesus Christ. He is not the truth among many, but the truth about God, the world and ourselves. Yet this truth is not our property to be handed over to those who seek it, but it is the speech of the living God that can be heard and received only through the power of God's Spirit.*[25]

Bloesch believed that evangelism is not charged with the task of finding points of identity between the gospel and the orientation of society. Nor should the church seek to simply answer society's questions with gospel laden answers. Instead, the church should "confront the religious claims of our hearers with the message of the gospel and call our hearers to break with their present commitments and embrace a message that is utterly new, disrupting and transforming."[26]

---

22. Bonhoeffer, *Life Together*, 80–82.
23. Bonhoeffer, *The Cost of Discipleship*, 206, 210.
24. Bonhoeffer, *The Cost of Discipleship*, 206, 210.
25. Bloesch, *The Church: Sacraments, Worship, Ministry, Mission*, 246.
26. Bloesch, *The Church: Sacraments, Worship, Ministry, Mission*, 248.

Indeed, Bloesch agrees with James Edwards: "All efforts to produce a gospel compatible with society have been disastrous for the church's witness and credibility."[27] The church cannot experience the renewal that is called for today without settling one account: confessing Christ as Lord means refusing that honour to anything else. Karl Barth's diagnosis of the modern church is similar. The church must cease trying to ensure its own survival and begin to share the good news that Christ has come to redeem the whole world. According to Barth, "a Church which is not as such an evangelizing Church, is either not yet or no longer the Church, only a dead Church, itself standing in supreme need of renewal by evangelization."[28]

Indeed, Barth made the point:

> *The Church is not in any sense to be understood as the divine institution for the satisfaction of needs related to . . . fulfilment . . . [Although we may say it includes this as well]. But on closer examination all this will be seen as subordinate. The Church has its true meaning, and therefore the man elected to life in the Church has his true personal determination, in the fact that, equipped and empowered by these benefits (that is, salvation from sin and death, justification and sanctification), instructed by this admonition and comfort, he is made serviceable to the Lord of the Church, and therefore, in the omnipotent lovingkindness of God realized and revealed in Him, to the rest of the world. That is to say, the Church as such, and every individual in the Church in his own place and manner, becomes a bearer and proclaimer of this name and this fact.*[29]

The consequence, claimed Barth, for those who do not believe, is a delivery, a handing over, according to which God in his wrath (Rom 1:18f) hands them over to judgment.[30]

Dale Moody spoke of the church in its relation to God, Jesus Christ and the Holy Spirit. Moody stipulated that the

> *question of the relationship between the church and God is raised by the use of the terms 'the church of God' (1 Cor. 1:2; 10:32; 15:9; 2 Cor. 1:1; Gal. 1:13; 1 Tim 3:5, 15) and 'the churches of God' (1 Thess. 2:14; 1 Cor. 11:16) in the New Testament. In 1 Peter 1:3–2:10, the church as the people of God is related to the Old Testament. Against the background of the work of the Father (1:3–6), the Son (1:7–9), and the Holy Spirit (1:10–12), God's redemption of his people is described in the figures of the exodus (1:13–21), a life (1:22–2:3), and a house (1:4–10). The description of the new exodus made possible by 'the precious blood of Christ' (1:19) is filled with allusions to the Old Testament Exodus.*[31]

27. Bloesch, *The Church*, 248. 249.
28. Bloesch, *The Church*, 248. 249.
29. Barth, *Church Dogmatics: II/2*, 428–9, 484–5.
30. Barth, *Church Dogmatics: II/2*, 428–9, 484–5.
31. Moody, *The Word of Truth*, 442.

The church is described by Paul to be the "body of Christ" with him as the head (1 Cor. 12; Col 1:24). Moody rightly asserted that the church, as the body of Christ, can best be understood in relation to the Hebrew concept of God's people comprising a corporate personality. Metaphors such as, the Servant of the Lord (Isa. 53), the Son of Man (Dan. 7:13–22), and Adam (Rom. 5:12–21) are eminent examples. For Paul, the members are of paramount importance, since they form a single identity under Jesus Christ as the head. Given the special status of this group, they come under specific scrutiny. For instance, the body of Christ is to maintain the highest standard of morality (1 Cor. 6:15f) since they are "members of Christ" as well as the temple of the Holy Spirit. "The fact that Christians constitute one body of which all are members is both the basis for saying the loaf at the Lord's Supper is a participation (koinonia) in the body of Christ and the reasons for Christians to separate themselves from pagan sacrifices (1 Cor. 10:14–22)."[32]

ELLEN WHITE'S THEOLOGY OF THE CHURCH

Like other biblical Christians, Ellen White saw the apostolic church as being the normative model for the Christian church in all ages. Most importantly, the apostles built the church on foundations laid by Christ.[33] Based on these foundations, the church has the important ministry of being Christ's representatives on earth.[34] The church is able to accomplish this ministry because its members have been baptized with the Spirit's power.[35] On this basis the church is able to teach Christianity in its purity[36] and present the plain preaching of God's word.[37] However, Mrs White noted the many challenges and difficulties that the early church faced. She highlighted a tendency for selfishness and ease-loving,[38] together with the waning of brotherly love[39] and the creeping in of coldness.[40] Jointly with these relational struggles, the early church faced doctrinal challenges that are described as poisonous errors.[41] Indeed, future apostasy was revealed to Paul.[42] To be sure, as Revelation . . . . attests,

---

32. Moody, *The Word of Truth*, 444.
33. White, *Acts of the Apostles*, 553.
34. White, *Acts of the Apostles*, 122.
35. White, *My Life Today*, 47.
36. White, *Testimonies: Vol. 5*, 166.
37. White, *Testimonies: Vol. 5*, 166.
38. White, *Testimonies: Vol. 8*, 26.
39. White, *Acts of the Apostles*, 548.
40. White, *Acts of the Apostles*, 580.
41. White, *The Sanctified Life*, 63–5.
42. White, *The Sanctified Life*, 395.

the early church lost its first love.[43] Nonetheless, a constantly enlarging work was entrusted to it.[44]

During the first centuries, the church is marked by increasing apostasy. Indeed, the acceptance of heathen rites and customs corrupted the church,[45] along with the allurements of temporal prosperity and worldly honor.[46] All in all, as the result of the subtle work of Satan to weaken and destroy,[47] there was a departure from the simplicity of the Gospel.[48] To be sure, Mrs White asserted that there was a compromise with paganism as they conformed to pagan practices to facilitate the acceptance of Christianity by the heathen.[49] In the process, Satan's banner was planted[50] under the cloak of pretended Christianity.[51] In spite of this, some Christians stood faithful.[52] Significantly, Ellen White pointed to the example of the Waldenses, who arrived at the truth in opposition to false dogmas and heresies.[53]

---

43. White, *Testimonies: Vol. 8*, 26.
44. White, *Testimonies: Vol. 8*, 90.
45. White, *Great Controversy*, 443.
46. White, *Great Controversy*, 42.
47. White, *Testimonies: Vol. 5*, 297.
48. White, *Great Controversy*, 384, 443.
49. White, *Great Controversy*, 384.
50. White, *The Story of Redemption*, 322.
51. White, *The Story of Redemption*, 322–4.
52. White, *Great Controversy*, 43.
53. White, *Great Controversy*, 64.

Chapter 28

THE CHURCH IN THE PLAN OF SALVATION

THE FIRST VATICAN COUNCIL REITERATED the Catholic Church's teaching that salvation is not found outside the church. This is clear in the pronouncement that "outside the Church no one can be saved . . . . Who is not in the ark will perish in the flood." As the Roman Catholic Tradition developed, salvation came to be seen more and more as not so much a free gift of the Spirit but as "a grace created by the Spirit and infused into people of faith through the rites and sacraments of the faith community." Therefore, Catholicism derives authority from itself. That is, God speaks through His church for His people. Indeed, the First Vatican Council confirmed the need for Reformation in which the primary authority for the church is God speaking through His Word to the church. "Cyprian articulated what was to be normative in Catholic theology: 'If someone has not the church for his mother, he has not God for his father.' Therefore, there is no salvation outside the church." This view has come under critical scrutiny in Catholic theology since the Second Vatican Council, which acknowledged that the Spirit of Christ works salvifically beyond the parameters of prescribed and officially sanctioned rites and ceremonies. Yet even in this theology, the church is envisioned as the redemptive agency of the Spirit by which seekers after the truth are brought to the full realization of their salvation. Indeed, Tertullian, as early as 210, held to a sacramental view of the Lord's Supper when he stated:

> The flesh, indeed, is washed [baptism] in order that the soul may be cleansed. The flesh is anointed so that the soul may be consecrated. The flesh is signed [with the cross] so that the soul may be fortified. The flesh is shadowed with the imposition of hands so that the soul also may be illuminated by the Spirit. The

flesh feeds on the body and the blood of Christ so that the soul likewise may feed on God.[1]

In response, Donald Bloesch has commented that from a biblical perspective even these newer forms of expression in the Catholic Church seem to "compromise the biblical doctrine of Solus Christus, Christ alone is the Savior of the world." Christ, Himself, pointed to Himself as the source of all salvation.

> *I am the living bread that came down out of heaven; if anyone eats of this bread, he will live forever; and the bread also which I will give for the life of the world is My flesh." Then the Jews began to argue with one another, saying, "How can this man give us His flesh to eat?" So Jesus said to them, "Truly, truly, I say to you, unless you eat the flesh of the Son of Man and drink His blood, you have no life in yourselves. He who eats My flesh and drinks My blood has eternal life, and I will raise him up on the last day.* (NASB) (John 6:51–54)

Indeed, "Martin Luther challenged the Catholicism of his time by insisting that grace is not a fluid or power dispensed by the church but the free bestowal of the Spirit of God who nonetheless condescends to meet us wherever the Word is truly proclaimed and the sacraments rightly administered." To be sure, the sacraments are not efficacious, but do have the ability to proclaim Christ when accompanied by the preaching of the Word. In a similar fashion, "Calvin propounded a theology of Word and Spirit in which the role of the Spirit is to illumine and bring home to us the meaning of the written Word of God." Therefore, faith is an awakening of the truth, worked within us by the Spirit. "It involves a conscious recognition and affirmation of Jesus Christ as Lord and savior of the elect people of God."[2]

Peter T. Forsyth, an English Congregationalist, sounded a biblical note when he stated that the "Church is not the continuation of Christ, but his creation and His response."[3] Karl Barth, in his early writings, held to a sacramental view of the church. As he progressed in his thinking, however, he emphasized more the ethical role of the church over its soteriological role. "Jesus Christ himself became the only sacrament—the visible sign of invisible grace, and the church and ordinances became testimonies of grace rather than means of grace."[4] Thomas Torrance was adamant that,

> *the invisible reality of the living Word cannot be reduced to the visible reality of the church and the sacraments . . . The sacraments do not as such contain or confer grace, but they are employed by the Spirit to direct us to the living Christ, the fount and source of all grace. Grace is not a created power that*

---

1. Bercot, *Dictionary of Early Christian Beliefs*, 573.
2. Bloesch, *The Church*, 50.
3. Sell, *Testimony and Tradition: Studies in Reform and Dissenting Thought*, 195.
4. Bloesch, *The Church*, 54.

can be controlled and dispensed by the clerics of the church, but it is the living Christ himself reaching out to us through sacramental acts of celebration and adoration.[5]

Donald Bloesch believed that the "church can be thought of as a redemptive community but not in the sense of being in itself a redeeming force in the world. It is the community of the redeemed but not the source of redemption. It plays an important role in directing sinners to Christ, but its ministrations and rituals do not effect redemption." In contrast to Catholicism, Bloesch did not believe that the church dispenses grace. It proclaims grace. "In this role, it may on occasion become the means through which people come to experience God's grace."[6]

THE PROCLAMATION OF THE CHURCH

In the second century Irenaeus (c. 130–200), Bishop of Lyons, wrote:

> *The church having received this preaching and this faith, although scattered throughout the whole world, yet, as if occupying but one house, carefully preserves it . . . For the churches which have been planted in Germany do not believe or hand down anything different, nor do those in Spain, nor those in Gaul. Nor those in the East, nor those in Egypt, nor those in Libya, nor those which have been established in the central regions of the world. But just as the sun, that creation of God, is one and the same throughout the whole world, so also the preaching of the truth shines everywhere, and enlightens all men who are willing to come to a knowledge of the truth.*[7]

Origen (c. 185–255), who followed Clement to lead the school in Alexandria, recognized the need of proclamation and the power of God. "The Word of God declares that the preaching is not sufficient to reach the human heart (even though it may be worthy of belief), unless a certain power is imparted to the speaker from God.[8]

A central focus for any Bible centered church will be an emphasis on evangelism as the focus of the church's outreach mission. It is certainly true to say that evangelism entails proclamation. As the foundation of equating evangelism with proclamation, Grenz did not seek to go any further than the great commission. "And he said unto them, go ye into all the world, and preach the gospel to every creature (Mk16:15)." We can also look to the prophecy of Jesus: "And this gospel of the kingdom shall be preached in all the world for a witness unto all nations; and then shall the end come (Matt 24:14)." Indeed, Paul rightly concluded, "How then shall they call on him in

---

5. Bloesch, *The Church*, 56.
6. Bloesch, *The Church*, 59.
7. Bercot, *Dictionary of Early Christian Beliefs*, 260–61.
8. Bercot, *Dictionary of Early Christian Beliefs*, 260–61.

whom they have not believed? and how shall they believe in him of whom they have not heard? and how shall they hear without a preacher? (Rom 10:14)."

There are a number of ways that the church stands as a sign to the world. Firstly, the church points to the divine reign of God when it gathers for worship. Secondly, the church is a sign when it lives as a community in the world. "As those who have responded to the gospel call and acknowledge the lordship of Christ, we seek to model what it means to live under the guidelines of divine reign. Kingdom principles include peace, justice, and righteousness. But above all, the divine reign is characterized by love." The church, as a community of believers, carries with it a prophetic dimension. "Insofar as we model community, our presence bears prophetic witness to the world. It issues an implicit call to society to measure itself against the divine reign under which it too must stand and against which it will be judged."[9]

Indeed, evangelism is one of the primary functions of the church. In Matthew 28:19 Jesus instructed them, "Therefore go and make disciples of all nations." In Acts 1:8 he says, "But you will receive power when the Holy Spirit comes on you; and you will be my witnesses in Jerusalem, and in all Judea and Samaria, and to the ends of the earth." This was the final point Jesus made to his disciples.

---

9. Grenz, *Theology for the Community of God*, 502—504.

CHAPTER 29

THE THREE ANGELS MESSAGE

THE THREE ANGELS MESSAGE IS the ministry of the Seventh-day Adventist Church. Found in Revelation 14, it describes the events surrounding the beginning of the movement at the time of the Great Disappointment. However, the three messages are to finally unfold in order and then combine to constitute a single message in the final days.

FIRST ANGEL

The first angel has the "everlasting Gospel to preach". It began in 1843, when people were called to decide for or against the truth regarding the soon return of Jesus Christ. Indeed, "servants of God were raised up in the power of Elijah to proclaim the message."[1] It will continue to sound towards the end but swell just before the close of probation. It calls upon people to repent of their sins before God and to commit their lives to Him as their Lord and Saviour. Further, it is a call for God's true people to leave the apostate churches and join God's Advent people. As Ellen White described it, "A great religious awakening under the proclamation of Christ's soon coming, is foretold in the prophecy of the First Angel's message of Revelation 14."[2] Indeed, the first angel's message is "designed to separate the professed people of God from the corrupting influences of the world, and to arouse them to see their condition of worldliness and backsliding."[3]

---

1. White, *Early Writings*, 233.
2. White, *Great Controversy*, 355.
3. White, *Great Controversy*, 379.

SECOND ANGEL

Following chronologically, the "second angel's message of Revelation 14 was first preached in the summer of 1844."[4] However, it was not completed then. It applies to those who were once faithful but have become corrupt. Babylon equates with confusion. It describes apostate Christianity aligned with the state. It is a religion that sacrifices truth to form an alliance with the world. That is, Protestants who come to follow the example of Rome. However, the "change is a progressive one, and the perfect fulfillment of Revelation 14:8, ("And there followed another angel, saying, Babylon is fallen, is fallen, that great city, because she made all nations drink of the wine of the wrath of her fornication"), is yet future."[5] Therefore, just before Jesus comes, the second application of the call to "come out of Babylon" will recede and then combine with the third angel's message. At that time, a love of the world will numb many believer's minds to spiritual things and there will be truth mixed with error. This is why the angel calls on God's people to "come out" and embrace the truth of a Gospel without compromise.

THIRD ANGEL

As Ellen White taught, "the third angel's message is to be regarded as of the highest importance. It is a life and death question."[6] It will be proclaimed in the context of Sunday Law, which will lead to keeping the Sabbath as being the last great test.[7] Mrs. White stipulated that it "is the last great message to all the world.[8] Indeed, the "third angel's message has been sent forth to the world, warning men against receiving the mark of the beast or his image in the foreheads or on their hands. To receive this mark means to come to the same decision as he beast has done, and to advocate the same ideas, in direct opposition to the Word of God."[9] For those who present the third angel's message an important warning is given. Mrs. White relayed that God had presented to her "the dangers that are threatening those who have been given the sacred work of proclaiming the third angel's message . . . Those who keep the commandments of God and have the faith of Jesus are the object of the wrath of this power."[10] Indeed, religious intolerance will gain control and church and state will unite to persecute those who keep the commandments of God.[11] However, the

---

4. White, *Great Controversy*, 389.
5. White, *Great Controversy*, 390.
6. White, *Selected Manuscripts 16, 1900*.
7. White, *Great Controversy*, 605.
8. White, *Great Controversy*, 390.
9. White, *Review and Herald July 13, 1897*.
10. White, *Selected Messages, 1902*, 135.
11. White, *Great Controversy*, 605.

third angel points believers to the Sanctuary where they will see the hope of Jesus Christ, and are promised an empowering from the Holy Spirit to finish the work.

CHAPTER 30

CHURCH ORDINANCES

RECEIVING MEMBERS

THE GATHERING OF MEMBERS, AND receiving them into the fellowship of the church, was first modeled by Christ when he gathered His disciples. Importantly, they were received for the purpose of being involved in the life, ministry and mission of the Gospel. Therefore, those received into membership are called to be followers and advocates of Jesus Christ. As ministers of Christ, all believers are endowed with power from the Holy Spirit so that the proclamation of the Gospel is accompanied by transformation and spiritual liberation.

The nature of the fellowship is further outlined in the activity of the early church as it is recorded in the Book of Acts. Meaningful fellowship and prayer are significant hallmarks. Following the resurrection of Jesus, they, without Judas Iscariot, "all joined together constantly in prayer, along with the women and Mary the mother of Jesus, and his brothers (Acts 1:14)." In addition, we note the centrality of preaching the Gospel of Jesus Christ in the power of the Holy Spirit. The aim, as outlined at the event of Peter's first post-Pentecost sermon, is conversion and baptism. After Peter's sermon on the Day of Pentecost, "those who received his word were baptized, and there were added (*prosetethesan*) that day about three thousand souls" (Acts 2:41). The early expectation of the church is that it would grow. As the word is proclaimed so are people added to the church's number. "And believers were the more added to the Lord, multitudes both of men and women (Acts 5:14)." "And the word of God increased; and the number of the disciples multiplied in Jerusalem greatly; and a great company of the priests were obedient to the faith (Acts 6:7)". "And the hand of the Lord was with them: and a great number believed, and turned unto the Lord (Acts 11:21)."

BAPTISM

In Greek, the basic verb is *bapto*, [while the verb used in the New Testament is *baptizo*] which has the meaning of "dip in or under" and also "dye". An associated word is *baptismos*. It refers to the act of washing and also refers to Jewish ablutions. In the Synoptic Gospels, the first reference to baptism occurs in relation to John. He is called the baptizer or Baptist in Mark 1:4 and Matthew 3:1. In Mark 1:5; Luke 3:3, John is preaching a baptism of repentance for the remission of sins. Matthew 3:2 puts it differently: John proclaims, "Repent, for the kingdom of heaven is at hand." All the Gospels have an account of the baptism of Jesus by John. "Matthew 3:14 adds that John was reluctant to baptize Jesus but consented when Jesus said it was fitting for them to fulfil all righteousness."[1] "All the Synoptics (Mk. 1:11f; Mt. 3:16f; Lk. 3:21f.) tell us that three things took place after the baptism: the opening of heaven, the descent of the Spirit like a dove, and the voice from heaven calling Jesus the beloved Son in whom God is well pleased."[2]

The Book of Acts opens with the promise of baptism with the Holy Spirit (1:5) and the summoning of the disciples to a worldwide ministry. After the people hear the message they are cut to the heart and ask what must be done. "Peter tells them to repent and be baptized for the forgiveness of sins (2:37f)." After Paul was granted his vision of the risen Lord and then brought blind to Damascus, Ananias, acting on divine command, went to him and laid hands on him, telling him that he, Ananias, had been sent in order that Paul might regain his sight and be filled with the Holy Spirit (9:3ff.,10ff.,17). Paul's sight was returned, and he rose up and was baptized (v.18).

In Philippi two baptisms are spoken of; being Lydia (16:15) and the jailer (16:33). In both of these instances the whole household was baptized. In Romans, Paul refers to baptism only once (6:3f). However, it is an important reference. In it Paul "interrelates the death and resurrection of Christ and the dying and rising of His people in and with Him . . . All who are baptized into Christ are baptized into his death (v.3). They are buried with Him by baptism into death so that as He rose again they can now 'walk in newness of life' (v.4). Consequently, union with Christ in death means union with Him in resurrection."[3]

---

1. Bromiley, *Baptism*, 411.
2. Bromiley, *Baptism*, 411.
3. Bromiley, *Baptism*, 411.

CHURCH ORDINANCES

There are a number of important references to baptism in 1 Corinthians. In chapter 1, Paul refers to baptism in response to the factionalism that was occurring there. It is not the person that is conducting the baptism that counts, but the event itself. Chapter 10 also mentions baptism as Paul makes a comparison with Israel. "Israel had its own baptism in the great act of deliverance out of Egypt. Israel was baptized into Moses in the cloud and the sea (10:2f). It also received spiritual food and drink (vv. 3f). Yet through its wicked acts it still came under God's displeasure (vv. 5ff). Christians should learn from this, especially by avoiding idolatry (vv11ff., 14ff)."[4]

Baptism is also an illustration used by Paul when discussing gifts in chapter 12. "By one Spirit we were all baptized into one body . . . and all were made to drink of one Spirit' (v.13)." "It should be noted that baptism and Spirit are closely associated here, that baptism is into Christ's body."[5]

In Galatians, baptism is only mentioned once (3:27) yet, like in Romans, it is a significant statement. "The line of thought is that in Christ, the one seed of Abraham, all are sons of God through faith, whether or not they fulfil the law (3:27). Baptism is, for all who receive it, a putting on of Christ (3:27). In Christ, all divisions are broken down." In Ephesians, unity is the issue (4:5f) and in Colossians Paul makes a connection between circumcision and baptism. (2:11ff). However, there is no indication that since infants were circumcised, so should they be baptized.

In the book of Hebrews (10:22) there is an allusion to baptism linking the outer and the inner action. Through Christ we may draw near to God in faith, having had our hearts sprinkled clean from a bad conscience, and having had our bodies washed with pure water. The physical washing during baptism has a spiritual counterpart. A similar thought reappears in 1 Peter 3:21. Here baptism is compared to the ark in which Noah and his party were saved. In baptism, we again have saving water. "The washing, however, is not a removing of bodily dirt. It is the answer of a good conscience, or the appeal for it, through the resurrection of Jesus Christ. An inner cleansing is again linked to the outer act."[6]

In the early church a theology of baptism soon emerged. Justin Martyr wrote c 160:

> *At our birth, we were born without our own knowledge or choice, but by our parents coming together . . . In order that we may not remain the children of necessity and of ignorance, but may become the children of choice and knowledge, and may obtain in the water the remission of sins formerly committed, there is pronounced over him who chooses to be born again, and has repented*

---

4. Bromiley, *Baptism*, 411.
5. Bromiley, *Baptism*, 411.
6. Bromiley, *Baptism*, 413.

of his sins, the name of God the Father and the Lord of the universe . . . And in the name of Jesus Christ . . . and in the name of the Holy Spirit.[7]

The mode of baptism, and rules surrounding its practice, was also an issue. The Didache (c 80–140) gives this instruction:

Concerning baptism, baptize in this manner: Having first said all these things, baptize into the name of the Father, the Son, and the Holy Spirit—in living water. But if you have no living water, baptize in other water. If you cannot baptize in cold water, baptize in warm. But if you do not have either, pour out water three times upon the person's head in the name of the Father, the Son, and the Holy Spirit. However, before the baptism, let the baptizer fast, and the one to be baptized, together with whoever else can. But you will instruct the one to be baptized to fast one or two days before [the baptism].[8]

A sacramental theology of baptism emerged early in the history of the church. Tertullian wrote in c 198;

It makes no difference whether a man is washed in a sea or a pool, a stream or a fountain, a lake or a trough . . . All waters . . . attain the sacramental power of sanctification. For the Spirit immediately supervenes from the heavens and rests over the waters, sanctifying them through Himself. And thus, being sanctified, they acquire at the same time the power of sanctifying.

Tertullian, however, did not advocate infant baptism.

And so, according to the circumstances, disposition, and even age of each individual, the delay of baptism is preferable. This is particularly true in the case of little children. For why is it necessary—if baptism itself is not so necessary—that the sponsors likewise should be thrust into danger? . . . Let the children come, then, while they are growing up. Let them come while they are learning where to come. Let them become Christians when they have become able to know Christ. Why does the innocent period of life hasten to the remission of sins? If anyone understands the weighty importance of baptism, he will fear its reception more than its delay. Sound faith is secure of salvation.[9]

Cyprian, bishop of Carthage, disagrees. In a clear departure from the biblical model, he advocated infant baptism and infers baptismal regeneration. In c. 250, eight years before his death, he wrote:

In respect to the case of the infants, you say that they should not be baptized within the second or third day after their birth—that the law of ancient circumcision should be regarded. So, you think that one who has just been born

---

7. Bercot, *Dictionary of Early Christian Beliefs*, 51.
8. Bercot, *Dictionary of Early Christian Beliefs*, 56.
9. Bercot, *Dictionary of Early Christian Beliefs*, 59.

should not be baptized and sanctified within the eighth day. However, we all thought very differently in our council . . . Rather, we all believe that the mercy and grace of God is not to be refused to anyone born of man . . . As far as we can, we must strive that no soul be lost, if at all possible. . . . Moreover, belief in divine Scripture declares to us that among all—whether infants or those who are older—there is the same equality of the divine gift . . . Otherwise, it would seem that the very grace which is given to the baptized is given either more, or less, depending on the age of the receivers. However, the Holy Spirit is not given with measure. Rather, it is given alike to all, by the love and mercy of the Father . . . For although the infant is still fresh from its birth, yet it is not such that anyone should shudder at kissing it in giving grace and in making peace.[10]

BAPTISM SINCE THE REFORMATION

The theology of baptism was developed during the time of the Reformation. Martin Luther made a connection between salvation and baptism.

In his treatise on baptism, 'The Holy and Blessed Sacrament of Baptism', Luther recognizes that the word baptismos means plunging in water. Immersion, then, is the proper mode of baptism. It expresses most vividly the drowning of the old man. Baptism is defined as 'an external sign and token' marking off Christians from others as 'a people of Christ, our Leader, under whose banner of the holy cross was continually fighting against sin'.[11]

Luther also emphasizes baptism's lifelong significance and its connection with sanctification and suffering.

The Anabaptists renewed the biblical model of believer's baptism. Menno Simons argued against infant baptism in his "Foundations of Christian Doctrine". "The starting point here, as so often, is the wording of the great commission, which puts preaching or teaching before baptism. Since one cannot preach to infants or teach them, logic demands that they should not be baptized."[12] "Against the appeal to circumcision Simons makes two points. First, Jesus was circumcised as an infant but was then baptized as an adult, not as an infant. Second, circumcision, in contrast to baptism, is limited to boys."[13] As a result of the teachings of the Anabaptists, John Calvin was more adamant in his emphasizing of infant baptism. Calvin found a relationship between Old Testament circumcision and the New Testament sign of baptism.

---

10. Bercot, *Dictionary of Early Christian Beliefs*, 50–57.
11. Bromiley, *Historical theology: An Introduction*, 270.
12. Bromiley, *Historical theology: An Introduction*, 274.
13. Bromiley, *Historical theology: An Introduction*, 274.

FOUNDATIONS OF THEOLOGY

> *The obvious differences are in externals only. Materially the signs are one and the same; they are one in promise (God's fatherly favor), in the thing represented (forgiveness), and in foundation. The giving of circumcision to children shows plainly that the covenant promises to pertain no less to them than to their parents. Since the covenant does not change (only the outer observance has changed) it obviously applies to Christian children too. 'Why then' asks Calvin, 'shall they be debarred from the sign?'*[14]
>
> *In a brief section Calvin lists three blessings of infant baptism. a. The parents receive from it assurance of the promise that God's mercy extends to their children, too b. It commends the children to the other members of the church. c. Later it spurs them to an earnest zeal for God. As Calvin sees it, the sign itself also carries with it a warning of divine judgement on those who refuse the proffered grace by despising the sign.*[15]

Otto Weber stated that both Luther and Calvin maintained "the medieval thesis of the concealed faith in children ('children's faith'). Further, the attempt was generally made to demonstrate that the baptism of infants was practiced in the New Testament period."[16]

Calvin's theology of baptism has been upheld in the Reformed tradition. Lois Berkhof asserted that even though there is no explicit mention of infants being baptized in the New Testament this does not mean that infant baptism is unbiblical. The Scriptural ground for it is found in the following data:

The Old Testament covenant was a spiritual covenant with circumcision as its sign. The covenant is still in force today. "By the appointment of God infants shared in the benefits of the covenant, and therefore received circumcision as a sign and seal ... (B)aptism is by divine authority substituted for circumcision as the initiatory sign and seal of the covenant of grace."[17]

A more biblical perspective was offered by Augustus Strong, who asserted that the "proper subjects of baptism are those only who give credible evidence that they have been regenerated by the Holy Spirit, -or, in other words, have entered by faith into the communion of Christ's death and resurrection." The proof of this is found in Matthew 28:19. Also, Scripture teaches that only those who have previously repented and believed can be baptized (Matt. 3:2–6). According to Strong, the mode of baptism must be immersion. This is so because the command to baptize is a command to immerse. This is seen from the Greek word, *baptizo*, to immerse. Strong quoted Marcus Dods, who defined baptism as "a rite wherein by immersion in water the participant symbolizes and signalizes his transition from an impure to a pure life, his death to a past he abandons, and his birth to a future he desires." For Strong,

---

14. Bromiley, *Historical theology: An Introduction*, 280.
15. Bromiley, *Historical theology: An Introduction*, 268–282.
16. Weber, *Dogmatics: Vol. 2*, 607.
17. Berkhof, *Systematic Theology*, 633.

baptism "symbolizes the previous entrance of the believer into the communion of Christ's death and resurrection . . . in other words, regeneration through union with Christ."[18] Therefore, baptism is a symbol of the death and resurrection of Christ. (Rom. 6:3; Matt. 3:13; Mk. 10:38; Lk. 12:50; Col. 2:12). and serves to demonstrate death and resurrection in the believer so as to deliver sinners from its penalty and power. (Rom 6:4).[19]

Donald Bloesch sounded a note from the Radical-Reformation when he declared that baptism "is not a ritual that automatically effects regeneration, but neither is it a barren symbol that simply points to regeneration. It is a sign that when joined to the Word of God and the outpouring of the Spirit effects what it symbolizes." Bloesch further commented that while many texts *seem* to support a sacramental understanding of baptism, they, in fact, do not. Water baptism is only a sign, though an essential one done in response to the command of Christ. Spirit baptism alone is equivalent to the new birth. As Paul stated in 1 Cor. 12:13. "By one Spirit we were all baptized into one body . . . and all were made to drink of one Spirit." Bloesch revealed his own opinion with the reflection: "Because pedobaptism today has virtually become a means of cheap grace, I personally favor the rite of believer's baptism . . . When baptism is given to believers, it does not impart salvation but confirms and ratifies a salvation already set in motion by the experience of conversion."[20]

Ellen White followed the Anabaptist reading of Scripture as she associated baptism with the dynamics of salvation. To be sure, it is a consequence of a true and full conversion. "Baptism commemorates Christ's resurrection and the candidate's new birth—The resurrection of Christ is commemorated by our being buried with Him by baptism, and raised up out of the watery grave in likeness of His resurrection, to live in newness of life".[21] The importance that Mrs. White places on the meaning of baptism is seen in her assertion that full instruction should be given before a candidate is baptized. Indeed,

> *Ministers should give each candidate plain instruction regarding baptism's meaning—Our churches are becoming enfeebled by receiving for doctrines the commandments of men. Many are received into the church who are not converted. Men, women, and children are allowed to take part in the solemn rite of baptism without being fully instructed in regard to the meaning of this ordinance. Participation in this ordinance means much, and our ministers should be careful to give each candidate for baptism plain instruction regarding its meaning and its solemnity.*[22]

---

18. Strong, *Systematic Theology*, 244.
19. Strong, *Systematic Theology*, 931–946.
20. Bloesch, *The Church*, 159.
21. White, *Early Writings*, 217.
22. White, *Review and Herald*, Oct. 6, 1904.

To be sure, the ordinance points to the transformation of the heart and renunciation of the world that conversion represents.

> *Baptism is a most solemn renunciation of the world. Those who are baptized in the threefold name of the Father, the Son, and the Holy Spirit, at the very entrance of their Christian life declare publicly that they have forsaken the service of Satan and have become members of the royal family, children of the heavenly King. They have obeyed the command: 'Come out from among them, and be ye separate, ... and touch not the unclean thing.' And to them is fulfilled the promise: 'I will receive you, and will be a Father unto you, and ye shall be My sons and daughters, saith the Lord Almighty' (2 Corinthians 6:17, 18).*[23]

Ellen White also called for a re-baptism by those who felt compelled to do so. This should never be forced upon a candidate but may well represent a new commitment to God as a result of a personal reformation that has taken place when embracing the present truth of the Three Angels Message.

> *The Lord calls for a decided reformation. And when a soul is truly converted, let him be rebaptized. Let him renew his covenant with God, and God will renew His covenant with him . . . Reconversion must take place among the members, that as God's witnesses they may testify to the authoritative power of the truth that sanctifies the soul.*[24]

THE LORD'S SUPPER

The precursor to the Lord's Supper[25] in the Gospels is found in the Old Testament Passover Meal. The Passover meal originated during Israel's nomadic period. "A one-year-old lamb or kid (Exod. 12:5) was killed by the head of the household on the fourteenth of Nisan at sundown (Exod. 12:6). Its blood was smeared on the doorposts, its flesh roasted and eaten by the family during the night of 14–15 Nisan (Exodus 12:8f). After Josiah's reform (621 B.C.) the killing of the Passover lambs and the Passover meal took place in Jerusalem (Deut. 16:5–7; 2 Kings 23:21–23). The Jewish Passover meal in the time of Jesus recalled the sparing of the houses marked with the blood of the Passover lambs and the redemption out of Egypt. At the same time the Passover meal looked forward to redemption in the future, of which the redemption from Egypt was the pattern. The Lord's Supper is in the setting of a Passover meal. (Matt. 26:17ff; Mk. 14:12, 14, 16; Lk. 22:7, 11, 12, 15). The institution of the Lord's Supper has been handed down in four forms. Matthew 14:22–25;

---

23. White, *Testimonies for The Church: Vol. 6*, 91.
24. White, *Letter 63, 1903*.
25. The expression, *the Lord's Supper*, occurs only in 1 Cor. 11:20.

Matthew 26:26–29; Luke 22:15–20; 1 Cor. 11:23–25). Indeed, the Supper is the oldest account of the passion.[26]

The Significance of the Lord's Supper is found in the Institution-Narratives. Firstly, it was meant to be a perpetual commemoration of Christ's sacrificial death. Secondly, it was intended to be a means of communion, and it was therefore fittingly come to be called Communion. Through this rite the disciples were to experience real fellowship with their Lord. The bread and wine were taken as symbols of the body and blood of Christ. The rite was a dramatic representation of the life of union with Christ. Further, the Supper was conceived as the covenant-meal of the new dispensation, in which, as in other covenant-meals, fellowship was established between the members of the covenant on the one hand, and also with one another and thirdly, it was a pledge that Christ would come again, and the sacramental experience was a foretaste of a fuller and deeper fellowship with Christ in His Consummated Kingdom.

The Teaching of Luther repudiated the Roman Catholic doctrine of the Mass, but attached a great deal of importance to the Eucharist. His mature doctrine took a number of years to evolve, but emerged from Luther's careful and detailed study of Scripture. While still supporting the doctrine of transubstantiation in 1519, it appears that in his 1520 *Treatise of the New Testament*, he clearly rejects this doctrine and moves, in contradistinction to Zwingli, to describe the state of the elements in terms of consubstantiation. That is, Christ is under, in and through the bread and wine, as an iron enters and is transformed by the heat while still remaining an iron. The bread and wine remain bread and wine, but after the consecration the actual flesh and blood of Christ co-exist in and with the bread and wine, just as a heated iron bar still remains an iron bar, though a new element, heat, co-exists in and with it. This connection is not permanent, but pertains only to the act of communion.

Zwingli regarded communion to be a memorial of our Lord's death, the bread and wine being the signs of the broken body and shed blood, and also as an act of renewed union with Christ (who is spiritually present) through faith, bread and wine being seals of this union. The opinion that the Supper is purely commemorative is commonly called Zwinglian. But this does not seem to do full justice to Zwingli's views. In his *Exposition of the Faith*, Zwingli defined the sacraments as "signs and symbols of holy things, but not . . . the things of which they are the signs". They are signs of real things, representing and recalling things which once took place literally and naturally. By the bread and wine "Christ is himself as it were set before our eyes, so that not merely with the ear, but with the eye and palate we see the taste that Christ whom the soul bears within itself and in whom it rejoices."[27]

---

26. Klappert, *Lord's Supper*, 520–538.
27. Schreiner, Crawford, *The Lords Supper,* 243.

Zwingli added another section to stress his positive evaluation of the sacraments. The supper has value because it was instituted by Christ, testifies to historical facts, has the name of which it signifies, represents a high thing, and stands in analogy to the thing signified—Christ our food, and ourselves, the one fellowship. It also augments faith even though it cannot give it . . . Finally, the sacrament as a pledge binds us together as "one body by the sacramental partaking of his body, for we are one body with him." The saying "This is my body" must be taken as a metonymy (that is, substitution for what it represents), meaning "This is the sacrament of my body," or "This is my sacramental or mystical body—the sacramental and representative symbol of the body which I really assumed and yielded over to death."[28]

Calvin emphasized the idea of the real spiritual presence of Christ in the Eucharist. The bread and wine are signs of the body and blood of Christ, but they are not mere signs; they are instrumental means of His presence. Because Christ is present there is a means for deepening our union with Him. "As Calvin acutely observes, the words 'given and shed for you' give the sacrament its force. The body and blood benefit us as they were given up for our salvation. The analogical relation is also important: 'As bread nourishes . . . the life of our body, so Christ's body is the only food to invigorate and enliven our soul.'"[29]

Methodist thought has in the main followed the line of Calvin's teaching. Maldwyn Hughes believed that the following would be generally accepted:

1. The Supper is a memorial of our Lord's dying on our behalf.

2. It is a renewal of the Christian's oath of allegiance to his or her Lord and Master.

3. It is the feast of the Holy Communion. Christ is really present in Spirit, and is apprehended by faith. The life of union with Christ is represented dramatically or symbolically by the eating of the bread and the drinking of the wine, and as we apprehend our Lord, who is really present, so does our union with Him deepen.

4. The Supper has a social significance. All social and other distinctions fall away among those who are guests at the Lord's Table, and those who are Christ's enter into fellowship with one another, as well as with their Lord. In the Holy Supper, we have a foretaste of a redeemed society.

5. It is a pledge that our Lord will come again to consummate His Kingdom. Hughes further clarified Methodist theology as he pointed out that evangelicals do not believe that the Lord's Supper is a channel of grace. The only "channel of grace" is fellowship with the Spirit. Sacraments and other ordinances may, and do, aid the realization of this fellowship.[30]

28. Bromiley, *Historical Theology*, 288–89.
29. Bromiley, *Historical Theology*, 295.
30. Hughes, *Christian Foundations*, 200–206.

During sixteenth-century England, Ridley played a key role in the development of the understanding of communion. "Appealing to "the word of God and the ancient fathers," Ridley saw the bread to be "the body of Christ in the remembrance of him and of his death". By remembrance he did not just mean the subjective act of recollection, for Christ makes the remembrance and by God's power "it far passeth all kinds of remembrance that any other man is able to make either of himself, or of any other thing."

Ridley seemed to hold closely to Calvin's understanding when he stated that Christ's body can be described as really present by the Spirit, even though bread remains bread and wine, wine.

> *Thus, the sacrament can be no naked sign, no purely human act of remembrance. Under the Holy Spirit it involves the presence of the whole Christ to his people in grace and power. What Ridley denies is what is for him the pseudo-miracle of substantial change. What he affirms is the true miracle of a real presence by the Word and Spirit.*[31]

The Heidelberg Catechism (1645) has a lengthy section on the Lord's Supper. According to the Catechism, the sacrament consists in the rite and the promise annexed to it, or in the signs and things signified.

> *The rite, or signs are the bread which is broken and eaten, and the wine which is poured out, and drunk. The things signified are the broken body, and shed blood of Christ, which are eaten and drunk, or our union with Christ by faith, by which we are made partakers of Christ and all his benefits, so that we derive from him everlasting life, as the branches draw their life from the vine. We are assured of this our union and communion with Christ by the analogy which there is between the sign and the thing signified: and also by the promise which is joined to the sign. This analogy declares, and exhibits in a particular manner the sacrifice of Christ, and our communion with him; because the bread is not only broken, but also given unto us to be eaten.*[32]

The Westminster Confession of Faith [Chap. XXIX, Sect. II] stipulates that in "this sacrament Christ is not offered up to the Father, nor any real sacrifice made at all for remission of sins of the quick or dead; but only a commemoration of that one offering up of himself by himself, upon the cross, once for all, and a spiritual oblation of all possible praise unto God for the same." [Sect. VII]

> *Worthy receivers, outwardly partaking of the visible elements in this sacrament, do then also inwardly by faith, really and indeed, yet not carnally and corporally, but spiritually, receive and feed upon Christ crucified, and all benefits of his death: the body and blood of Christ being then not corporally or*

---

31. Bromiley, *Historical Theology*, 300–301.
32. *Heidelberg Catechism*, 378.

carnally in, with, or under the bread and wine; yet as really, but spiritually, present to the faith of believers in that ordinances as the elements themselves are to their outward senses.[33]

Adolf Schlatter (1852–1938) averred that Christ instituted the Lord's supper at the time of the Passover so that he could "institute the new covenant on the day of commemorating the old." Schlatter further discussed Paul's claim in 1 Cor. 11:23–25. It was that the entire church has as its foundation the word of Jesus. Paul

saw therein an imperishable gift that was granted not only to them but to his entire community and that would never again be taken away from them. God's new covenant would remain forever and was in effect for all who belonged to the Christ, and forgiveness of sins was acquired for them all by his death. They also were not to experience the blessed power of his death in such a way that they would forget its basis and origin. It reminded them of his human life and his earthly deed, therefore making what he then did for them a means by which they could direct their memory to him again and again. Thereby he made direct connection with the way in which the old covenant possessed its continual attestation in the annually repeated covenantal meal.[34]

According to Dietrich Bonhoeffer, the Lord's Supper fosters and sustains Christians in fellowship and communion in the body of Christ. Furthermore, communion, like baptism, flows from the true humanity of our Lord Jesus Christ. Communion is closely linked with his word. The Lord's Supper proclaims the death of Christ for us (Rom. 6:3ff; 1 Cor. 11:26).

Both baptism and the Lord's Supper give us far more than the forgiveness of our sins. It would be better to describe the gift of the sacraments as the gift of the very Body of Christ in the Church . . . in contrast to our present practice, the administration of the two sacraments was not combined by the apostles with the proclamation of the Word in New Testament times, but was performed by the congregation itself (1 Cor. 1:1, 14ff; 11:17ff). Baptism and the Lord's Supper belong to the fellowship of the body of Christ alone, whereas the Word is intended not only for believers but also for unbelievers. The sacraments belong exclusively to the Church.[35]

According to James Torrance the concept of remembering must be considered. The remembrance at communion must amount to our "participation in the past event" as well as seeing our destiny and future as bound up with it. "For example, when the Jews in their worship remember the Passover and the exodus from Egypt,

---

33. *Westminster Confession*, 292–302.
34. Schlatter, *The History of the Christ*, 353–362.
35. Bonhoeffer, *The Cost of Discipleship*, 251.

they do not think of it as simply an irretrievable date from over three thousand years ago. Rather, they remember it in such a way that they confess:

> *We were once Pharaoh's bondsmen, but by the grace of God, we are a people whom God brought up out of the land of Egypt. . . . So at the Lord's table we do not merely remember the passion of our Lord as an isolated date . . . (W)e remember it in such a way that we know by the grace of God we are the people for whom our Saviour died and rose again, we are the people whose sins Jesus confessed on the cross, we are the people with whom God has made a new covenant in the blood of Christ . . . This work of memory, or realizing our participation and fellowship in the sufferings of Christ, is the work of the Holy Spirit.*[36]

According to Alister McGrath, the sacraments have a number of functions. Firstly, they strengthen faith. "The sacraments represent the promises of God, mediated through objects of the everyday world." Secondly, they enhance unity and commitment within the church. "Luther asserted that a central function of the sacraments was to reassure believers that they are truly members of the body of Christ, and heirs of the kingdom of God." Luther wrote: "To receive this sacrament in bread and wine, then, is nothing else than to receive a sure sign of this fellowship and union with Christ and all the saints." According to Luther, the liturgy of the Eucharist makes three vitally important points. It affirms the promises of grace and forgiveness; identifies those to whom those promises are made; and declares the death of the one who made those promises.[37] Alternatively, Zwingli advocated that "the purpose of the sacraments is primarily to demonstrate that an individual belongs to the community of faith." Furthermore, communion is "a public demonstration of the believer's allegiance to that church and its members." Thirdly, the sacrament reassures us of God's promise. However, it was the Anabaptists who revived a solidly biblical perspective free of the error that had accompanied the established churches.

THE ANABAPTISTS

In Luther's contribution to the Reformation he sought to cleanse the church from all that contradicted scripture. Zwingli went further by only embracing that which he believed to have scriptural foundation. But there were those who sought to go further still. They were Zwinglian originally before splitting over beliefs about baptism. Their theology of communion, however, remained essentially Zwinglian.

Anabaptists saw in Scripture a marked contrast between the church and its surrounding society that the so-called "Magisterial Reformers" had not addressed. Ever since the time of Constantine, accommodationalism had beset the church and led

---

36. Torrance, *Worship, Community and The Triune God of Grace*, 74–75.
37. McGrath, *Christian Theology: An Introduction*, 438–439.

into the mire of compromise and error. Therefore, what was being called for was a total separation of church and state. Consequently, the Anabaptists argued that although one is born into the state by the mere fact of being born in a particular place, one couldn't belong to the true church without a personal decision of faith. The two were separate. "In consequence, infant baptism must be rejected, for it takes for granted that one becomes a Christian by being born in a supposedly Christian society. This obscures the need for a personal decision that stands at the very heart of the Christian faith."[38]

The Anabaptists first came to public attention in Zurich when "a group of believers urged Zwingli to undertake a more radical reformation."[39] When it appeared that he was not going to take that course of action, some of the "brethren" decided to take matters into their own hands and start a congregation. "George Blaurock, a former priest, asked another of the brethren, Conrad Grebel, to baptize him. On January 21, 1525, at the fountain that stood in the square in Zurich, Grebel baptized Blaurock, who then did the same for several others."[40]

FOOT WASHING

Some Anabaptised practiced foot washing at communion. Sebastian Franck's "Chronical" of 1531 appears to be the earliest reference to its observance in reformation Germany. "Marpeck's 'Verantwortung' refers to the practice, and the oldest Anabaptist song book, the 'Ausbung' of 1564, contains a hymn for its observance."[41] Its revival can be traced back to the teaching of Jesus. In the time of Jesus, it was customary for the host to make provision for the washing of the feet of guests (Luke 7:44–46), but without religious significance. Jesus turns this custom into a commandment to be observed at communion. He instructed: "Ye also ought to wash one another's feet. For I have given you an example, that ye should do as I have done to you" (John 13: 14, 15). Foot washing was practiced in the early church. Tertullian (145-220), in his *De Corona,* is the first Church Father to indicate that foot washing was practiced. Most significantly, the Albigenses who arose in Southern France in the 11th and 12th centuries, apparently observed foot washing following the communion service. Among the Waldenses, it was the custom to wash the feet of visiting ministers, but there is no evidence of the practice of the ordinance by the members. The Bohemian Brethren, or Hussites, also practiced it, at least in the 16th century. The ordinance was not introduced into the new Reformation state churches, but it was adopted by the Anabaptists. From the beginning (1525–35) some Anabaptists

---

38. González., *The Story of Christianity: Vol. 2,* 54.
39. González., *The Story of Christianity: Vol. 2,* 52.
40. González., *The Story of Christianity: Vol. 2,* 55.
41. Packull, *An Introduction to Anabaptist Theology,* 214.

practiced foot washing, but it was not universal. It was most common in Holland and the related or descendant groups in Northwest Germany, West and East Prussia, and Russia.[42]

Ellen White's biblical teaching clearly outlined the origins and meaning of communion. As Christ,

> *ate the Passover with His disciples, He instituted in its place the service that was to be the memorial of His great sacrifice. The national festival of the Jews was to pass away forever. The service which Christ established was to be observed by His followers in all lands and through all ages . . . . Till He shall come the second time in power and glory, this ordinance is to be celebrated.*[43]

Further, communion is to be a service of spiritual nurture and uplifting.

> *It is at these, His own appointments, that Christ meets His people, and energizes them by His presence . . . . All who come with their faith fixed upon Him will be greatly blessed. All who neglect these seasons of divine privilege will suffer loss. Of them it may appropriately be said, 'Ye are not all clean.' . . . But the Communion service was not to be a season of sorrowing. This was not its purpose . . . . They are not to recall the differences between them and their brethren. The preparatory service has embraced all this . . . . Now they come to meet with Christ. They are not to stand in the shadow of the cross, but in its saving light. They are to open the soul to the bright beams of the Sun of Righteousness. With hearts cleansed by Christ's most precious blood, in full consciousness of His presence, although unseen, they are to hear His words, 'Peace I leave with you.'*[44]

The biblical perspective of the Anabaptists is seen in the teaching of Ellen White, as she promoted the significance of practicing the pattern of the entire Last Supper.

> *Christ in the fullness of His grace is there [during the ordinance of humility] to change the current of the thoughts that have been running in selfish channels. The Holy Spirit quickens the sensibilities of those who follow the example of their Lord. As the Savior's humiliation for us is remembered, thought links with thought; a chain of memories is called up, memories of God's great goodness and of the favor and tenderness of earthly friends. Blessings forgotten, mercies abused, kindnesses slighted, are called to mind. Roots of bitterness that have crowded out the precious plant of love are made manifest. Defects of character, neglect of duties, ingratitude to God, coldness toward our brethren, are called to remembrance. Sin is seen in the light in which God views it. Our thoughts are not thoughts of self-complacency, but of severe self-censure and humiliation. The mind is energized to break down every barrier that has caused alienation.*

---

42. Bender, *Footwashing*, 347–351.
43. White, *The Desire of Ages*, 653–4.
44. White, *The Desire of Ages*, 656.

FOUNDATIONS OF THEOLOGY

> *Evil thinking and evil speaking are put away. Sins are confessed, they are forgiven. The subduing grace of Christ comes into the soul, and the love of Christ draws hearts together in a blessed unity.*[45]

In June and July of 1897, Ellen White wrote a number of articles for the *Review and Herald*, regarding the ordinances of the Lord's Supper, Foot washing and baptism. She pointed to the biblical exposition that the Lord's Supper takes the place of the Passover and in so doing marks the point of transition between two economies and their two great festivals. The former, the Passover of the old covenant, was closed forever, however the new memorial was to take its place and continue as a memorial of His death.[46] "On these occasions heaven is brought very near". Indeed, "the love of Jesus, with its convincing power, is to be kept fresh in the memory. We must not forget Him who is our strength and sufficiency."[47] Indeed, the gospel of salvation through Jesus Christ is at the heart of the church's remembrance and our need to repent of sin and put our faith in Christ's atoning sacrifice.

> *The first look, the first act, of contrition and repentance that you direct toward Christ, does not escape His notice. The first step you take toward Him will bring Him more than a step toward you. All things, especially on this occasion, are ready for your reception. He will meet you in your weakness, repenting, broken hearted soul, with His divine strength; He will meet your emptiness and spiritual poverty with His inexhaustible fullness.*[48]

This state of mind naturally leads to foot washing. The importance of foot washing accompanying communion is highlighted by the fact that this ordinance does not cleanse the participants of sin, but is a test as to whether or not their hearts have been cleansed. "Christ gave His disciples to understand that the washing of their feet did not cleanse away their sin, but that the cleansing of their heart was tested in this humble service. If the heart was cleansed, this act was all that was essential to reveal the fact."[49]

---

45. White, *The Desire of Ages*, 650–1.
46. White, *Review and Herald*, June 22, 1897.
47. White, *Review and Herald*, June 22, 1897.
48. White, *Review and Herald*, June 14, 1898.
49. White, *Review and Herald*, June 14, 1898.

CHAPTER 31

WORSHIP

WORSHIP IS A VITAL PART of the Christian life and ministry of the Church. Jesus calls upon His people to worship the Father in spirit and in truth (John 4:23-24). Worship is an act in response to the liberation from sin, and entering into a new life in the Spirit that Jesus promises to all who believe in Him. The book of Revelation describes worship as another aspect of the Christian's destiny and an integral part of the fulfilment and end of salvation.

> *And I saw another sign in heaven, great and marvellous, seven angels having the seven last plagues; for in them is filled up the wrath of God. And I saw as it were a sea of glass mingled with fire: and them that had gotten the victory over the beast, and over his image, and over his mark, and over the number of his name, stand on the sea of glass, having the harps of God. And they sing the song of Moses the servant of God, and the song of the Lamb, saying, Great and marvellous are thy works, Lord God Almighty; just and true are thy ways, thou King of saints* (Rev. 15:1-3).

The Bible is filled with references to worship, ultimately pointing to it as an essential and unavoidable expression of Christian life. In the Old Testament, the people of God were a worshipping community. Since the wilderness wanderings, the life of Israel centred around the place of worship. There are two significant words worthy of comment. Firstly, *shachah*—to bow down (Gen 24:26, 48; Deut. 29:26; Exodus 4:31, 12:27; Psalm 95:6); and *abodah*—service (Num. 4:24, 26, 8:25; 2 Kings 10:19-23). Worshippers are servants who serve God in praise. In the New Testament, the focus turns to Jesus Christ. *Proskuneo*—to kiss the hand toward—originally used of a person prostrating themselves on the ground before another to kiss their feet (Matt 2:11, 4:9-10, Mk. 15:19; Jn. 4:23; 1 Cor. 14:25; Rev. 5:14); *latreuo*—to serve (in reverence) (Matt. 4:10; Luke 1:74, 2:37; Heb. 9:14; Rev. 7:15); and *thusia*—sacrifice (Rom. 12:1; 1 Peter 2:5; Phil. 4:18; Heb. 13:15). In Scripture we find that worship is to be given to God because of who He is as our creator (Gen 1:1ff; Rev. 4:11); the Holy One (Is. 6:1-3; Rev. 4:6-8); Gracious (Psalm 145:10; Deut. 7:7-8); because of His uniqueness and eternity (Rev. 4:8) and because of what He has done in Redemption (Exodus 15:1-18; Rev. 5:9ff). Scripture describes the various elements of worship: Praise, prayer and thanksgiving (Ps. 22:22, 138:2, 149:1, 35:18, 100:4, 116:17; Acts 2:42); Reading and Exposition of Scripture (Acts 13:15, 27; 15:21, 20:7-12); and The Lord's Supper (Acts 2:42, 20:7; 1 Cor. 11:17ff). Worship must be conducted in the church in Spirit and in truth (Jn. 4:23-24; 1 Cor. 14:15; Phil. 3:3). Further, worship is to be loved by God's people (Ps. 27:4, 84:1-4, 10, Zec. 8:21) and therefore believers should prepare for worship (Ex. 19:10-13, 21-24, 20:24-25; Lev 10:3; Isa. 56:6-7).

In the early church, Clement of Alexandria wrote c. 195:

> *We are commanded to reverence and to honor the same One, being persuaded that He is Word... We do not do this on special days, as some other persons do. Rather, we do this continually in our whole life, and in every way... For that reason, not in a specified place, or selected temple, or at certain festivals and on appointed days, but during his whole life, the spiritual man honors God. He does this in every place—even if he is alone by himself. He does this wherever he has with him any of those brethren who have exercised the same faith.*[1]

Lanctantius (c. 250-325), a prominent Roman teacher of rhetoric who later converted to Christianity, wrote that if

> *anyone thinks that vestments, jewels, and other things that are considered precious are valued by God, he is altogether ignorant of what God is ... That which is spiritual must be offered to God, for he accepts this. His offering is innocency of soul. His sacrifice is praise and hymns. Since God is not seen, He should be worshipped with things that are not seen ... Therefore, the chief ceremonial in the worship of God is the praise from the mouth of a just man directed towards God.*[2]

According to James Packer,

> *Worship in the Bible is the due response of rational creatures to the self-revelation of their Creator... It involves praising him for what he is, thanking him for what he has done, desiring him to get himself more glory by further acts of mercy, judgement, and power, and trusting him without concern for our own and others' future well-being.*

Packer added that moods of awestruck wonder and grateful celebration are all part of worship (2 Sam. 6:14-16; 7:18). "The basis of worship is the covenant relationship whereby God has bound himself to those whom he has saved and claimed.[3]

---

1. *The Stomata, Book II.*
2. Bercot, *Dictionary of Early Christian Beliefs*, 699.
3. Packer, *Concise Theology*, 99.

WORSHIP

James Torrance averred that the Christian community, in her worship, recapitulates the history of salvation;

> *In her worship, the Church sets forth by word and action that perfect life or Worship which we see in Jesus Christ. As her response to the Worship and Ministry of Christ, she sets forth objectively in her liturgical life what God has done for her and for the world. In worship we sum up, we recapitulate, we echo the Offering, the Prayers, the Praises of Him who is our Leitourgos (the one who leads us into worship), in our self-offering, prayers and praises uniting with the whole company in heaven and on earth who worship God as 'the Lamb upon the Throne.' . . . Thus, our worship has the character of witness—liturgical witness to grace, according to the divinely given ordinances of grace." Worship is the very life and essence of the church. Humanity is never more fully human in worship. In worship, there is the raising to all the heights of human dignity, "and all God's purposes in Creation in Creation and in Redemption are fulfilled in us as together in worship we are renewed in and through Jesus Christ.*[4]

For Ellen White, worship in the church takes on a particular importance.

> *To the humble, believing soul, the house of God on earth is the gate of heaven. The song of praise, the prayer, the words spoken by Christ's representatives, are God's appointed agencies to prepare a people for the church above, for that loftier worship into which there can enter nothing that defileth. The house is the sanctuary for the family, and the closet or the grove the most retired place for individual worship; but the church is the sanctuary for the congregation. There should be rules in regard to the time, the place, and the manner of worshiping. Nothing that is sacred, nothing that pertains to the worship of God, should be treated with carelessness or indifference. In order that men may do their best work in showing forth the praises of God, their associations must be such as will keep the sacred distinct from the common, in their minds. Those who have broad ideas, noble thoughts and aspirations, are those who have associations that strengthen all thoughts of divine things. Happy are those who have a sanctuary, be it high or low, in the city or among the rugged mountain caves, in the lowly cabin or in the wilderness.*[5]

---

4. Torrance, *The Place of Jesus Christ in Worship*, 362–63.
5. White, *Testimonies fo the Church: Vol. 5*, 491.

CHAPTER 32

THE SABBATH

As Wilfred Stott observed, the derivation of the word, Sabbath, is uncertain. However, it is most likely the word is derived from the verb *sabat*, to cease or to pause. This explanation seems to be inferred in Genesis 2:2, "And on the seventh day God ended his work which he had made; and he rested (*wayisbot*) on the seventh day from all his work which he had made. And God blessed the seventh day and sanctified it: because in it he had rested (*sabat*) from all his work which God created and made."[1] In the Old Testament there is no other commandment as strongly emphasised as this one. Indeed, the death penalty was to be carried out for any infringement (Ex. 31:14).

As Stott further stated, the "emphasis on the aspect of rest from labour in both forms of the Decalogue and in Exodus 34:21 shows that its main purpose was the cessation of ordinary work for one day in seven."[2] In addition, in Exodus 31:17, the Sabbath is viewed as a sign between God and Israel. In that sense, it is understood as a sign of the covenant and of covenant faithfulness. "As B. S. Childs pointed out, 'the Sabbath as a sign is a reminder both to God and Israel of the eternal covenant relationship which was the ultimate purpose of creation' (*Exodus*, 416)."[3]

In the New Testament there is no annulment of this most significant commandment. Indeed, "it appears that Jesus kept the Sabbath faithfully by attending the synagogue and by teaching (Mk. 1:21; 6:2; Lk. 4:16, 31)."[4]

When the Pharisees condemned Jesus for breaking the Sabbath (Matt. 12:1–14; Jn. 5:1–21) He did not respond by announcing the cessation of the Sabbath, but gave instruction as to how God intended it to be kept. To be sure, Jesus maintained

---

1. Stott, *Sabbath*, 405.
2. Stott, *Sabbath*, 406.
3. Stott, *Sabbath*, 406–407.
4. LaSor, *Sabbath*, 251.

a biblical approach to Sabbath keeping, in distinction to the legal code of the Pharisees that they had devised for themselves. They had primarily done this to elevate their experience of piety. Christ began His public ministry on the Sabbath when He preached in the synagogue. "It is noteworthy that in the Gospel of Luke the ministry of Christ not only begins on the Sabbath—the day which, according to Luke (4:26), Christ habitually observed—but also ends on 'the day of preparation as the Sabbath was beginning' (23:54)."[5] He clearly expected His followers in the future to be Sabbath keepers when He told them to pray that they would not have to flee Jerusalem on the Sabbath; an event that would not take place for another 40 years. Therefore, Jesus emphasised Sabbath ministry, as well as worship and rest. Significantly, after the crucifixion, Jesus rested on the Sabbath before rising to life on the next day (Lk. 23:54–24:4). The keeping of the Sabbath was also a feature of the early Christians as recorded in the Book of Acts, where Sabbath keeping is maintained by Paul as he "continued to observe the Sabbath by preaching in synagogues" (Acts 13:14, 42, 44; 17:2; 18:14).

The situation in the early church, after experiencing many years of severe persecution, was one of an apostasy brought about by compromise and syncretism. Ellen White outlined this turn of events in "The Great Controversy".

> *In the early part of the fourth century the emperor Constantine issued a decree making Sunday a public festival throughout the Roman Empire. The day of the sun was reverenced by his pagan subjects and was honored by Christians; it was the emperor's policy to unite the conflicting interests of heathenism and Christianity. He was urged to do this by the bishops of the church, who, inspired by ambition and thirst for power, perceived that if the same day was observed by both Christians and heathen, it would promote the nominal acceptance of Christianity by pagans and thus advance the power and glory of the church. But while many God-fearing Christians were gradually led to regard Sunday as possessing a degree of sacredness, they still held the true Sabbath as the holy of the Lord and observed it in obedience to the fourth commandment. The archdeceiver had not completed his work. He was resolved to gather the Christian world under his banner and to exercise his power through his vicegerent, the proud pontiff who claimed to be the representative of Christ. Through half-converted pagans, ambitious prelates, and world-loving churchmen he accomplished his purpose. Vast councils were held from time to time, in which the dignitaries of the church were convened from all the world. In nearly every council the Sabbath which God had instituted was pressed down a little lower, while the Sunday was correspondingly exalted. Thus, the pagan festival came*

---

5. Bacchiocchi, *A Historical Investigation of The Rise of Sunday Observance in Early Christianity*, 19.

finally to be honored as a divine institution, while the Bible Sabbath was pronounced a relic of Judaism, and its observers were declared to be accursed.[6]

The final decree condemning the seventh day Sabbath was declared at the Council of Laodicea in 354 A.D. The Synod comprised of thirty bishops, who gathered to settle a number of issues, including the Sabbath question. "Of the fifty-nine Canons of this council, the sixteenth and twenty-ninth canons mentioned the Sabbath. Later, the Council of Chalcedon (451 CE) confirmed these canons, imbuing them with ecumenical force."[7] Laodicea asserted that the Sabbath promoted Judaizing of the faith and laziness. Although the decree of Laodicea came about as a culmination of years of discussion, from this point on, the seventh-day Sabbath became a heresy.[8] The early church fathers re-enforced this general line of thinking. Justin Martyr eruditely summarized the sentiment. "There was no need of circumcision before Abraham. Nor was there need of the observance of Sabbaths, or of feasts and sacrifices, before Moses. Accordingly, there is no need of them now."[9]

During the Reformation, Sabbatarianism emerged by way of the Sabbath keeping Anabaptists in continental Europe. It was around the years 1527/8 that "Andreas Fischer adopted the Sabbatarian beliefs of Oswald Glait in Nikolsburg, Moravia, and became thenceforth Glait's principal co-labourer."[10] There is also evidence of Sabbath keeping Christians existing at this time in Ethiopia and Syria. "Other areas in which Seventh-day observance appeared in the sixteenth century included Poland, particularly Lithuania, Bohemia (as noted by Erasmus), and especially Transylvania."[11]

The first known Sabbath keeper in England was John Traske, who also produced, along with Theophilus Brabourne, one of the first publications promoting seventh day observance, *A Defence of the Seventh Day* (1632). Brabourne had earlier published, *A Discourse upon the Sabbath Day* (1628).

These first Sabbath keepers, however, understood themselves to be leaders in a movement that was the "natural outgrowth of a medieval Sabbatarian emphasis, maturing at a time when respect for the Bible as God's authoritative word had received new life."[12]

Ellen White referred to the Sabbath as a literal day, from sunset to sunset (Lev. 23:22) with associations to God's creative work. Indeed, on "the basis of Genesis

---

6. White, *The Great Controversy*, 54.
7. O'Hare, *The Sabbath Complete: And the Ascendency of First-Day Worship*, 258.
8. O'Hare, *The Sabbath Complete*, 258.
9. Dods, *The Sacred Writings of Justin Martyr*, 80. Bercot, *Dictionary of Early Christian Beliefs*, 571.
10. Ball, *The Seventh-Day Men—Sabbatarians and Sabbatarianism in England and Wales, 1600-1800*, 37.
11. Ball, *The Seventh-Day Men*, 38.
12. Ball, *The Seventh-Day Men*, 20.

THE SABBATH

2:1–3 Ellen White describes the seventh day as a memorial of God's creative work."[13] Further, the institution of the Sabbath as a day of rest was laid as a foundation at the creation of the earth. In addition, Mrs White strongly emphasised the Sabbath as being a commandment of God. Significantly, she pointed to the keeping of this commandment as constituting the seal of God (Ez. 20:12), which, together with the infilling of the Holy Spirit, separates those who are loyal to God and therefore worthy of protection during the events of the end times, as the Hebrews were protected against the Angel of Death at the Exodus by the sign of blood over their doorposts.[14] In *Testimonies for the Church*, Ellen White stipulated that "(t)he fourth commandment alone of all the ten contains the seal of the great Lawgiver, the Creator of the heavens and the earth."[15] She also wrote that the "observance of the Lord's memorial, the Sabbath instituted in Eden, the seventh-day Sabbath, is the test of our loyalty to God."[16] To be sure, "(t)hose who receive the seal of the living God and are protected in the time of trouble must reflect the image of Jesus fully."[17] The Sabbath, therefore, points to Jesus Christ, who is the Lord of the Sabbath (Mk. 2:28) and its creator (John 1:3). "To see Christ in the Sabbath is to call to mind the lost peace of Eden and the peace restored through the saviour (DA 288, 289)."[18]

---

13. *The Ellen G. White Encyclopedia*, 1116.
14. *Bible Commentary: Vol. 7*, 969.
15. White, *Testimonies for the Church: Vol. 6*, 350.
16. White, *Letter 94, 1900*.
17. White, *Early Writings*, 71.
18. Fortin and Moon, *The Ellen G. White Encyclopedia*, 1117.

CHAPTER 33

SPIRITUAL AGENTS

ANGELS

IN THE OLD TESTAMENT THE Hebrew for angel, *malak*, is derived from the meaning to send. According to Genesis angels are significantly and intimately involved in human affairs. Angels visited Abraham and Sarah and told them that a child would be born to them and made a visit to Lot at Sodom. The message the angel brought saved the lives of Lot and his family. "And when the morning arose, then the angels hastened Lot, saying, arise, take thy wife, and thy two daughters, which are here; lest thou be consumed in the iniquity of the city (Gen. 19:15)." An angel also brought about a wife for Isaac. "The LORD God of heaven, which took me from my father's house, and from the land of my kindred, and which spake unto me, and that sware unto me, saying, unto thy seed will I give this land; he shall send his angel before thee, and thou shalt take a wife unto my son from thence (Gen. 24:7)." In the Book of Exodus angels went before and behind the Israelite armies (14:19) and before the children of Israel as they travelled to the Promised Land. "Behold, I send an Angel before thee, to keep thee in the way, and to bring thee into the place which I have prepared (23:10)." However, there are also destroying angels.

In the book of Samuel angels are said to have destroyed Jerusalem through a plague.

> When the angel stretched out his hand to destroy Jerusalem, the Lord relented concerning the disaster and said to the angel who was afflicting the people, "Enough! Withdraw your hand." The angel of the Lord was then at the threshing floor of Araunah the Jebusite.
>
> When David saw the angel who was striking down the people, he said to the Lord, "I have sinned; I, the shepherd have done wrong. These are but sheep. What have they done? Let your hand fall on me and my family." (NIV) (2 Sam. 24:16–17).

SPIRITUAL AGENTS

Indeed, according to the Psalms there are both guardian (91:11) and destroying angels (78:49).

In two instances, angels are mentioned by name. Gabriel literally means "a man of God", and appears to Daniel for the interpretation of his dream (8:16) and while he was being given skill and understanding. "Yea, whiles I was speaking in prayer, even the man Gabriel, whom I had seen in the vision at the beginning, being caused to fly swiftly, touched me about the time of the evening oblation. And he informed me, and talked with me, and said, O Daniel, I am now come forth to give thee skill and understanding (9:21–22)."

The angel Michael is mentioned three times in the Book of Daniel (10:13; 21; 12:1). Israel is described as Israel's particular protector (ch.12:1). His identity is not definitely stated here, but a comparison with other scriptures identifies Him as Christ. Jude 9 terms Him "the archangel". According to 1Thess. 4:16, the "voice of the archangel" is associated with the resurrection of the saints at the coming of Jesus. Christ declared that the dead will come forth from their graves when they hear the voice of the Son of Man (John 5:28). Therefore, it appears that Michael is none other than the Lord Jesus Himself.[19] In the New Testament there are many references to angels. It was Gabriel who announced the birth of John the Baptist to his father Zechariah (Lk. 1:11–20).

According to Ellen White, "Angels are sent on missions of mercy to the children of God."[20] They are sent by God to protect God's people against the Satan's attacks by providing assurance of salvation; "God's people, exposed to the deceptive power and unsleeping malice of the prince of darkness, and in conflict with all the forces of evil, are assured of the unceasing guardianship of heavenly angels. Nor is such assurance given without need. If God has granted to His children promise of grace and protection, it is because there are mighty agencies of evil to be met—agencies numerous, determined, and untiring, of whose malignity and power none can safely be ignorant or unheeding."[21] Indeed, each believer is provided with a guardian angel. "A guardian angel is appointed to every follower of Christ. These heavenly watchers shield the righteous from the power of the wicked one."[22]

Therefore, the children if God are called upon to separate themselves out for God's service by not resisting or inhibiting the work of angels by our thoughts or actions.

> *Angels of God are all around us . . . . Oh, we want to know these things, and fear and tremble, and to think much more of the power of the angels of God that are watching over and guarding us than we have done hitherto . . . . Angels*

---

19. White, *Early Writings*, 164. White, *The Desire of Ages*, 421.
20. White, *Great Controversy*, 512.
21. White, *Truth About Angels*, 11.
22. White, *Great Controversy*, 512.

of God are commissioned from heaven to guard the children of men, and yet they draw away from their restraining influences and go where they can have communication with the evil angels.... Oh, that we might all obey the injunction of the apostle (Wherefore come out from among them, and be ye separate, saith the Lord, and touch not the unclean thing; and I will receive you. And will be a Father unto you, and ye shall be my sons and daughters, saith the Lord Almighty. 2 Corinthians 6:17, 18).[23]

SATAN

The early church referred to the spiritual battle that each Christian must undertake. While the devil might test the servants of God, he is no match for those who have a strong faith in the power of God to overcome and who are filled with the Spirit of Christ. Rather, he goes to those who are empty, and finding a way to enter, produces in them whatever he wishes, and they become his servants. Assurance was given by the second century Christian, Hermas, author of "The Shepherd". In it he stated that Satan "cannot hold dominion over the servants of God, who with all their heart place their hope in Him [Christ]. The devil can wrestle against them. But he cannot overthrow them."[24]

Ellen White averred that before the entrance of evil there was peace and joy throughout the universe, with all being "in perfect harmony with the Creator's will."[25] In this perfect state God desired that all His creatures served Him in love and bring "homage that springs from an intelligent appreciation of His character. He takes no pleasure in a forced allegiance, and to all He grants freedom of will, that they may render Him voluntary service."[26] In this environment there was one who chose to pervert this freedom. "Sin originated with him who, next to Christ, had been most honored of God, and who stood highest in power and glory among the inhabitants of heaven".[27] Lucifer had been first among the covering cherubs, full of wisdom and beauty. However, he became proud and filled with self-exaltation.[28] A warning was given out of the storehouse of God's infinite love and mercy. But this only "aroused a spirit of resistance" as Lucifer continued his jealousy of Christ with increasing determination. This resulted in a gradual drift into a place that Lucifer himself was uncertain of. From misrepresentation of the words of Christ came direct falsehood and accusation. "God in His wisdom permitted Satan to carry forward his

---

23. White, *Manuscript Releases: Vol. 5*, 125.
24. Hermas (2:29), in Bercot, *Dictionary of early Christian Beliefs*, 592.
25. White, *Great Controversy*, 493.
26. White, *Great Controversy*, 493.
27. White, *Great Controversy*, 493.
28. Ez. 28:12–15,17; 28. Isa. 14:13–14.

work, until the spirit of disaffection ripened into active revolt. It was necessary for his plans to be fully developed, that their true nature and tendency might be seen by all."[29] Ultimately, Lucifer rebelled against God, which led to a war in heaven. He was defeated and he and a third of the angels of heaven where thrown out (Rev.12:7-9). They sought to deceive other beings of other worlds, but ultimately found willing subjects in the garden of Eden. "God's government included not only the inhabitants of heaven, but of all the worlds that He had created; and Satan thought that if he could carry the angels of heaven with him in rebellion, he could carry also the other worlds."[30]

While defeated at the cross, Satan, the adversary, thrashes around in the pains of death, seeking to take as many as possible with him to his fiery end (Rev. 20:7-9).

Ellen was well aware of the roll that angels, whether holy or evil, play in the Great Controversy between good and evil in which every believer is called to take part.

> *I am instructed to say that in the future great watchfulness will be needed. There is to be among God's people no spiritual stupidity. Evil spirits are actively engaged in seeking to control the minds of human beings. Men are binding up in bundles, ready to be consumed by the fires of the last days. Those who discard Christ and His righteousness will accept the sophistry that is flooding the world. Christians are to be sober and vigilant, steadfastly resisting their adversary the devil, who is going about as a roaring lion, seeking whom he may devour. Men under the influence of evil spirits will work miracles. They will make people sick by casting their spell upon them, and will then remove the spell, leading others to say that those who were sick have been miraculously healed. This Satan has done again and again.*[31]

In his comprehensive article discussing Ellen White's teaching on confronting spiritual powers, Marc Coleman discerned six distinct principles.

> 1. *In one of the few comments she made directly about the casting out of demons she strongly discouraged those who claim to have the gift of setting people free as their unique ministry to do it. She further says that such manifestations in themselves can be a deception of the enemy. Her silence elsewhere on the need for highly ritualistic and formal exorcism services is instructive. Some would deduce from this that not everyone who has been a tool of the enemy needs an exorcism to be free from the influence of Satan.*

---

29. White, *Great Controversy*, 497.
30. White, *Great Controversy*, 497.
31. White, *Letter 259*, 1903.

2. *The Scriptures are the primary element to be used in breaking Satan's chains. The battle is chiefly a battle for the control of the mind and Ellen White says that it is truth that frees the mind from Satan's lies. Through the preaching of the gospel, Satan and his angels are cast out from people's minds. Through faith in the preached Word people are enabled to gain the victory, and the devil loses his hold upon them. Satan will eventually lose his power over all who continue to believe and trust in God. Satan's kingdom totters and falls before the presentation of sanctified truth (1905b: Letter 119, para. 29).*

3. *When God's people confront evil spirits they should never work alone. Christ is greater and Satan is a defeated foe but Christians are not Christ and are liable to make mistakes and to become proud.*

4. *Evil spirits should be confronted openly only when necessary and this should be done with much humility, faith in Christ, and in the company of others who can pray with and for the servant of God.*

5. *For some it is possible that the ability to cast out devils is viewed as a magically formula to use as a replacement for the preaching of the Gospel (see Ellen White's comments in The Acts of the Apostles concerning the Sons of Sceva (1911b:287, 288).*

6. *The ultimate goal in delivering those who are under the control of demons is to get the individual to grasp by faith the power of Jesus and therefore be delivered; no demon or the devil himself can hold anyone in their cruel grip when that soul clings in faith to Jesus, the Savior of all who come to him in faith. In one case Ellen White said that a demonized man was possessed but the moment he would turn to Christ in faith and surrender to him he would be free. In her personal experience when dealing with a demon possessed man she encouraged him to look to Christ and be free of the evil spirits that were troubling him.*[32]

---

32. Coleman, E. *Ellen White on Confrontation with Evil Spiritual Powers.*

Chapter 34

ESCHATOLOGY

As Alister McGrath rightly pointed out, the "New Testament is saturated with the belief that something new has happened in the history of humanity, in and through the life and death of Jesus Christ, and above all through his resurrection from the dead."[1] Indeed, world history finds its true meaning and a clear trajectory towards its conclusion, through the evident, victory and power that accompanies Christ's resurrection. The resurrection of Jesus Christ results in Him continuing in His ministry in the Heavenly Sanctuary until such a point that he returns to finish His work. Indeed, a "belief in a consummation of some type has always been a vital part of Christian theology."[2] The basis of the return of Christ is His sovereign rule over all creation.

A hope in God as sovereign in life and history is well anchored in the Old Testament and extends to the end of the Canon. Foundational to the scriptural witness is a belief in the universal sovereignty of God. It is He who rules over all creation, and particularly over humanity. As Walter Conner surmised:

> *This universal sovereignty or rule of God is necessarily involved in the biblical conception of God. There is only one true God and He is sovereign over the universe. He is everywhere present and has all power. He is infinite in wisdom and goodness. He reigns over the universe which He has created. All nations... are subject to His moral law and must account to Him for their deeds... There is no point in space or time, no member of the human race, no part of any... life, that is not subject to His righteous rule.*[3]

---

1. McGrath, *Christian Theology*, 466.
2. Moody, *The Word of Truth*, 481.
3. Conner, *Christian Doctrine*, 298.

While this rule may now appear hidden, it will be self-evident and unavoidable at the coming of the Lord.

THE DAY OF THE LORD

The final coming of Jesus Christ finds its origins in the Old Testament, which clearly articulates the concept of the Day of the Lord. In the Book of Isaiah, the destruction of God's enemies is seen to correlate with this day. "Come near, ye nations, to hear; and hearken, ye people: let the earth hear, and all that is therein; the world, and all things that come forth of it. For the indignation of the Lord is upon all nations, and his fury upon all their armies: he hath utterly destroyed them, he hath delivered them to the slaughter (Isaiah 34:1–2)." Similar themes are found in Jeremiah (46:2–12) Ezekiel (30:1–26) and Amos (8:9–14), but particularly Zephaniah, who saw in the invasion of the barbaric Scythian hordes from the north, the judgment of the Lord upon Judah. "The great day of the Lord is near, it is near, and hasteth greatly, even the voice of the day of the Lord: the mighty man shall cry there bitterly. That day is a day of wrath, a day of trouble and distress, a day of wasteness and desolation, a day of darkness and gloominess, a day of clouds and thick darkness (Zephaniah 1:14–15)." This destruction is, importantly, coupled with the survival of the people of God.

> *Therefore, wait ye upon me, saith the* LORD, *until the day that I rise up to the prey: for my determination is to gather the nations, that I may assemble the kingdoms, to pour upon them mine indignation, even all my fierce anger: for all the earth shall be devoured with the fire of my jealousy. For then will I turn to the people a pure language, that they may all call upon the name of the* LORD, *to serve him with one consent (Zephaniah 3:8–9).*

Indeed, Daniel introduced the hope that the Day of the Lord would be the Day of the Son of Man; a theme consistently in the teaching of Jesus. Daniel stated:

> *I saw in the night visions, and, behold, one like the Son of man came with the clouds of heaven, and came to the Ancient of Days, and they brought him near before him. And there was given him dominion, and glory, and a kingdom, that all people, nations, and languages, should serve him: his dominion is an everlasting dominion, which shall not pass away, and his kingdom that which shall not be destroyed (Dan. 7:13–14).*

THE MILLENNIUM

While Christians hold much in common, nothing differentiates Christendom more than the doctrine of the millennium. It is the thousand-year reign of Christ described in Revelation 20:2–7. Donald Bloesch summarized the three main schools of thought as follows:

> *Those who adhere to a millennial kingdom in earthly history inaugurated by the Cataclysmic coming of Jesus Christ in power and glory are known as premillennialists. Those who contend for a millennial period of peace and justice prior to Christ's visible coming in glory are postmillennialists. Those who conceive of a millennial kingdom already realized in history in the flowering of the church are amillennialists.*[4]

The first of the postmillennialists has been identified as Daniel Whitby, who authored "A Paraphrase and Commentary on the New Testament." This two-volume set was first published in 1703.[5] Prominent advocates of Whitby's position were Jonathan Edwards, Robert Lewis Dabney, Charles Hodge and A.H. Strong. However, the general pessimism following World War One saw postmillennialism go into decline. Today, it is rarely embraced. By contrast, Amillennialism flourishes among many evangelicals and tends to be the hallmark of evangelical moderation. Generally, the term "amillenial" refers to "not a thousand years by the calendar."[6] While there are a number of different variations, the origins of Amillenialism can be traced back to Augustine of Hippo, who settled on the view that the "symbolic" thousand years represented a time between the two advents of Christ, or the so-called church era. However, Premillennialism envisages a literal thousand-year reign of Christ.

Importantly, Premillennialism is well attested in the teachings of the early church. Justin Martyr, Irenaeus and Tertullian were all advocates. "According to Tertullian, there will be an earthly, post-resurrection kingdom for one thousand years centered in Jerusalem."[7] Ellen White presents her understanding of the millennium in both *Early Writings* and *The Great Controversy*. Continuing with Millerite doctrine, she argued in favour of premillennialism, following a particular series of events outlined in biblical prophecy. The second coming of Christ ushers in the beginning of the millennium with the destruction of the wicket and the resurrection of the righteous. At the commencement of the thousand years every eye shall see Him (Revelation 1:7). Indeed, "they shall see the Son of man coming in the clouds of heaven with power and great glory (Matt. 24:30)." He will come with the entire host of heaven.

> *For the Lord, himself shall descend from heaven with a shout, with the voice of the archangel, and with the trump of God: and the dead in Christ shall rise first: Then we which are alive and remain shall be caught up together with*

---

4. Bloesch, *The Last Things*, 88.
5. Whitby, *A Paraphrase and Commentary on the New Testament: Vol.s. 1 and 2*.
6. Garrett, *Systematic Theology: Vol. 2*, 763.
7. Garrett, *Systematic Theology: Vol. 2*, 751.

them in the clouds, to meet the Lord in the air: and so, shall we ever be with the Lord (1 Thess. 4:16–17).

Those who have been translated reign with Christ for a thousand years, while Satan is bound on earth (Lev. 16:21–22; Rev. 20:1–3) and those who, at the return of Christ, are unredeemed, will be destroyed (Isa. 11:4; 2 Thess. 1:7–8; Rev. 20:5). During the thousand years the saints sit in judgment over the wicked. John refers to this when he states that the resurrected saints will sit on thrones "and judgment was committed to them (Rev. 20:4)." During this time Satan and his angels will be judged (2 Peter 2:4; Jude 6). This correlates with Paul's exhortation that the saints would sit in judgement over the world and even the angels (1 Cor. 6:2, 3). The purpose of this judgement is not to decide the fate of the wicked. This has already been decided. It is to enlighten the saints as to the reason behind the fate of the lost, thereby providing full confidence in the process that God has set in place. Satan's accusation that God is unfair is finally put to rest and negated.

Finally, the thousand years is followed by a second resurrection of the unrighteous dead, the destruction of Satan and a second death for the un-justified (John 5:28–29; Rev:20:4–10).[8]

END TIME EVENTS—THE UNFOLDING OF PROPHECY

Observing the signs of the times is a Seventh-day Adventist emphasis and is strongly grounded in the teaching of Jesus Christ. In Matthew 24, Jesus warns His disciples about those who will deceive the brethren. From this beginning point, conditions for God's people become worse. They will come in Christ's name but they will not be from God. In the time just before the return of Christ, there will be times of geo-political conflict and natural disasters. Worse than these will be martyrdom, the betrayal of the brethren, continuing deception and a coldness towards the truth. Importantly, all those who persevere through these times will be saved. Therefore, Jesus places a condition upon salvation, by clearly inferring that salvation can be lost as much as it can be maintained. Believers must choose their path in the face of overwhelming conditions against them. Through these times, advice is given for believers. As in the days of the Roman conquest of Jerusalem, so will it be in the time of the end. Believers must flee and find protection.

> *Immediately after the tribulation of those days shall the sun be darkened, and the moon shall not give her light, and the stars shall fall from heaven, and the powers of the heavens shall be shaken: And then shall appear the sign of the Son of man in heaven: and then shall all the tribes of the earth mourn, and they shall see the Son of man coming in the clouds of heaven with power and great glory* (Matthew 24:29–30).

8. Fortin and Moon, *The Ellen White Encyclopaedia*, 983.

ESCHATOLOGY

The belief in the imminent return of Christ is given impetus in the Book of Daniel. In the second chapter, Nebuchadnezzar's statue takes the reader through the empires of history up until the present day. Babylon, Medo-Persia, Greece and Rome are followed by the ten toes of the statue which represent the division of the Roman Empire into ten regions. The legs of iron, representative of the pagan Roman Empire become iron mixed with clay in the feet. Here the iron represents papal Rome that seeks to "mix" with the state to form a religio-political system. The ten toes of Chapter Two correlate with the ten horns of Chapter Seven (Alemanni, Franks, Suevi, Vandals, Burgundians, Visigoths, Anglo-Saxons, Ostrogoths, Lombards, Heruli). Importantly, more information is given. The head of gold in chapter two is represented by the Babylonian symbol of a lion with wings. In chapter seven the silver chest of the statue is replaced by a bear, leaning to one side and with three ribs in its mouth. The leaning to one side symbolises the dominance of Persia in the Medo-Persian alliance. The three ribs taken in the mouth may be representative of the three kingdoms Medo-Persia conquered in the establishment of its extended borders: Babylon, Lydia and Greece. The Leopard with four heads points to the Greek Empire under Alexander the Great. After the Emperor's untimely death, the Greek Empire was divided into four regions, each one under the jurisdiction of Alexander's four generals (Cassander, Ptolemy, Antigonus, Seleucus). The beast with iron teeth correlates with the iron legs of chapter two. This is clearly Pagan Rome. However, the ten toes are represented now as ten horns. Three of these ten horns are plucked up and replaced by a little horn. This little horn speaks pompous words and changes times and laws. Out of these ten three are plucked up and replaced with a little horn power. The little horn power is the papacy. Historically, the papal states replaced the three kingdoms of the Heruli, Vandals and Ostrogoths. This power persecutes God's people.

The starting date to determine the meaning of prophetic days in relation to the papacy is 538 A.D. In that year, Emperor Justinian decreed that the Church has authority in all spiritual matters and has the power to prosecute heretics. The Catholic Church became the official religion of the state, with church and state becoming intentionally intertwined. However, this persecution comes to an end in 1798 (Dan. 7:25; 12:7; Rev. 12:14). In that year the pope was arrested by General Berthier under the direction of Napoleon. The time period between 538 A.D and 1798 represents 1260 years of fierce persecution. Indeed, prophetically, this power, being established in 538 A.D., receives a fatal wound after a period of 1260 years. This sequence is also represented as 42 months (Rev. 11:2; 13:5,8) and time (1 year), times (2 years) and half a time (6 months) (Daniel 7:25; 12:7; Rev. 12:14). Prophetic time translates three and a half years into 1260 Years (Rev. 11:3). This power, however, will be revived in the end times when the wound is healed. At that time persecution against God's people will re-commence. However, God's people to be persecuted will be His own

Sabbath keeping people, who keep the commandments of God and have the faith of Jesus (Rev. 14:12). "A striking illustration of Rome's policy toward those who disagree with her was given in the long and bloody persecution of the Waldenses, some of whom were observers of the Sabbath."[9] Clearly, in the end times, the papacy is the controlling power; drawing together an alliance or confederacy which includes Protestants, Spiritualists, leaders and merchants (Rev. 16:13). Indeed, through

> two great errors, the immortality of the soul and Sunday Sacredness, Satan will bring the people under his deception. While the former lays the foundation of Spiritualism, the latter creates a bond of sympathy with Rome. The Protestants of the United States will be foremost in stretching their hands across the gulf to grasp the hand of Spiritualism; they will reach over the abyss to clasp hands with the Roman power; and under the influence of this threefold union.[10]

However, this controlling power, described as Babylon and the embodiment of all the empires of history who have persecuted God's people, will be defeated. In the dream of Daniel 2, a stone cut out, but not by human hands, destroys the statue and grows into a great mountain. This stone is usually referred to as Christ. This is true; however, the text does not support this entirely; since Christ always works through His people. Christ is not cut out of a larger entity, nor does He anywhere in Scripture grow larger. However, the remnant will be 'cut out' of the populace and grow in number. To be sure, the stone represents the Christ in His remnant, or 144,000, who take the message forward in the power of Christ. It is these, empowered by the Holy Spirit in the Latter Rain (Joel 2:23-29), who will carry the Three Angels Message forward and defeat deceitful Babylon with the truth of God. It is this small group that will grow, as the body of Christ, into a "great mountain", as they are joined by a great multitude. The 144,000 will be those who have not succumbed to temptation and have remained steadfast in their faith. They will be the commandment keeping people of God who remained in the church through its shaking (see also Ezekiel 9), because they proclaimed the straight testimony.[11]

In *Early Writings*, Ellen White stated: "I asked the meaning of the shaking I had seen and was shown that it would be caused by the straight testimony called forth by the counsel of the True Witness to the Laodiceans. This will have its effect upon the heart of the receiver, and will lead him to exalt the standard and pour forth the straight truth. Some will not bear this straight testimony. They will rise up against it, and this is what will cause a shaking among God's people."[12] She further encouraged all in the church to strive to be part of the 144,000. "Let us strive with all the power

---

9. White, *Great Controversy*, 578.
10. White, *Great Controversy*, 588.
11. White, *1 Testimony*, 181.
12. White, *Early Writings*, 270.

that God has given us to be among the hundred and forty-four thousand. And let us do all that we can to help others to gain heaven."[13]

Before these great events take place, time prophecies must first be fulfilled. The time prophecies are centred on Daniel 8 and 9, but extend beyond this. The decree to return and re-build Jerusalem in 457 B.C. (Ezra 7:1–7) is the key beginning date from which all are built. The pre-condition for calculating these times is the year for a day principle (Numbers 14:33–34; Ezekiel 4:4–6). It is the foundation of a historicist view of prophecy as distinct from a symbolic interpretation. It is well attested in Christian history. Indeed, "John Wycliffe, John Knox, William Tyndale, Martin Luther, John Calvin, Ulrich Zwingli, Phillip Melanchthon, Sir Isaac Newton, Jan Hus, John Foxe, John Wesley, Jonathan Edwards, George Whitefield, Charles Finney, C. H. Spurgeon, Matthew Henry, Adam Clarke, Albert Barnes, E. B. Elliot, H. Grattan Guinness, and Bishop Thomas Newton."[14] Daniel outlines the first segment of the prophetic line in the 70-week prophecy. In Daniel 9:24–27, 70 weeks is translated into 490 days which, in prophetic time, becomes 490 years.

> *Seventy weeks are determined upon thy people and upon thy holy city, to finish the transgression, and to make an end of sins, and to make reconciliation for iniquity, and to bring in everlasting righteousness, and to seal up the vision and prophecy, and to anoint the most Holy. Know therefore and understand, that from the going forth of the commandment to restore and to build Jerusalem unto the Messiah the Prince shall be seven weeks, and threescore and two weeks: the street shall be built again, and the wall, even in troublous times. And after threescore and two weeks shall Messiah be cut off, but not for himself: and the people of the prince that shall come shall destroy the city and the sanctuary; and the end thereof shall be with a flood, and unto the end of the war desolations are determined. And he shall confirm the covenant with many for one week: and in the midst of the week he shall cause the sacrifice and the oblation to cease, and for the overspreading of abominations he shall make it desolate, even until the consummation, and that determined shall be poured upon the desolate.*

The important beginning date to return and rebuild determines the subsequent dates that build upon it in years. The return to re-build Jerusalem was given by Artaxerxes King of Persia in 457 B.C (Ezra 7:1–27).

From there is added the totality of the 70-week, or 490 years, that complete the prophetic segment. This takes the prophetic date to 34 A.D. On that date Stephen is stoned to death and the Gospel goes to the Gentiles (Dan 9:24; Acts 7:59). One week, or seven prophetic years, prior to this Jesus is anointed at His baptism. This is the year 27 A.D (Dan. 9:25). In the midst of the week, 31 A.D (Dan. 9:26–27), He is

---

13. White, *Review and Herald*, March 9, 1905.
14. Gregg, *Revelation: Four Views*, 34.

crucified, thereby bringing an end to the sacrificial system in His ultimate payment for the atonement of sin. This prophetic date is extended in Daniel 8:14, with a 2300-day prophecy. From the beginning date of 457 B.C. the 2300 prophetic years takes the time prophecy to 1844. It is a time in which, according to the prophet, the sanctuary shall be cleansed (or vindicated). Indeed, the word, vindication, often used in translations, does not detract from the ministry of the day of Atonement, since that day did in fact act as a vindication of the ministry that had taken place in the Sanctuary throughout the year. Therefore, the event described in the sanctuary is clearly the yearly day of Atonement prescribed in Leviticus 16. Since the earthly sanctuary was destroyed in 70 A.D. the description clearly refers to the original sanctuary in heaven (Heb. 8:5; 9:23–24).

The cleansing (or vindication) of the sanctuary is termed an Investigative Judgement. That is, the lives of God's people are investigated. Did they truly commit their lives to Christ and live as regenerated believers dressed in the life of Christ? Such people have their names entered into the Book of Life (Ex. 32:33; Luke 10:20; Phil. 4:3; Rev. 20:12; 21:27). In the Great Controversy, Ellen White referred to the earthly Sanctuary service which serves to point to its ultimate fulfilment in the Heavenly.

> *In the typical service, only those who had come before God with confession and repentance, and whose sins, through the blood of the sin offering, were transferred to the sanctuary, had a part in the service of the Day of Atonement. So, in the great day of final atonement and investigative judgment the only cases considered are those of the professed people of God. The judgment of the wicked is a distinct and separate work, and takes place at a later period.*[15]

Satan would accuse God's people of their sin, but Christ's atoning sacrifice is sufficient to cleanse them of their sin. Their deeds are placed in the Book of Remembrance (Mal. 3:16). However, faith must be sustained. Perseverance is a choice. Those who are not in the Book of Life after the close of probation (When Christ ceases His heavenly ministry and prepares to return as King) will be placed in the Book of Death (Ex. 32:33; Rev. 3:5; 20:12–15). Indeed, "We know not how soon our names may be taken onto the lips of Christ, and our cases be finally decided."[16] Parallels in the ministry of Jesus which describe this event are found in the parable of the wedding guests (Matthew 22; 25). In order to be ready, the professing Christian must meet the conditions of repentance and faith. However, these must be more than outward declarations. God required more than a change of language and culture. A profession of faith only has value as saving faith if it is an expression of a changed heart (Ezekiel 36:26). As Jesus told Nicodemus, "Except a man be born of water and of the Spirit, he cannot enter into the kingdom of God. That which is born of the flesh is flesh; and that which is born of the Spirit is spirit." John 3:5–6.

15. White, *The Great Controversy*, 480.
16. White, *Selected Messages: Vol. 1*, 125.

ESCHATOLOGY

Ultimately, those who hold the faith that has been delivered by God through His Spirit will bear the testimony of Jesus and keep His commandments (Rev. 14:12). The core of the commandments is its seal, and the seal is the fourth commandment (Ezekiel 31:13). Indeed, Ellen White instructed that the "Sabbath will be the great test of loyalty; for it is the point of truth especially controverted."[17]

Closely associated with the cleansing of the sanctuary, beginning on October 22, 1844, is the Three Angels Message of Revelation 14. The call to preach the Gospel relates with the historical call to join the Advent Message and prepare for the return of Christ. The people of the world are called upon to "fear God and give glory to Him". They do these by obeying the law (Prov. 28:9; Eccl. 12:13; 1 John 5:3). That is, God's people will be identified in the end times as they that keep the commandments of God, since He is the Creator.[18] Consequently, God's end time people are called to be Sabbath keepers and are identified as such. They are those who will decide for the truth. Before Jesus returns, the First Angel's message is "designed to separate the professed people of God from the corrupting influences of the world, and to arouse them to their condition of worldliness and backsliding."[19] Indeed, it is the work of judgment, immediately preceding the second Advent, that is announced in the First Angel's message.[20] Therefore, the Gospel message, in the light of God's judgment, becomes the only hope of the world. The first outworking of the First Angel was in 1843, among those who heard the Advent message and were led to either accept or reject Advent truth.[21] The Second Angel's declaration of the fall of Babylon relates to those churches who rejected the message. It applies to religious bodies that were once pure but have become corrupt. They are the unfaithful church who have broken covenant and violated their marriage vow with Christ.[22] They do so by sacrificing truth and forming an alliance with the world.[23] They are called Babylon, confusion and falsehood, and these apply to the Catholic and Sunday keeping Protestant churches who will ultimately align themselves with the state. Its first outworking was preached in the summer of 1844 and applies to Protestants who rejected the Advent message. This message is a progressive one, as the realm of Babylon increases with an increase in apostasy until it reaches its full measure.[24] Conversely, from 1844 many left their churches and accepted that "Babylon is fallen".[25] However, the message of the fall of Babylon will be repeated. Indeed, there will be a great rejection of the

---

17. White, *Great Controversy*, 605.
18. White, *Great Controversy*, 436.
19. White, *Great Controversy*, 379.
20. White, *Great Controversy*, 357.
21. White, *Great Controversy*, 282.
22. White, *Great Controversy*, 381.
23. White, *Great Controversy*, 383.
24. White, *Great Controversy*, 390.
25. White, *Early Writings*, 237.

truth. "The minds of the people will become darker, their hearts more stubborn, until they are entrenched in the infidel hardihood."[26] The third Angel's call to keep the commandments of God relates to the beginning of God's end time movement. The decline in the faithfulness of the church will lead to weak teaching, political alignments and ultimately Sunday Law.[27] Therefore, in this context, keeping the Sabbath will be the final and ultimate test.[28] Those who are filled with the Spirit of God and keep the Sabbath will receive the seal of God. Those who do not keep the Sabbath will receive the mark of the beast.[29] Those who live in the Spirit and keep the Sabbath will be marked as God's people and the destroying angel (Ezekiel 9:7–11) will pass over them like in the days of Moses during the exodus.

It will be the later rain that will empower God's people to go forth and call people to keep the commandments of God and have the faith of Jesus. Indeed, Jesus is seen as the great hope of all. The Third Angel points to the Sanctuary where we find Jesus.[30] However, it is the last warning[31] to accept the mercy of God as it is delivered by His servants.[32] Consequently, the Third Angel's message is regarded as of the highest importance. It is a life and death question.[33] "When the Third Angel's message closes, mercy no longer pleads for the guilty inhabitants of the earth. The people of God have accomplished their work. They have received 'the later rain', 'the refreshing from the presence of the Lord', and they are prepared for the trying hour before them."[34] Therefore, these will be perilous times for God's people who will need to throw themselves entirely upon the sustaining power of God. Ellen White foresaw this in prophecy: "God has presented to me the dangers that are threatening those who have been given the sacred work of proclaiming the third angel's message… Those who keep the commandments of God and have the faith of Jesus are the object of the wrath of this power."[35]

The Three Angel's Message will be repeated at the very close of earth's history before finally coming together to form a single message. (Rev. 14:6–9, 20). Preaching the Gospel will be followed by a new world order, an alignment of powers, which will constitute an end time Babylon (Rev. 16:13; 18:9,13,15; 16:14). Concurrent with these events, Sunday Law will be introduced and a shaking in the church will occur

---

26. White, *Great Controversy*, 603.
27. White, *Great Controversy*, 604, 607–608.
28. White, *Great Controversy*, 605.
29. White, *Great Controversy*, 450, 605.
30. White, *Early Writings*, 255.
31. White, Great Controversy, 611.
32. White, *Great Controversy*, 609.
33. *Ellen White Manuscripts (MS) 16, 1900*.
34. White, *Great Controversy*, 613.
35. White, *Ellen White Manuscripts, 135, 1902*.

(Rev. 13:11; 14:16; Ez. 9:1–7). Ellen White provided significant prophetic insight to this when she wrote the

> *class that have provoked the displeasure of Heaven will charge all their troubles upon those whose obedience to God's commandments is a perpetual reproof to transgressors. It will be declared that men are offending God by the violation of the Sunday-Sabbath; that this sin has brought calamities which will not cease until Sunday observance shall be strictly enforced; and that those who present the claims of the fourth commandment, thus destroying reverence for Sunday, are troublers of the people, preventing their restoration of divine favour and temporal prosperity. Thus, the accusation urged of old against the servant of God will be repeated.*[36]

The shaking will be triggered by these events coupled with a preaching of the straight testimony.[37] American Protestantism and Spiritualism will combine under its power. Concurrent, will be the compliance of world leaders (Rev. 18:9; 16:14) and merchants (Rev. 18:13,15). However, this system will fall and be destroyed. God's remnant will let out a call to come out of Babylon and keep the commandments of God, identified primarily by the seal of God—the indwelling of the Spirit and the keeping of the Sabbath (1 Peter 4:17; Ez. 9:1–7). The remnant people of God, who keep His commandments (including keeping the Sabbath) and have the testimony of Jesus (which is the Spirit of Prophecy), are referred to as the 144, 000. They, with more power in the Holy Spirit than the days of Pentecost, will take the Three Angels Message, now combined into one message, through to the end of world history. They, through their testimony, will gather a great multitude from all the nations of the earth. Jesus will return for His bride, the church (Rev. 21), at the sounding of the 7th trumpet. At that time God's faithful suffering people will be rewarded for their steadfastness at the last moment.

> *With shouts of triumph, jeering, and imprecation, throngs of evil men are about to rush upon their prey when, lo, a dense blackness, deeper than the darkness of the night, falls upon the earth. Then a rainbow, shining with the glory from the throne of God, spans the heavens, and seems to encircle each praying company. The angry multitudes are suddenly arrested. Their mocking cries die away. The objects of their murderous rage are forgotten. With fearful foreboding, they gaze upon the symbol of God's covenant, and long to be shielded from its overpowering brightness.*[38]

These events will take place at midnight. The midnight cry at the Great Disappointment, will be replaced with the midnight song of joy, clear and melodious.

---

36. White, *The Great Controversy,* 590.
37. White, *Early Writings,* 270. White, *Testimonies for The Church: Vol. 1,* 181.
38. White, *Great Controversy,* 636.

Their words are simple, "Look up." "It is at midnight that God manifests His power for the deliverance of His people. The Sun appears, shining in its strength. Signs and wonders follow in quick succession."[39]

At His coming there will be special resurrections. Those who pierced Christ (Rev. 1:7) and those who die in the Three Angels Message (Dan. 12:2). "Graves are opened, and 'many of them that sleep in the dust of the earth . . . awake, some to everlasting life, and some to shame and everlasting contempt' (Dan. 12:2)." At Christ's appearing those who are righteous will rise from the grave. The resurrection of the unrighteous will occur at the conclusion of the 1000 years. To be sure, all "who have died in the faith of the third angel's message come forth from the tomb glorified, to hear God's covenant of peace with those who have kept His law. "They also which pierced Him,' those that mocked and derided Christ's dying agonies, and the most violent opposers of His truth and His people, are raised to behold Him in His glory, and to see the honor placed upon the loyal and obedient."[40] Indeed, those who drove in the nails and thrust the sword into His side will "behold these marks with terror and remorse."[41] Following, the dead in Christ will rise first (1 Thess. 4:16) "with the freshness and vigor of eternal youth,"[42] and the unrighteous living will be slain (Rev. 19:20–21). In fact, the very instruments set aside to kill God's people will be used to destroy their enemies. The time finally arrives for God to vindicate the authority of His downtrodden law. Indeed, the false watchmen, who professed to be spiritual guardians of the people, are the first to fall (Ez. 9:10–6).[43] Following, will be all who deny Christ. They will be blotted from the face of the whole earth, "consumed with the spirit of His mouth, and destroyed with the brightness of His glory."[44] Finally, the whole earth will appear as a desolate wilderness. Then there will be a thousand years (a millennium) during which Satan will be bound (Rev. 20:2). This desolate earth will be the home of Satan and his evil angels. "Limited to the earth, he will not have access to other worlds, to tempt and annoy those who have never fallen. It is in this sense that he is bound: there are none remaining, upon whom he can exercise his power."[45] Further, during this time the saints will judge the wicked (Rev. 20:4; Dan. 7:22). "The apostle Paul points to this judgement as an event that follows the second advent. "Judge nothing before the time, until the Lord come, who both will bring to light the hidden things in darkness, and will make manifest the councils of the heart" (1 Cor. 4:5). Daniel declares that when the Ancient of days came "judgement was given to the saints of the Most High" (Dan. 7:22). At this

39. White, *Great Controversy*, 636.
40. White, *Great Controversy*, 637.
41. White, *Great Controversy*, 643.
42. White, *Great Controversy*, 645.
43. White, *Great Controversy*, 656.
44. White, *Great Controversy*, 657.
45. White, *Great Controversy*, 659.

time, the righteous reign as kings and priests unto God. John in the Revelation says: "I saw thrones, and they sat upon them, and judgment was given unto them. 'They are priests of God and of Christ, and shall reign with Him a thousand Years" It is at this time, as foretold by Paul, "the saints shall judge the world" (Rev. 20:4, 6; 1 Cor. 6:2–3). After the thousand years Satan will be let loose (Rev. 20:7) and the unrighteous will be raised (Rev. 20:5) They will rise up against the Holy City which has descended from heaven, but they will be defeated (Rev. 20:8–9). This will culminate in the second death (Rev. 20:5,10). Finally, there will be a new heaven and earth (Rev. 21–22). Ultimately, as promised (Zech. 14:5,4,9) Christ will descend upon the Mount of Olives, from where He ascended. He will come with the New Jerusalem in all its dazzling splendour. It will rest upon the place purified and made ready to receive it, and Christ, with His people and angels, will enter the city.[46] Ellen White pointed to this day when she wrote in *Great Controversy*,

> *At the close of the thousand years, Christ again returns to the earth. He is accompanied by the host of the redeemed and attended by a retinue of angels. As He descends in terrific majesty He bids the wicked dead arise to receive their doom. They come forth, a mighty host, numberless as the sands of the sea. What a contrast to those who were raised at the first resurrection! The righteous were clothed with immortal youth and beauty. The wicked bear the traces of disease and death. Every eye in that vast multitude is turned to behold the glory of the Son of God. With one voice the wicked hosts exclaim:*
>
> *Blessed is He that cometh in the name of the Lord!" It is not love to Jesus that inspires this utterance. The force of truth urges the words from unwilling lips. As the wicked went into their graves, so they come forth with the same enmity to Christ and the same spirit of rebellion. They are to have no new probation in which to remedy the defects of their past lives. Nothing would be gained by this. A lifetime of transgression has not softened their hearts. A second probation, were it given them, would be occupied as was the first in evading the requirements of God and exciting rebellion against Him. Christ descends upon the Mount of Olives, whence, after His resurrection, He ascended, and where angels repeated the promise of His return.*[47]

Following the descent of the Heavenly Jerusalem

> *Satan prepares for a last mighty struggle for the supremacy . . . He will marshal all the armies of the lost under his banner and through them endeavor to execute his plans . . . He proposes to lead them against the camp of the saints and to take possession of the City of God . . . By command of Jesus, the gates of the New Jerusalem are closed, and the armies of Satan surround the city and make ready for the onset . . . As soon as the books of record are opened, and*

---

46. White, *Great Controversy*, 663–664.
47. White, *Great Controversy*, 663.

the eye of Jesus looks upon the wicked, they are conscious of every sin which they have ever committed . . . The whole wicked world stand arraigned at the bar of God on the charge of high treason against the government of heaven. They have none to plead their cause; they are without excuse; and the sentence of eternal death is pronounced against them . . . Upon the wicked He will rain coals; fire and brimstone and a burning wind shall be the portion of their cup." Psalm 11:6. Fire comes down from God out of heaven. The earth is broken up. The weapons concealed in its depths are drawn forth. Devouring flames burst from every yawning chasm. The very rocks are on fire. The day has come that shall burn as an oven. The elements melt with fervent heat, the earth also, and the works that are therein are burned up. (See Malachi 4:1; 2 Peter 3:10.) The earth's surface seems one molten mass—a vast, seething lake of fire. It is the time of the judgment and perdition of ungodly men— "the day of the Lord's vengeance, and the year of recompenses for the controversy of Zion." Isaiah 34:8 . . . The wicked receive their recompense in the earth. Proverbs 11:31. They "'will be stubble. And the day which is coming shall burn them up,' Says the Lord of hosts." Malachi 4:1 . . . All are punished "according to their deeds." Jeremiah 25:14 . . . In the cleansing flames the wicked are at last destroyed, root and branch—Satan the root, his followers the branches. The full penalty of the law has been visited; the demands of justice have been met; and heaven and earth, beholding, declare the righteousness of Jehovah.[48]

THE NEW HEAVEN AND EARTH

In the New heaven and earth God will be seen face to face, behold the Divine perfections, and delight in them.[49] The transformation of the Christian to complete holiness of character and physical perfection, will be complete and there will be a direct knowledge of God unrestricted by a sinful world.[50] However, a complete knowledge of God will also be accompanied by a complete fellowship. "And I heard a great voice out of heaven saying, Behold, the tabernacle of God is with men, and he will dwell with them, and they shall be his people, and God himself shall be with them, and be their God (Rev. 21:3)." The context of this fellowship is the complete absence of sin, characterised by pain, sorrow, suffering and death. The people of God will live in a perpetual Sabbath;

> *Let us therefore fear, lest, a promise being left us of entering into his rest, any of you should seem to come short of it. For unto us was the gospel preached, as well as unto them: but the word preached did not profit them, not being mixed with faith in them that heard it. For we which have believed do enter*

---

48. White, *Great Controversy*, 663ff.
49. Shedd, *Dogmatic Theology*, 816.
50. Garrett, *Systematic Theology: Vol. 2*, 817.

into rest, as he said, As I have sworn in my wrath, if they shall enter into my rest: although the works were finished from the foundation of the world. For he spake in a certain place of the seventh day on this wise, And God did rest the seventh day from all his works. And in this place again, if they shall enter into my rest. Seeing therefore it remaineth that some must enter therein, and they to whom it was first preached entered not in because of unbelief: Again, he limiteth a certain day, saying in David, to day, after so long a time; as it is said, today if ye will hear his voice, harden not your hearts. For if Jesus had given them rest, then would he not afterward have spoken of another day. There remaineth therefore a rest to the people of God. For he that is entered into his rest, he also hath ceased from his own works, as God did from his. Let us labour therefore to enter into that rest, lest any man fall after the same example of unbelief (Hebrews 4:1–11). Ellen White wrote: "*the rest here spoken of is the rest of grace, obtained by following the prescription, labour diligently . . . Those who are unwilling to give the Lord faithful, earnest, loving service will not find spiritual rest in this life or in the life to come. Only from earnest labor comes peace and joy in the Holy Spirit happiness on earth and glory hereafter.*"[51]

The movement came to the conviction of Christ's return, and events that unfold to its lead up, unfolded early in its formation. By the end of 1850 the new group of Sabbatarian Adventists held to the belief that,

Christ would take resurrected and living saints to heaven at the beginning of the millennium; the earth, to which Satan would be confined, would be desolate for a thousand years; the saints would participate in judging the wicked angels and humans; at the end of the millennium the Holy City would descend to earth where Satan and the resurrected would unsuccessfully attack it; and after fire destroyed the wicked and the old earth, a new earth would arise.[52]

In Ellen White's description Eden is restored.

Then they that have kept God's commandments shall breathe in immortal vigor beneath the tree of life; and through unending ages the inhabitants of sinless worlds shall behold, in that garden of delight, a sample of the perfect work of God's creation, untouched by the curse of sin—a sample of what the whole earth would have become, had man but fulfilled the Creator's glorious plan. Adam is reinstated in his first dominion. Transported with joy, he holds the trees that were once his delight—the very trees whose fruit he himself had gathered in the days of his innocence and joy. He sees the vines that his own hands have trained, the very flowers that he once loved to care for. His mind grasps the reality of the scene; he comprehends that this is indeed Eden restored. Restored to the tree

---

51. White, *Manuscript 42, 1901*.
52. Land, *The A to Z of the Seventh-Day Adventists*, 192.

of life in the long-lost Eden, the redeemed will "grow up" to the full stature of the race in its primeval glory. The last lingering traces of the curse of sin will be removed, and Christ's faithful ones will appear in "the beauty of the Lord our God" (Psalm 90:17), in mind and soul and body reflecting the perfect image of their Lord. Oh, wonderful redemption! long talked of, long hoped for, contemplated with eager anticipation, but never fully understood.[53]

---

53. White, *God's Amazing Grace*, 360.

BIBLIOGRAPHY

Aalen, S. "Glory." In *The New International Dictionary of New Testament Theology- Vol 2.* Edited by C. Brown, Grand Rapids, Michigan: Zondervan, 1986.

Arminius, J. "Orations of Arminius: Oration 1." In *The Works of James Arminius: Vol. 1.* Quezon City: New Century Books, 2010.

Arminius, J. et al. The Works of James Arminius, DD, Formerly Professor of Divinity in the University of Leyden. New York: Derby, Miller, & Orton, 1853.

Arminius, J. *The Works of James Arminius:Vol. 1.* Quezon City: New Century Books, 2010.

Articles of Religion of the Wesleyan Church: https://www.wesleyan.org/about/articles-of-religion

Augsburger, M. S. *Christian Pacifism.* Westmont, Illinois: Intervarsity, May 07, 2004.

Aune, D. E. "Son of Man." In *The International Standard Bible Encyclopaedia- Vol. 4.* Edited by G. W. Bromiley. Grand Rapids, Michigan: Eerdmans, 1988.

Bacchiocchi, S. A. *Historical Investigation of The Rise of Sunday Observance in Early Christianity.* Rome: The Pontifical Gregorian University Press, 1977.

Ball, B.W. *The Seventh-Day Men- Sabbatarians and Sabbatarianism in England and Wales, 1600-1800.* Cambridge: James and Clarke, 2009.

Bangs, C. *Arminius: A Study in the Dutch Reformation.* Wilmore, KY: Frances Asbury Press, 1985.

Barth, K. *Dogmatics in Outline.* Translated by G. T. Thomson, London: SCM, 1966.

Baus, K. et al. "The Imperial Church from Constantine to the Early Middle Ages." In *History of the Church: Vol. 2.* Edited by Hubert Jedin and John Dolan. Translated by Anselm Biggs. New York: The Seabury Press, 1980.

Banks, J. S. *A Manuel of Christian Doctrine.* London: Charles Kelly, 1902.

Bender, H. S. "Footwashing." In *The Mennonite Encyclopedia.* Edited by Harold Bender and Henry Smith. Scottdale, PA: Mennonite Publishing House, 1955.

Bercot, D. W. ed. *A Dictionary of Early Christian Beliefs.* Massachusetts: Hendrickson, 1998.

Beasley-Murray, G. R. *Word Biblical Commentary: John.* Dallas, TX: Word, 1991.

Berkhof, L. *Systematic Theology,* Grand Rapids, Michigan: Eerdmans, 1996.

Bloesch, D. G. *Essentials of Evangelical Theology, Vols. 1 and 2.* San Francisco: HarperCollins, 1978.

———. *A Theology of Word and Spirit.* Illinois: IVP, 1992.

———. *God the Almighty: Power, Wisdom, Holiness, Love.* Illinois: IVP, 1995.

———. *Jesus is Victor! Karl Barth's Doctrine of Salvation.* Nashville, TN: Abingdon, 1976.

———. *Jesus Christ: Saviour and Lord.* Illinois: IVP, 1997.

———. *The Last Things: Resurrection, Judgment, Glory.* Illinois: IVP, 2004.

BIBLIOGRAPHY

———. *The Church: Sacraments, Worship, Ministry, Mission*. Illinois, IVP, 2002.

Boettner, L. *The Person of Christ*. Eugene, OR: Wipf & Stock, 2009.

Bonhoeffer, D. *Life Together*. London: SCM Press, 1995 (1954).

———. *The Cost of Discipleship*. New York: Simon and Schuster 1995 (1959).

Bragg, E. C. *Systematic Theology- The Doctrine of God*. Class Notes, N.D.

Bromiley, G. *Introduction to the Theology of Karl Barth*. Edinburgh: T. & T. Clark, 1979.

Bromiley, G. W. "Atone, Atonement." In *The International Standard Bible Encyclopedia- Vol.1*. Edited by G. W. Bromiley. Grand Rapids, Michigan: Eerdmans, 1979.

———. *Historical Theology: An Introduction*. Edinburgh: T. & T. Clark, 1978.

———. "Baptism." In *TISBE: Vol. 1*. Edited by G. W. Bromiley, Grand Rapids, Michigan: Eerdmans, 1979.

Brown, C. *The New International Dictionary of New Testament Theology: Vol. 3*. Milton Keynes, UK: Paternoster, 1992.

Brooks, J. A., and Winbery, C.L. *Syntax of New Testament Greek*. University of America Press, 1988.

Brunner, E. "The Christian Doctrine of Creation and Redemption." Translated by O. Wyon. Cambridge: James Clarke and Co, 1952.

Calvin, J. "Institutes I.10.1-3." In *Reformed Reader: A Source book in Christian Theology*. Edited by W. S. Johnson and J. H. Leith. Louisville, KY: Westminster/ John Knox Press, 1993.

———. "Institutes of the Christian Religion- Book IV." In *Historical Theology*. Edited by G. W. Bromiley, Edinburgh: T. & T. Clark, 1994.

Canfield, L. H. *The Early Persecutions of the Christians*. The Lawbook Exchange, 2005.

Cairus, A. E. "Human Nature." In *The Ellen G. White Encycopedia*. Edited by D. Fortin, J. Moon. Hagerstown, ML: Review and Herald, 2014.

Canale, F. L. "Doctrine of God." In *Handbook of Seventh-day Adventist Theology*. Edited by G. W. Reid. Hagerstown, ML: Review and Herald, 2013.

Caulley, T. S. "Holy Spirit." In *Evangelical Dictionary of Theology*. Edited by W.A. Elwell. Grand Rapids, Michigan: Baker Books, 1984.

Chadwick, H. *The Pelican History of the Church- The Early Church*. London, UK: Penguin, 1967.

Chung, P. K. *Rise of the Remnant: The Formation of the Seventh-day Adventist Church from the Era of Slavery and the Civil War*. California State University, Fullerton, ProQuest Dissertations Publishing, 2005.

Coenen, L. "Church." In *The New International Dictionary of New Testament Theology: Vol. 1*. Edited by Colin Brown. Grand Rapids, Michigan, 1986.

Conner, W. T. *Christian Doctrine*. Broadman Press, 1937.

Coleman, E. "Ellen White on Confrontation with Evil Spiritual Powers." *Journal of Adventist Mission Studies* Vol 11 [2015] No 2 Art 8.

Daane, J. *The Freedom of God*. Grand Rapids, Michigan: Eerdmans, 1973.

Dando-Collins, S. *The Great Fire of Rome: The Fall of the Emperor Nero and His City*. Cambridge, MS: De Capo Press, 2010.

Davidson, R. M. "Doctrine of the Sanctuary." In *The Ellen White Encyclopedia*. Edited by D. Fortin, and J. Moon. Hagerstown, ML: Review and Herald, 2013.

———. "The Old Testament in The Church?" In *Understanding Poets and Prophets- Essays in Honour of George Wishart Anderson*. Journal for the Study of The Old Testament, Supplement Series 152. Sheffield, UK: Sheffield Academic Press, 1993.

BIBLIOGRAPHY

Dederen, R. "The Church: Authority and Unity." *Ministry* May 1995,

Dever, M. et al. *Preaching the Cross*. Crossway. 2007.

Douglass, H. E. "Covenants." In *The Ellen E. White Encyclopedia*. Edited by D. Fortin, and J. Moon. Hagerstown. ML: Review and Herald, 2013.

Drake, H. A. "The Impact of Constantine on Christianity." In *The Cambridge Companion to the Age of Constantine. Vol. 13*. Edited by N. Lenski. Cambridge, UK: Cambridge University Press, 2006.

Durant, W. *The Story of Civilization: The Reformation- Vol. VI*. New York: Simon and Shuster, 1957.

Ekeke, E. C. "Persecution and Martyrdom of Christians in the Roman Empire from AD 54-100: A Lesson for the 21st Century Church." *European Scientific Journal* July Vol 8 No 16 2012.

Elliott, L. *The Renaissance in Europe*. New York: Crabtree Publishing Company, 2009.

Elton, G. R. "Reformation Europe 1517-1559." In *Blackwell Classic Histories of Europe*. Second Edition, Hoboken, NJ: Blackwell, 1999.

Erickson, M. *Introducing Christian Doctrine*. Grand Rapids, Michigan: Baker Book House, 1992.

———. *Christian Theology*. Second Edition, Grand rapids, Michigan: Baker Books, 1999.

Estep, W. R. *Renaissance and Reformation*. Grand Rapids, Michigan: Eerdmans, 1986.

Ferguson, E. *Encyclopaedia of Early Christianity- Vol. 1*. Taylor and Francis, 1998.

———. *Backgrounds of Early Christianity*. Third ed. Grand Rapids, Michigan: Eerdmans, 2003.

Finger, T. N. *A Contemporary Anabaptist Theology: Biblical, Historical, Constructive*. Westmont, IL: Intervarsity, 2004.

Finney, C. G. *Lectures on Systematic Theology*. Edited by G. Redford. London: W. Tegg and Co. 1851.

Forlines, F. L. *Biblical Systematics*. Nashville, TN: Randall House Publications, 1975.

Franzmann, M. *Jesus in the Nag Hammadi Writings*. Edinburgh: T. & T. Clark International, 1996.

Gane, E. R. *The Arian or Anti-Trinitarian Views Presented in Seventh-day Adventist Literature and the Ellen G. White Answer*. Unpublished Master's Thesis June 1963 Andrews University.

Garrett, J. L. *Systematic Theology: Biblical, Historical and Evangelical: Vol. 1*. Grand Rapids, Michigan: Eerdmans, 1990.

Gelzer, H. *The Life of Martin Luther and the Reformation in Germany*. Philadelphia: Lindsay and Blakiston, 1857.

Gillett, E. H. *The Life and Times and John Huss*. Boston: Gould and Lincoln, 1864.

González, J. *The Story of Christianity- Volume 1, The Early Church to the Dawn of The New The Reformation*. San Francisco: Harper 1984.

———. *The Story of Christianity- Vol. 2: The Reformation to the Present Day*. San Francisco: Harper 1985.

Gordon, P. A. "William Miller." In *The Ellen G. White Encyclopedia*. Edited by D. Fortin, and J. Moon. Hagerstown, ML: Review and Herald, 2013.

Gregg, S. *Revelation: Four Views*. Nashville: Grand Rapids, 1997.

Grenz, S. *Theology for the Community of God*. Grand Rapids, Michigan: Eerdmans,1994.

———. *Renewing the Center: Evangelical Theology in a Post-Theological Era*. Grand Rapids, Michigan: Baker books, 2000.

Gunther, W. "Sin." In *The New International Dictionary of New Testament Theology: Vol. 3.* Edited by Colin Brown. Milton Keynes, UK: Paternoster, 1992.

Hamburger, P. *Separation of Church and State.* Cambridge MS: Harvard University Press, 2002.

Harrison, E. F. "Glory." In *The International Standard Bible Encyclopedia- Vol. 2.* Edited by G. W. Bromiley. Grand Rapids, Michigan: Eerdmans, 1982.

Hendrix, S. H. *Martin Luther: Visionary Reformer.* New Haven, CN: Yale University Press, 2015.

———. "Luther." In *The Cambridge Companion to Reformation Theology.* Edited by D. Bagchi and D. C. Steinmetz. Cambridge, UK: Cambridge University Press, 2004.

Hill, C. E. "The New Testament Canon: Deconstructio Ad Absurdum." *Journal of the Evangelical Theological Society.* 52/1, March 2009.

Hillerbrand, H. *The Reformation: A Narrative History Related by Contemporary Observers and Participants.* Grand Rapids, Michigan: Baker Book House, 1992.

Hoeksema, H. "An Exposition of The Heidelberg Catechism, Part 2." *The Standard Bearer* Vol XX1 No 13 April 1 1945.

Hoever H. ed. *Lives of the Saints, For Every Day of the Year.* New York: Catholic Book Publishing Co., 1955.

Hughes, M. *Christian Foundations.* Epworth, 1933.

Hynson, L. O. *Through Faith to Understanding.* Lexington, KY: Emeth Press, 2005.

Jeramias, J. "The Prayers of Jesus." *Abba in the Old Testament.* JETS 31/4 December 1988.

Johnson, J. H., and Leith, J. H. eds. *Reformed Reader.* Louisville, KY: John Knox Press, 2002.

Kauffman, D. *Doctrines of the Bible: A Brief Discussion of the Teaching of God's Word.* Scottdale, Pennsylvania: Herald Press, 1956.

Kirby, A. "The Death of Postmodernism and Beyond." *Philosophy Now.* Issue 58 2006.

Klappert, B. "Lord's Supper." In *TNIDNTT, Vol 2.* Edited by Colin Brown. Grand Rapids, Michigan: Paternoster, 1971.

Kraybill, D. B. *Concise Encyclopedia of Amish, Brethren, Hutterites, and Mennonites.* John Hopkins University Press, 2010.

Ladd, G. E. "Kingdom of Christ, God, Heaven." In *Evangelical Dictionary of Theology.* Edited by W. A. Elwell. Grand Rapids, Michigan: Baker Books, 1984.

Land, G. *The A to Z of the Seventh-Day Adventists.* Maryland: Scarecrow Press, 2005.

LaSor, W.S. "Sabbath." In *The International Standard Bible Encyclopedia, Vol. 4.* Edited by G. W. Bromiley. Grand Rapids, Michigan: Eerdmans, 1988.

Latourette, K. S. *A History of Christianity- Vol. 1: Beginnings to 1500.* Harper, 1975.

Layton, B. The Gnostic Scriptures. London: SCM Press, 1987.

Lehner, U. L. et al. eds. *The Oxford Handbook of Early Modern Theology, 1600-1800.* Oxford: Oxford University Press, 2016.

Leith, J. H. ed. *Creeds of the Church: A Reader in Christian Doctrine from The Bible to The Present.* Third Ed. Louisville, KY: John Knox Press, 1982.

Lindberg, C. *The European Reformations.* Second Ed. Grand Rapids, Michigan: Wiley-Blackwell, 2010.

Lindsay, T. M. *History of the Reformation-Vols.1 and 2.* Edinburgh: T. & T. Clark, 1907.

Little, F. H. *The Anabaptist View of the Church: A study in its Origins and Sectarian Protestantism.* Boston: Star and King, 1958.

Lohse, B. *Martin Luther's Theology: Its Historical and Systematic Development.* Translated by R. Harrisville. Edinburgh: T. & T. Clark, 1999.

BIBLIOGRAPHY

Lovci, R. *Michael Servetus: Heretic or Saint: The Life and Death of a Renaissance Man*. Jaffa, Israel: Prague House: 2008.

Lumpkin, W, *Baptist Confessions of Faith*. Jusdon, 1969.

Luther, M. D. "Martin Luther's Werke: Kritische Gesamtausgabe. Vol. 5." In *The Christian Theology Reader*. Edited by A. McGrath. Massachusetts: Blackwell, 1995.

———. "The Babylonian captivity of the Church- 1520." In *The Annotated Luther- Volume 3*. Edited by in P. W. Robinson, Minneapolis, MN: Fortress Press, 2016.

———. *To the Christian Nobility of the German Nation- 1520*. Mineapolis, MN: Augsburg Fortress 2016.

Malony, H. N. *The Amazing John Wesley: An Unusual Look at an Uncommon Life*. Westmont, ILL: InterVarsity, 2012.

Manross, J. E. *Sebastian Castello: Apostle of Tolerance in the Sixteenth Century*. The University of Arizona, 1961.

Markham, P. M. *Rewired: Exploring Religious Conversion*. Eugene, OR: Wipf & Stock, 2007.

Marshall, I. H. *Jesus The Saviour: Studies in New Testament Theology*. London: SPCK, 1990.

Mbanisi, V. N. *Baptism and the Ideal of Unity and Universality of the Church in St. Augustine's Ecclesiology: An Exposition of His Theology of Baptism in the Light of Donatist Controversy*. Dissertation for Fordham University, New York, March, 2008.

McGrath, A. E. *Christian Theology: An Introduction*. Grand Rapids, Michigan: Blackwell, 1994.

———. *Historical Theology: An Introduction to the History of Christian Thought*. Grand Rapids, Michigan: Blackwell, 1998,

———. *Luther's Theology of the Cross: Martin Luther's Theological Breakthrough*. Hoboken, NJ: Wiley-Blackwell, 1991.

———. *The Christian Theology Reader*. Massachusetts: Blackwell, 1995.

McKim, D. K. ed. *Readings in Calvin's Theology*. Eugene, OR: Wipf & Stock, 1998.

Miley, J. *Systematic Theology, Vols. 1 and 2*. New York: Hunt and Eaton, 1892.

Miller, W. *The Midnight Cry*. Dec 5, 1844.

Moore, H., and McCormack, P. "Domitian (Part i)." *IBS* 25 2003 Issue 2.

Morgan, D. "Following the Prince of Peace in a Time of War." *Adventist Review* June 12 2007.

Morris, L. *The Epistle to The Romans*. Grand Rapids, Michigan: Eerdmans, 1988.

———. *New Testament Theology*. New York: Harper Collins, 1990.

Mullins, E. *The Christian Religion: In Its Doctrinal Expression*. Philadelphia: The Judson Press, 1959 (1917).

Murray, J. *The Life of John Wycliffe*. Edinburgh: John Boyd, 1840.

Murphy, T. F. *Religious Bodies, 1936: Pt 1*. U.S. Government Printing Office, 1941.

Moody, D. *The Word of Truth: A Summary of Christian Doctrine Based on Biblical Revelation*. Grand Rapids, Michigan: Eerdmans, 1981.

Nouse, N. R. "Moravian Musical Origins." In *Pleasing for Our Use*. Edited by C. A. Traupman-Carr, Associated University Press, 2000.

Norris, R. "The Later Middle Ages." In *A History of the Christian Church*. Edited by W. Walker et al., Fourth Edition, New York: Charles Scriber's Sons, 1985.

Oden, O. *John Wesley's Scriptural Christianity: A Plain Exposition of His Teaching on Christian Doctrine*. Grand Rapids: Michigan: Zondervan, 1994.

Oden, T. *Life in the Spirit: Systematic Theology, Volume Three*. New York: HaperCollins, 1994.

O'Hare, T. D. *The Sabbath Complete: And the Ascendency of First-Day Worship*. Eugene, OR: Wipf & Stock, 2011.

BIBLIOGRAPHY

Owen, J. "Exposition of Psalm 130." In *The Works of John Owen, Vol. 6*. Edited by W. Gould, et al., 1851.

Olsen, R. E. *The Story of Christian Theology- Twenty Centuries of Tradition and Reform*. Apollos, 1999.

———. *Arminian Theology: Myths and Realities*. Westmont, IL: InterVarsity, 2009.

Packull, W. O. "An Introduction to Anabaptist Theology." In *The Cambridge Companion to Reformation Theology*. Edited by D. Bugchi and D. Steinmetz. Cambridge University Press, 2004.

Packer, J. I. *Concise Theology: A Guide to Historic Christian Belief*. Wheaton, IL, Tyndale, 1993.

Parker, J. *The People's Bible*. BiblioBazaar, 2009 (1885).

Parker, T. H. L. *John Calvin: A Biography*. Louisville, KY: Westminster/John Knox Press, 1975 and 2006.

Patterson, P. "What Contemporary Baptists can Learn from Anabaptists." In *The Anabaptists and Contemporary Baptists: Restoring New Testament Christianity, Essays in Honour of Paige Patterson*. Edited by in M. Yarnell. Nashville: Broadman and Holman, 2013.

Peisker, C. H. "Prophet." In *The New International Dictionary of New Testament Theology*. Edited by Colin Brown. Milton Keynes: Paternoster Press, 1992.

Pelikan, J. *The Christian Tradition (A History of the Development of Doctrine): Reformation of Church and Dogma (1300-1700)*. Chicago, IL: University of Chicago, 1984.

———. *The Christian Tradition, A History of the Development of Doctrine: The Emergence of the Catholic Tradition (100-600)*. Chicago, IL: University of Chicago Press, 1971.

Pfandl, G. "The Remnant Church." *Journal of the Adventist Theological Society* 8/1–2 1997.

Pinnock, C. "New Directions in Theological Method." in *New Dimensions in Evangelical Theology: Essays in Honor of Millard Erickson*. Edited by David Dockery. Downers Grove, IL: InterVarsity, 1998.

Pinson, J. M. "The Nature of Atonement in the Theology of Jacobus Arminius." *JETS* 53/4 December 2010.

Platinga, A. "The Twin Pillars of Christian Scholarship." in *Seeking Understanding- The Stob Lectures, 1986-1998*. Grand Rapids, Michigan: Eerdmans 2001.

Prosser, K. *Was Jesus Crucified?* Take Heart, 2016.

Rengstorf, K. H. "Jesus Christ." In *The New International Dictionary of New Testament Theology, Vol. 2*. Edited by Colin Brown. Michigan: Paternoster, 1986.

Ralston, T. *Elements of Divinity*. Louisville, KY: E. Stevens, 1851.

Ramm, B. L. *The Christian View of Science and Scripture*. Exter, Devon, UK: Paternoster Press, 1967.

———. *The Pattern of Religious Authority*. Grand Rapids, Michigan: Eerdmans, 1957.

———. *After Fundamentalism: The Future of Evangelical Theology*. San Francisco: Harper and Row, 1993.

———. *An Evangelical Christology: Ecumenic and Historic*. Grand Rapids, Michigan: Thomson Nelson, 1985.

Rengstorf, K. H. "Jesus Christ." In *The New International Dictionary of New Testament Theology, Vol. 2*. Edited by Colin Brown. Michigan: Paternoster, 1986.

Rice, R. *The Reign of God*. Andrews University Press, 1985.

Rogers, J., and McKim, D. K. *The Authority and Interpretation of the Bible: An Historical Approach*. Eugene, OR: Wipf & Stock, 1999.

BIBLIOGRAPHY

Schattenmann, J. "Fellowship." In *TNIDNTT: Vol. 1*. Edited by Colin Brown. Milton Keynes: Paternoster, 1971.

Scheepers, P. "Acts and the Mission of the Church." *Vox Reformata* 2010.

Schlatter, A. *The Theology of the Apostles*. Translated by A.J. Kostenberger. Grand Rapids: Michigan: Baker Books, 1999.

———. *The History of the Christ*. Translated by A. J. Kostenberger. Grand Rapids, Michigan: Baker 1997.

Schnabel, E. J. "Jewish Opposition to Christians in Asia Minor in the First Century." *Bulletin for Biblical Research* 18:2 2008.

Schreiner, T. R., and Crawford, M. R. *The Lords Supper*. B and H Publishing, 2011.

Sell, A. P. F. *Testimony and Tradition: Studies in Reform and Dissenting Thought*. Eugene, OR: Wipf & Stock.

Shank, R. L. *Elect in The Son*. Missouri: Westcott Publishers, 1970.

Shaw, R. *An Exposition of the Confession of Faith of The Westminster Assembly of Divines*. Ross-shire: Christian Focus Publications (1885), 1980.

Sheehan, J. *The Enlightenment Bible: Translation, Scholarship, Culture*. Princeton University Press, 2013.

Shelley, B. *Church History in Plain Language*. Dallas, TX: Word, 1982.

Somerville, B. A. *Martin Luther: Father of the Reformation*. Compass Point Books, 2006.

Southy, R. *The Life of Wesley; and the Rise and Progress of Methodism*. London: Paternoster-Row, 1820.

Spener, P. J. *Pia Desidaria*. Minneapolis, MN: Fortress Press, 1964.

Steinmetz, D. C. "The Theology of John Calvin." In *A Cambridge Companion to Reformation Theology*. Edited by D. Bagchi and D. C. Steinmetz. Cambridge University Press, 2004.

Stevick, D. B. *Jesus and His Own: A Commentary on John 13-17*. Grand Rapids, Michigan: Eerdmans, 2011.

Stott, W. "Sabbath." In *The New International Dictionary of New Testament Theology, Vol. 3*. Edited by Colin Brown. Grand Rapids, Michigan: Zondervan, 1993.

Strong, A. *Systematic Theology*. London: Pickering and Inglis, 1958(1907).

Taylor, V. *Forgiveness and Reconciliation*. London: Macmillan, 1946.

Tertullian, "On Idolatry." In *Early Latin Theology: Selections from Tertullian, Cyprian, Ambrose, Jerome*. Edited and Translated by S. L. Greenslade. The Westminster Press, 1956.

Thorsen, D. *The Wesleyan Quadrilateral*. Lexington, KY: Emeth Press, 2005.

Torrance, T. F., and Walker, R. T. eds. *Incarnation: The Person and Life of Christ*. Milton Keynes: Paternoster, 2008.

Torrance, T. F. "The Place of Jesus Christ in Worship." In *Theological Foundations for Ministry*. Edited by Ray Anderson. Grand Rapids, Michigan: Eerdmans, 1979.

———. *Atonement: The Person and Work of Christ*. Paternoster and IVP Academic, 2009.

Torrance, J. *Worship, Community and The Triune God of Grace*. Carlisle: Paternoster, 1996.

Traver, A. G. "Agricola, Johann (1494-1566)." In *Renaissance and Reformation: 1500-1620, A Biographical Dictionary*. Edited by J. E. Carney. Westport, CN: Greenwood Press, 2001.

Tuttle, R. G. "Wesley, John." *Evangelical Dictionary of Theology*. Edited by W. A. Elwell. Grand Rapids, Michigan: Baker, 2001.

Ursinus, Z. *The Commentary of Dr. Zacharias Ursinus on the Heidelberg Catechism*. Columbus, 1852.

BIBLIOGRAPHY

Vermeulen, T., and van den Akker, R. "Notes on Metamodernism." *Journal of Aesthetics and Culture* Vol 2 2010.

Vine, W. E. *Expository Dictionary of New Testament Words*. Massachusetts: Henrickson, no date.

Waggoner, E. J. *The Signs of the Times*. Vol 22 June 11 1896.

Walker, W. et al. *A History of the Christian Church*. Fourth Edition, New York: Charles Scribner's Sons, 1985.

Watson, T. *A Body of Divinity*. Edinburgh: The Banner of Truth (1692), 1992.

Wawrykow, J. P. *The Westminster Handbook to Thomas Aquinas*. Louisville, KY: Westminster/John Knox Press, 2005.

Weaver, J. D. "Pacifism." In *Evangelical Dictionary of Theology*. Edited by W. A. Elwell. Grand Rapids, Michigan: Baker Books.

Weber, O. *Foundations of Dogmatics- Vols. 1&2*. Translated by D. L. Gruder. Grand Rapids, Michigan: Eerdmans, 1981.

Webster, S. *Practical Christian Spirituality, No. 1 Spiritual Disciplines Are Never Out of Date*. St Michaels North Carlton, undated.

Wesley, J. *Journal*. January 25, 1736.

———. *Journal*. May 24, 1738.

———. *Thoughts Upon Slavery*. 1775.

Wesley, J. *John and Charles Wesley: Selected Prayers, Hymns, Journal Notes, Sermons, Letters and Treaties*. Edited by Frank Whaling. Mahwah, NJ: Paulist Press, 1981.

Wesley, J. *The Works of the Rev. John Wesley A.M.: Sermons*. Carlton and Porter, 1831.

Whitby, D. *A Paraphrase and Commentary on the New Testament-Volumes 1 and 2*. London: Bower and Churchill, 1703.

White, E. G. *Early Writings*. Washington, D.C.: Review and Herald, 1882

———. *Publications*. https://whiteestate.org/books/egw-books/.

———. *Colporteur Ministry*. Mountain View, Cal.: Pacific Press, 1953.

———. *Evangelism*. Washington, D. C.: Review and Herald Publishing Association, 1946.

———. *Ellen White Letters: Archives*. https://whiteestate.org/resources/archives/.

———. *Manuscripts*. https://m.egwwritings.org/en/book/61.2.

———. *Life Sketches of Ellen White*. Mountain View, Cal.: Pacific Press, 1915.

———. *Review and Herald: Archives*. https://documents.adventistarchives.org/Periodicals/.

———. *Selected Messages, Book One*. Washington, D. C.: Review and Herald Publishing Association, 1958.

———. *Testimonies for the Church*. Mountain View, Cal.: Pacific Press Publishing Association, 1909.

———. *The Great Controversy*. Mountain View, Cal.: Pacific Press, 1888.

———. *The Sanctified Life*. Washington D.C.: Review and Herald, 1889.

Willard, G. W. *The Commentary of Dr. Zacharias Ursinus on The Heidelberg Catechism*. Grand Rapids, Michigan: Eerdmans, 1956.

Wood, L. W. *The Meaning of Pentecost in Early Methodism*. Lanham, ML: Scarecrow Press, 2002.

Wright, N. T. *Jesus and the Victory of God*. Minneapolis, MN: Fortress Press, 1996.

———. *The New Testament and the People of God*. Minneapolis, MN: Fortress Press, 1992.

Wright, D. F. "Calvin's Role in Church History." In *The Cambridge Companion to John Calvin*. Edited by D. K. McKim. Cambridge, UK: Cambridge University Press, 2004.

BIBLIOGRAPHY

Yarnell, M. B. ed. *The Anabaptists and Contemporary Baptists: Restoring New Testament Christianity.* Nashville, TN: Broadman and Holman, 2013.

Zhodiates, S. *The Complete Word Study New Testament.* Chattanooga, TN: AMG Publishers, 1991.

www.ingramcontent.com/pod-product-compliance
Lightning Source LLC
Chambersburg PA
CBHW080545230426
43663CB00015B/2709